The Press
as Guardian of
the First Amendment

The Press
as Guardian of
the First Amendment

BY JOHN LOFTON

UNIVERSITY OF SOUTH CAROLINA PRESS

Library of Congress Cataloging in Publication Data

Lofton, John.
  The press as guardian of the first amendment.

  Bibliography: p.
  1. Liberty of the press—United States—History.
2. Press law—United States—History. I. Title.
KF4774.L64   342.73′0853   80–10617
ISBN 0–87249–389–X

For my sons:
Jack and Charlie

Contents

Acknowledgments

FOR PERMISSION TO REPRINT in chapter 11 an excerpt on the *Myron Farber* case from "The Talk of the Town," the author extends grateful acknowledgment to *The New Yorker*. Appreciation is expressed to Dr. William Landau and to James Millstone, assistant managing editor of the *St. Louis Post-Dispatch*, for reading portions of the manuscript. Curt Matthews of the Baltimore *Sun* contributed useful research to the chapter dealing with the 1812 mob attack on the *Federal Republican* in Baltimore. Cathy Vespereny of the *Post-Dispatch* aided immeasurably with proofreading. Katherine Rhodes deserves credit for her meticulous work as a typist.

Introduction

"FREEDOM OF THE PRESS," like holy writ, has been invoked with reverence by Americans since the founding of the republic. But the concept has been quickly ignored by politicians and people alike when it seemed to be inconvenient.

George Washington, who has been exalted as the preeminent American, once grumbled about "that rascal Freneau," as he agonized over ways to silence Philip Freneau, the editor of a newspaper that constantly criticized his administration. John Adams readily signed the Alien and Sedition Laws and applauded their use to prosecute journalistic critics of his administration. Thomas Jefferson, who has been honored as the champion of freedom of expression, wrote in 1803: "I have . . . long thought that a few prosecutions of the most prominent offenders would have a wholesome effect in restoring the integrity of the presses."

If even these towering figures among the founding fathers were guilty of lapses in their commitment to a free press, it should not be surprising that ordinary Americans have sometimes showed a total lack of sympathy with the spirit of the First Amendment. The amendment's guarantee of freedom of expression was ignored when mobs attacked abolitionist presses in the 1830s, when citizens during World War I reported to the government the alleged disloyal utterances of their neighbors, when alleged Communists were driven from their jobs in the 1950s because of the supposedly subversive views they espoused.

Yet for all of the vicissitudes that freedom of expression has suffered, an avowed commitment to the principle has survived. The principle is enunciated not only in the United States Constitution but in every state constitution. It has been expressed variously by generations of Americans in idealistic terms that have come to be accepted in the abstract as self-evident truths. Sculptured in concrete and emblazoned on mastheads, aphorisms on press freedom have become so prevalent as to be part of our political ethos.

"The only security of all," wrote Thomas Jefferson in 1792, "is in a free press. . . . No government ought to be without censors; and where the press is free no one ever will."

"Freedom of conscience, of education, of speech, of assembly are among the very fundamentals of democracy," declared Franklin D. Roosevelt, "and all of them would be nullified should freedom of the press ever be successfully challenged."

Whatever their lapses, Americans have recognized in their most clear-eyed moments that the protection of the First Amendment is essential to democratic self-government. Without a free and informed electorate, democracy cannot function; that kind of electorate cannot exist without freedom of expression even for the idea that may be hateful or subversive. As with democracy, individual creativity in science, art, and literature are dependent on uncontrolled expression.

More than any other institution, the press is the vehicle and the symbol of unfettered expression. As such, its fights with governmental authorities and other would-be suppressors have been chronicled often and at length. The erratic records of public figures with respect to the First Amendment have also been documented.

Considering the provocations on the one hand and the temptations of power on the other, the uneven record of politicians from George Washington to Jimmy Carter is perhaps not surprising. But if our foremost political leaders have not been undeviating defenders of freedom of the press, what about newspapers? As the most obvious beneficiaries of the constitutional guarantee of freedom of expression, they might be expected to be the foremost promoters of press freedom in practice. Yet so far as I have been able to discover, the historical record of the press from the founding of the republic to the present as supporter or nonsupporter of the First

Amendment has never been systematically studied and documented. The purpose of this book is to examine how the American press has performed when confronted with the application of the amendment to practical events.

I have accepted as axiomatic the often espoused proposition that the dissemination of information and the discussion of conflicting ideas are vital to the survival of a free, democratic society. The importance of freedom for the expression of adversary views was recognized by James Madison, the author of the First Amendment, when he wrote: "Could it be so arranged that every newspaper, when printed on one side, should be handed over to the press of an adversary, to be printed on the other, thus presenting to every reader both sides of every question, truth would always have a fair chance. But such a remedy is ideal."

If Madison's remedy was idealistic, the lesser remedy of press championship of the freedom of others to express dissenting views should not be unrealistic. The truest measure of the press's commitment to freedom of the press is its willingness to defend the First Amendment rights of those with opinions differing from its own or of the proponents of unpopular views, whoever they are. Taking this definition of commitment as a standard, this study focuses on how leading American newspapers have met the test of upholding the First Amendment throughout this nation's history.

In order to be sure that the threat to freedom of expression was one with which editors of newspapers under study might be expected to be familiar, I searched for First Amendment issues that were reported in the press of the time and place in question. To be certain that the issue was thrust before editors in a manner presumably requiring some response from them, I concentrated on threats to freedom for newspapers, as distinguished from other kinds of impediments on free expression. My survey, however, was not wholly limited to direct threats to newspapers. Some assaults on free expression were so important symbolically for the First Amendment that they merited editors' attention even though no newspaper was involved. Such a case was the prosecution under the 1917 Espionage Act of Socialist party leader Eugene Debs, for the views he expressed in a single speech. Other examples of suppression, though newspapers were not the direct target, were so clearly a forewarning to the daily press as to deserve editorial comment. Such a case was a 1972 court injunction against a book about the Central Intelligence Agency.

My survey of nearly 200 years of press reaction to First Amendment issues has led to some surprising and some not so surprising findings. Whether the press was faithful or faithless toward the constitutional principle that is most entitled to its allegiance, its performance should teach us valuable lessons as to how to keep freedom of expression and democratic government alive.

JOHN LOFTON

The Press
as Guardian of
the First Amendment

1

Seed Ground for the First Amendment

Americans living during the era of the nation's birth had several significant object lessons in the value of freedom of the press. The early political campaigns for resistance to British laws and then for independence were transformed into effective national movements by the press. The Declaration of Independence itself was made known to the people through the press. First printed on the night of July 4, 1776, by the presses of John Dunlap's *Pennsylvania Packet*,[1] the Declaration was soon reprinted by other papers and its electrifying message spread across the land. The founding fathers would have been well aware that, had the British been able to control the press, such a stirring appeal as theirs for a defiance of authority could never have been effectively communicated. The usefulness of an unfettered press not only in arousing popular support for the revolutionary cause but also in shaping new national political institutions was clearly demonstrated.

In the century in which the First Amendment was formulated, American editors and their newspapers were engaged in many battles for freedom of the press. But even in their fierce disputes on the issue, neither editors nor political leaders were clear about what freedom of the press really meant. Eighteenth-century editors, as well as politicians, were divided over the concept of seditious libel, which —like national security today—was used by government as an all-purpose weapon for curbing the press. A review of the ideological battles over seditious libel and other free press issues is important to an understanding of what the First Amendment meant to contemporaries of its drafters and to what it later came to mean.

The first major national dispute over the press occurred a decade before the American Revolution. As events developed, the British themselves were to help make the American press into an instrument for revolution. Journalists, as a result of the Stamp Act of 1765, were among the first to be antagonized by the British government. The act required all legal documents, official papers, books, and newspapers to be printed on stamped paper that carried a special tax. For each copy of a two-page newspaper, the tax was a half penny; for each four-page paper, a penny—with an additional two-shilling tax being imposed on each advertisement. This was a heavy tax in proportion to the value of the item being taxed.

Printers and editors were soon up in arms and, besides organizing their own forms of protest, they opened their columns to letters condemning the Stamp Act and to news of the various meetings and other activities launched throughout the colonies to resist the tax. Using the traditional symbol of journalistic mourning, some newspapers set off their columns with heavy black margins on the day before the tax was to be enforced. Papers in Massachusetts, Pennsylvania, and Maryland printed silhouetted skulls and crossed bones as signs of a dead free press.[2]

From the first acts of resistance to the end of the Revolution, newspapers were in the forefront of the ideological struggle that led to independence. Sam Adams, one of the chief propagandists of the Revolution, met regularly in the office of the Boston *Gazette* with other members of the Caucus Club, a group intent on agitating and directing political action. Writing under pen names, they used the columns of the *Gazette* to stir their countrymen's animosity toward the British and to promote their political strategy. As John Adams put it, they "cooked up paragraphs" and "worked the political engine."[3]

Farther south, where a more restrained and reasoned approach was the pattern, John Dickinson of Philadelphia contributed a series of twelve influential articles to the *Pennsylvania Chronicle*.

Entitled "Letters From a Farmer," lawyer Dickinson's articles argued cogently against Parliament's infringements of the rights of the colonists. The Dickinson letters were extensively reprinted in other newspapers during 1767 and 1768.

In every colony the advocates of political resistance and then of revolution reached the public through the press. Their organ in Charleston, the South's largest city, was the *South Carolina Gazette*, which showed its sentiments by enclosing a report of the 1770 Boston "massacre" in heavy black borders. Peter Timothy, its editor, was made a prisoner of war by the British in 1780, after he had left the paper.[4]

Tom Paine, who was to become the most renowned publicist of the Revolution, burst into public notice in January 1776 with the publication of his pamphlet, *Common Sense*. Reprinted piecemeal in newspapers, *Common Sense* quickly became the most widely read document in America. As a fervent condemnation of monarchy and an appeal for action, it galvanized public opinion in favor of a concerted stand against the British. In December of the same year, Paine's *Crisis* paper, published in the *Pennsylvania Journal*, gave currency to the now well-known phrases: "These are the times that try men's souls. The Summer soldier and the Sunshine Patriot will, in this crisis, shrink from the service of their country; but he that stands it now deserves the love and thanks of man and woman." Paine's appeal was used by Washington to rally his troops before the Battle of Trenton.

Throughout the war, poet Philip Freneau, who was to become famous as the editor of the *National Gazette*, used his writing gifts against the British, letting his "best arrows at these hell-hounds play." His verses were widely published in the press, copied on slips of paper, distributed in the army, and posted in conspicuous places to encourage despairing soldiers.[5]

Following the war an uninhibited press played a key role in the determination of what kind of government was to be used to hold the new states together. Nationalists employed the press to publicize the failures of the Articles of Confederation and to urge revision. They were answered in the press by those who feared tyranny from too strong a national government.[6]

After the new Constitution was drafted in 1787, the value of the press in fostering its ratification became immediately apparent.

Alexander Hamilton, James Madison, and John Jay wrote a series of articles for newspaper publication, arguing the case for ratification of the charter. These were to become known as the *Federalist* papers. Phrased in an elegant style and pitched at a high level of philosophical discourse, they were reprinted throughout the country after their initial appearance in the New York *Packet*, the *Independent Journal*, and the *Daily Advertiser*.[7] Besides presenting the case for ratification, *The Federalist*, in book form, became a classic and often-used contemporary exposition and defense of the Constitution.[8]

One might assume that Americans during the eighteenth century arrived at a sophisticated definition of freedom of the press in the light of their experience with the usefulness of the press in political protest, revolution, and constitution-making. American editors of that time were indeed committed to something called "freedom of the press." But in their ringing appeals for freedom of the press, editors and political leaders never arrived at the unequivocal position—now generally accepted—that newspapers and writers should be immune from penalties for criticism that brought government into disrepute. Moreover, the eighteenth-century defenders of freedom were even more blithely inconsistent about who should enjoy freedom of expression than are free press rhetoricians today.

One of the most passionate expositions of the value of free expression came in 1737 from James Alexander, lawyer, editor of Peter Zenger's New York *Weekly Journal*, and a staunch defender of Zenger when that printer was prosecuted by royal authorities for his paper's attacks on Governor William Cosby. Alexander proclaimed that: "Freedom of speech is a *principal Pillar* in a free Government: when this Support is taken away, the Constitution is dissolved, and Tyranny is erected on its ruins." Yet Alexander also wrote, in another article in the same series, that "to infuse into the minds of the people an ill opinion of a just administration is a crime that deserves no mercy."[9]

William Bradford—who had earlier championed freedom of the press in Pennsylvania when he himself was prosecuted for seditious libel—moved to New York, became a royal printer, and founded the New York *Gazette*, in which he attacked Zenger for having published "pieces tending to set the province in a flame, and to raise sedition and tumults."[10]

Benjamin Franklin, the most eminent of colonial printers, declared in an "Apology for Printers," published early in the eighteenth century, that "when Men differ in Opinion, both Sides ought equally to have the Advantage of being heard by the Publick . . . when Truth and Error have fair Play, the former is always an overmatch for the latter." But Franklin noted in the same article, "I have avoided such Things as usually give Offence either to Church or State." Many years later Franklin was to declare that he favored as much discussion as possible of "public measures and political opinions," but recommended harsh treatment for anyone calumniating the government or affronting its reputation.[11]

As the colonies moved toward a break with Great Britain, the press was recognized as a potent propaganda vehicle. Newspapers doubled in number between 1763 and 1775. While the quarrel with Britain was in its earlier stages, colonial papers vigorously represented conflicting points of view. Editors freely opened their columns to both Whigs and Tories. As long as Britain remained in firm control, Whig editors staunchly upheld the value of open debate. But as the anti-British cause gained in strength, Whig journalists began to challenge the Tories' right to espouse their cause in the press. Liberty of speech, they contended, was the right of those who spoke the speech of liberty. Tory editors were subjected to more than verbal harassment, as legislatures proscribed their activities and confiscated their property.[12]

In 1770 Alexander McDougall, one of the commanders of the Sons of Liberty in New York, was prosecuted for seditious libel against the colonial assembly. The New York *Journal* supported freedom of discussion and defended McDougall, but another local paper, the New York *Mercury*, backed the assembly against McDougall. Five years later McDougall, who earlier had posed as an American Wilkes (in the manner of John Wilkes, English champion of a free press), led a band of armed men who destroyed the press of James Rivington, a Tory publisher.[13] The Rivington episode was symptomatic of the growing American intolerance of an opposition press during the Revolutionary period.

Political leaders, who earlier had extolled freedom of the press, became equally intolerant. John Adams in 1765 had urged the publishers of the Boston *Gazette* not to be intimidated but to publish "with the utmost freedom *whatever* can be warranted by the laws of your country." But in 1776 he favored requiring adherence to independence as a test of loyalty, which would mean that the opposition press would "produce no more seditious or traitorous speculations. Slanders upon public men and measures will be lessened."[14]

In 1774 the Continental Congress addressed the inhabitants of Quebec on the value of a free press: "The last right we shall mention regards the freedom of the press. The importance of this consists, besides the advancement of truth, science, morality and arts in general, in its diffusion of liberal sentiments on the administration of government."[15] Only two years later, however, the Congress was calling upon the states to pass laws to prevent the people from being "deceived and drawn into erroneous opinion."[16]

The history of the colonial period provides much evidence that Americans were far from hospitable to unorthodox opinions. And they certainly did not view government as being properly open to the same scrutiny from the press as it is today. The Continental Congress, on November 9, 1775, adopted a secrecy resolution providing that any member who violated the agreement by divulging any part of the proceedings without consent was to be expelled from Congress and "deemed an enemy to the liberties of America."[17] If there was justification for this caution lest the members be later charged with seditious or traitorous activity against Great Britain, the same reason did not apply to the convention that drafted the Constitution. Yet early in the 1787 debates, Pierce Butler of South Carolina moved that the House provide against "licentious publications of their proceedings." The next day, May 29, the convention adopted a rule that "nothing spoken in the House be printed, or otherwise published, or communicated without leave." There was no very pointed objection from the press, and the most important convention in American history went unreported.[18] The closed-door rule, although it may have served the members' purposes, hardly indicated a commitment to the value of public debate in shaping the document.

At the Constitutional Convention efforts by George Mason of Virginia and Charles Pinckney of South Carolina to incorporate in the nation's charter a bill of rights, including a guarantee of freedom of the press, were defeated. The rationale for not protecting the press was that the power of Congress did not extend to the press and that, in any event, state declarations of rights were in effect and adequate.[19] Yet prior to the Revolution the most notorious prosecutors of the press had been the colonial legislatures, and at the time of the convention twelve states left freedom of speech unprotected and four states provided no constitutional protection for freedom of the press.[20]

In Massachusetts, which had a constitutional exhortation of freedom of the press, George Brock and Gideon Pond were indicted for libeling the government in 1787, after they had published articles in sympathy with Shay's Rebellion, but their cases never came to trial. Other criminal libel indictments were handed down in the same state in 1791, 1798, and later. In Pennsylvania, the only state among the original thirteen to guarantee both freedom of speech and press, those guarantees were not considered as repudiating the common law injunction against libels on the government. In 1788, Judge Thomas McKean convicted Eleazer Oswald of contempt for libeling the Pennsylvania state court. McKean's ruling that the common law of libel was not incompatible with the constitutional guarantee of freedom of the press was upheld by the state assembly. Not until 1790 did Pennsylvania adopt a constitution that allowed a jury rather than the judge to decide whether an accused's statement was libelous as a matter of law and that made truth a defense in a prosecution for criminal libel. Even then Pennsylvania still accepted the concept that a republican form of government could be politically libeled and that the offender could be criminally prosecuted.[21] As it turned out, enlargement of the jury's power provided only limited protection for free expression.

When the new federal Constitution was referred to the states, one of the most important single objections to ratification was the document's failure to provide a bill of rights. Yet as the first Congress was meeting in 1789 to provide for the organization of the new national government, not all of the members were as committed as was James Madison to the drafting of a bill of rights. In the House of Representatives, William L. Smith of South Carolina thought it would be impolitic to go into the consideration of amending the government before it was organized. James Jackson of Georgia said the members ought not to be in a hurry with respect to altering the Constitution. Speaking for Connecticut, Roger Sherman said his constituents desired no amendments, adding that no advantage could arise from them. Alexander White of Virginia said he believed a majority of the district that elected him did not require alterations.[22]

Little is known about what was said in the Senate about the desirability of a bill of rights, since that body, like the Constitutional Convention itself, met behind closed doors, and the Senate journal, which was required by the Constitution, showed only official action and provided no record of debates.

In the House, Madison apologized for taking the time of the members, but explained that he had made a promise to his constituents and held strong personal convictions on securing the liberties of the people. One of the great bulwarks of liberty, said Madison, was freedom of the press. This great right and the right of freedom of conscience were not safeguarded in the British constitution. The American constitution, however, should protect the right to speak, to write, and to publish, against infringement by the national government, particularly the legislative branch. He added that freedom of the press should also be protected against violation by the states. In a display of insight that marked him as a prescient civil libertarian, Madison observed that protection ought to extend not just against government itself but to that quarter where the greatest danger lies—namely, to the body of people operating as a majority against the minority.[23]

But Jackson saw no danger to liberty of the press. Had not the newspapers attacked a member of the House for sentiments delivered on the floor? Yet the lawmakers had not ordered any writer before them even for a breach of privilege, although the Constitution provided that a member should not be questioned in any other place for any speech or debate in the House. (In less than a decade an editor was to be summoned before Congress.) Edanus Burke of South Carolina thought they were wasting time on the proposed amendments, and Thomas Sinnickson of New Jersey conceded at one point that the discussion had become so desultory that he had lost track of the question altogether.[24]

Madison persisted, nevertheless, and eventually the House not only adopted his proposed injunction against federal violation of freedom of speech and press but expanded his proposed ban against state infringement of freedom of the press to include freedom of speech as well. An attempt by Thomas Tucker of South Carolina to eliminate the provision on the states was rebuffed by the House, but the Senate refused to accept this prohibition, even though Madison had considered it the most valuable provision of the whole list.[25] As the amendment emerged in final form, its now familiar injunction said "Congress shall make no law . . . abridging the freedom of speech or of the press." Yet its prohibition was hardly broad enough or explicit enough to effectuate the objective held by Madison in debate when he said: "The right of freedom of speech is secured; the liberty of the press is expressly declared to be beyond the reach of this Government."[26]

In his draft Madison had not used the more inclusive language recommended by the Virginia ratification convention to the effect that the liberty of the press "cannot be cancelled, abridged, restrained or modified by any authority of the United States." Although both the Madison proposal and the final draft of the amendment did contain the mandatory "shall make no law" phraseology rather than the merely declaratory "cannot" phraseology of the Virginia resolution, the press guarantee as adopted said nothing about branches of the new national government other than Congress. It left unanswered the questions of whether the executive branch, acting through federal attorneys, might prosecute for the common law crime of seditious libel, or whether, as a corollary, the federal courts had jurisdiction to try such cases.

In their debates, the framers did not discuss such questions as whether the mails should be open to the transmission of seditious or pornographic material or whether speakers or writers should be free to incite violence immediately and directly against the United States. "The framers," wrote Zechariah Chafee, "would probably have been horrified at the thought of protecting books by Darwin or Bernard Shaw."[27] If this was so, one cannot infer this from the debates; nor can one infer that they meant to ensure a totally unfettered press.

As in the ratification discussion before the drafting of the Bill of Rights, the debates in the first Congress on the meaning of a free press guarantee were vague and lacking in thorough exposition.[28] Newspapers themselves contributed little to clarifying the objective.

Obviously then, the First Amendment did not spring in burnished glory from the heads of the founding fathers like Athena from the forehead of Zeus. Indeed, the record of the origins of the amendment—especially that part that guarantees freedom of the press—

indicates that its meaning was neither clearly defined nor its implications for the future fully understood either by its framers or by the press of that time.[29]

To say that the free press guarantee did not spring into life, full-blown and adapted to the coverage of all exigencies, is not to denigrate the work of its drafters but merely to suggest the obvious—that the framers were human and that their constitutional language was a product of their own experience and of compromise. Although many reputable historians and judges have contended that the First Amendment was intended to bring about a radical change in the law on the press, the revisionist historian, Leonard Levy, makes a stronger case for the view that the amendment was intended to do little more than affirm the principle, already established in English law, that the press could not be restrained prior to publication. Even if the amendment was intended to bar Congress from imposing by statute any postpublication penalty on the press, its language did not clearly preclude federal common law prosecutions of the press after the publication of offending words.

The more liberal interpretation of the amendment as a bar to prosecutions for so-called seditious libel came later, as the Jeffersonian party's response to the Alien and Sedition Laws of 1798.[30] And, of course, the First Amendment's expansion to cover ramified issues of free expression, either not considered at the time or not existing, came only through a long history of national experience and, later, through judicial interpretation. There was little judicial discussion of the free speech and free press clauses before 1917.[31]

At the time a bill of rights for the new Constitution was being considered, Americans were thoroughly familiar with the notion of seditious libel—defined as any comment about public affairs that could be construed as having a tendency to lower the public's esteem for the government or one of its branches or officials. Prosecution for seditious libel was the principal means for muzzling editors. It was employed by the common law courts, by governors and their councils, but most of all, by legislative bodies. This did not mean, however, that Americans, as they prepared to establish a new form of government, were primed to write into its charter an absolute prohibition against interference with the press.

The Bill of Rights, including the First Amendment, was ultimately adopted, not because of a universal belief in its necessity but as a compromise in the struggle between anti-Federalists, who opposed the new Constitution, but insisted, for sometimes obstructionist purposes, that one was needed, and Federalists who supported the Constitution and committed themselves to guarantees of rights as a way of getting support for the new charter of government.

Although the value of a free press had been widely proclaimed in America both during the colonial period and during the interim between the Revolution and the adoption of the Bill of Rights, the history of the period, as has been shown, does not indicate that the First Amendment meant to Americans of that time what it means today or even what it came to mean only a few years later when a national political battle erupted over the Alien and Sedition Laws.

Political experience in the new nation in the last decade of the eighteenth century was to have a profound influence in shaping attitudes toward what the newly adopted First Amendment stood for. The era was one of change in journalism as well as one of political transition in which Americans had to adjust to living under a unifying national government instead of a loose confederation of sovereign states. Newspapers played a role in this political transition. Between the end of the war and the beginning of the nineteenth century, many of the old papers disappeared, but about 450 new ones were started. The *Pennsylvania Evening Post*, on May 30, 1783, became the first newspaper to begin daily publication.[32]

This period was marked by the emergence of editors who, through their own writings and selection of items to be printed, stamped their newspapers with their own personalities. Prior to the 1790s nearly all newspapers had been started as auxiliaries to printing establishments, whose proprietors printed and distributed communications from outside contributors and routine selections of domestic and foreign intelligence from other papers. By the turn of the century, however, newspapers came more and more to be the voices of political parties, with editors assuming responsibility for choosing and coordinating their contents.

National policies were being formulated for the first time under the administration of George Washington. One of the most hotly debated was the plan of Washington's secretary of the treasury, Alexander Hamilton, who proposed to have the federal government assume the public debt, foreign and domestic, and pay off creditors at the face value of their securities. By this means, he hoped not only to put the nation's credit on a sound footing but also to ensure the continuing loyalty of "the rich and well-born" (Hamilton's phrase) to the new government. Since wealthy merchants and financiers had acquired government securities at greatly depreciated value, the Hamilton plan, when adopted, served to enrich them still further and to bind them to the emerging Federalist party. Farmers, petty shopkeepers, former soldiers, and others had been forced during hard times to sell at ruinous discounts their government securities, which represented goods supplied or services rendered by them during the war. Infuriated at seeing their lost holdings paid off at par with taxes levied against them, they began to form an opposition party, which came in time to be led by Thomas Jefferson.[33]

As in the case of the plan for national funding of debts, partisan differences developed over United States relations with Great Britain and France. In France, which had aided the American colonies in their war for independence, the revolution against the monarchy had begun in 1789 with the meeting of the estates-general. At first, almost all Americans viewed the French Revolution with friendly sympathy. Meanwhile, relations with Britain were sour because of boundary and trade disputes that still remained unsettled, although Britain was considered of ranking importance for American commerce. When Britain declared war on France in 1793 and both the British and French began seizing American vessels, popular opinion in the United States became divided. The beheading of Louis XVI in 1793 and the growing excesses of the Revolution, however, cooled the sympathies of many Americans for the French.

Hamilton despised the French Revolution, and he and his friends constantly avowed their admiration for the British Constitution and society. The Hamilton partisans in particular, the Federalists generally, wanted to maintain peace with Britain at almost any price. To the Republicans, or Jeffersonians, the French Revolution seemed a clear-cut contest between autocracy and democracy. They wanted to remain friendly to France. American opinion was further polarized by Washington's 1793 declaration of neutrality in the war between Britain and France and by the 1794 Jay Treaty between the United States and Britain, which was denounced by many, including some Federalists, because it did nothing about the impressment of American seamen and won little from the British other than their promise to withdraw from forts on the American side of the frontier, which they had already pledged to do under the 1783 treaty ending the American Revolution.[34]

Strong differences over this series of events—Hamilton's financial plans, the French Revolution, the neutrality proclamation, and Jay's Treaty—furthered the development of political parties, with newspapers serving as vehicles for increasingly vehement partisan battles. In the early years of Washington's administration, the Federalists controlled nearly all of the papers.[35] The paper that was to become the leading Federalist organ, the *Massachusetts Centinel*, was founded in Boston in 1784 by Benjamin Russell. Later renamed the *Columbian Centinel*, the paper pushed Massachusetts toward ratification of the Constitution. Russell, its editor, was pro-British and an advocate of an American nobility. Idolizing Washington, he proposed that Washington be addressed as "His Majesty, the President." Although Russell was sympathetic with the French Revolution in its early stages, he was horrified by the execution of the king. As encounters between American and French vessels occurred, he indulged in warlike rhetoric against the "French pirates." He defended the Jay Treaty with as much fervor as the Republicans attacked it.

When the new federal government was established with the capital in New York, that city had no strong paper of Federalist convictions. Thus, when John Fenno, a former Boston school teacher, arrived in New York with letters from leading Boston Federalists praising his editing and writing abilities, he was encouraged to start a paper. The first issue of his *Gazette of the United States,* a semiweekly, came out on April 15, 1789. Evidently fancying himself as editor of a kind of "court journal," he treated Federalist leaders as nobility and was accused of favoring monarchy. His paper soon became the mouthpiece for the administration and when the seat of government was moved to Philadelphia in 1791, the *Gazette* followed. Upon suffering financial difficulties, Fenno in 1793 appealed to Hamilton for a loan and aid was apparently forthcoming, since the paper was soon transformed into a daily.

With the establishment on March 4, 1797, of *Porcupine's Gazette* by William Cobbett, the capital had another Federalist organ that was to make a vitriolic splash on the national scene until November

1799, when its editor had to leave town because of a libel judgment against him. Meanwhile, in New York the *American Minerva*, founded in 1793 and edited by Noah Webster, was emerging as a powerful Federalist voice. In 1797 its name became the *Commercial Advertiser*. In New England another undeviating supporter of Federalist positions was the *Connecticut Courant* (founded in 1764) of Hartford.

On the Republican side, the leading newspaper in New England was the *Independent Chronicle*, which had been published in Boston since the Revolution. But the Jeffersonians had no strong voice in the nation's capital until October 31, 1791, when Philip Freneau, known as the poet of the Revolution, founded the *National Gazette* in Philadelphia.[36] He had been helped by his appointment by Jefferson to a parttime job as translator in the State Department. With the demise of the *National Gazette* in 1793, the chief organ of the Republicans became the Philadelphia *Aurora*, which had been founded on October 1, 1790, by Benjamin Franklin Bache, grandson of Benjamin Franklin, as the Philadelphia *General Advertiser*. In 1795 Thomas Greenleaf founded another Republican paper, the New York *Argus*. By 1797 Freneau was back in the thick of the political fray as editor of the *Time Piece* in New York, where he remained until his retirement from journalism in 1798.

These, then, were the chief journalistic jousters in the early years of the new nation. John Fenno set the objective of the *Gazette of the United States* when he said his task was, "by every exertion, to endear the GENERAL GOVERNMENT TO THE PEOPLE." Hamilton, John Adams, and other leading Federalists contributed anonymously to its columns. Referring to Freneau's *National Gazette*, James Madison, Jefferson's most prominent supporter, said, "Our main object in encouraging it, was to provide an antidote against Fenno's paper, which was devoted to monarchy. . . ."

The opposing papers squared off against each other on Hamilton's financial measures, with the Federalist press supporting them and the *National Gazette* attacking them. Freneau castigated Federalist speculators who had bought the frontier citizens' government bonds for an eighth of their true value before news of Hamilton's plan to fund the national debt could reach the back-country.

Stung by Freneau's attacks, Hamilton sought to silence the *National Gazette* by placing an anonymous letter in Fenno's paper questioning the ethics of an editor who vilified the administration while receiving a salary from the government. He charged that the *National Gazette* was Jefferson's personal organ. Freneau responded by denying that Jefferson, the secretary of state, had ever written a line for his paper, which was more than Fenno could say about the secretary of the treasury. He labeled Fenno "a vile sycophant," who received "emoluments from government far more lucrative than the salary alluded to." Freneau was referring to Fenno's printing contract with the Senate and treasury and his alleged business connections with the Bank of the United States. Jefferson, in a letter to Washington, denied that he had ever written for the *National Gazette* and, alluding to Freneau's criticism of governmental measures, declared that "no government ought to be without censors and where the press is free, no one ever will." Neither side seemed to be sensitive to the implications for freedom of a press subsidized by government.

The controversy over Hamilton's financial plans was one of the first to engage the opposing papers. Fierce press disputes were also triggered by the French Revolution, which, according to Thomas W. Higginson, "drew a red hot plow through the history of America." In his first issue, Freneau had praised the French revolutionists and Tom Paine, author of the *Rights of Man*, a response to Edmund Burke's attack on the French Revolution.[37]

Having helped to ignite the French upheaval by its own revolutionary movement, America was now reacting to the transatlantic reverberations from Paris. Press exhortations to the American public over the meaning of events in France helped to determine the character of American political institutions. Freneau's ardent advocacy of the cause of the French revolutionists was an attempt to offset the contempt for democracy being voiced by the Federalists in the *Gazette of the United States*. Jefferson, on returning in 1790 from his post as minister to France, had expressed his "wonder and mortification" over the all but unanimous "preference for the kingly over the republican government." Hamilton held that the masses were "turbulent and changing; they seldom judge or determine right."

The arrival in the spring of 1793 of "Citizen" Edmond Charles Genêt, minister to the United States from the French Republic, served to crystallize American public opinion. Received like a conquering hero upon his arrival at Charleston, Genêt initiated arrangements to make the United States a base for privateering operations in behalf of the French even before he presented his credentials at Philadelphia. Rebuffed at the capital but inflated by his evident popularity, Genêt appealed to public opinion over the head of the president. Freneau, whose ancestry was French Huguenot, and Bache, who had been educated in France, aligned their papers with Genêt. Russell's *Columbian Centinel* in Boston denounced the Frenchman and his American followers.

Meanwhile, even Jefferson and Madison recoiled against Genêt's antics. To Washington, the sentiments being published in Freneau's and Bache's papers were "outrages to common decency." But Freneau was undaunted. He reminded the president that he was only a "public servant" but was "so buoyed up by official importance as to think it beneath his dignity to mix occasionally with the people." "Why," he continued, "all this outcry against Mr. Genet for saying he would appeal to the people? . . . The minister of France, I hope, will act with firmness and with spirit. . . . The people are sovereign in the United States."

The president summoned Jefferson to complain that there "never had been an act of government . . . which that paper had not abused." Jefferson recorded later that he took Washington's intention to be that the secretary "should interpose in some way with Freneau; perhaps withdraw his appointment as translating clerk." Jefferson declared: "I will not do it. His paper has saved our constitution, which was galloping fast into monarchy, and has been checked by no other means so powerfully as by that paper." On October 26, 1793, Freneau, faced with financial difficulties following the reaction to Genêt, discontinued the *National Gazette*.

As with the Genêt episode, partisan feeling ran high when the Jay Treaty was signed with Great Britain in 1794. So unpopular was the treaty in the United States that the Senate, even though it had already been ratified and much of its contents were known, resolved not to make its text public until the president should decide. But Bache of the *Aurora* acquired a copy from anti-Federalist Senator Stevens T. Mason of Virginia and, ignoring the official strictures against disclosure and the presumed harm to the national interest, published the treaty in full. Other newspapers widely reprinted the document in a 1795 equivalent of the Pentagon Papers episode of 1971, except that the Washington administration sought no court injunction to stop the presses.

The Republican press damned the accord, the Charleston *City Gazette* calling it "degrading to the national honor, dangerous to the political existence and destructive to the agricultural, commercial, and shipping interests of the people of the United States." Noah Webster and Alexander Hamilton defended the treaty in the *American Minerva*. The Federalist attitude was reflected in the comment of one of their partisans who declared that opposition to the pact was the work of a "violent Jacobin Party" that was determined "either to throw this country into war and anarchy, or reduce us to a Province of France."[38]

Thus the political lines were drawn during Washington's administration between those who rallied behind Hamilton and those who followed Jefferson, between those who were for Federalism and Britain or for Republicanism and France, for capitalism and Britain or agrarianism and the Revolution. As summed up by historians Samuel Eliot Morison and Henry Steele Commager:

Hamilton wished to concentrate power; Jefferson to diffuse power. Hamilton feared anarchy and thought in terms of order; Jefferson feared tyranny and thought in terms of liberty. Hamilton believed republican government could only succeed if directed by a governing class; Jefferson that republicanism was hardly worth trying if not fused with democracy. Hamilton took a gloomy view of human nature; Jefferson, the hopeful view of Jean-Jacques Rousseau.[39]

Washington, who entered the presidency enjoying universal acclaim and whose two elections were unaccompanied by electioneering, ended his administration with Bache's *Aurora*, his most partisan critic, subjecting him to bitter attack: "If ever a nation has been debauched by a man, the American nation has been debauched by Washington. . . . Let his conduct then be an example to future ages. Let it serve to be a warning that no man may be an idol. . . ."

John Adams, vice-president under Washington, had already been deflated by Freneau's *National Gazette*. In reply to Adams's ponderous *Discourses of Davila*, published in Fenno's *Gazette of the United States,* Freneau wrote:

When you tell us of kings,
And such petty things,
Good Mercy! how brilliant your pages!
So bright is each line
I vow that you'll shine
Like—a glow-worm to all future ages.

Adams, with the support of four-fifths of the newspapers, was chosen president in 1796 by the narrow margin of three electoral votes. The Federalists feared that their papers' preponderance in numbers would not guarantee them success. Numbers of newspapers and such circulation figures as are available for this period do not truly reflect the influence of the press in the last quarter of the eighteenth century. Newspapers of all kinds at the start of the Revolution probably went into fewer than forty thousand homes. Fenno's and Freneau's papers each had a circulation of only about fifteen hundred. Most newspapers were widely distributed. Copies of papers were passed from hand to hand, were read in inns and coffee houses, and their articles widely discussed.[40]

During the colonial and the immediate post-Revolutionary periods, the press had been used as a vehicle for espousing the interests of one group against those of another—colonists against royal governors, revolutionists against Tories, and generally outsiders against insiders in government. Each group vied for the favor of the public through the press, with the challenging side extolling freedom of the press because its chances for ascendancy depended on reaching the public with its message, and with the dominant side feeling threatened and using its power, when it was sufficient, to stifle press criticism.

Royal authorities and colonial legislatures alike had used their power to inhibit press voices of dissident groups. When the revolutionists gained the ascendancy, they too used their authority, directly or indirectly, to suppress the Tory press. Thus, with the establishment of a new national government, its potential for misusing power was suspected by enough people to force the adoption of a free press guarantee. The First Amendment's explicit proscription of congressional power over the press meant that those in official positions functioned under a charter leaving far less ambiguity about governmental authority over newspapers than had instruments of government prior to 1791. Although the First Amendment could not supply clear answers to the multitude of questions that would arise, it did provide a powerful rationale for the supporters of freedom of expression in the first major attempt at suppression—the Sedition Act of 1798. As the nation moved toward what was to become an epic political battle over that law, newspapers were mobilized to play a role in determining what the First Amendment would mean for the future of democratic government.

2
Sedition and the Press

A hint of trouble for freedom of expression under the new federal government came as early as 1794. In his annual message to Congress that year, Washington, in words penned by Hamilton, blamed "certain self-created societies" and their "arts of delusion" for the Whiskey Rebellion, in which Pennsylvania farmers had violently protested against federal excise taxes on whiskey. Eager to align Congress on the side of the administration against emerging critics, Representative Thomas Fitzsimons of Philadelphia moved to insert in a pending congressional resolution a passage saying that legislators could not withhold their "reprobation of the self-created societies" that had "risen up" in some parts of the country, were "misrepresenting the conduct of the government, . . . disturbing the operation of the laws, and . . . by deceiving and inflaming the ignorant and the weak, may naturally be supposed to have stimulated and urged the insurrection."

The so-called self-created societies were the initial organizations of the emerging Jeffersonian party, and Fitzsimons's proposal was a way of suggesting that Congress did not look with favor on criticism of the government. Taking the lead against the Fitzsimons motion, Representative Madison saw the attack on the organizations as an infringement of the reserved rights of the people and noted that opinions should not be the objects of censure by a legislative body. Otherwise, he warned, congressional action "may extend to the liberty of speech and of the press." In a system of republican government, he said, "the censorial power is in the people over the Government, and not in the Government over the people." The Fitzsimons resolution was overwhelmingly defeated.[1]

Washington's neutrality proclamation of 1794 had done nothing to reconcile political divisions over United States relations with the British and the French. Republicans, as partisans of the French, were dubbed "Jacobins" by their critics; and Federalists, as apologists for Britain, were called "monarchists." In addition to debates on neutrality, trade relations, and European politics, newspapers were filled with accounts of popular demonstrations. In 1794 and 1795 alien and sedition laws aimed at French sympathizers were adopted in England. By early 1796 Fenno's *Gazette of the United States* was commenting favorably on the British Sedition Act, which was later to provide an example for the Federalists. When John Adams assumed the presidency in 1797, after a period marked by electioneering essays and invective, partisan feeling was still running high. War with France was expected.

In this tense atmosphere, Thomas Iredell, associate justice of the United States Supreme Court, sitting as a circuit judge in Richmond in the spring of 1797, denounced the members of Congress who had published letters to their constituents criticizing the Adams administration for its belligerent attitude toward France. Stirred by the judge's charge, a federal grand jury in Richmond indicted Representative Samuel J. Cabell for seditious libel on the grounds that he had disseminated "unfounded calumnies against the unhappy government of the United States." Attorney General Charles Lee prepared a memorandum on "Libellous Publications," arguing on the strength of British legal authorities Blackstone and Mansfield that freedom of the press consisted of printing without prior restraint. He added that in this definition he concurred with "the learned judge." Iredell himself, when asked at the North Carolina ratifying convention nine years earlier whether the new Constitution might not allow Congress to punish its critics, had assured his questioners that Congress was

barred from such action by the silence of the Constitution as completely as could be done "by the strongest negative clause that could
be framed."

The grand jury's assault on free speech, less than three months
after the inauguration of Adams, was protested in a resolution
drafted by Vice-President Jefferson, approved by Madison, signed
throughout the district, and adopted by the Virginia House of Delegates. Denouncing the action against Cabell as the perversion of a
legal institution into a political one, the petition went on to warn that
the move amounted to a "usurpation of power . . . and a subjection
of a natural right of speaking and writing freely." Apparently deterred by the protest, Lee dropped the prosecution.[2]

But sentiment against the Republicans and against freedom for
the expression of their ideas continued. A leading organ of the Federalist press, which had been filled with vituperation of Jefferson
during and after the election of 1796, reflected Federalist feeling in
June of 1797, while the Cabell affair was brewing. "There is a liberty
of the press," declared the *Columbian Centinel* of Boston after
quoting a "treasonable" statement by the Republican *Independent
Chronicle*, "which is very little short of the liberty of burning our
houses."[3]

Bache of the *Aurora*, who consistently opposed war and urged a
settlement of difficulties by diplomacy rather than by arms, was
denounced by Federalists as a hireling of France and barred from
the floor of the House throughout the 1797–1798 session—a move
condemned by the editor as an "act of tyranny" that both injured
the press and kept the public uninformed. Cobbett, in *Porcupine's
Gazette*, claimed that the French intended to overthrow the United
States government through the agency of the Republican newspapers
and, in March 1798, urged the administration to "regenerate" the
press. To prevent Republican editors from distributing their cor-
roding poison throughout the Union, he thought strict postal control
might work in time, but the most immediate method, he suggested,
might be for Federalist merchants to withdraw their advertising
from the opposition press.

Despite the war fever being generated by the Hamilton partisans,
Adams personally hoped to avoid conflict. To this end, he had sent
emissaries to France in the fall of 1797, only to have the mission produce an imbroglio, known as the XYZ Affair, that was to provide

further rhetorical ammunition for the war hawks. The American envoys reported that French agents (whom they labeled X, Y, and Z) demanded loans and gifts amounting to $240,000 from the United States. Following the transmission to Congress of papers in the XYZ Affair, the lawmakers, in the spring of 1798, authorized the president to raise an army of ten thousand volunteers. Washington was appointed lieutenant general and the head of the army; Hamilton was named second in command.

Meanwhile, the administration prepared to deal with its enemies at home. Adams, in a communication published in Fenno's paper, wrote that "the delusions and misrepresentations which have misled so many citizens, must be discountenanced by authority as well as by the citizens at large."[4] Congress during the early summer of 1798 passed in quick succession: (1) the Naturalization Act, extending the term of residence required before naturalization from five to fourteen years; (2) the Alien Act, giving the president the power to deport or imprison any alien whom he regarded as dangerous; and (3) the Alien Enemies Act, authorizing the president to deport or restrain subjects of any country with which the United States might be at war. The new laws, passed despite Republican protests that they would violate due process, were aimed at large numbers of French émigrés, as well as English and Irish refugees, many of whom were considered hostile to the administration's point of view. Among the potential targets were several leading Republican journalists, including William Duane, who was to succeed Bache as editor of the *Aurora*, and John Burk, editor of the New York *Time Piece*. Duane, though born in colonial New York, had spent twenty-two years abroad as a British citizen. Burk was born in Ireland.[5]

Another bill was to be aimed specifically at the press. Abigail Adams, wife of the president, had written to her sister on April 28, 1798, that she presumed Congress would pass a sedition bill because every issue of the two leading Republican newspapers, the Philadelphia *Aurora* and the Boston *Independent Chronicle*, contained statements that "might have been prossecuted [*sic*] as libels upon the President and Congress." On the same day Jefferson was writing to Madison to warn that a sedition bill would soon be proposed, the object of which would be "the suppression of the Whig presses. Bache's [*Aurora*] has been particularly named."[6]

Initially, proscriptions against sedition were included in an omnibus alien and sedition bill reported by a House committee on June 4. Among other things, the bill would have punished "any person, whether alien or citizen, who shall . . . openly combine . . . with an intention of opposing any measure of the Government of the United States, which are or shall be directed by the proper authority." Without specifying force or violence, the measure applied to any opposition and singled out any writing, printing, or advised speaking. Thus, the authors of a petition for repeal of a law they thought to be unconstitutional could have been prosecuted for criminal behavior.

On June 6 the *Aurora* simply quoted the First Amendment in full and followed it with the text of the bill presented without comment. While the omnibus bill was being considered, the Federalist press became apoplectic over the departure on June 13 for France on a one-man peace mission of Dr. George Logan, a Philadelphia Republican and an ardent Quaker. "Recollect," said *Porcupine's Gazette*, "that seditious Envoys from all the Republics that France has subjugated first went to France and *concerted measures with the despots*. . . . Take care; or, when your blood runs down the gutters, don't say you were not forewarned of the danger."

On June 16, two days before Adams notified Congress of the receipt by the American envoys of a mollifying communication from the French foreign minister, Talleyrand, the publication of the Tallyrand letter in the *Aurora* was taken by the Federalists as a sign that the Republicans were serving as French agents. Bache swore, however, that the Talleyrand letter came into his possession not from France but from a gentleman in Philadelphia. While the furor over the Talleyrand letter was in progress, the House postponed action on the omnibus bill in order to take up the Senate's alien bill.[7]

Senator James Lloyd of Maryland received permission on June 23 to introduce a bill "to define more particularly the crime of treason, and to define and punish the crime of sedition." The Lloyd bill designated the government and people of France as enemies of the United States and declared that adherence to them and giving them aid and comfort was treason, punishable by death. For the first and only time in American history a legislative attempt was made to establish by law the concept of treason in peacetime. The bill also provided that, if any person should "by any writing, printing, or speaking threaten" any federal officeholder "or person in public trust, with any damage to his character, person or property, or shall counsel, advise, or attempt to procure any insurrection, riot, unlawful assembly or combination, whether such conspiracy . . . advice or attempt should have the proposed effect or not," he would be guilty of a high misdemeanor and subject to fine and imprisonment. The bill branded as "seditious or inflammatory" any declarations or expressions tending to produce a belief among the citizens that the federal government had been led to pass any law by motives "hostile to the constitution, or liberties and happiness of the people." Any persons who attempted to defame the president or any federal court by declarations "directly or indirectly tending to criminate their motives in any official transaction," were made subject to fine and imprisonment.

Two days later, on June 29, Alexander Hamilton labeled the bill politically inexpedient because it would make martyrs of Republicans. By that time a Senate committee under Lloyd, evidently having reached the same conclusion, had revised the bill to omit the treason portions that prescribed the death penalty for Americans convicted of adhering to the government or people of France. The sections on sedition were retained.

Bache, taking note earlier of the progress of Federalist legislation, observed in the *Aurora* that "to laugh at the cut of a coat of a member of Congress will soon be treason." The New York *Argus* attacked the Senate bill as a gross violation of the First Amendment and asked: "If I know that a member is actuated by motives hostile to the constitution, as they must be on the present occasion, have I not a right to say so, and if I now have this right can such freedom of speech be abridged? Certainly not." The Boston *Independent Chronicle* commented to the effect that the fear of criticism being exhibited by the administration suggested that it had "insufficient confidence in its own integrity," and went on to denounce the sedition bill as the last gasp of an "expiring Aristocracy." The editor predicted that liberty would "eventually arise with renovated lustre," so that citizens could speak openly of their government. On July 3 the *Aurora* condemned the sedition bill for "making it criminal to expose the crimes, the official vices or abuses, or the attempts of men in power to usurp a despotic authority."

Across the nation on July 4 the Republicans drank toasts to freedom of speech and press. Federalists in Newburyport, Massachusetts, marked the Fourth by burning copies of the *Independent Chronicle*. On that same day the Senate passed the Lloyd bill by a straight party vote of 16 to 6.[8] Senator Harry Tazewell of Virginia, in a masterpiece of understatement, remarked that it was "an unauspicious event to have happened on the 4th of July."

In its issue of July 4, the Federalist *Columbian Centinel* paid its respects to the Republican views of the *Independent Chronicle*. "How long," the paper asked, "will these fools [*Chronicle* writers] continue to keep alive the public contempt by such artless efforts at deception!"[9] The *Chronicle* proclaimed the next day that the Federalists were "creating a balance inimical to liberty" with "pensioned presses."[10] The next issue printed a speech by Republican Representative Edward Livingston of New York in which he attacked the alien bill, saying its provisions "are not only unauthorized by the constitution but are in direct violation of its fundamental principles and contradictory to some of its most express prohibitions."[11]

The House began consideration of the Lloyd sedition bill on July 5, with newspapers being the focus of much of the discussion. Unlike the Senate, where press access was restricted, the House allowed its debates to be reported. Federalist arguments for the bill were presented by Representatives John Allen and Samuel Dana of Connecticut, Harrison Gray Otis of Massachusetts, and Robert Goodloe Harper of South Carolina. Republican spokesmen were Albert Gallatin of Pennsylvania, Nathaniel Macon of North Carolina, and John Nicholas of Virginia.

Otis and Harper argued that the federal government, under the original Constitution, had inherent power to protect itself against sedition and libels. "Every independent Government," said Otis, "has a right to preserve and defend itself against injuries and outrages which endanger its existence." Acts tending directly to the destruction of the Constitution, he noted, were listed as offenses in section one—namely, unlawful combinations formed to oppose governmental measures, to intimidate federal officers, to incite insurrection, or to counsel or advise these deeds. Arguing the justification for section two on grounds of indirect causation, Otis said that "all means calculated to produce these effects, whether by speaking, writing, or printing, were also criminal."

To buttress their position further, the Federalists argued that authority for the proposed law was derived not only from inherent power but from the Constitution's grant to Congress of the authority to make all laws "necessary and proper" for carrying into execution all powers vested in the government of the United States or in any department or officer thereof. Otis also claimed that the Constitution conferred on the federal courts common law jurisdiction over criminal cases, including sedition—his argument being based on the judicial article (Article III) that said the powers of the federal judiciary extended to cases arising under the Constitution and under the laws of the United States. Since cases arising under the Constitution could not be the same as cases arising under the laws, he argued that the former phrase must refer to cases under the common law as derived from England. Republicans were quick to point out that, if the federal courts had common law jurisdiction over seditious libel, which the Republicans denied, no statute was necessary.

As for the First Amendment, the Federalists contended that its purpose was merely to prohibit any restraints on the press prior to publication, which was the meaning of freedom of the press as defined in Blackstone's famous *Commentaries*. This freedom, said Otis, "is nothing more than the liberty of writing, publishing, and speaking one's thoughts, under the condition of being answerable to the injured party, whether it be the Government or an individual, for false, malicious, and seditious expression, whether spoken or written, and the liberty of the press is merely an exemption from all previous restraints." Subsequent punishment for seditious words, he said, was therefore no violation of this freedom.

Noting that the states had constitutional guarantees similar to the First Amendment, Otis said they had given legislative and judicial interpretations of these guarantees in accordance with Blackstone's definition, and they all agreed that freedom of the press meant freedom from censorship prior to publication and not freedom from prosecution for defamatory and seditious libels.

To support their claim that a sedition law was needed the Federalists pointed to what they called a conspiracy of Republican newspapers, congressmen, and others. Allen made it plain who they were talking about when he said:

If ever there was a nation which required a law of this kind, it is this. Let gentlemen look at certain papers printed in this city [Philadelphia] and elsewhere, and ask themselves whether an unwarrantable and dangerous combination does not exist to overturn and ruin the Government by publishing the most shameless falsehoods against the Representatives of the people of all denominations, that they are hostile to free Governments and genuine liberty, and of course to the welfare of this country; that they ought, therefore, to be displaced, and that the people ought to raise an *insurrection* against the Government.

As evidence of newspaper incitement to revolt, Allen then quoted a paragraph from the *Aurora* which said: "It is a curious fact, America is making war with France for not treating, at the very moment the Minister of Foreign Affairs [Talleyrand] fixes upon the very day for opening a negotiation with Mr. Gerry. What think you of this, Americans?"

The danger in the *Aurora's* paragraph, said Allen, was that its intent "is to persuade the people that peace with France is in our power . . . on proper terms, but that we reject her offers, and proceed to plunge our country into a destructive war." He saw a combination to achieve this purpose between Bache of the *Aurora* and Representative Livingston, who several days earlier had made a motion requesting that President Adams direct Mr. Gerry to treat with France. This motion reflected the fact that Talleyrand had refused to treat with all three American commissioners, regarding two of them as partisans of Britain, but was willing to negotiate with Gerry, a Republican. Livingston had pointed out that Gerry had authority to deal with the French, since the powers given the commissioners were "joint and several."

Allen, however, saw Bache and Livingston as engaged in a conspiracy to persuade the people as to certain facts which a majority of the House and the people at large, according to his belief, knew to be unfounded. Moreover, further proof that "a revolution is intended," said Allen, was provided by an *Aurora* statement on the sedition bill, in which the editor commented that it would soon be "difficult to determine, whether there is more safety and liberty to be enjoyed at Constantinople or Philadelphia."[12]

The Connecticut representative was convinced that "a conspiracy, against the Constitution, the Government, the peace and safety of this country" was "in full operation." He quoted from a speech Livingston made against the alien bill: "If we exceed our powers we become tyrants, and our acts have no effect. Thus, sir, one of the first effects of measures such as this, will be disaffection among the States; and opposition among the people to your Government; tumults, violations, and a recurrence to first revolutionary principles."

To show that Bache was aiding Livingston in promoting insurrection, Allen referred to a letter that the *Aurora* had published in which the writer had asked whether it was reasonable to expect aliens to join the provisional army and fight in defense of a country that proscribed them. Bache's intention, said Allen, could have been to inflame the passions of Irish aliens and encourage them to join the ranks of an invading French army once it had landed.

Extending his view of the conspiracy beyond Bache and Livingston, Allen cited an item in the New York *Time Piece*, now edited by John Burk, in which President Adams was referred to as "a person without patriotism, without philosophy, and a mock monarch," and suggested that he had been elevated to his position by an "ominous combination of old Tories with old opinions and old Whigs with new." These, then, according to Allen, were "awful, horrible" examples of "the liberty of opinion and freedom of the press. . . . God deliver us from such liberty, the liberty of vomiting on the public floods of falsehood and hatred to everything sacred, human and divine."

The real reason for Allen's excitement became apparent, however, when, without naming Jefferson, the leader of the Republicans, he insinuated that the vice-president was advising Bache in midnight closet conferences. His hearers knew what he meant, since a Federalist newspaper, hinting at dark conspiracy, had made such an accusation. Jefferson freely conceded that he met Bache, along with others, in a public room in which the door was open to anyone who should call. The real basis for Allen's concern was evidently not an insurrection but a political transfer of power at the next election, with the Republicans, aided by the press, winning control from the Federalists. Since the Republicans (whose newspapers, incidentally, were still outnumbered two to one by those on the Federalist side)[13] sought to keep the weapon of the press in their hands, Allen said the business of the Federalists was "to wrest it from them."

Federalist lawmakers were joined in their attack on the Republican press by Federalist newspapers. The *Gazette of the United States* in Philadelphia, the New York *Gazette*, the New York *Commercial Advertiser*, the Albany *Centinel*, the *Connecticut Courant* in Hartford, the Boston *Columbian Centinel*, and *J. Russell's Gazette* in Boston (published by a brother of the *Centinel* publisher) all endorsed the sentiments of the Fourth of July toast offered by Federalists of Deadham, Massachusetts: "Freedom of speech—let the revilers of our government have *rope* enough. For honest men of all parties the cord of friendship; for traitors and foreign spies the hangman's cord."

In their speeches opposing the sedition bill, the Republicans answered the Federalist arguments point by point. Under the Federalist theory of inherent power, the Republicans said, Congress had a sort of undefined general legislative power to punish offenses against government, which would mean that federal officials might label as a crime any act they found obnoxious and make it punishable. Instead of granting Congress any such general power, the Constitution, Gallatin observed, listed the cases in which Congress could define and punish offenses; and sedition was not one of the cases enumerated. Nor did the "necessary and proper" clause confer such power, he said. For in order to infer such a grant from this clause, he added, the proponents would have to show the specific power given to Congress or the president by some other part of the Constitution, which would be carried into effect by a law against seditious libel; and this they had not done.

Denying flatly that there was any common law of the United States, the Republicans asserted that the common law of England had been received in each colony and had been modified in every one according to its needs. Because the common law now varied from state to state, the Constitution, they said, could not have adopted the common law of all the states. Nor could the Constitution have adopted the common law of England, they argued, since the convention would not in so doing have rejected the American modifications without comment.

Otis's contention that Article III conferred on the federal courts jurisdiction over common law crimes was also rejected by Gallatin, who noted that the Constitution specified the kinds of cases to which the judicial authority extended and, in addition to these, mentioned cases arising under the Constitution and laws. The reference to cases arising under the Constitution, Gallatin said, was not meant generally to include common law crimes but only those cases in which construction of the Constitution might be in dispute. Moreover, declared Gallatin, the First Amendment was added to the Constitution to remove any shadow of a doubt as to whether the original charter might possibly have given Congress any power over the press. The amendment, he added, was intended not only to preserve the pre-Revolutionary victory abolishing censorship prior to publication but to provide a new protection guaranteeing free discussion of public men and measures. The amendment, he said, not only repudiated the English common law concept of libels against the government but also forbade Congress to add any restraint, either by previous restriction, subsequent punishment, alteration of jurisdiction, or mode of trial. The Federalists, it appeared to him, evaded the Constitution when they said: "We claim no power to abridge the liberty of the press; *that*, you shall enjoy unrestrained. You may write and publish what you please, but if you publish anything against us, we will punish you for it. So long as we do not prevent, but only punish your writings, it is no abridgement of your liberty of writing and printing."[14]

Gallatin argued that the Federalists had failed to prove the existence of any criminal conspiracy against the government or of any alarming seditious disposition among the American people. He charged that the "only evidences brought by the supporters of this bill consist of writings expressing an opinion that certain measures of Government have been dictated by an unwise policy, or by improper motives, and that some of them are unconstitutional." Was the administration, he asked, afraid to leave these questions open to argument, afraid that error could not be successfully opposed by truth? Macon observed that if anything appeared in the *Aurora* that was unfounded, it would always be contradicted in another journal because there were papers on both sides of the political fence.

In defense of Livingston's speech, which seemed to so alarm the Federalists, Gallatin said it simply set forth the general proposition that the people have a right to resist, and would resist, unconstitutional and oppressive laws. This doctrine, he thought, was neither seditious nor treasonable. He reminded his hearers that Americans had just celebrated the Fourth of July, a commemoration of the right to resist unconstitutional laws.

Nicholas observed that the people of the United States were competent judges of their own interests, and the press should remain perfectly free to provide them with information on those interests. He was willing, he said, to give liberal support to Federalist defense measures, especially if war came, but he was not ready "to create a *domestic tyranny.*"

As the debate progressed, the bill was amended to permit a defendant in any prosecution to give evidence as to the truth of the matter charged as libel; and the jury, rather than the judge, was empowered to determine the law and the facts of the case.[15] Gallatin observed, however, that criticism of government and its measures almost always intermixed facts and opinions. "And how," he asked, "could the truth of opinions be proved by evidence."[16] Moreover, Gallatin said, the jury in some states would be selected by a federal marshal who owed his tenure to the president. What chance would a citizen have, he asked, if the jury was picked, and possibly packed, by "a creature of the Executive"?

Nicholas noted that the presiding judge would also be appointed by the president and declared that the sedition bill would lead "to the suppression of every printing press in the country, which is not obsequious to the will of Government," Gallatin concluded, "this bill must be considered only as a weapon used by a party now in power in order to perpetuate their authority and present places."[17]

On July 10 the House approved the sedition bill by a vote of 44 to 41. Two days later Congress passed a little-noticed supplement to the Sedition Law authorizing all federal judges to bind persons to good behavior in cases arising under the laws of the United States. Thus accused violators of the Sedition Act could be required to post bond, which would deter alleged offenders from repeating their criticism, since such action might lead to forfeiture of the bonds. With federal judges exercising discretionary power over the amount of the surety and the length of the binding, this legislation imposed an economic sanction on criticism of the government during the interval set by the judge.

Although a one-year limit on the Sedition Law had been proposed in the House, the bill was altered before passage to extend the life of the act, not for the duration of the crisis with France but until March 3, 1801—the expiration date of the Adams administration. Significantly, the act would extend through the period of the next presidential election, in which the Federalists presumably hoped to benefit from its restraints on their opponents. But if the Republicans should win, the law would no longer be available for their use against the Federalists. President Adams, who willingly signed the statute on July 14, was to eagerly urge its enforcement.

The new law made criminal "any false, scandalous and malicious" writings, utterances, or publications against the government, Congress, or the president, with intent to defame them, bring them into contempt or disrepute, or excite against them the hatred of the people. Anyone convicted under the act was made subject to a fine of up to $2,000 and imprisonment of up to two years.[18]

Republican newspapers greeted the law with ridicule and defiance. On the day before it was to be approved by the president, the New York *Time Piece* called it a "harmonizer of parties . . . they must all sing the same tune!" The Boston *Independent Chronicle* (July 11) declared that it was the duty of citizens to speak their sentiments, and added, "may the hand be palsied that shrinks back from its duties" regardless of whether the "threats of the SERVANTS OF THE PEOPLE become ever so vociferous to controll [sic] it." The Philadelphia *Aurora* denounced the Federalists as "the majority of three" (the margin of votes by which the bill was passed in the House) and warned Americans that they "had better hold their tongues and make tooth picks of their pens." On the day the act was signed, the *Aurora* ran an "Advertisement Extraordinary!!!"

Orator Mum takes this very orderly method of announcing to his fellow citizens that a thinking Club will be established in a few days at the sign of the *Muzzle* in *Gag* street. The first subject for cogitation will be:

"Ought a Free People to obey the laws which violate the constitution they have sworn to support?"

N. B. No member will be permitted to think longer than fifteen minutes.

Leading the chorus calling for enforcement of the act were Federalist newspapers: the *Gazette of the United States* in Philadelphia, the New York *Commercial Advertiser*, the New York *Gazette*, the

Albany *Centinel*, the *Connecticut Courant*, and in Boston, the *Columbian Centinel* and *J. Russell's Gazette*.[19] The *Columbian Centinel*, four days after the law took effect, exclaimed: ". . . when your Adams . . . is insulted beyond example by the rulers of France, and their incendiaries among you . . . is it not time to . . . call to an account these monsters of ingratitude, these enemies of order; these friends of darkness:—Is it not time to silence their tongues, or dash them to the earth."[20]

The Albany *Centinel* defined sedition as an attempt "to weaken the arm of Government, by undermining the confidence of the community in its measures." Even the silence of the Republicans was suspect in the view of the *Connecticut Courant*. The paper warned that when the Jacobins were silent, it was "ominous of evil. The murderer listens to see if all is quiet, then he begins. So it is with the Jacobins." As the weeks went by, the *Columbian Centinel* continued its campaign, declaring that it "is patriotism to write in favor of our government—it is sedition to write against it." Referring to the Republican papers as the promoters of the anarchical and despotic principles of France, the New York *Gazette* called these papers "the greatest curse to which free governments are liable." Those who circulated falsehoods about men chosen by the people, said the *Gazette*, "should be ferreted out of their lurking places, and condemned to punishment merited by every patricide from the days of Adam to our own." *J. Russell's Gazette* saw several members of the House, Albert Gallatin and William Findley of Pennsylvania and Matthew Lyon of Vermont, as fitter subjects for the execution of the Sedition Law than for the framing of statutes.

As the Sedition Law was being applied to silence their political opposition, the Federalists displayed a remarkable blindness toward the implications of the enforcement campaign for a nation boasting a constitutional guarantee of free speech and free press. Not a single Federalist is known to have questioned the constitutionality of the act, and only one, John Marshall, doubted its wisdom. With the exception of Marshall, every Federalist favored use of the statute against Republican spokesmen, including congressmen, editors, and less influential citizens. In rulings on circuit during the period, 1798–1800, every member of the Supreme Court, all then Federalists, held the law constitutional. Every Republican, with the exception of Attorney General James Sullivan of Massachusetts, thought the act to be unconstitutional.[21]

The supervisor of enforcement for the Adams administration was Secretary of State Timothy Pickering, a zealot who was so convinced of the rightness of Federalist policies that he could not recognize that there was another side. As one of his biographers put it, to Pickering "there was right and wrong, and the eternal battle between them; there could be nothing else." Pickering systematically read Republican newspapers in search of material that might form a basis for prosecution.

As the campaign to suppress the dissemination of opposition views went forward, there were prosecutions for seditious libel under both the common law and the new sedition statute. Twenty-five arrests were made under the Sedition Act itself. There were at least seventeen verifiable indictments—fourteen under the Sedition Act and three under the common law, two before and one after the passage of the statute. Fifteen actions resulted in convictions, eight of them related to newspapers. Most of the prosecutions were begun in 1798, but the majority of cases did not come to trial until the spring of 1800—the year of the presidential campaign between Adams and Jefferson.[22]

While the Federalists were readying the Sedition Law for use as a weapon against the opposition press, they were so incensed over what they called the licentiousness of two major Republican newspapers that they did not wait to act until the statute was enacted. Their first target was Bache's Philadelphia *Aurora*; and their next was John Daly Burk's New York *Time Piece*, which had only been taken over by him on June 13, 1798.

The pretext that was decided upon at first as a basis for action against Bache was his publication of Talleyrand's letter, which they said he had obtained in a secret and treasonable correspondence with the French foreign office. Bache was able to prove, however, that a packet addressed to him from the French foreign office that allegedly contained the Talleyrand letter actually consisted of two innocuous pamphlets on British affairs. The editor was able to show, moreover, that the packet containing the reputed evidence of treason was not ever in his hands at the time of the publication of the Talleyrand letter but had been diverted to the secretary of state through a meeting with the courier by Secretary of Treasury Oliver Wolcott. When Bache defended himself by accusing two cabinet officers, who were creatures of the president, "subject to his will and pleasure," of illegally detaining his property and attempting to use it in a baseless effort to defame him the editor's words were seized upon for use in a sedition prosecution under the common law. Bache was arrested on June 26 and charged with "libelling the President and the Executive Government, in a manner tending to excite sedition, and opposition to the laws, by sundry publications and re-publications."

Following Bache's publication of the Talleyrand letter, the capital's leading Federalist papers, the *Gazette of the United States*, and *Porcupine's Gazette*, both sought to tar the Republican editor with the brush of treason. *Porcupine's Gazette* charged further that Bache, in connivance with the French, had printed the conciliatory communication "for the express purpose of *drawing off the people from the Government*, of exciting discontents, of strengthening Republican opposition, and to procure a *fatal* delay *of preparation for war*." Labeling Bache a "prostitute printer," Porcupine asked: "ought such a wretch to be tolerated at this time?"

Republican papers came to Bache's support, the Boston *Independent Chronicle* declaring that his defense against "the botched up charge of conspiracy" had defeated the malignant intentions of his traducers. The New York *Time Piece* went further, contending that even if Bache had obtained the letter directly from Talleyrand, he would have committed no crime. After all, said the *Time Piece*, the two countries were at peace; but even if they were at war, the editor continued, nothing would hinder an American editor from procuring from any person, "no matter whom, intelligence, useful to America." Republican newspapers took the position that Bache had frustrated the Federalist warmongers by revealing France's willingness to negotiate with Gerry.

A delay in the initial hearing of his case having been secured, Bache appeared with his counsel before United States District Judge Richard Peters on June 29 and declared that the federal courts lacked common law jurisdiction, a position the judge promptly rejected. The editor was released upon the pledging of $4,000 as security for his later appearance, and his trial was set for the October term of court. Meanwhile Bache had sworn that "prosecution no more than persecution" would silence him. True to his word, he continued to attack Adams administration measures, particularly the Alien and Sedition Laws. Claiming that the liberty of the press was at stake, he accused the administration of a concerted attempt to suppress his paper by official and unofficial action. Having already suffered two mob attacks on his house that year as well as two physical assaults on his person, Bache remained at his post during the politically tumultuous summer of 1798, the season when a raging yellow fever epidemic struck Philadelphia. Although others left, to escape infection, Bache stayed in the city, and on September 5 caught the fever. Five days later he was dead at the age of twenty-nine. The Republican press echoed the sentiments of the Boston *Independent Chronicle*, which proclaimed that "the real friends of their country cannot but lament the loss of so valuable a citizen." Federalist editors, who had been gloating over the prospect of Bache's coming trial while deploring the continuing circulation of his paper, tended to agree with *J. Russell's Gazette*, which greeted the news of the Republican editor's death with the comment: "The Jacobins are all whining at the exit of the vile Benjamin Franklin Bache; so they would do if one of their gang was hung for stealing. The memory of this scoundrel cannot be too highly execrated."[23]

Although the *Aurora* was suspended at the time of Bache's death, publication of the paper was resumed on November 1, 1798, under the editorship of William Duane, who had been Bache's assistant since 1796 and who was to marry his widow. Duane's wife had died of the fever. The new editor of the *Aurora* was soon to come under fire by the administration.

Meanwhile, the administration had been proceeding with an attack on its second major Republican target, John Burk, editor of the New York *Time Piece*. Burk, born in Ireland about 1775, had emigrated to the United States in 1796 as a political refugee from his native land, where he had been expelled from the University of Dublin for his republicanism and deism and was being sought for a sedition prosecution after participating in an attempt to rescue a political prisoner being led to execution. Becoming editor of Boston's first daily newspaper, *The Polar Star and Boston Daily Advertiser*, Burk avoided partisan politics, but his libertarian sympathies were suggested by his comment that he abhorred "that gloomy and monastic system of politics" which condemned those who differed in opinion "to the Inquisition and Bastille." When his daily newspaper project failed, Burk moved to New York, where on June 13, 1798, he became editor of the *Time Piece*.

Burk promptly became involved in the controversy over the pending Alien and Sedition Laws and other administration measures. In his first issue, Burk said the *Time Piece,* which he proposed to convert to a daily, would support the Constitution, but he pledged that "its Federalism will not be of that kind which displays itself in mere sycophantic compliance with every act of Administration, in clamoring for war, taxes, standing armies and a government of Terror, in efforts to suppress the liberty of speech and the press." Within five days, Noah Webster's Federalist *Commercial Advertiser* was denouncing Burk "for his turbulent, revolutionary Jacobin sentiments," and suggesting that the alien editor should be run out of town.

Like Bache of the *Aurora*, Burk soon ran into trouble with the administration because of his opposition to war with France. After President Adams had transmitted to Congress a letter from Elbridge Gerry in which the remaining American envoy in Paris said it would be futile for him to stay on, Burk published the letter on the front page but intimated that certain passages had been altered "to promote certain ends in this country." Claiming to have grounds for believing that a continuing diplomatic role in France for Gerry would not be useless, that Gerry could see that channels for communication were still open and did not wish to be recalled, the editor questioned whether it was "sedition to say the President is incorrect in a part of History." Two days later, on the Fourth of July, Burk observed that the people have every right to criticize their elected officials and concluded that it was deplorable that Federalist administrators should be able to charge their opponents with Jacobinism because the latter refused to grant the "heaven born genius of an Adams."

As a result of Burk's claim that the Gerry letter had been altered, Secretary of State Pickering called the attention of the federal attorney in New York, Richard Harrison, to what he said was the editor's "false" charge that the president had falsified the envoy's letter. Pickering charged that Burk's comment was "inflammatory" and of a "seditious tendency," and asked the prosecutor to examine the *Time Piece* for other seditious material. The secretary also told the prosecutor of a speech Burk was said to have made in which he said that he hoped the French would invade America and that "every scoundrel in favor of this government would be put to the guillotine." Calling upon Harrison to determine Burk's citizen status, Pickering suggested that if he was an alien, "no man is a fitter object" for deportation under the Alien Act. But, he added that deportation might be too lenient for a foreigner who edited a vehicle of "atrocious slander of the Government . . . a ready instrument of sedition." It might be better, he advised, to punish him for his libels before deporting him.

Harrison, however, had already shown himself to be in tune with the wishes of the government. On July 6, before hearing from Pickering, Harrison had Burk arrested in the name of the president and charged under the common law with seditious and libelous utterances against Adams. Burk's publishing partner, Dr. James Smith, was also arrested. On appearing before United States District Judge John Sloss Hobart, they were released under $4,000 bond. Noah Webster's *Commercial Advertiser* promptly proclaimed that, though "justice has been slow, . . . we hope she will not check her step till she has dragged the guilty to condign and *exemplary* punishment." The Republican New London *Bee*, in noting the arrest of Bache, Burk, and Smith, contrasted these events with what the American envoys in Paris had told Talleyrand when he demanded that the United States government discountenance anti-French comments in Federalist newspapers: "In the United States no individual fears to utter what his judgment or his passions dictate, and an *un-restrained press* conveys alike to the public eye the labours of virtue and the efforts of particular interests."

Burk, as the *Time Piece* continued to appear, maintained that he and Smith were being prosecuted because of their championship of freedom of the press and, like Bache, declared that prosecution would not force him into "sycophancy or silence." He published long extracts from essays on liberty of the press, including quotations from Thomas Erskine, the British lawyer who had defended Tom Paine in 1792 against a charge of seditious libel in Great Britain.[24]

With the new sedition law having been passed by this time, Noah Webster defended it as "the fruit of opposition." Burk, in continuing attacks on the statute, charged that it subjected printers to prosecution for every sentence "which the eye of a jealous government can torture into an offence." He declared that the law "will tend to the suppression of every press, however congenial with the constitution, if it be not obsequious to the will of government."

The Federalist prosecution and Burk's continuing outspokenness in the *Time Piece* led to a quarrel between Smith and Burk, and the combined effect of the dispute and the action of the government was hard on the fortunes of the paper. By the end of August 1798 its last issue was published. Its anticipated demise was greeted by the Federalist New York *Daily Advertiser* with the exultant comment: "May such be the fate of every paper, that under the hypocritical vizer of false patriotism and hallow-hearted professions of attachment to the people, aim at the subversion of our fair fabric of law, government, individual security and domestic enjoyment."

With his paper having been put out of business, Burk offered to depart voluntarily from the United States in return for the dismissal of his case and release from his bail requirement. Foreseeing the probability of conviction because he was an alien and concluding that, even if he were acquitted of the charge of sedition, he would be "at the mercy of the President," who might deport him at any time, the former editor decided that his chances for justice were slight if he remained. The administration did not reveal whether it was satisfied with the death of the *Time Piece* or unsure of its ground under the common law, but the prosecution was not pressed. Nevertheless, in accepting Burk's proposal, transmitted through Aaron Burr, Pickering remained fanatic in his attitude that this "turbulent mischievous person" ought to leave the Western Hemisphere and insisted that he be prosecuted if he should turn up anywhere on United States territory. Fearing seizure by British agents while aboard ship Burk did not leave the United States but instead went into hiding under an assumed name until the expiration of the Alien and Sedition Laws.

In their eagerness to silence the Philadelphia *Aurora* and the New York *Time Piece*, the Federalists had proceeded against the editors of these papers without waiting for passage of the Sedition Act. Thomas Adams, the editor of the Boston *Independent Chronicle*, was the first important journalist to be indicted under the law. A strong critic of the Adams administration and of the Alien and Sedition Laws, he was an open target in Federalist New England. He was arraigned on October 23, 1798, and pleaded not guilty to a charge of "sundry libellous and seditious publications . . . tending to defame the government of the United States." His trial was set for June 1799. Meanwhile, the *Chronicle* pledged itself to support the rights of the people and the liberty of the press and continued to attack the Federalists. When the Massachusetts legislature rejected the Virginia Resolutions, which condemned the Alien and Sedition Laws, the *Chronicle* accused the legislators of violating their oaths of office by not supporting the right of the states to decide on the constitutionality of acts of Congress. For this attack, Adams and his older brother, Abijah Adams, the bookkeeper for the paper, were indicted by Massachusetts for seditious libel on February 28, 1799. Thomas Adams was too ill to stand trial; Abijah was tried and convicted in March. With the scheduled federal trial less than a month away, ailing Thomas Adams on May 2 was forced to sell the *Chronicle*. A week later Adams died, leaving the Federalist prosecutor without a defendant.

By the summer of 1799, with the New York *Time Piece* having ceased publication the summer before, the New York *Argus* came under the eye of Secretary of State Pickering as the third leading Republican paper, after the *Independent Chronicle* and the Philadelphia *Aurora*. He instructed the federal attorney in New York to examine the paper for "audacious calumnies against the government" and to prosecute it for any libel on the government or any of its officers. Thomas Greenleaf, the founder of the paper having died in the 1798 yellow fever epidemic, his widow, Ann, was now its publisher. In the fall of 1799 federal attorney Richard Harrison secured an indictment against her for the paper's advocacy of the right to erect liberty poles, its denunciation of the Alien and Sedition Acts, and its contention that the federal government was "corrupt and inimical to the preservation of Liberty." Because of Ann Greenleaf's illness and a yellow fever epidemic in New York, her trial was postponed until April 1800.

The Federalists, however, were not content to wait for a resolution of the federal case against Ann Greenleaf. When the *Argus* reprinted from another paper an article saying Alexander Hamilton was behind a scheme to buy the Philadelphia *Aurora* and suppress it, Major General Hamilton was instrumental in initiating a New York state criminal prosecution of David Frothingham, the paper's foreman, on the ground that libelous comments in the article threatened to overturn the government of the United States. Frothingham was tried on November 21, 1799, and sentenced to four months' imprisonment. Mrs. Greenleaf denounced the New York prosecution in the *Argus*, calling it part of a system of persecution of all printers who dared support the "cause of freedom and the rights of man." But under the pressure of the combined federal-state legal attacks, Mrs. Greenleaf felt compelled to sell the *Argus*, which ceased publication under that name in the spring of 1800. Fearing the political repercussions from the prosecution and jailing of a widow, the Federalists in the spring of 1800 dropped the case against Mrs. Greenleaf.

While other prosecutions were going forward, the Federalists had not overlooked William Duane, the new editor of the Philadelphia *Aurora*, the most visible target among the opposition papers. After Duane, Bache's successor as *Aurora* editor, appeared at St. Mary's Catholic Church on February 9, 1799, to get signatures of the Irish communicants on a petition for repeal of the Alien Law, he and others in his group were arrested and charged under state law with inciting a seditious riot. Although Duane had not been involved in the disturbance in the church yard, the prosecutors were ready to seize on any pretext for harassing the detested editor. A jury acquitted Duane and the three other defendants.

In the *Aurora* of July 24, 1799, Duane deplored the influence of British intrigue in American politics and claimed to have proof of British success in the form of a letter that President Adams had written in which he lamented the London government's effectiveness in gaining the appointment of an American official it favored. The editor went on to charge that the British secret service had spent $800,000 in the United States in 1798 to influence American policy. For these remarks, Duane was arrested on July 30 for seditious libel. President Adams approved the federal prosecution, as did former President Washington, then living in retirement at Mt. Vernon. The trial was postponed until June 1800. By the fall of that year, however, federal authorities decided to drop the prosecution, evidently fearing that the trial would bring about the publication of the embarrassing letter (a copy of which Duane possessed) in which Adams had complained in 1792 that the British had brought about the appointment of Thomas Pinckney as ambassador to England. During Duane's ordeal, Federalist editors denounced the *Aurora* as the "speaking trumpet of the devil" and its editor as a "lying paragraphist and conceited coxcomb." Republican papers defended him. Duane next enraged the Federalists by procuring and publishing on February 19, 1800, the text of a Senate bill through which they planned to create a packed special committee to count the electoral votes in the presidential election and thus, the editor said, deprive the people of a fair election. For this editorial audacity, the Senate on March 18, 1800, condemned Duane for a "high breach" of its privileges and found him guilty of seditious libel for words with the "bad tendency" of bringing its members into contempt and exciting against them the hatred of the people. Again the partisan press took sides, with Republican papers deploring the Senate's "star chamber proceedings" and Federalist editors lauding the Senate's action and calling the *Aurora* "that prostitute of newspapers" and "mother of abominations." Duane himself stoutly defended the right of a free press to discuss the Senate's proceedings.

Summoned to appear before the Senate but denied the assistance of counsel to challenge that body's jurisdiction to bring a case against him, Duane refused to present himself and was declared by the Senate on March 25 to be in contempt. The editor went into hiding and evaded the Senate's process server until Congress adjourned, meanwhile continuing to write for his paper. When the House rejected the Senate's electoral count bill, Duane saw this as vindication of a free press. Having failed to get Duane arrested, the Senate called on President Adams to have him prosecuted under the Sedition Law for his article on the electoral bill. The editor was indicted on October 17, 1800, but the trial was postponed. By the time of the next court session in May 1801, Jefferson had succeeded Adams as president and ordered the prosecution dropped.

The Federalists were not content with prosecutions of editors of major Republican papers. William Durrell, publisher and editor of the upstate New York *Mount Pleasant Register*, was prosecuted and convicted for reprinting from another paper a paragraph critical of President Adams. At the urging of the editors of the Federalist *Connecticut Courant*, Charles Holt, editor of the New London, Connecticut, *Bee*, was convicted for publishing a letter from a reader condemning the federal forces as a standing army. Anthony Haswell, editor of the *Vermont Gazette*, was convicted for publishing an advertisement seeking to raise money to cover the fine and court costs of Congressman Matthew Lyon, a victim of another Sedition Act prosecution.

Two other Republican writers were the targets of sedition proceedings, but their alleged offenses did not consist of their newspaper contributions. Thomas Cooper, who was editor for a brief time of the Sunbury and Northumberland *Gazette* in Pennsylvania, was tried and convicted for publishing an antiadministration handbill in answer to a Federalist attack on one of his earlier newspaper articles. James Thomas Callender, a writer for the Richmond *Examiner*, was convicted on a charge of maliciously planning to defame the president in certain passages of his book, *The Prospect before Us.*

As a result of Federalist prosecutions, a leading Republican paper, the New York *Time Piece*, ceased publication; two others, the Boston *Independent Chronicle* and the New York *Argus*, were sold; a smaller paper, the *Mount Pleasant Register*, folded; the New London *Bee* suspended operation from April to August, 1800, while its editor served a sedition sentence.

While the sedition prosecutions were going forward, the Jeffersonians launched a polemical counterattack on the Alien and Sedition Acts aimed at turning public opinion against them. In 1798, Jefferson drafted the Kentucky Resolutions and Madison the Virginia Resolutions attacking the constitutionality of the repressive federal laws. Adopted by the legislatures of Kentucky and Virginia respectively, these resolutions called on the states to resist the challenged laws and to seek their repeal.[25] The resolutions, after being sent to the other states, were censured by five New England states and Delaware; the other states remained silent. In 1799, Kentucky issued a brief counterreply mentioning "nullification" as the "rightful remedy." The Virginia response, drafted by Madison in 1799 and approved by the Virginia legislature early in 1800, marshalled all of the constitutional arguments against the acts and espoused the new libertarian theories on freedom of political opinion.[26]

In this Virginia report, Madison contended that a free, republican government cannot be libeled and that the freedom of speech and press guaranteed by the First Amendment was absolute so far as the federal government was concerned.[27] In addition to these legislative tracts, individual Jeffersonians during this period also wrote and had published several lengthy treatises arguing the case for an unfettered press. Among the authors were George Blake, counsel for Abijah Adams when he was prosecuted for seditious libel; George Hay, a member of the Virginia House of Delegates; and Tunis Wortman, a New York lawyer.[28] Significantly, these scholarly works, taking radical positions on freedom of the press, were all written by lawyers rather than editors.

The story of seditious libel prosecutions in the early years of the new nation would not be complete without a reference to the switch in position by some Jeffersonians once they achieved power in 1801, at which time the Alien and Sedition Acts expired. While Jefferson was president—and with his explicit encouragement in at least one case—Federalist editors were prosecuted for seditious libel in state courts in New York and Pennsylvania and in federal court in Connecticut.

In New York in 1803, Harry Croswell, editor of *The Wasp*, was indicted under common law and convicted for printing an allegation that Jefferson had paid James T. Callender to denounce Washington as "a traitor, a robber, and a perjurer" and Adams as "a hoary-headed incendiary." On appeal, Alexander Hamilton, as attorney for Croswell, argued for a new trial, contending that the jury should have been allowed to decide the criminality of an alleged libel and that freedom of the press consisted "in the right to publish, with impunity, truth, with good motives, for justifiable ends, though reflecting on government, magistracy, or individuals." Although Hamilton lost the case in court, the state legislature in 1805 enacted a law adopting his proposed standards for libel prosecutions.

Jefferson in 1803 wrote a letter to Governor Thomas McKean of Pennsylvania in which he complained that the Federalists were pushing their press into licentiousness and urging a few prosecutions of the most eminent offenders. Joseph Dennie, Federalist editor of the *Port Folio* in Philadelphia was subsequently indicted in a state court for seditious libel against the state and national governments for publishing an essay calling democracy "contemptible and vicious" and predicting that it would bring civil war, despotism, and anarchy. Dennie was acquitted.

In Connecticut the Jeffersonians were oblivious to their own 1798 position that there was no federal common law and that the First Amendment had repudiated the notion of seditious libel against the government. At the urging of United States District Judge Pierpont Edwards, who had been named to the bench by Jefferson, a federal grand jury in that state in 1806 returned indictments against six defendants for the common law crime of seditious libel of President Jefferson. Those indicted included Thomas Collier, publisher of the *Litchfield Monitor*, and Barzillai Hudson and George Goodwin, editors of the Federalist *Connecticut Courant*.[29]

As Jefferson prepared to assume office in 1801, the *Courant* had greeted the forthcoming event with two-and-a-half columns of invective in verse. The philippic, which included a denunciation of *Aurora* editor William Duane, a Jeffersonian, was typified by the following stanza:

> While to the Union's utmost bounds,
> The Jacobinic Tocsin sounds,
> Thieves, traitors, Irish renegades,
> Scape-gallowless, and desperadoes,
> All sorts of rogues stripped off the mask
> And entered on the glorious task . . .[30]

Thomas Seymour and six other Jefferson supporters from Connecticut had written to the president in December 1806:

Federal Editors have unceasingly issued from their presses, libels as unprecedented in number and grossness, as they were unfounded in truth. . . . The professed friends of Order in Connecticut had screened their own, by Juries openly and avowedly selected for the purpose. While for publishing the truth about them, in language not abusive but decent, a Republican printer had been compelled to pay One Thousand Dollars; while another Printer and another Editor had been fined and Imprisoned. Bills were found [in federal court] against a Judge, two political Priests, and three Federal printers, who were corrupting the taste and morals of the people.[31]

The press, Jefferson's correspondents explained, "we consider as essential to *our* Liberties; *its* liberty is inviolable. . . . but not to charge . . . [government officials] with motives subversive of the liberties and happiness of the Nation."[32] Jefferson replied, saying:

"that a spirit of indignation and retaliation should arise when an opportunity should present itself, was too much within the human constitution to excite either surprise or censure, and confined to an appeal to truth only, it cannot lessen the useful freedom of the press."[33]

In 1808 the government dropped the prosecutions of all of the defendants except Hudson and Goodwin, whose case prior to trial was appealed to the Supreme Court for a decision on whether federal courts possessed jurisdiction over the common law crime of seditious libel. In keeping with the earlier Jeffersonian argument on this question, the Supreme Court, with Justice William Johnson, a Jeffersonian appointee, speaking for the bench, ruled in 1812 against federal common law jurisdiction.

Although there is positive evidence (indicated by the letter to Governor McKean) that Jefferson himself approved the Dennie prosecution, no proof that he personally condoned the others during his administration has been found. Eight seditious libel indictments, two state and six federal, are known to have been brought during Jefferson's tenure as president. Only one resulted in a conviction. The record suggests that, although the Jeffersonians were not consistent in adherence to principle on seditious libel, they were less zealous than their Federalist predecessors in prosecution.

After the federal seditious libel prosecutions of the early 1800s, there were no federal proceedings against citizens for defamation of the government until the passage of the Espionage Act of 1917 and the amending Sedition Act of 1918. The Federalist hysteria, generated by the prospect of war with France and reinforced by their desire to stay in power, created a crisis for freedom of the press that fortunately passed without implanting a permanently restrictive constitutional doctrine. Indeed, the battle over the Sedition Law was important because early in the life of the republic, it forced the champions of free expression to articulate for future generations doctrines of freedom that were far more carefully reasoned than were the verbal exchanges at the time the First Amendment was adopted.

3

First Wartime Test of the First Amendment

The declaration of war on Great Britain by Congress on June 18, 1812, produced the circumstances for the first test of the First Amendment under conditions of armed conflict. Whether the war actually provided a meaningful test of the viability of the constitutional guarantee under stress, however, is a matter of doubt. A real test of protection for freedom of expression on war would have been provided only if public opinion was overwhelmingly committed to one side of the issue, which was not true of the War of 1812. The nation was deeply torn by differences over the wisdom of hostilities. President Madison—even if he was inclined to attempt the silencing of his newspaper critics, which in his case is questionable—may have realized that the country was so divided that a crackdown on the press would have made matters worse.

In any event, Madison neither sought, nor did Congress enact, any espionage, sedition, censorship, or other law designed to curb dissent. And dissent ran wide and deep. While the war was cheered in some parts of the country, the president was jeered elsewhere as the instigator of what became known as "Mr. Madison's War"—a conflict which actually he had sought with reluctance in his message to Congress on June 1.

While lawmakers from the states of the northeastern seaboard had opposed war, a group of newly elected, young House members from the lower South and the West had promoted it. But their talk of defending American maritime rights was not greeted with universal enthusiasm even from their home areas. Representative John Randolph of Virginia spoke for many when he referred to their invocation of rights as a "cant of patriotism" to mask their real motive —a lust for land. The war hawks' denunciations of the impressment of American seamen were coupled with cries of "on to Canada." War, they thought, was a way to expand U.S. territory by seizing Canada from Britain and wresting Florida from Spain, Britain's ally. Although constituting a minority in the House, the war hawks had been able to gain control of key committees and to propel the nation into a war that was vocally opposed by many of their countrymen who were more interested in the profits of commerce with Britain than in vindicating American rights or in expanding U.S. frontiers.

Opposition to the war was particularly intense in New England, where the conflict was viewed as ruinous to shipping and commercial interests. This view and the notion that the war was dictated by Napoleon was propagated in the New England press. The *Columbian Centinel* of Boston complained of the "waste of blood and property" in a "useless and unnecessary war." Other Federalist newspapers took up the cry.[1] The Boston *Gazette* trumpeted rhetorically: "Is there a Federalist, a patriot, in America, who conceives it his duty to shed his blood for Bonaparte, for Madison or Jefferson, and that Host of Ruffians in Congress who have set their faces against the United States for years . . .?"[2] Matching deeds with words, the New England states withheld militia from federal service, sold large quantities of provisions to the British invaders, and in other ways impeded the American war effort.

As the war continued, newspapers even in other sections were appealing to citizens who had pistols and other military articles to turn them over to the commissaries so that troops could be equipped. Despite the desperate situation, exacerbated by the opposition press, the government took no action to suppress the critical journals.[3]

In other parts of the country, where the war was more popular than in New England, the citizenry was not so tolerant of dissent. Baltimore provided an example of extralegal popular action against dissent. On June 20, 1812, two days after the declaration of war by Congress, the *Federal Republican*, a Federalist newspaper in Baltimore, denounced the decision to launch hostilities. In a city where the mayor and most local officials favored the war, Alexander Hanson, the publisher, flung defiance with his antiwar editorial:

Without funds, without taxes, without an army, navy or adequate fortifications, with one hundred and fifty millions of our property in the hands of the declared enemy, without any of his in our power, and with a vast commerce afloat, our rulers have promulgated a war, against the clear and decided sentiments of a vast majority of the nation. . . . We mean to represent in as strong colors as we are capable that it is unnecessary, inexpedient, and entered into from partial, personal motives. . . . We mean to use every constitutional argument and every legal means to render as odious and suspicious to the American people, as they deserve to be, the patrons and contrivers of this highly impolitic and destructive war, in the fullest persuasion that we shall be supported and ultimately applauded by nine tenths of our countrymen, and that our silence would be treason to them. . . .[4]

Republican partisans in Baltimore responded to this challenge by assembling at Hanson's printing shop. The crowd soon grew into a mob, which by evening, uncontained by any show of opposition from the authorities, swarmed into the premises, smashed the type, destroyed the presses, and tore down the building.[5]

The Baltimore *Federal Gazette* reacted to the attack on Hanson's printing plant by holding the city up to shame. Noting that this "alarming" episode had occurred in a land alleged to be the only one where true liberty exists" and in a city styled the "most Republican in the United States," the *Gazette* went on to observe that the mob had done its work in the presence of Baltimore's judges, magistrates, and military officers, "in open defiance of the dictates of Reason and of all laws, divine and human."[6]

In New York the *Commercial American* sharply reminded Republicans that it was they who wanted the war and whose wishes had now been gratified, and that they should be the last to embark on scenes of "turbulence and outrage" and the first to set an example of obedience to the laws.[7] The next day the *Commercial American* charged that the mayor of the city and the judge of the criminal court had witnessed "the flagrant outrage" without attempting to restrain it.[8]

No such concern for the rule of law was exhibited by the leading Republican organ in South Carolina, a state that had sent some of the most vocal war hawks to Congress. One of them, Representative John C. Calhoun, had introduced the bill formally declaring war against Great Britain. News of the attack on Hanson's paper was published in the Republican *City Gazette* of Charleston in the form of a letter from a citizen of Baltimore. Reporting the Baltimore mob actions with approval, the letter writer concluded that the treatment of the *Federal Republican* showed that "the citizens of Baltimore are not quite lost to all sense of patriotism." Below the letter, the *City Gazette* reprinted the offending editorial from the *Federal Republican*, with an editorial explanation that it was "the obnoxious article . . . which drew upon its authors the vengeance of an insulted community."[9]

After the destruction of his plant, Hanson, fearing for his life, fled to Rockville. Within a month he had made arrangements to have his paper printed in Georgetown and sent to him in Baltimore, where he planned to distribute it from a house that he had rented on Charles Street. In its first issue, the revived *Federal Republican* reviewed the events culminating in the rioters' destruction of the paper's office a month before and castigated the mayor of Baltimore and the governor of Maryland for their failure to preserve order. A long article, under the heading, "A Mobocracy," referred to the constitutional protection that was supposed to be afforded freedom of the press and quoted the Maryland Bill of Rights on the subject, adding that freedom of the press had been "extinguished in Maryland."

"The Editors," the article continued, "will not stoop to enquire what degree of liberty of speech and discussion may be enjoyed in a state of war, nor will they degrade themselves or dishonor the virtuous cause they support, by an examination of the rights which a change of foreign relations cannot abridge or impair." Exhibiting a staunch determination not to be intimidated, the *Federal Republican* editors declared that they would continue to consider "freedom of the press as the palladium of reason, as the distributor of light and learning," and to remember that "where the law halts with dread, the freedom of the press advances." The article closed with an impassioned declamation in the words of the poet William Cowper:

> How shall I speak thee, or thy power address,
> Thou God of our idolatry, the Press!
> By thee, Religion, Liberty and Laws,
> Exert their influence and advance their cause.[10]

Hanson's reappearance served as fresh fuel for the firebrands of Baltimore. Another mob gathered, and Hanson and a group of friends and Federalist supporters prepared to defend themselves in the rented house if the Baltimore police and militia would not provide protection. Among the defenders were two Revolutionary War veterans, Generals Richard Henry (Light Horse Harry) Lee and James Maccubin Lingan. Lee, who had been a friend of Hanson's father, was a Federalist and opposed the war—although he was prepared to don his uniform again once it started.

During a siege of the house by the mob on the night of July 28–29, Lee commanded the defense, telling the armed occupants not to fire except as a last resort. When the attackers battered in the front door, a volley of fire from inside repulsed them. By morning, with the militia on hand but doing nothing to disperse the mob, the rioters had brought up a cannon and aimed it at the second floor. Thomas Wilson, a local Republican editor, stood nearby, a pistol in each hand, and urged the cannoneer to fire the weapon, all the while yelling "blood for blood."[11] Finally, with the mayor and militia leaders declaring that they could not disperse the mob and could only protect Hanson and his supporters if they would allow themselves to be escorted to jail, the defenders of the press were marched off to prison.

Despite the promise of protection, the local authorities stood by and did nothing as the mob gathered again at the jail that night. Crying "Tory," the rioters broke into the building and fell upon Hanson and his friends. As the embattled Federalists sought to escape the jail, many were clubbed and kicked until they were unconscious. Members of the mob stuck pen knives in their faces and poured grease from dripping candles in their eyes. The torturing continued for nearly three hours. Finally one of several physicians who had arrived on the scene persuaded the mob to disperse. General Lingan was dead and Lee was maimed for life. About thirty-five were left injured.

Soon after Lee was carried back to his home in Alexandria, President Madison paid a call and issued a public statement denouncing the rioters as "barbarians and hypocrites who have done nothing to advance our national cause, but instead spent their wrath on a citizen whom this nation will forever honor."

In reporting the Baltimore outrage, the Republican press tended to excuse the mob by blaming the Federalists for provoking such actions. The Federalist press denounced the atrocity and reminded the Republicans that it was they who were supposed to be champions of a free press.[12] General Lee was hailed as a martyr who had fallen in defense of liberty of the press.[13]

At the scene of violence the Baltimore *Whig* lauded Baltimore as a city that had excited the "hatred of the enemies of civil liberty" and went on to exclaim that these foes of liberty had resolved to mar the city's "felicity"; they had established "two presses (inimical to the rights of man) afterwards united by the name of the 'Federal Republican.' . . ." This paper, the *Whig* declared, had reviled republican principles, spouted poisoned slander, vilified and defamed the government. The operators of the *Federal Republican* were referred to as "atrocious offenders from *Montgomery county*" who had "flung defiance in the teeth" of the community of Baltimore and who as "fomenters of mischief" had "dyed the streets with innocent blood, killing one man and wounding between 20 and 30." For this, continued the *Whig*, the "guilty scoundrels" had provoked a "horrible retaliation," but the city could be thankful that the result was not so terrible as the rumor. Only one had been killed and several prisoners "considerably wounded." If the "insulted crowd" had gotten hold of the "Montgomery conspirators" at the time of the fray at Hanson's house, the *Whig* said, the members could not have been blamed for putting them "to instant death."[14]

In nearby Washington, the Republican *National Intelligencer*, while claiming that it was stating the facts impartially, could not refrain from coloring the event to excuse the conduct of the rioters. The populace, the *Intelligencer* surmised in its issue of August 1, may have taken umbrage at the reappearance of the *Federal Republican* or may have been roused by the "garrisoning of an armed citadel in the midst of their city." But in any event, the paper went on, the crowd—which some reported to have been composed chiefly of boys at first and of curious onlookers—was provoked to revenge when the defenders of the house fired upon those besieging them. Once this had happened, said the *Intelligencer*, even the most respectable and influential citizens could not save Hanson and his friends from "the rage of the people, so much had they been infuriated by the sight of their dying and wounded fellow citizens."

The Washington paper, while unduly emphasizing the initial passivity of the crowd and exaggerating the number wounded in the firing from the house, overlooked the fact that passions had had twenty-four hours to cool before the mob set upon the jailed defenders of the *Federal Republican*. In its columns of that issue, the *Intelligencer* had no comment on the question of press freedom.[15] In its issue of August 13, 1812, the *Intelligencer* published a report of the various Baltimore events prepared by a panel of the city council and obviously designed as an apology for the authorities.[16]

By the time of its issue of August 13, the *Intelligencer* felt compelled to respond to a resolution adopted at a town meeting in Boston's Faneuil Hall in which the participants addressed themselves to "the alarming attack on the liberty of opinion and of the press at Baltimore" and suggested that the Washington paper had implied approval and justified the outrages in Baltimore. The *Intelligencer* declaimed that it never had been and never would be an advocate of mobs, especially when one was directed against freedom of the press. "This," the paper continued, "is one of those unalienable rights which, as republicans, we will always support; and, as conductors of a press, if attempted to be violated thro' us, we will not cease to defend to the last extremity." The *Intelligencer* then went on to denounce the Boston Federalist press for printing "the most foul and slanderous" falsehoods about the "transactions at Baltimore" and any other subject "capable of distortion."[17]

In its next issue, the *National Intelligencer* found itself once again answering an attack from Boston on the Washington paper's stance on freedom of the press, this time from the Boston *Gazette*. While insisting that it had unequivocally condemned the lawless proceedings in Baltimore, the *Intelligencer* went on to indicate its approval of one of its correspondent's statements that during war public opinion must assume a patriotic tone and disaffection or toryism must be put down "not by mobs; but by the correct exercise of the same political right which disaffection abuses when it raises its voice against its own government."[18]

Opposing papers in New York argued over responsibility for the bloodshed in Baltimore. The *Columbian*, a Tammany paper, made excuses for the mob action, saying Hanson should have applied to the civil authority for protection and that, by taking arms inside the house and firing on the assailants, he and his associates were "guilty of murderous intent, and wilfully exciting the popular vengeance."[19] In a furious response, the *New York Evening Post*, which opposed the war, castigated Charles Holt, the *Columbian* editor, declaring that not one of the propositions laid down by Holt as the law of the land was true, and going on to assert that the civil authority in Baltimore was probably in league with the mob.[20] The *Post* had already made clear its position that Hanson was attacked because he dared to exercise his rights and the civil authorities were too timid to provide the protection they had pledged.[21]

The Republican *Independent Chronicle* in Boston, apparently in an effort to disown the rioters, reported that a Baltimore paper had stated that the mob there was composed almost wholly of foreigners. The *Chronicle* went on to charge that in Boston exaggerated accounts of the Baltimore riots were printed in a handbill and distributed in a manner calculated to excite ruffians.[22] Two days later the *Chronicle* was complaining that "the federalists pretend to reprobate mobs, but what could have a greater tendency to create them than their conduct in Boston?"[23]

The Federalist *Columbian Centinel* in Boston published an account of the Baltimore affair under the heading, "History of Government Mob," and observed that, while Hanson and his fellow citizens were defending freedom of the press against the mob, they were not backed by the authorities.[24] In Hartford the Federalist *Connecticut Courant* also voiced indignation in many columns devoted to the Baltimore events.[25] The Boston *Reportory*, another Federalist paper, extolling General Lee for his attempt to rescue the nation from itself, referred to the Baltimore mob as "more monstrous than any that ever maddened France."[26]

In Charleston rival papers revealed their partisan leanings by the way they treated the events in Baltimore. The Republican *City Gazette* printed correspondence from Baltimore suggesting that Hanson, Wagner, and others had provoked the attack on themselves by following General Lee's orders to fire on the mob "with powder and ball," killing eight and wounding twelve or fifteen. General Lee, according to a letter writer, "left his home and came to Baltimore with Hanson, to compel the citizens to receive his treasonable publications. . . ."[27]

The Federalist *Charleston Courier*, on the other hand, lamented that the sway of the mob "over the liberty of the press and freedom of speech in that city [Baltimore] is terrible and ominous." Continuing in the same vein, the *Courier* noted that in consequence of mob threats, Hanson and a few friends, about thirty "gentlemen," had gone to the house where the paper was to be issued "with a view to support the liberty of the press guaranteed to him by the Constitution and Laws of his country. . . ." The dwelling, the paper said, "was surrounded by a lawless banditti and violently assaulted for at least two hours before any resistance was made." On the same page the *Courier* reprinted an article from the *Federal Republican*, headed "Another Enormity Upon Our Press," which reported the attack on the Charles Street house.[28]

As the war continued, the Federalists in New England began to talk of disunion. On January 13, 1813, the *Columbian Centinel* declared: "We must no longer be deafened by senseless clamors about a Separation of the States. . . . *The States are separated in fact* when one section . . . perseveres in measures fatal to the interests and repugnant to the opinion of another section."[29]

In December 1814, New England Federalists, representing mainly Massachusetts, Connecticut, and Rhode Island, met in secret at the Hartford Convention. Talk of secession was in the air, but moderates restrained the hotheads among the delegates. The convention contented itself with denouncing the Madison administration and the war, inviting the New England states to nullify the conscription bill then before Congress, and proposing several constitutional amendments. If the nation had not been so divided, as this convention indicated, the Federalist press might not have been allowed so much latitude to promote New England's extreme antiwar activities.

An episode in another part of the country, as the war was ending, revealed the difference in attitude toward the press when authority was not under political constraint. After the defeat of the British in the Battle of New Orleans, the *Louisiana Gazette* on February 21, 1815, announced that the American commander, General Andrew Jackson, had received word that peace had been negotiated. Jackson, who had imposed martial law on the city, sent a peremptory note to Godwin B. Cotten, the editor, saying: "Henceforth it is expected that no publication of the nature of that herein alluded to and censured will appear in any paper of this city unless the editor shall have previously ascertained its correctness and gained permission for its insertion from the proper sources."[30]

The editor was also commanded to destroy "every copy of so *unauthorized and improper* a notice" and to publish a retraction which Jackson had dictated. Jackson was miffed over what he considered a premature leak of the news of peace, fearing that discipline in his army might collapse.[31]

Cotten's response was to publish the required retraction, accompanied by an introductory paragraph in which he commented:

Every man may read for himself, and think for himself—[Thank God! our thoughts are as yet unshackled!!], but as we have been officially informed that New Orleans is a camp, our readers may not expect us to take the liberty of expressing our opinion as we might in a free city. We cannot submit to have a censor of the press in our office, and as we are ordered not to publish any remarks without authority, we shall submit to be silent until we can speak with safety—except making our paper a sheet of shreds and patches—a mere advertiser for our mercantile friends.[32]

When news of Jackson's action reached New York in late March, the *New York Evening Post* reprinted the item from the *Louisiana Gazette*. But the editor of the *Evening Post* added no comment of his own.[33] In Washington the *National Intelligencer* laconically reported that Jackson's order had been issued as a result of "certain injudicious publications in the New Orleans papers." The order was said to characterize Jackson's "wariness and energy" during his military career. The restriction on the press, the *Intelligencer* said simply, "appears to have excited some dissatisfaction."[34]

Jackson's muzzling of the press did not end with his move against the *Louisiana Gazette.* The prelude for the next episode of suppression began with the efforts of French citizens, chafing under military service once they believed the war was over, taking steps to secure their discharge from the militia. They did so by registering their nationality at the French consulate. Perceiving the advantage of the same procedure, Creoles (French colonists born in Louisiana) applied to the French consul, Louis de Tousard, for French citizenship papers. As the consul was busily granting such papers, Jackson, on February 28, ordered all French citizens to remove themselves within three days to a distance of 120 miles from the city and not to return until ratification of the peace treaty had been officially published. When the French consul protested, he was also banished.[35]

On March 3 the *Louisiana Courier* published an anonymous letter, complimenting General Jackson on his defense of New Orleans but denouncing the banishment of Frenchmen from the city and calling for the lifting of martial law. The letter writer noted that "when every one laments such an abuse of authority, the press ought to denounce it to the people," and concluded by saying that "the citizens of this State should return to the full enjoyment of their rights. . . . we do not feel much inclined, through gratitude, to sacrifice any of our privileges, and less than any other, that of expressing our opinion of the acts of his [Jackson's] administration."[36]

Ordering the editor of the paper to appear at his headquarters, Jackson demanded to know the name of the contributor and was told that it was Louis Louaillier, a member of the legislature and a naturalized Frenchman who had distinguished himself by his support of the war. Two days later Jackson sent a military detail to arrest Louaillier as the author of "the seditious publication."[37] Louaillier's lawyer, Pierre Louis Morel, who had witnessed the arrest, immediately asked United States District Judge Dominick A. Hall for a writ of habeas corpus for the legislator's release. The judge, who in earlier cases had already shown his lack of sympathy with the proclamation of martial law, granted the writ.[38] But when the writ was served on Jackson, he not only seized the original document (giving the court officer a certified copy) but ordered Judge Hall arrested and imprisoned along with Louaillier for aiding and "abetting and exciting mutiny within my camp." An attorney who

applied to a state judge for Hall's release on habeas corpus proceedings was ordered arrested along with the state judge.[39]

Although a courier on March 6 brought Jackson reliable, but
still unofficial, word of peace, the general nevertheless had Louaillier court-martialed on seven serious charges, including the ridiculous one that he was a spy. After proceedings of two days, the court,
presided over by Brigadier General Edmund P. Gains, declared itself
lacking in jurisdiction in six of the charges, and on the remaining
charge, that of being a spy, acquitted the defendant. Furious over
the outcome, Jackson rejected the decision and sent the legislator
back to prison in the military barracks. In general orders on March
10 reviewing the scope of martial law, Jackson adopted the British
view, which virtually equated martial law with the will of the general, although in every case in which the subject had been taken
to court during the War of 1812, judges had rejected this view and
announced limitations designed to reduce the arbitrariness of martial law.[40]

As a result of the *Courier* letter and Jackson's actions in response
to it, the general was within a few days being subjected to considerable popular criticism. Other arrests were ordered. Realizing by
March 11 that Judge Hall would probably not be convicted by a
court-martial, Jackson the next day had him escorted by military
guard four miles outside the city limits and released with orders not
to return until peace was regularly announced or the enemy had
departed from the coast.[41] On Monday, March 13, Jackson received
what he considered sufficiently official notification that the Treaty
of Ghent had been ratified. He immediately revoked martial law
and ordered Louaillier and other such prisoners released. New Orleans, which had been bubbling with unrest, turned once again to
adulation of the commanding general.

Judge Hall returned to his courtroom, and on March 21 he issued
a summons directing Major General Andrew Jackson to show cause
why he should not be held in contempt of court for disregarding the
writ of habeas corpus in the case of Louis Louaillier, for disrespect-
fully wresting the judge's order from the clerk, and for imprisoning
the judge. After ten days of legal fencing between Jackson's counsel
and United States Attorney John Dick, Jackson, on March 31, presented himself before Judge Hall and announced himself ready to

receive the sentence of the court. When jeers arose from the crowd of Jackson admirers upon the appearance of the judge, the general, now in civilian attire, called upon them to be quiet.

Judge Hall, born in Great Britain but a staunch defender of the United States and its law, was determined to vindicate the supremacy of civil authority. Acknowledging the defendant's important services to the country, the judge said that imprisonment would form no part of the sentence. "The only question," he said, "was whether the Law should bend to the General or the General to the Law." Whereupon he adjudged Andrew Jackson in contempt and imposed a fine of $1,000.

Outside and surrounded by a cheering crowd, Jackson addressed the gathering: "Considering obedience to the laws, even when we think them unjustly applied as the first duty of a citizen, I did not hesitate to comply with the sentence you have heard, and I entreat you to remember the example." Jackson sent a check to the court for $1,000 and refused a purse raised by supporters to reimburse him for the fine.

By the time Americans in the East were reading about the clashes in New Orleans between Jackson and protesters against his iron rule, the events there were over. On April 11, 1815, the *New York Evening Post* reported arrests in New Orleans under martial law. Although observing that at such a distance and with little information, it was incompetent to judge, the paper went on to say: "One thing we know, that the state of society there (foreigners composing nearly a majority of the people) is very different from anything we see here and may require very different method [*sic*] of government."[42] By April 17 the *Evening Post* was saying: "The proceedings [in New Orleans] have been disgraceful . . . and a complete prostration of what is commonly called constitutional rights."[43]

Meanwhile in Washington, the *National Intelligencer* published, on April 15, a letter from New Orleans dated March 8, reporting that the city was still under martial law. The correspondent went on to note that there had been "a little trouble" with certain partisans who were refusing to serve against "his Britannic majesty." As a consequence, said the writer, "the general has ordered them and their consul, who first began it, out of the city." On April 27 the *National Intelligencer* reprinted an item from New Orleans that had been published in the Philadelphia *Gazette*, relying on that paper to provide news and comment. Some of Jackson's actions were said to have been "arbitrary if not tyrannical." But the report went on to observe that Jackson had behaved well when summoned into court on contempt charges and fined $1,000.

In Charleston the *Courier* noted that it was "concerned to learn" that General Jackson by the severity of his discipline had created dissatisfaction among the citizens of New Orleans. The paper went on to observe that the "man, who but a few weeks previous had been hailed as the Saviour of the country, is now reviled as a Military despot. Martial law still continued and numerous convictions and imprisonments had taken place under slight and frivolous pretense. . . ."[44]

Congress in 1844 was to pass a bill remitting Jackson's fine and providing that it should be returned with interest. Jackson, old and debt-ridden, had let his friends know that he would accept the refund because of the effect such an act of Congress might have on the country's future safety at a time when it would be the duty of an army commander, ringed about with foes, to assume extraordinary powers. A check for $2,732.90 was sent to the former president at the Hermitage. Thus, in effect, was Judge Hall's symbolic victory for law repudiated. A sign stretched across Broadway in New York City proclaimed:

JUSTICE TO THE BRAVE

Judge Hall's
Sentence on
GENL JACKSON
Repudiated by the
Nation
Feb. 14th 1844[45]

The nation had remembered what seemed an affront to a military hero but had forgotten a confrontation over a free press in which the First Amendment lost.

4
Judicial Abuse of the Press

By the time the Bill of Rights was twenty-five years old, its First Amendment guarantee of press freedom had already been undermined by all three branches of government under the Sedition Law of 1798 and by mobs and a military commander during the War of 1812. In another ten years the judiciary was to be involved in a press suppression episode, insignificant by itself but important as an issue because it drew the attention of Congress to judicial abuse of the press and resulted in the passage of an act restricting the contempt power of the federal courts.

The controversy involving a Missouri federal judge and a newspaper grew out of an effort to settle contested land claims in Missouri. Then on the nation's western frontier, Missouri was admitted to the Union in 1821 as one of the states carved out of the Louisiana Purchase. As a frontier territory, its lands had become subject to eager speculation. The earlier pioneers knew that in the East land had risen in price as more settlers came, and they assumed that the same thing would happen in Missouri. When immigrants arrived, they placed most of their money in land purchases and mortgaged their holdings to buy more cheap land. In the early frontier period, almost everyone in Missouri was a speculator of sorts. The specula-

tors included some of the most prominent citizens of early Missouri.
Land acquisition in Missouri was complicated, however, by un-
certainty of ownership stemming from the time when the Louisiana
Territory had been under French or Spanish control. Under both of
these governments, land had been transferred from public to private
ownership under loose policies aimed only at getting the territory
settled. Grants were made and registered under the authority of various royal agents, but the concessions were often not surveyed.
Sometimes surveys were not accompanied by plats and were not
sanctioned by proper authority. Under the last two Spanish lieu-
tenant governors, land grants had become more extensive, and were
often based on schemes by which Spanish officials could make a
profit for themselves and for land speculators. Zenon Trudeau, lieu-
tenant governor of Upper Louisiana (including Missouri) from
1792 to 1799, had been induced by speculators to sign a number of
blank sheets of paper, which were later used as a basis for claims
covering thousands of acres in Missouri, including some of the richest mineral lands in the state. Legitimate documents were defaced
and many grants were antedated by crooked speculators to make
them appear legitimate. Bona fide claims were bought for insignificant amounts from holders who did not realize their potential increase in value.

As late as 1795, only eight years before the transfer to the United
States, little progress had been made in surveying the vast lands
of Upper Louisiana, including the 43,985,280 acres in what is
now Missouri. When Antoine Soulard was appointed first surveyor-
general of the territory in 1795, he attempted to bring order to
the formerly haphazard surveying practices. (His own practices,
however, were later to be questioned.) He appointed deputy sur-
veyors in the several districts, fixed a system of fees, and established
an office for registering surveys. But in 1801 when the Louisiana
Territory was ceded by Spain back to France (which had held it
until 1762), titles to land claims in the area were far from settled.
When Upper Louisiana was transferred to the United States in 1804,
land claimed under registered French and Spanish titles amounted
to 1,463,259 acres. Of this total, only 738,455 acres had actually
been surveyed, and only about one-twentieth of all claimants had
acquired complete titles from the Spanish authorities. Despite the
irregularities that had existed, the Spanish commissioners at New

Orleans, on delivering Louisiana to the French in the presence of American authorities, had proclaimed that all concessions of property given by the governors of the province were confirmed. This blanket confirmation, complicated by the lack of surveys and the prevalence of incomplete titles, was to lead to a half century of litigation over Spanish land claims in Missouri. When the United States acquired the Missouri territory through the Louisiana Purchase, prevailing official opinion had seen the public domain as a way of raising revenue. Land, which had had no value under French and Spanish regimes, except as a means of attracting settlers, was immediately valuable. Speculators saw that, either by confirming titles to land they already held or by acquiring land while it was still cheap, they stood to realize big profits. Older immigrants—who had already established claims to land, however tenuous they might be—were pitted against newer arrivals who were eager to acquire land by cheap purchase and therefore resented the large claims of the earlier immigrants.

By 1819, with Missouri's petition for admission as a state still pending in Congress, the contest over land was dramatized in the area near the town of Franklin. There squatters had made small improvements on the land to enhance their entitlement as purchasers while they waited for its sale as public land. These settlers, mostly from Kentucky and Tennessee, were then able to purchase land at two dollars an acre, with one-fourth to be paid in cash and one-fourth in each of the second, third, and fourth years after purchase.

Missouri politics of the time revolved around disputes over land, and newspapers spoke for one faction or another. The *Western Journal*, founded in 1815, became the *Western Emigrant* in 1817 and the next year acquired still another name, the *St. Louis Enquirer*, and a new editor, Thomas Hart Benton.[1] Benton, a lawyer who had moved to St. Louis from Tennessee in 1815, used the paper to promote his driving political ambition. He called for adjustment of the Spanish land claims, particularly the surveyed concessions that had not been confirmed by the American authorities, a position that would endear him to established leaders in St. Louis. But recognizing the value of political support from small farmers, he dubbed them in the *Enquirer* as "the chosen of God," and said it should be the object of a good government "to increase, by all possible means, the members of this useful class of citizens." Therefore, he said, "the refuse lands of the Republic" should be made "the subject of donation to such as will cultivate them," and a new policy should be built on the interests of actual settlers.[2]

Benton made the *Enquirer* a vigorous competitor of the older *Missouri Gazette*, which had been founded in 1808 in St. Louis as the first newspaper west of the Mississippi. The *Gazette's* editor, Joseph Charles, sneered at his rival's flowery rhetoric and his grandiose political visions. "What a prodigy this editor is," Charles said of Benton, "who can alone see better into the interests of the nation, from the point he occupies near the mouth of the Missouri River, than . . . Mr. Adams [President John Quincy Adams]."[3]

Although nearly everyone in Missouri who was politically active called himself a Democratic-Republican, there were local divisions. One group, composed of French business leaders and holders of large acreages under Spanish land grants, was called the "little junto" by editor Charles. The *St. Louis Enquirer*, like its predecessor, the *Western Emigrant*, was considered a projunto paper, although Benton tried to appeal to both groups. The antijunto faction, for which the *Missouri Gazette* was often the spokesman, was composed largely of American settlers who had come to St. Louis since the Louisiana Purchase—among them the more recently arrived land speculators and their allies. This group opposed confirmation of the Spanish grants. Land policy was the chief subject of their dispute, the outcome of which would determine control over the still vast unsettled land of Missouri.[4]

Despite the fact that he was an attorney for Spanish land claimants, Benton, by his adroit political preachments, managed to be elected as one of Missouri's first two United States senators with the support of members of the antijunto group, including David Barton, who was chosen as the other senator. Barton sponsored former Tennessee lawyer James H. Peck for appointment as the first judge of the federal court for the district of Missouri. Peck, who had settled in St. Louis in 1818, was to become the main figure in an impeachment trial growing out of a newspaper controversy involving land claims.

Early in 1822 Benton raised the land title matter in the Senate, introducing a bill to authorize the federal district court in Missouri to dispose of the claims and settle them on the basis of Spanish or French legal procedures rather than British or American. Although he got the bill through the Senate that year, it was tabled in the House. Not until 1824 was the bill adopted, and Benton was able during the debate to write to a St. Louis claim-holder and assure him of his successful effort "to oblige . . . my individual friends."

With the passage of the 1824 act, the stage was set for intense litigation over disputed titles to a large portion of the land of Missouri. Luke E. Lawless, an Irish born lawyer who had moved to St. Louis in 1816 or 1817 and was a close friend of Benton, represented some of the most important Spanish land claimants. As attorney for the widow and heirs of Antoine Soulard, he filed suit to confirm the validity of his clients' claims to some ten thousand acres of Missouri land. Judge Peck in December 1825 ruled against the Soulards and in favor of the United States, whereupon Lawless appealed to the United States Supreme Court.[5]

Since the Peck decision jeopardized the titles of numerous land claimants, including some of the most influential people in Missouri, it was immediately a subject of vocal controversy—especially among the more than twenty lawyers already practicing in St. Louis, then a town of only five thousand inhabitants. On March 30, 1826, Judge Peck—undoubtedly aware of the sentiments being expressed against his decision—had published in the *Missouri Republican*, successor paper to the antijunto *Missouri Gazette*, a long article in which he set forth the reasons for his decree. Lawless promptly took up the argument in print. In an article signed "A Citizen," published in the *Missouri Advocate and St. Louis Enquirer*, the paper Benton had edited before going to the Senate, Lawless presented what he contended were eighteen erroneous assumptions of fact and doctrine on the part of the judge.[6]

The Soulards, represented by Lawless, were heirs of the late surveyor general, who had been closely associated with the St. Louis junto and whose surveys were reported by his successor to contain numerous inaccuracies, erasures, and apparent alterations. Among other holders of unconfirmed Spanish land titles to sizable acreages were Auguste Chouteau, Charles Gratiot and Bernard Pratte—all members of the so-called junto and of the coterie of French families who had long dominated affairs in St. Louis.

The letter from Lawless, therefore, represented the views of no mere dissenting crank. When the federal court reconvened in St. Louis on April 17, Judge Peck ordered Stephen A. Foreman, editor and publisher of the *Missouri Advocate and St. Louis Enquirer*, to appear the next morning and show cause why he should not be punished for contempt for having published "a false statement," tending to "bring odium on the court, and to impair the confidence of the public in the purity of its decisions." As commanded, Foreman appeared in court, with Lawless as his volunteer counsel. Although the letter had been couched in mild language, Peck was visibly outraged. According to later reports, he repeatedly and rudely interrupted Lawless as he attempted to defend the validity and propriety of the letter. After two days of abuse from the bench, Lawless gave up. Another attorney concluded the argument, citing the First Amendment of the U.S. Constitution and the Missouri Bill of Rights. He was promptly overruled. Despite private advice from his friend, U.S. attorney Edward Bates, "to let the matter drop as easily as possible," Peck pressed on.[7]

On April 20, Foreman, having been released by Lawless from his pledge of confidence, identified the lawyer as the letter writer. Lawless commented later that he had consented to the disclosure to protect Foreman from having an attachment made against his press. As soon as Lawless was revealed to be the offending letter writer, Peck ordered him to appear the next day and defend himself against a charge of contempt of court. Upon the refusal of the judge to permit any discussion of the truth of what Lawless had written, Lawless instructed his defense counsel to defend him on the ground that, even if the letter was "false and malicious," the guarantee of a free press and the right to trial by jury barred the judge from punishing him in a "summary" manner.

Ignoring the defense arguments, Peck unleashed a tirade against Lawless and called on Bates to read the allegedly libelous letter paragraph by paragraph, whereupon Peck delivered his own comment on each as it was read. Lawless, having been denied an opportunity to offer a defense, exhibited a bit of audacity by leaving for another court to try a state case. The judge had him brought back by a marshal and demanded that he purge himself of contempt. Upon the lawyer's refusal to grovel, Peck sentenced him to jail for twenty-four hours and to an eighteen-month suspension from practice in the district court. Lawless was immediately lodged in jail, where he remained from 4 P.M. to 9 P.M., at which time he was discharged on a legal technicality. A state judge ordered him released after Lawless had pointed out that the order of commitment had no judicial seal or signature.

During the furor over the Lawless letter, the *Missouri Republican*, where the controversy had its beginning, had nothing to say about the implications for freedom of speech and press of Judge Peck's strictures against the right of a newspaper and a writer to discuss a judicial opinion in print. Not only was the *Republican* silent on the constitutional question, but it also ignored the subject as news.

Whatever his professional competence may have been, Peck's evident eccentricity did not aid his reputation for personal stability. According to accounts of contemporaries, he labored under the delusion that, if he exposed his eyes to light, he would go blind. Hence, he kept a blindfold over his eyes when the light was deemed to be too bright, and had a servant lead him around. He even sat upon the bench blindfolded at times. Although he was said to be tall and fine looking, one contemporary observer characterized him as "pompous in his language, manner and carriage." His irascible behavior during the proceedings on the Lawless letter suggested an extreme sensitivity to anything that he might consider an affront to his dignity.

Five months after his confrontation with Judge Peck, Lawless— still chafing under the restrictions that barred him from practicing in the district court—wrote a "memorial" to the House of Representatives setting forth what he described as Judge Peck's violations of "the liberty of speech and of the press" and requesting that the "conduct and proceedings" of Judge Peck be inquired into by the House. When Congress met in December 1826, the memorial charging Peck with tyranny, oppression, usurpation of power and violation of "the liberty of speech and of the press" was presented to the House by John Scott, Missouri's first U.S. Representative and also, incidentally, politically aligned with the St. Louis junto.[8]

In 1826 and again in 1828, Lawless's petition was referred to the House Judiciary Committee, which each time neglected to act on it. On December 15, 1829, with new members on the committee, Representative George McDuffie of South Carolina brought up the matter again. This time the committee launched an inquiry. On March 23, 1830, Representative James Buchanan of Pennsylvania, presented a committee report concluding that, as a result of evidence collected, the members were of the opinion that Judge Peck should be impeached for "high misdemeanors in office."

Judge Peck, in a letter to the House, responded that the short notice given him by the Judiciary Committee had not allowed him time to make an adequate statement and that he wanted an opportunity to present "a full exposition of the facts." Courts, he contended, must have the power to punish for contempt or "lose all their value and sink into inevitable contempt and insignificance." He noted that some of the ablest men in Congress, including Daniel Webster, had found no grounds for proceeding against him in prior attempts. Only after extensive debate did the House vote to permit the judge to make a written or oral statement, whereupon Peck submitted a lengthy letter of explanation. In it the judge implied that the dispute over his opinion had arisen because of the existence of rival presses in St. Louis.[9] "The 'liberty of the press'," said Peck, "is among the greatest of blessings, civil and political, so long as it is directed to its proper object—that of disseminating correct and useful information among the people. But this greatest of blessings may become the greatest of curses, if it shall be permitted to burst its proper barriers."[10]

Unmoved by the Peck letter, the full House—where, incidentally, the status of western lands was now a political issue—voted 123 to 49 in favor of Buchanan's impeachment resolution. The resolution said Peck's arbitrary actions had constituted a "great disparagement of public justice, the abuse of judicial authority, and . . . the subversion of the liberties of the people of the United States."[11]

Buchanan and McDuffie, along with Henry R. Storrs and Ambrose Spencer of New York and Charles A. Wickliffe of Kentucky, were named managers to conduct the prosecution. On May 4, 1830, three days after the adoption of the articles of impeachment in the House, the Senate convened as a "high court of impeachment" with Vice President John C. Calhoun presiding. But as a result of delays and a recess by the Senate, the trial was not begun until December 20. The case attracted national attention as one more chapter in the prolonged debate in Congress over the status of western land grants, during which the federal courts were repeatedly attacked.

With the entire House observing, McDuffie launched the prosecution. McDuffie, whose face, according to John Quincy Adams, reflected a "gloomy churlishness," was a fiery orator who spoke with a powerful voice and pounded the air with his fists as he talked. His speeches, delivered as if he were in a frenzy of passion, were characterized by extravagant phrases and denunciatory sallies. Pitted against McDuffie, Buchanan, and the others were William Wirt, former United States attorney general and one of the most eminent lawyers in the country, and Jonathan Meredith, arguing the case for the defense.

Calling Peck "a petty provincial judge" who had acted like an "hereditary monarch," McDuffie said: "We have so long enjoyed the blessings of a free press that we seem to be more disposed to censure its unavoidable excesses than to appreciate its vast and inestimable advantages." (Only five years later McDuffie was so oblivious to the principles of press freedom that, as governor of South Carolina, he suggested that abolitionist editors be put to death without benefit of clergy.[12]) On December 22, Lawless appeared before the Senate and related what had happened in Peck's courtroom five years earlier. He referred, among other things, to his defense of the editor of the *Missouri Advocate and St. Louis Enquirer* on grounds of freedom of the press.[13] After several days devoted to cross-examination of Lawless, other witnesses testified against the judge. Half the members of the St. Louis bar made the long trip to Washington, D.C., to be witnesses in the case.

James Buchanan, who had become chairman of the House Judiciary Committee after playing a prominent part in the Jackson campaign of 1828, was perhaps the most effective spokesman for the prosecution. In a thrust designed to show Peck's hostility toward press freedom, Buchanan quoted the judge as having said: "The liberty of the press has always been the favorite watchword of those who live by its *licentiousness*. It has been from time immemorial, is still, and ever will be, the perpetual *decantatum* on the lips of all libellers." The quotation, taken from Peck's letter to the House, gave Buchanan an opportunity to observe that "the licentiousness of the press has always been a favorite watch-word of those who are afraid of its liberty."[14]

"The people of this country," declared Buchanan during the

course of his presentation, "love their judiciary well, but they love the freedom of the press still better; and if these two great branches of our civil policy shall be placed in hostile array against each other by the decision of the Senate upon this impeachment, Judge Peck has been the last man in the United States to exercise this power, and Mr. Lawless has been its last victim." (Only five years later Buchanan was to favor a proposed law giving the states the power to keep abolitionist newspapers out of the mail.) [15] Wickliffe too emphasized the importance of freedom of the press.

William Wirt, Peck's defense counsel, referred to the same words of the judge that Buchanan had quoted, and sought to make a distinction between liberty and license of the press. Peck's censure of the press, he said, was not on "*liberty of the press, but an abuse of that liberty* [italics in original]." Peck, he continued, "feels as deep a reverence for the liberty of the press as its loudest panegyrist can vaunt." [16]

Through exhaustive arguments by the five managers, every phase of the controversy was covered. But the crux of the matter in dispute was whether courts could punish only for contemptuous conduct in the presence of the judge and immediately disruptive of proceedings or, as Peck did, also for constructive contempt (outside the courtroom, in the form of a newspaper article) that did not interfere with the proceedings. Authority to punish for constructive contempt would give the courts as much latitude to curb expression in their own sphere as the government had once claimed in seeking to punish for seditious libel.[17]

As important as the contempt argument was for freedom of expression, the outcome would depend on how the Senate interpreted the meaning of impeachable offenses. Buchanan granted that, for the Senate to convict, the managers would have to prove that Peck violated the Constitution or some known law of the land. But he contended that "this violation of law" might consist in "the abuse, as well as in the usurpation of Authority." Offering the hypothetical case of a man found guilty of ordinary assault and battery who was thereupon fined by a judge a thousand dollars and committed to prison for a year, Buchanan asked whether the judge who exercised such tyrannical and arbitrary power should not be subject to conviction for an impeachable offense. His example, said Buchanan, was analogous to the charge against Judge Peck. Counsel for the judge, he noted, had "labored for hours" to show that the "perfectly decorous" article by Lawless was a libel even though it imputed no criminal intention to the judge in his ruling on the land claim. Buchanan suggested that the article was not libelous.

Yet, even admitting the power of the judge to punish for such an article, he asked, was it not a "cruel and oppressive use of authority" to degrade the author of the article by imprisonment and to deprive him of the means of earning bread for himself and his family for eighteen months? "A gross abuse of granted power and an usurpation of power not granted are offenses equally worthy of and liable to impeachment." By punishing Lawless in "an arbitrary and oppressive manner, and without the authority of law," Peck had committed an act that was in itself criminal, Buchanan declared. The Pennsylvanian asked whether such an act—"the product of a jaundiced mind and wounded vanity"—did not permit the inference of criminal intent.[18] The acquittal of Peck, he said, would make the impeachment provision the "scare-crow of the constitution."[19]

Speaking for the defense, William Wirt emphatically rejected Buchanan's contention that his client had acted in an arbitrary and oppressive manner. Peck, he said, was "innocent and simple-hearted as a child, . . . amiable, patient and forbearing." He might have made an error, but Wirt could not believe that such an error would be "a high misdemeanor in the sense of the Constitution of the United States." Wirt stressed the absence of any criminal intent. "Even if the judge were proved to have mistaken the law, he said, "that would not warrant a conviction unless the guilt of the intention be also established. For a mere mistake of the law is no misdemeanor in a judge. It is the intention that is the essence of every crime."

Buchanan's conclusion was keyed to the protection of liberty:

I ask for the conviction of Judge Peck in the name of the judiciary whose pure character he has sullied and whose independence he has endangered. I ask for it in the name of the people of the United States whose constitution and laws he has violated by tyranny and oppression. Should he be acquitted I shall never cease to believe that it will establish a precedent dangerous in the extreme to the rights and liberties of the American people.

Wirt's peroration was keyed to the preservation of the independence of the judiciary:

The question before you is not that of Judge Peck alone. It is the question of the independence of the American judiciary. Is this Court prepared to suspend the sword by a hair over the heads of our judges, and constrain them to the performance of their duties amidst fear and trembling from the terrors of an impeachment? Or will you rather, by your decision, maintain them in that firm, enlightened and honest discharge of their duties, which has heretofore so pre-eminently distinguished them?[20]

On January 31, 1831, Vice-President Calhoun called the roll of senators: the resulting vote was 21 for a verdict of guilty and 22 for a verdict of not guilty, which by any measure was well short of the votes needed for conviction under the Constitution's requirement of two-thirds of the members present. Of the 48 senators, three, John Rowan and George M. Bibb of Kentucky and Ezekiel F. Chambers of Maryland, were not present; two, John M. Robinson of Illinois and Thomas Hart Benton of Missouri, were excused from voting.[21] Senator Benton, who had appeared as attorney for the Soulards in the appeal of their case to Supreme Court in 1830, had asked to be excused from voting on the verdict. He did not vote in any of the recorded votes during the trial either. Senator Barton, who had sponsored Peck for appointment to the bench, voted for acquittal. The trial had lasted for nearly six weeks and created a record of more than 500 pages. In early March the Senate ordered 100 copies of the report of the trial of Judge Peck.[22]

St. Louis papers, hampered by the intervening distance, published belated accounts of various stages of the proceedings.[23] During the course of the trial the St. Louis *Beacon*—successor to the *Missouri Advocate and St. Louis Enquirer*, the paper that had started it all by publishing the Lawless article—quoted an article from the *Cincinnati Gazette* in which the writer said Peck and Lawless were both wrong and that Lawless should have stayed in Ireland. But the *Beacon*, in its own locally written article, said that Lawless should be thanked for taking his case to the House of Representatives and contributing to "public justice" by seeking to insure "punishment of a petty judicial tyrant."[24]

The *Missouri Republican*, the paper that had published Judge

Peck's opinion, reported that the trial was expected to end in acquittal and went on to say: "The torrent of odium which was let loose upon him [Peck] by Mr. McDuffie, was made to return upon his persecutors, by the invincibility of truth and the eloquence of his counsel."[25]

On February 21, the news having finally reached St. Louis, the *Beacon* reported the acquittal of Peck and the names of senators who answered the roll call and how they voted. The next day the *Missouri Republican* carried the news. On March 10 the St. Louis *Beacon* reprinted comments from other papers around the country on the Peck acquittal; the news had long since been published in eastern papers.[26] Apparently neither the *Beacon* nor the *Missouri Republican* saw fit to comment further on the case themselves.

The *National Intelligencer* reported the acquittal and observed: "We have never witnessed a more dignified proceeding in any public body."[27] The *Intelligencer* quoted with approval the final passage of an account of the trial by a writer in the New York *Commercial Advertiser*: "senators voted sincerely. . . . the votes were marked neither by sectional lines, nor party distinctions. Men of the same political views . . . voted different ways."[28]

A different view, however, was expressed by the *Courier and Enquirer* in New York, that city's largest circulation newspaper. It perceived a cleavage between the Jacksonians and the emerging Whig Party of Henry Clay and declared the vote to be along party lines, with all of the opponents of the Jackson administration voting to acquit and only a few Jackson senators so voting. Although the *Courier and Enquirer* concluded that there were sufficient grounds for convicting Judge Peck, the paper (which had begun as a Jackson paper and then turned against him on the bank issue) saw as a matter of regret that the Jackson party—which had been "so loud in its professions to keep politics and the judiciary separate"— should have deemed it advisable or proper to interfere in the case. Despite its reservations as to political interference with the judiciary, the paper saw a need to protect the people from "the worst of tyrannies"—that exercised by a judge, who can insult lawyers and imprison them for contempt and "can only be reached by impeachment." Expressing the hope that the admonitory lesson for Judge Peck would have its effect on other judges, the editor concluded by saying that Lawless had done his duty.

In Richmond, the *Whig*, a Clay paper, was outraged over the verdict. "Can we imagine a more high handed offence," asked the editor, "than that committed by Judge Peck! An offence which struck in the same blow, at the express guarantees of the Constitution, the freedom of the Press, and the personal liberty of the citizen!" The *Whig* made a point of noting that it differed with the majority of those with whom it generally sided, presumably the Clay partisans in the Senate who voted to acquit. The paper thought Peck should have been convicted, not just to punish the judge but as a vindication of the Constitution.

In Washington, the *Globe*, the voice of the administration in the nation's capital, observed caustically that Judge Peck had "escaped with impunity" because "every member of the opposition" had voted to shield him and were aided by Senators Felix Grundy and Hugh Lawson White, Tennessee Democrats, who, the paper suggested, had voted to acquit out of feelings of sympathy for a fellow Tennessean. Noting that Senator Benton and some other party members had declined to vote because they had prejudged the case, the *Globe* exclaimed wryly that Daniel Webster and David Barton, who had decided in favor of Peck before the trial, had nevertheless sat in the trial and voted. If Benton and the others of his party who declined to vote had done the same as the Peck partisans, said the editor, "there would have been a majority against the Judge."

In Boston, the *Courier*, a Clay paper, found the acquittal verdict as distasteful as did the paper of similar persuasion in Richmond. Judge Peck, the *Courier* declared sardonically, now had permission to "go back to Missouri and imprison all the lawyers and printers in the state, if they should ever dare to question the soundness of his opinions, whether promulgated from the Bench which he disgraced, or from the columns of a newspaper in which he chose to appear in defence of his official proceedings." The *Courier* perceived the acquittal "as much of an imposition upon the liberty of the Press, as the edicts of Charles the Tenth which cost him his crown and sent him an exile to Great Britain." (Presumably the *Courier* was referring to Charles X of France, who in 1830 had been forced into exile after imposing restrictions on the press and taking other authoritarian steps.)

Noting that Senators John M. Clayton of Delaware and Asher Robbins of Rhode Island, antiadministration lawmakers, had voted with nineteen Jackson men to convict, while Grundy, White, William Hendricks of Indiana and Littleton W. Tazewell of Virginia (Democrats) had voted with the opposition for acquittal, the *Courier* observed that it did not seem to have been "entirely a political question."[29]

Clearly the papers that saw the Peck acquittal as a sign of Senate insensitivity to freedom of the press were not limited to Jackson organs. Some papers, however, were themselves apparently insensitive to the First Amendment issue. The *National Intelligencer* evidently was not stirred enough to offer a comment of its own when it reported the verdict. Nor were the Charleston *Courier* or the Charleston *Mercury* in South Carolina, the state represented by George McDuffie, one of the most zealous prosecutors of Peck.[30]

Members of Congress, however, had evidently been feeling some heat on the question of judicial heavy-handedness. On February 1, the day after Peck's acquittal, Representative Joseph Draper of Virginia introduced a resolution directing the House Judiciary Committee to inquire into the expediency of defining by statute offenses that might be punished as contempts of the courts. It was promptly amended, with his permission, to have the statute limit punishments for contempt. Draper presented a passionate argument on the importance of the right of citizens to respond to publications by officials justifying their actions.[31] Later in the same month Buchanan introduced a bill to limit the contempt power of federal judges.

On March 2, 1831, Congress gave final approval to "An Act Declaratory of the Law Concerning Contempts of Court." The law said simply:

That the power of the several courts of the United States to issue attachments and inflict summary punishments for contempts of court, shall not be construed to extend to any cases except the misbehaviour of any person or persons in the presence of the said courts, or so near thereto as to obstruct the administration of justice, the misbehaviour of any of the officers of the said courts in their official transactions, and the disobedience or resistance by any officer of the said courts, party, juror, witness, or any other person or persons, to any lawful writ, process, order, rule, decree, or command of the said courts.[32]

A brief second section subjected to indictment and prosecution anyone who attempted to interfere with the courts by corruption or by threats or force directed against officers of the court or participants in litigation.

The speedy congressional action to prevent a recurrence of petulant judicial citations of the press evoked no outpouring of hurrahs from newspapers. The *National Intelligencer* briefly mentioned the passage of the contempt act, but offered no comment either then or in its next few issues.[33] The Richmond *Enquirer* mentioned House action on the bill without comment.[34] The *Missouri Republican* reported passage of the bill but had nothing to say editorially.

Although the Peck trial and the ensuing contempt act did not resolve permanently the continuing struggle between the press and the courts over the power of judges to inflict summary punishment for indirect or out-of-court contempt, the two events did herald a period of press ascendency in the confrontations between press and courts. Convictions for contempt by out-of-court publication were rare during the next thirty years.

Judges in early American cases had convicted editors for publications that attacked courts or litigants while cases were pending on the grounds that such comments would prejudice the public mind and possible jurors. But by 1830, even before the Peck trial, two Pennsylvania convictions and other actions in New York had led to state statutes sharply limiting the power of courts to punish for out-of-court contempt.[35] The movement to curb the courts was given further impetus when William Wirt argued in defense of Peck that the federal judge was following in good faith the firm precedents of the common law as embodied in the writings of Britain's Justice John Eardley Wilmot and Sir William Blackstone—namely, that courts had an inherent right to punish for so-called constructive contempt in order to protect the integrity of their procedures. Congress firmly rejected this rationale by adopting the 1831 law.

Luke Lawless eventually won not only on the principle of his dispute with the judge but also on his contention over the land claims. Congress in 1832 passed an act providing for a new board of land commissioners to decide on all remaining land claims, with instructions to follow a policy of confirming any claim that it thought would have been perfected by the Spanish authorities had they remained in possession of Louisiana. In this way many of the holders of old claims obtained confirmation of their titles. The decisions of the board were ratified by another act of Congress in 1836. Also in

1836, the Supreme Court, which had reserved the Soulard case for future decision, again considered the matter and reversed the ruling of the Missouri federal district court.[36]

The final irony in the Lawless saga came that same year (1836) when Lawless—by this time a judge in the second judicial circuit of Missouri—appeared as plaintiff in a libel suit against the Missouri *Republican*. He demanded $10,000 in damages for defamation of character that he said he had suffered as a result of the *Republican*'s publication of a communication complaining of the short sittings of the court over which he presided. Lawless lost.[37]

5
Slavery and Freedom of the Press

Slavery prompted more repression against the press than any other issue during the nineteenth century. The chief target of repressive efforts was the abolitionist press. Although newspapers devoted to the antislavery cause were being published as early as the second decade of the century, the great expansion of the abolitionist press came in the late 1830s and early 1840s, and it was in this period that significant efforts at restraint flourished.

Between thirty and forty abolitionist newspapers were published between 1830 and 1860. Abolitionists also published pamphlets, magazines, and other periodical publications. A measure of their printed output was provided by the third annual report of the American Anti Slavery Society, which revealed that during the fiscal year ending May 1836 the society printed and circulated more than a million pieces of antislavery literature. At this time distribution of the material was primarily by mail.

Not surprisingly, therefore, the abolitionists' use of the mails drew the censorial fire of those who perceived a threat to their interests or lives from abolitionist newspapers or other printed material. The circulation of such newspapers encouraged slave revolts, according to the often-repeated complaints from the slave-owning

South. Abolitionist editors insisted, however, that their publications were not intended to incite slave uprisings and, in fact, did not do so. They pointed out that slaves could not receive mail and that most of them could not read. Moreover, they noted that their papers explicitly disavowed violence.

Despite its avowed objective of change by peaceable means, the abolitionist press had to fight for acceptance in the North, to say nothing of the South. Abolitionist editors were the targets of anonymous threats and were harassed by libel suits. Abolitionist reporters were sometimes evicted from meetings and physically assaulted. Their papers were victimized by brick-throwing and other individual acts of vandalism and by mob actions, including attacks in such supposed citadels of liberal thought as Boston.[1] Many citizens in the North favored some legal control of the abolitionist press.

Although there were parts of the South, such as border areas with few slaves, where mild antislavery sentiment had been tolerated before 1830, the appearance of passionate abolitionist literature soon transformed the whole region into fiercely hostile territory for the discussion of issues deemed likely to undermine the slave system. The two publishing events that had the greatest impact were the appearance in 1829 of an *Appeal to the Colored Citizens of the World*, an eloquent antislavery pamphlet by David Walker, a free black of Boston; and the launching in 1831 of William Lloyd Garrison's abolitionist newspaper, *Liberator*.[2]

Citing Walker's and Garrison's uncompromising language and pointing to Nat Turner's slave uprising in Virginia in 1831, southerners called for an immediate reexamination of freedom of expression as it affected slavery. By 1836 movements for the repression of material "tending to incite insurrection" had appeared in all the states of the lower South. A Charleston, South Carolina, meeting in 1835 came to the conclusion that abolitionist editors were "no more entitled to the protection of the laws than the ferocious monster or venomous reptile."

From Virginia to Louisiana, older statutes were strengthened or new ones passed to impose the death penalty for printing or circulating anything tending to incite slave insurrections.[3] The laws varied on whether the ultimate penalty was prescribed for a second or third offense. The lash or imprisonment were specified for first offenses. In Georgia free Negroes were barred from working in print shops or newspapers. In Mississippi fines and jail sentences were provided for expressing "sentiments likely to produce discontent among the colored class." In South Carolina a penalty of $1,000 and one year in jail was made applicable to the white man who published or possessed abolitionist literature. In Louisiana the law provided penalties for publishing, speaking or writing "in court, bench, stage, or pulpit," anything tending to excite slaves. In Virginia postmasters and justices of the peace were empowered to censor the mails. Although these laws were justified on grounds that they were needed to protect the white population against slave insurrections, they actually reflected the dominance of the slaveholding class and its desire to protect its vested economic interests in cotton and slaves.

From the outset abolitionist editors regarded themselves as defenders of freedom of the press and constantly invoked their constitutional rights. They believed, with good reason, that the maintenance of freedom of the press for minorities was of vital importance to the American tradition. They often asserted that one of the evils of slavery was the denial in the South of freedom of speech and opinion in regard to it. In its *Declaration of Sentiments and Constitution* of 1835, the American Anti Slavery Society reprinted all federal and state constitutional guarantees of free speech and press. Abolitionists also warned that the continued existence of slavery would threaten the existence of a free press in the North as well as the South.

Among the better known abolitionist editors (who in many cases moved around and were connected with more than one paper during their careers) were Benjamin Lundy, James G. Birney, Gamaliel Bailey, John Greenleaf Whittier, James Russell Lowell, and William Lloyd Garrison. Viewing an end to slavery as his primary objective, Garrison at one point advocated disunion, referring to the constitutional "compact" with the South as "a covenant with Death and an agreement with Hell."[4] He countenanced no neutrality on the issue. His florid rhetoric, aimed at certain of his opponents, was enough to send them into a rage. They were, he said "the human hyenas and jackals of America, who delight to listen to negro groans, to revel in negro blood, and batten upon human flesh." He denounced some southern editors as "rum-drinkers, lechers, pimps, and knaves."

Garrison's courage, single-mindedness, and vigor made his *Liberator*, published in Boston, one of the half dozen most influential abolitionist newspapers in the country. Among the others were the Cincinnati *Philanthropist,* edited by Birney and later by Bailey; the Philadelphia *Pennsylvania Freeman,* later absorbed by *The National Anti Slavery Standard,* edited by Whittier and others; *The National Anti Slavery Standard* of New York City; and the Washington, D.C., *National Era,* edited by Bailey. Indicating their belief in the clash of ideas, abolitionist editors regularly published editorial selections from the southern press, speeches by proslavery men, and extracts from proslavery books. The abolitionist editors' method was either to allow the proslavery spokesmen in effect to condemn themselves by their own words, or to debate their opponents in parentheses or in footnotes.

One of the first incidents to precipitate a national controversy touching on press freedom for abolitionists occurred at Charleston in July of 1835. Prompted by reports that the mail steamer had brought in a number of packages of "incendiary" materials, a group of citizens entered the United States post office at Charleston, seized the packages, and burned them publicly on July 30.[5] Charleston Postmaster Alfred Huger immediately wrote to Postmaster General Amos Kendall informing him that he was detaining inflammatory tracts on slavery and asking for instructions on the disposition of future shipments of antislavery publications.

Kendall, one of President Jackson's advisors and a former newspaper editor himself, replied in a letter, dated August 4:

Upon a careful examination of the law, I am satisfied that the postmaster general has no legal authority to exclude newspapers from the mail, nor prohibit their carriage or delivery on account of their character or tendency, real or supposed. Probably, it was not thought safe to confer on the head of an executive department a power over the press, which might be perverted and abused.

But I am not prepared to direct you to forward or deliver the papers of which you speak. . . .

We owe an obligation to the laws, but a higher one to the communities in which we live, and if the *former* be perverted to destroy the *latter,* it is patriotism to disregard them. Entertaining these views, I cannot sanction, and will not condemn the step you have taken.[6]

Kendall's letter, in effect advising postmasters to disregard the law if they felt it necessary, was widely published and set off a wave of comment. But the letter was by no means generally condemned even in the northern press. Southern newspapers, as might have been expected, greeted it with approbation. The *Richmond Whig* revealed the tenor of southern opinion, writing: "The law is defective, and to supply its omissions until Congress meets, the people and postmasters must act upon their own responsibility. All men will acknowledge that the circulation of these incendiary tracts is out of the question."[7] The *Baltimore Republican and Commercial Advertiser* reported a proposal by the *Charleston Patriot* to use "lynch law" with respect to "incendiary publications." The Baltimore paper then went on to comment mildly that it seemed that already "Judge Lynch has been exercising authority in that city."[8]

The *Daily Albany* (N.Y.) *Argus*, a Jackson administration paper, having already approved the "summary seizure and destruction" of abolitionist literature by southerners as "a matter of justifiable self defence," said on August 13 that the Kendall view of the subject was "the only one which could be taken of the case."[9] Much the same view was expressed by the *Albany Daily Advertiser*.[10]

In Boston the *Daily Advertiser* said, "Our advice is to abstain altogether from the discussion of these questions [slavery and abolition], not so much because the people of the South complain of us, as because it can do no good."[11] During the controversy over the Kendall letter the Boston *Daily Evening Transcript* contented itself with an expression of concern over abolitionist agitation;[12] whereas the *Boston Atlas* declared: "There was but one course for the postmaster general to have pursued; and that is to have directed his subordinate to follow the law as it was laid down, and leave the result to the law. Instead of this, he tells him that it is *patriotism, sometimes, to disregard the law.*"[13]

In New York City the *Evening Star* thought the abolitionists' "vile pamphlets should be seized as common nuisances against the morality and peace of the community" in order to "secure the public from being contaminated or exasperated by their inflammatory doctrines, either through the press or the postoffice, or any other medium." The New York *Commercial Advertiser*, on the other hand, challenged Kendall for authorizing "the assumption of a dangerous authority that may be pleaded in *other* instances." The

National Gazette of Philadelphia asserted that "the head of one of the chief offices of the government 'will not condemn' a violation of law, and announces a principle subversive of all order."[14]

Perhaps the most stinging newspaper comment came from the *New York Evening Post*, a paper generally friendly to the Jackson administration, which denounced Kendall for "establishing a *censorship of the press* in its worst possible form, by allowing every two penny postmaster through the country to be the judge of what species of intelligence it is proper to circulate, and what to withhold from the people. A less evil than this drew forth, in former days, the *Areopagitica* from the master mind of Milton; but we little dreamed that new arguments in favour of the freedom of speech and of the press would ever become necessary in our country."[15] The editor of the *Evening Post* at the time was William Leggett, a markedly independent journalist.

Although there were scattered attacks on Kendall's ruling as a threat to freedom of expression (mostly from anti-Jackson papers), the Northern press was fairly unanimous in condemning the abolitionists' use of the mails to disseminate their materials.

Meanwhile, across the country, public meetings were convened to denounce the abolitionists' use of the mails as an abuse of this method of communication. In August a city-wide mass meeting in Charleston adopted a resolution viewing "with *abhorrence* and *detestation* the attempt to deluge our State with Incendiary publications." A committee, headed by former Governor Robert Y. Hayne, was appointed to inspect the mails in cooperation with the postmaster and to burn any objectionable matter. Similar meetings were held in Richmond and other places in Virginia and in various towns in Alabama and Mississippi. As far away as Missouri, Elijah Lovejoy, editor of the St. Louis *Observer*, was threatened with violence for an editorial comment on the Charleston incident. The majority of southern meetings, however, suggested that control of the mails ought to be established by some type of law and not by mob action.

Meetings to condemn the transmission of abolitionist publications through the mails were not limited to the South. Gatherings were also held in Philadelphia, New York City, Newark, New Jersey, Portsmouth, New Hampshire, Portland, Maine, and in Faneuil Hall in Boston, where a denunciatory resolution was adopted. The press, therefore, seemed to be merely reflecting popular opinion against facilitating freedom of expression for abolitionists, rather than defending their right to disseminate their views.

Public opinion was brought to a new boil by the delivery on December 7, 1835, of President Jackson's seventh annual message to Congress in which he appealed for a federal law prohibiting the circulation of "incendiary publications intended to instigate the slaves to insurrection." Jackson, a slaveowner himself, referred to the activities of the abolitionists as "unconstitutional" and declared it "proper for Congress to take such measures as will prevent the Post-Office Department, which was designed to foster an amicable intercourse and correspondence between all members of the Confederacy, from being used as an instrument of an opposite character."[16]

In a reply addressed to Jackson, the Executive Committee of the American Anti Slavery Society reiterated the abolitionists' arguments that they were opposed to violence in the abolition of slavery and that their message was not directed to slaves. The society suggested that a special congressional committee inspect its publications and try to discover a single inflammatory passage in any of them. Finally, the group declared: "We never intend to surrender the liberty of speech, or of the press, or of conscience—blessings we have inherited from our fathers, and which we mean, so far as we are able, to transmit unimpaired to our children."

Although a study of antislavery literature would have substantiated the abolitionists' contention that their publications intended for distribution in the South were not designed for slave consumption or to incite revolts, the antiabolitionist press was unmoved. The Columbus, Georgia, *Republican Herald* trumpeted: "The Press with its herculean power is rolling off sheet after sheet of vile and incendiary matter which is scattered like firebrands over the land."

The *Charleston Courier* printed the entire Jackson message and commented: "On the Abolition question, the Message holds language properly and patriotically indignant."[17] In the same issue in which it printed the message, the *Baltimore Republican* concluded that no "true hearted American" could read it "without deriving from it unalloyed pleasure and satisfaction."[18] The *Daily Albany* (N.Y.) *Argus*, after printing a long communication from Kendall justifying his recommendation of postal censorship, praised his stand.[19] The *National Gazette* of Philadelphia, with respect to the proposal in the Jackson message, said simply: "The paragraphs concerning the regulation of the Post Office department, with reference to the Slavery question, are of much consequence."[20] The *Daily Evening Transcript* of Boston reported the Jackson censorship proposal without comment.[21]

Senator John C. Calhoun of South Carolina managed to get the issue of postal treatment of abolitionist literature referred to a special Senate committee, of which he was a member. He argued that a federal law would infringe upon the states' reserve powers, that it might imply that Congress could legislate upon the subject of slavery in the states. "If Congress may this year decide what incendiary publications are," he said, "they may decide next year what they are not, and thus laden the mails with real or corrupt abolitionism. It belongs to the States, and not to Congress, to determine what is or what is not calculated to disturb their security."

Pursuant to this line of reasoning, Calhoun introduced a bill designed to give the states regulatory power over the mails within their borders. It provided that no deputy postmaster should receive or transmit "any pamphlet, newspaper, handbill, or any other paper, printed or written, or pictorial representation, touching the subject of slavery, addressed to a person or postoffice in a state, territory, or district whose laws forbade such material or to deliver such to anyone except those entitled by state law to receive it."

The Calhoun proposal provoked immediate opposition, some of it even in the South. Senator John Davis of Massachusetts pointed out quite logically that if state law could define what was "incendiary," the Declaration of Independence could already be legally barred from the mails in several southern states. Arguing in support of his bill, Calhoun said that the principle of such postal regulation could never be applied to matters of morals and religion. He insisted that no rights of free speech or press were violated by his measure, declaring that few postmasters would abuse their new authority by prying into personal mail.

But the Natchez, Mississippi, *Courier* maintained that a man would much rather "receive a bushel of abolitionist literature, which could easily be burned, than have his own private affairs pried into by every rascally deputy postmaster or clerk, who might choose to say he suspected they contained incendiary matter." The Boston *Daily Advocate* termed the proposal "an absurdity . . . as abhorrent to our free notions as a censorship of the press." The Philadelphia *Evening Star* characterized the bill as "a conspiracy against the rights of freemen."

The Dayton, Ohio, *Republican* commented on the broad restrictive implications of the proposed law:

The next step will be to stop the circulation of all antimasonic papers, then those that are opposed to the administration. This done, and their censorship fairly established, we will become the *white* slaves of the masters of the black slaves of the South. Lynch law will become the exclusive law of the land, and will be enforced against any who dare to utter sentiments not in accord with those of their masters.

As debate over the measure continued, public opinion against the Calhoun proposal was sufficient to force a reversal. The House passed a bill that prohibited, under penalty, any postmaster from detaining "any letter, package, pamphlet, or newspaper with intent to prevent the delivery of same." The Senate accepted the House bill with a few minor changes, and in July the measure became law. The post office was now under federal mandate not to interfere with the mails. The Richmond *Compiler* moaned that "no law can ever be constitutionally passed for the purpose of restraining the fanatics of the North in their crusade against our rights."

Despite the 1836 law, antislavery publications and even some publications of general coverage continued to be detained in the South and sometimes were destroyed. At Wirt Courthouse, Virginia, (now Elizabeth, West Virginia) the Pittsburgh *Dispatch* was burned. Among northern publications banned from the mails in certain localities in the South were the Boston *Atlas*, the Boston *Courier*, the Springfield, Massachusetts, *Republican*, the Philadelphia *Daily Republic*, the Philadelphia *Saturday Evening Post*, the New York *Herald*, the New York *Eagle*, and Horace Greeley's *New York Tribune*. The federal mails law of 1836 became largely a dead letter in the South.[22]

At the same time that Congress was debating the proposed postal censorship law, an editor in Ohio was beginning a publishing venture that was to contribute to another polarization of opinion on the abolitionist press. James G. Birney, an Alabama slave-holder who had been converted to the abolitionist cause, first tried to establish an antislavery newspaper in Danville, Kentucky. He was forced by popular opposition and by the refusal of job printers to set his type, to give up the project, although he appealed for respect for the "right secured by the Constitution to every citizen 'to speak, write, and print on any subject.' " Birney then made plans to start his newspaper, the *Philanthropist*, in Cincinnati and asserted that the project was as vital to the maintenance of freedom of the press as it was to the spreading of abolitionist sentiments.

When publication of the *Philanthropist* was begun in January 1836, Cincinnati's reaction was for the most part unfavorable. The *Post*, the *Whig*, and the *Republican* of that city all opined that the *Philanthropist* was definitely dangerous. Although Ohio's constitution plainly guaranteed Birney's right to publish, only Hammond's *Gazette* among local newspapers defended his right. Charles Hammond, the editor, did so despite his personal support for Ohio's "black laws" and for fugitive slave laws and his opposition to the organized abolition movement.

Soon after the *Philanthropist* began appearing, the *Republican* declared that "the interference of individuals not residing in those states where slavery is recognized, and who are not ameanable [*sic*] to their laws . . . is unjust, unpatriotic, unchristian, and revolutionary in its tendency." The *Whig* proposed a mass meeting of citizens to discuss the advisability of allowing Birney's paper to continue. On January 22 the first in a series of mass meetings, encouraged and egged on by the local press, was held. These gatherings, which were convened from time to time over a period of months, were not the work of rude and vulgar agitators but were promoted and participated in by civic and political leaders. They feared the effect of Birney's paper on the economy of Cincinnati, which enjoyed a highly profitable trade with the slave states of the Mississippi Valley, states that might retaliate with a boycott against an area where abolitionism flourished.

The *Republican* put their interests plainly when on January 22 it pointed out that "Southern feeling is strong in this city, and the interests of her *merchants*, her *capitalists*, and her *tradesmen*, are too deeply interwoven with the interests of the slave states . . . to admit of the *uninterrupted* operation of a society tending to separate the ties which connect the city to those states." The same paper a week later called on citizens to "put down abolition and abolitionists, *peaceably if we can, and forcibly if we must.*" The agitation of the Cincinnati press was such that the Steubenville, Ohio, *Herald* felt called upon to warn the papers of Cincinnati that they were encouraging a mob.

In time popular action did turn from resolutions of censure against Birney to mob attacks. A group broke into the *Philanthropist* offices on July 12 and destroyed some printing equipment. Handbills and placards containing thinly veiled threats against abolitionists appeared. Even Charles Hammond, whose *Gazette* in January had said "we are not afraid to hear the advocates of these [abolitionist] measures speak," had retreated in his defense of free speech by July. While deploring the attacks on Birney, he advised the abolitionist editor that slavery was the business of the slave states with "which the people of the free States have *nothing* to do."

In other places in the Midwest, however, the threat to press freedom roused editors to vigilance. Antimob editorials appeared in the Lexington, Kentucky, *Intelligencer*, the Greensburgh, Iowa, *Repository*, and the Piqua, Ohio, *Western Courier*. The *Western Courier* asserted: "We care nothing for the abolitionist because he is such, but we would protect him in his full exercise of the freedom" secured by the Constitution and all the civil institutions of the country.

With lynch law being encouraged by some of Ohio's leading citizens, the Ohio Anti Slavery Society, sponsor of Birney's paper was asked by a citizens' committee after the July 12 mob action whether it intended to continue the *Philanthropist*. The society replied that it had become the custodian of liberty of the press and was determined to go on with publication. More meetings followed, and after a large assembly on July 23 a committee of prestigious members was appointed to meet with Birney. The committee—which included Jacob Burnet, former United States senator and former justice of the Ohio Supreme Court; D. T. Disney, former Speaker of the Ohio House of Representatives; Josiah Lawrence and Robert Buchanan, bank presidents; and Nicholas Longworth, the city's richest man— was to inform the abolitionist editor of the danger of continuing to publish his paper. The meeting having failed to persuade Birney or the Anti Slavery Society to suspend publication, editor Charles Ramsay of the *Republican* pointedly told Birney: "There are points beyond which public sentiment, even in a free government, may not be trifled with with impunity."

The city's leadership having clearly signaled that it was not prepared to uphold the law and indeed was virtually condoning violence, a mob two days later, on July 30, broke into the shop where the *Philanthropist* was printed, destroyed the press and scattered the type. The mob then went to the black section of the city, where they broke into two homes and wrecked a saloon. Finally requested to disperse by the mayor, "lest it disturb the respectable parts of the city," the mob dissolved.[23]

The Cincinnati press, with one exception, in effect applauded the attack on the abolitionist paper. In its August 1 issue, the *Republican* voiced the opinion that the attackers had been "the most systematic, orderly, and wellbehaved mob we have ever witnessed." The next day the *Whig* said "few seem to be dissatisfied with the result, or [have] the slightest sympathy with the sufferers." Only Hammond's *Gazette* castigated the Cincinnati mass meeting and the mob attack against Birney. Editor Hammond had stern words not only for the mob but for the *Whig*, a rival newspaper in Cincinnati:

In Saturday's *Whig*, we have nearly two columns of editorial, which, so far as I can understand it, may be reduced to this syllogism: "The liberty of the press is subject to responsibility for its licentiousness"—to print and publish in favor of abolitionism is licentious, therefore, for this licentiousness, an abolition press may be torn down by the high hand of violence—I cannot waste time discussing such a proposition as this, no matter in what multitude of words it is submerged.[24]

As the first major attack on the abolitionist press in the North, the Cincinnati riot prompted a considerable amount of press comment across the nation. Hezekiah Niles, whose weekly *Register* in Baltimore seldom had sharp editorial remarks, had a comment on the Cincinnati affair but, in a curious balancing of blame, laid more condemnation on the abolitionists than the mob. The riots, he said, "evince a settled determination on the part of the people not to tolerate incendiary attempts to excite the fears of the sister states, but they have taken a direction hardly less censurable than the course pursued by the abolitionists themselves."

The *New York Evening Post*, under the editorship of William Cullen Bryant, concluded: "We hold that this combination of the few to govern the many by terror of illegal violence is as wicked and indefensible as a conspiracy to rob on the highway." In a more realistic assessment of the strength of the popular opposition to Birney, the New York *Sun* said the mob had established the thoroughly dangerous precedent "that a real or pretended opinion of the majority of the people should be the governing principle, even though it be in opposition to existing law." The Pittsburgh *Gazette* said: "we hold in utter abhorrence every unlawful infringement upon the rights of the press, whether it be devoted to slavery, anti-slavery, religion or politics."

In Ohio the editorial reaction was no less trenchant. The Cleveland *Advertiser* declared: "However numerous, or respectable those may be who get up the spirit of mobocracy, we consider it none the better, but worse on this account . . . he who countenances mobocracy is doing the most in his power towards uprooting our free institutions, and scattering firebrands, arrows and death amongst the community." The Dayton *Journal* remarked that "such an outrage should have been committed on that palladium of liberty, the press, cannot be too sharply deplored. The spirit of mobocracy could not have been more unfortunately directed."[25] The Dayton *Republican* concluded that the mob had accomplished nothing except to gain support for the abolitionists.

Whatever their feelings about the abolitionist cause, editors were beginning to see—as they did on the postal censorship issue—that panic-induced suppression of the abolitionist press could eventually affect their own papers as well. That many northern editors saw the Cincinnati incident as a danger sign for the press was indicated by the fact that Birney was able to collect and reprint editorials from twenty-three northern papers expressing disapproval of the mob and pointing out the threat to freedom of the press.[26]

But the fight for freedom of the press for abolitionists was not yet won even in the North. Efforts were mounted by antiabolitionists, North and South, to impose legal controls on the antislavery press. In early 1836 southern legislatures transmitted to the legislatures of northern states, where abolitionist publishers were especially active, memorials requesting that official action be taken against the antislavery papers. From the South Carolina legislature came a typical petition asking the northern states to "make it highly penal to print, publish, and distribute newspapers, pamphlets, tracts, and pictorial representations, calculated and having an obvious tendency to excite the slaves of the slave States to insurrection and revolt." With the exception of Vermont, all of the petitioned legislatures seemed at first to favor the southern point of view, although they recognized that the proposed legislation would encounter constitutional difficulties.

As might have been expected, the Richmond *Enquirer* and the *Charleston Patriot* thought the southern memorials were asking nothing that violated editorial freedom of expression. But newspaper support for repressive legislation was not limited to the South. The Boston *Courier* at one point advocated legislation specifically to suppress Garrison's *Liberator*. (At another time, however, the *Courier* thought "the mere suggestion of legal interference with the press" would be "a signal for revolution.") In New York City the *Evening Star* proposed for presentation to the state legislature a bill defining as a misdemeanor the printing of any material tending to incite insurrection.

The *New York Evening Post* declared, however, that secession would be preferable to a gag law on the press. The New York *Sun* asserted: "Although we are decidedly opposed to the fanatical course of the immediate abolitionists, . . . we shall nevertheless raise our arm in fearless independence against the insolent invasion of the dearest and most sacred rights of our free states." And the New York *Plain Dealer* proclaimed that the North would "never surrender the right of free discussion of slavery, nor any other subject." Despite a flurry of legislative activity, all of the northern states eventually rejected the proposed laws.

More than any other case, that of Elijah Lovejoy, editor of the *Observer* in Alton, Illinois, helped to turn the tide of northern opinion toward support of freedom of the press for abolitionists. Lovejoy, a Presbyterian minister and a native of Maine, had been editor of the St. Louis *Observer*, a religious weekly, beginning with its first issue on November 22, 1833. At that time the editor had proclaimed in his paper that: "Truth is its object. . . . It will seek no controversy, and it will decline none when by so doing it might compromise the purity of that faith once delivered to the saints." Although not an abolitionist, Lovejoy, in his paper's columns, did condemn what were, by his lights, sins: intemperance, greed, slaveholding and Sabbathbreaking, as well as so-called papist pretensions and errors.[27]

For two years the *Observer* prospered despite its occasional strictures against slavery in a slave state. But in the fall of 1835 word came from Jefferson City that a box of Bibles mailed to the Cole County Bible Society by the Missouri Bible Society in St. Louis, of which Lovejoy was the secretary, had been filled with violent abolitionist literature. Immediately the editor of the St. Louis *Observer* became a marked man. The *Missouri Argus* in St. Louis declared that Lovejoy had forfeited all rights to courtesy as a newspaper editor.[28] The St. Louis *Commercial Bulletin* denounced the *Observer* editor in an editorial ending with the threat: "Let then the abolitionists, their emissaries and their tools beware! They are watched, their slightest movement will bring upon them a summary punishment. *They will be put down.*"[29]

Meanwhile, Lovejoy had already taken his stand in the *Observer* in which he quoted the Missouri constitution on freedom of the press and protested "all these attempts . . . to frown down the liberty of the press and forbid the expression of opinion."[30] In early November a meeting of citizens in St. Louis passed a resolution saying: "Freedom of speech and press does not imply a moral right to . . . freely discuss the subject of slavery, . . . a question too nearly allied to the vital interests of the slaveholding States to admit of public disputation."[31]

Faced with the intense local opposition stirred by mob psychology, the *Observer's* prominent Presbyterian backers in St. Louis in early October had already asked Lovejoy "to pass over in silence every thing connected with the subject of slavery."[32] Lovejoy, as a result, handed in his resignation as editor, but not before he had published an issue of the *Observer* containing an account of what had happened, setting forth his views on slavery, and affirming his strong commitment to freedom of the press. He explained that in packing the Bibles for Jefferson City he had filled the extra space in the box with loose papers gathered at his office and that among these was inadvertently included a copy of an abolitionist paper. But, after asserting that the enclosure had been inadvertent, he added sardonically that no law forbade his sending to a friend or citizen any document he pleased despite the fashion in certain parts of the country of breaking open the post office and taking from it "such documents as the mob should decide ought not to pass unburned." He stated that he was not an abolitionist, which he took to mean one who wished to have slaves *immediately* set free, but added candidly that he was an emancipationist, by which he meant that he favored the eventual termination of the system of slavery.[33] Referring to the meeting at which it had been resolved that slavery was not a subject for discussion, he declared:

> Tomorrow another meeting decides it is against the peace of society that the principle of property be discussed. . . . The next day a decree is issued against speaking against distilleries, dram shops, and drunkenness. And so on to the end of the chapter. The truth is, my fellow citizens, if you give ground a single inch, there is no stopping place.
>
> I deem it, therefore, my duty to take my stand upon the Constitution.[34]

As the *Observer* reached its readers, threats against the paper mounted. But Lovejoy also found, as a number of young men offered to defend him, that he had made some friends in St. Louis. Although most of the proprietors were ready to sell the *Observer* at auction, one of them decided to underwrite the paper alone and offered the editorship again to Lovejoy. However, he suggested that the paper be moved to the safety of a free state.

Meanwhile, Lovejoy's spirited defense of freedom of the press had won him admirers among abolitionists. His reply to those who would deny him the right to discuss slavery was reprinted in newspapers across the country. Papers in Boston, Philadelphia, New York, and Cincinnati commented favorably.

Although Lovejoy had decided to move his paper across the Mississippi to Alton, Illinois, he was to have more trouble in St. Louis before the move. His local critics were still not appeased, although he opened his pages to both proslavery and antislavery opinion, the former point of view being represented by a fiery speech by Gov-

ernor McDuffie of South Carolina in which the governor proclaimed
the advantages of slavery and called abolitionists "wicked monsters and deluded fanatics."[35]

On April 28, 1836, a mob in St. Louis lynched a black man who
had been arrested for homicide by stringing him up to a tree and
burning him to death. In the *Observer* of May 5, 1836, Lovejoy had
a scathing comment on mob actions in Charlestown, Baltimore,
Vicksburg, and St. Louis. In St. Louis, he wrote, the mob "forces
a man—a hardened wretch certainly, and one that deserved to die,
but not *thus* to die—it forces him from beneath the aegis of our
constitution and laws, hurries him to the stake and burns him
alive!" He urged a return to the constitution and laws and warned
that otherwise "ALL IS GONE!"

Less than a month later a grand jury was convened in St. Louis
and was addressed by Luke E. Lawless, the same man who had
championed freedom of the press in the Peck case and who was
now a judge of a Missouri circuit court. Speaking of the lynch mob,
Lawless presented the grand jury with a rationale and circumstances
under which they need not bring an indictment for the lynching.
He blamed abolitionists for arousing in the lynch victim passions
which caused him to resist authority. He referred to the abolitionist
press in St. Louis, held up a copy of the St. Louis *Observer*, and
cited its contents as examples of material "calculated to fanaticize
the Negro and excite him against the white man. . . ." He condemned
the paper for printing sermons against slavery and a sermon on
"Liberty of the Press." The judge, in his charge to the grand jury,
said he was in favor of freedom of the press, but he believed the law
should protect society from the abuses of the press as well as from
the abuse of any other means.[36]

Lovejoy's response in the *Observer* was a personal attack on
Lawless, in which the judge was called "a papist." Referring to the
judge's charge, the editor said:

A horrid crime must not be punished because, forsooth, it would be
difficult perhaps to do. The principles of justice and of constitutional
law must yield to a doubtful question of present expediency. . . .
Property in its essential principles is incompatible with regulated civil
or religious liberty.

To establish our institutions of civil and religious liberty, to obtain freedom of opinion and of the press guaranteed by constitutional law cost thousands, yea tens of thousands of valuable lives. And let them not be parted with at least for less than cost.[37]

Feelings in the town were stirred to a frenzy by the quarrel between the editor and the judge. During the summer of 1836, the *Observer* office was the target of repeated mob attacks. Type was scattered and the press damaged. Lovejoy's home was invaded and the furnishings vandalized.

In July the *Observer* press was shipped to Alton and, while it was standing on the dock at night awaiting delivery the next day, it was shattered and thrown into the river by a mob. Despite his difficulties, Lovejoy was welcomed to Alton by many of its citizens. He was able to publish his paper for some time on a new press without any serious problems. By the spring of 1837 the *Observer* had adopted a militantly abolitionist position. The *Missouri Republican*, across the river, began hammering away at the *Observer*, saying that Lovejoy merited the full measure of his community's indignation and had "forfeited all claims to the protection of that or any other community."[38]

In July a mass meeting of citizens of Alton appointed a committee to warn Lovejoy against continuing his outspoken course. Once more Lovejoy invoked the rights of a free press, saying no public meeting "could dictate what sentiments should not be discussed in a duly authorized newspaper." As tension mounted during August, Lovejoy was threatened twice. On August 23 his office was invaded and his press destroyed. The *Alton Spectator* came to the defense of the mob, implying that it was the avenger for an "insulted community." The *Missouri Republican* warned of the danger to Alton's commerce with the slave states if the town continued to tolerate an abolitionist.[39]

In an appeal to subscribers and friends of the *Observer*, Lovejoy asked for donations for a new press, basing his request on a plea to maintain freedom of the press in Illinois. The necessary $1,500 was raised in less than a month. Meanwhile, Lovejoy's cause was again receiving attention in the east and support from newspapers in localities where abolitionist sentiment was a growing force. His determined defense of press freedom also won support from at least two newspapers in Kentucky.

The Louisville *Gazette* said: "Mr. Lovejoy has the right of publishing his paper even in Alton, and however we may differ with him in relation to his tenets, we certainly admire the tenacity with which he clings to them, and the pertinacity with which he asserts his right to disseminate his principles."[40] The Lexington *Intelligencer* declared:

We agree with our friend of the Louisville *Gazette*, that the rights of Mr. Lovejoy have manifestly been violated. And we will add a query for the consideration of the *violators*. Do you not admit the truth and moral force of the sentiments promulgated, when you resort to illegal, animal, or brute force to postpone their promulgation?[41]

Scarcely had Lovejoy's new press, the third, arrived when, on September 21, it was also destroyed by a mob, and again an appeal went out for funds to buy another. Twice more during the weeks immediately following Lovejoy was the target of threats. And in early October, while visiting his wife in St. Charles, Missouri, where she had gone for a rest, he was pursued by a mob and barely escaped injury.

Later that same month the Illinois Anti Slavery Convention met in Alton and resolved that "the cause of human rights, the liberty of speech and of the press imperitively [*sic*] demands that the press of the Alton *Observer* be reestablished at Alton with its present editor." By this time many of Alton's influential citizens were alarmed by the prospect of the *Observer's* continued operation. They sponsored two public meetings, on November 2 and 3, under the leadership of the attorney general of Illinois for the purpose of finding some way to silence the paper.

Despite Lovejoy's attendance and moving speech in his own defense, the assembled citizens resolved that they held a "sacred regard for the great principles contained in our Bill of Rights. . . . No discussion of slavery, by any paper or editor, would be permitted in Alton." Moreover, they concluded that the peace and harmony of the community required that Lovejoy no longer be identified with "any newspaper enterprise" in their city. Lovejoy promptly expressed his intention to ignore the warning, saying he would "insist on protection" in the exercise of his rights, and adding: "If the civil authorities refuse to protect me, I must look to

God, and if I die, I have determined to make my grave in Alton."[42]

Lovejoy's fourth press arrived on November 5. At the request of Mayor John Marshall Krum, who had initially welcomed Lovejoy to Alton, the new press was placed in a warehouse, pending its removal to the Observer offices. Learning of plans to destroy the press, Lovejoy gathered a group of armed supporters who barricaded themselves in the warehouse to protect it. On the evening of November 7 a mob gathered at the warehouse. Shots were exchanged and Lyman Bishop, one of the attackers, was killed. (The mayor later said the first shot came from the building and was the one that killed Bishop. A Cincinnati *Journal* eyewitness account and others asserted, however, that the mob fired first.) The mob withdrew and returned with ladders for use in setting fire to the roof of the warehouse. Several of the defenders rushed out, fired a few shots, and sought to mount the ladders and extinguish the fire. Lovejoy, standing in the doorway, was fired upon and fell with five bullets in his body.

News of Lovejoy's murder reverberated across the nation and strongly identified abolitionist publishing with freedom of the press in a manner that made it difficult for editors, in the North at least, to ignore the implications of growing mob activity for a basic constitutional guarantee. An outpouring of editorials in northern papers condemned the Alton mob and labeled Lovejoy a martyr for freedom of the press. The *New York Evening Post* thundered:

We regard this not as a question connected with the Abolition of slavery, in the South, but as a question vital to the liberties of the entire Union. For our own part, we approve, we applaud, we would consecrate, if we could, to universal honor, the conduct of those who bled in this gallant defence of the freedom of the press. Whether they erred or not in their opinions, they did not err in the conviction of their right, as citizens of a democratic government, to express them, nor did they err in defending this right with an obstinacy which yielded only to death and utmost violence.[43]

Horace Greeley wrote in his weekly *New Yorker* that "for the act of inflexibly maintaining the common rights of every citizen in defiance of the audacious tyranny of the multitude, he may well be deemed a martyr to public liberty." The Pittsburgh *Times* declared:

we believe we are borne out by the truth, in affirming that the Alton murder has made ten thousand accessions to the cause of Abolition. In this number, we do not include ourselves; but, although opposed to their cause, we are in favor of extending, to every portion of our fellow-citizens, the same right that we claim for ourselves, freedom of thought and the right of expressing our opinions.[44]

In Louisville the *Herald* called on the press to rally to the cause of freedom:

Is a citizen of the United States to have his house—his castle—assailed by an armed mob, and is he to be murdered for defending the rights guaranteed to him by the constitution of his country? Are such things to be tolerated, and will the presses of the country, which can find so much gall and wormwood, and so many maledictions for political opponents, pass by this outrage with a bare expression of cold regret?[45]

There were indeed papers that appeared to regret Lovejoy's death more because of what it would do for the cause of abolitionism than for what it signified about the status of press freedom. The Louisville *Journal* moaned:

Let those, who oppose the Abolitionist, take warning from this event, and let them ever remember that the only weapons with which these zealots can be successfully encountered, are truth, reason, moderation, and tolerance—and these are the only means to disarm them of their fanaticism; and that violence, outrage, and persecution will . . . inflame their zeal, enlarge their numbers, and increase the power of their dangerous doctrines.[46]

In St. Louis the *Commercial Bulletin* expressed a similar opinion:

Be the offences of Lovejoy what they may, if he has violated every law of the land, and outraged every feeling of society, and every principle of moral and social duty—the end of his unfortunate career—the mode and measure of his punishment has changed the offender to a martyr, and the presuming, daring sinner to an apostle of righteousness and a saint. His martyrdom will be celebrated by every Abolitionist in the land, and the only consolation we have is, that it was inflicted upon him in a non-slave-holding State.[47]

But the great majority of papers were unequivocal in condemning the Alton mob. *The Emancipator*, between November 23, 1837, and February 8, 1838, reprinted 161 editorials. The *Liberator*, between November 24 and December 22, 1837, reprinted more than 50. Of the many editorials on the Lovejoy murder, fewer than a dozen (those reprinted in *The Emancipator* of January 18, 1838) expressed the view that Lovejoy deserved his fate.

The murder of an editor standing guard over his press had dramatized the issue of freedom of expression in a way that demanded attention. Ralph Waldo Emerson "sternly rejoiced that one was found to die for humanity and the rights of free speech and opinion." Former President John Quincy Adams said Lovejoy's death set off "a shock as of an earthquake throughout this continent, which will be felt in the most distant region of the earth." Numerous sermons throughout the North were devoted to the "martyr of Alton."

The rallying cry for the defense of press freedom was not taken up by editors, however, until the threat had become obvious to many others. Lovejoy's death by gunfire was simply the tragic climax of a rash of riotous events in the 1830s, events that included the mob manhandling of editor Garrison of the *Liberator* in Boston in 1835, the sacking of the office of the Utica, New York, *Standard and Democrat*, an abolitionist paper, in 1835; the mobbing of Birney's *Philanthropist* in Cincinnati in 1836.[48]

Whenever abolitionists were merely a troublesome minority with no way of relating the suppression of their presses to larger interests, their cases were often ignored by general circulation papers. As late as 1840, an important editor like James Gordon Bennett of the New York *Herald* could see nothing inconsistent in arguing for freedom of expression during the so-called moral war against *Herald* sordidness, while being oblivious to the throttling of abolitionist editors.

Although abolitionist journalism encountered little significant difficulty in the North after 1840, occasional outrages against abolitionist publications continued until the Civil War. Except for Horace Greeley and a few others, nonabolitionist editors in the North either refused to allow abolition material in their columns or actively opposed the cause.

In the South, where editors with any abolitionist tendencies were almost universally restrained by overwhelming public pressure and the threat or fact of mob action, most newspaper editors accepted and applauded restrictions on the press where slavery was concerned and helped to ferret out and incite feeling against antislavery spokesmen. The *Georgia Telegraph* in 1835 proposed banning all northern newspapers from the state. The *South Carolinian* of Columbia, warning in 1849 that the *National Anti Slavery Standard* and the *Pennsylvania Freeman* were circulating in the state, suggested mob action. In the South, slaveholders, comprising a minority of the population but holding powerful economic leverage, were able to control legislatures and mold public opinion in a way that enabled them to effectively nullify federal and state constitutional guarantees of free speech and press. Southern editors came to accept the rationale that the duty of the press was to respect the interests of the community, which in this instance were identified with slavery.

During the critical period of testing for freedom of the press, from 1830 to 1850, the brunt of the struggle to uphold constitutional guarantees of free expression was borne by abolitionist editors, not by the press in general. Editors of nonabolitionist papers were fairly outspoken in defense of freedom for the abolitionist press when it was the victim of violence or when it was the target of suppression that might also affect the press in general, as in the case of postal censorship, but even in these kinds of cases, editors were far from unanimous in perceiving the free press guarantee as a shield especially needed for the protection of an unpopular point of view.

6

War and the First Amendment: New Tests

As in the case of the War of 1812, the war with Mexico, 1846–1848, found the nation far from united in support of the conflict. Whigs and antislavery people generally opposed the war, seeing it, with good reason, as being motivated by a desire for westward and southward expansion at the expense of Mexico. Whig members of Congress, including Abraham Lincoln, denounced the war.[1]

Like the people and politicians, the press took opposing positions. "LET US GO TO WAR," the New York *Journal of Commerce,* a proslavery paper, declared in a blunt editorial. The *New York Morning News* also was in favor of fighting. The American people, according to the Richmond *Enquirer,* were for "a full and thorough chastisement of Mexican arrogance and folly." In a righteously bellicose comment, the New Orleans *Commercial Bulletin* said the "United States have borne more insult, abuse, insolence and injury, from Mexico, than one nation ever before endured from another." Therefore, said the paper, the United States was left "no alternative but to extort by arms the respect and justice which Mexico refuses. . . ."[2]

Other papers were equally vehement on the opposite side. "People of the United States," the *New York Tribune* warned, "your rulers are precipitating you into a fathomless abyss of crime and calamity. Why sleep you on its verge?" James Russell Lowell castigated the war in the Boston *Courier*.[3] The Boston *Atlas* declared: "It would be a sad and woeful joy, but a joy nevertheless, if the hordes under [General Winfield] Scott and [General Zachary] Taylor were, *every man of them, swept into the next world*."[4]

Such fierce antiwar sentiments, which were considered treasonous in other times, were tolerated by the government, not because of any extraordinary respect for the First Amendment but because there was no strong popular majority demanding suppression.[5] There was, however, military suppression of small papers on the Mexican fighting front.[6]

Not until the Civil War was the First Amendment again to be tested in wartime and the press challenged to take a stand on the amendment's meaning for freedom of the press under such circumstances. The Civil War, however, was different from any other American war in that the survival of the United States, as organized in 1789, was more severely threatened than in any other conflict. The critical nature of the threat seemed to justify severe measures. Yet, while the threat was real, the nature of the war complicated the choices between strict or lenient government treatment of the press. The federal government had to be concerned not only about how to restrict the publication of military information of possible value to the armies of the Confederacy but about whether to restrict the publication of political criticism and comment that might win or lose the allegiance of various groups in parts of the country. This was especially important in the border states, where public opinion was far from united behind the Union cause. Even if the administration had been philosophically inclined to put a total gag on the press in the interest of preventing the publication of potentially harmful information or comment, it could see that rigid across-the-board restraints might have the effect of antagonizing some newspapers that were useful to the cause or of alienating segments of the population whose loyalties wavered in the fierce fratricidal struggle.

As a result, there was no consistent enforcement from Washington of any fixed body of rules to control the press. No censorship, espionage, or sedition laws were enacted. Of course, freedom of expression for individuals was widely affected by Lincoln's suspension of the writ of habeas corpus and the subsequent arrest and imprisonment without trial of thousands of citizens suspected of disloyal words or deeds (some estimates put the figure as high as thirty-eight thousand). Sometimes harsh restrictions and suppression were visited upon the press by both civil and military authorities in various parts of the country, often without direction from Washington.[7] Various newspapers were also the victim of mob attacks. The upshot, however, was that, without centralized regulation, the northern press was remarkably free to criticize civil leaders and generals, to assess the direction and success of the war effort, to publish military information of value to the other side and even to urge abandoning the pursuit of the war. Yet probably no other American war brought as many individual instances of restraint of the press by local governmental or military authorities or by the people.[8]

Censorship power over messages sent via telegraph lines was assumed early in the war by the War Department and later by the State Department. The postmaster general, in capricious exercises of judgment, denied the use of the mails to newspapers deemed disloyal, and in the process scores of papers found themselves temporarily or permanently suspended. Papers affected included the *New York Daily News*, the New York *Journal of Commerce*, the New York *Day-Book, Freeman's Journal*, the Brooklyn *Eagle*, the Franklin, New York, *Gazette*, the South Bend, Indiana, *Forum*, and the *Missouri State Journal* in St. Louis.

In Baltimore, the *Exchange*, the *South*, the *Maryland News Sheet*, the *Republican*, the *Daily Gazette*, the *Transcript*, the *Evening Post*, and the *Evening Loyalist* were all suppressed by military action. In Philadelphia, the *Evening Journal* was suppressed by order of Brigadier General Robert C. Schenck, and the *Christian Observer* was seized and suppressed by the United States marshal. The Chicago *Times* was seized and suspended by order of Major General Ambrose E. Burnside.

In St. Louis, the *War Bulletin* and the *Missourian* were suppressed by Major J. McKinstry, the provost marshal in the area. In Boone County, Missouri, the property of the *Standard* was confiscated. In New Orleans (which was in occupied territory), the *Bee*, the *Crescent*, and the *Delta* were suppressed by order of Union military authorities. So were the *Argus* and the *Avalanche* in Memphis. Mobs attacked the *Crisis* in Columbus, Ohio; the *Democratic Standard*, in Concord, New Hampshire; the *Democrat*, in Bangor, Maine; the *Jeffersonian*, in Westchester, Pennsylvania.[9]

Most of the papers that were suppressed by military or civil authorities or attacked by mobs were not targeted for giving direct aid to the enemy, such as by publishing useful military information. Rather, they were suppressed for expressing views that were deemed to be hindering the war effort, such as discouraging enlistment in the Union army, protesting against the draft, or opposing federal bond issues. Those publications whose opinions reflected a strong sympathy for the South were called "copperhead papers" (equivalent to the poisonous snake). Among the publications that were unabashedly in sympathy with the South, some were newspapers of general and sometimes large circulation. The papers that were victims of suppression, however, were by no means all chargeable with aiding the South in a military sense but were often merely exercising their First Amendment right to criticize the government in a manner offensive to Unionists.[10]

Yet, because of intense divisions within the Union and differing perceptions of what kinds of publication constituted a real danger, the suppression of papers, as recorded by history, do not always present in retrospect clear-cut examples of unwarranted interference with press freedom. By singling out cases in which the president himself made a decision to lift restraints that had been imposed on individual newspapers, we should be justified in assuming that editors should have been no less willing to recognize freedom of expression for those papers. There were two prominent cases in which President Lincoln revoked the suspension of papers by military authorities. The reaction of editors to these cases should be instructive as to their commitment to freedom of the press.

The first case was that of the Chicago *Times*. The *Times* had been purchased in 1861 by Wilbur F. Storey, who had previously published the Detroit *Free Press*. Storey, who hailed from Vermont, had been connected with half a dozen newspapers before moving to Chicago. A striking figure with thick white hair and white beard, Storey was tall and athletic, well endowed to defend himself against the frequent assaults upon his person. (Lydia Thompson, star of the "British Blondes," one of the famous burlesque troupes of the period, once tried to horsewhip Storey as punishment for some disparaging comments attributed to him. During the fracas the *Times* editor nearly strangled one of the two women who set upon him and almost broke the neck of one of their male companions. But Storey was never quite able to live down the story that he was soundly horsewhipped by the irate show girl.) A target of frequent libel suits as well as personal assaults, Storey seemed to hold public opinion in contempt. He rarely went out unarmed; in anticipation of possible attack, he kept loaded muskets and hand grenades on hand in the editorial rooms and rigged up a device to fill the floor below with scalding steam in case of assault.

Whatever his faults as an individual, Storey was an editor who made his paper a force to be reckoned with. By placing special emphasis on telegraphic news, he challenged the *Chicago Tribune.* He was reported to have once sent one of his war correspondents a message saying: "Telegraph fully all news you can get, when there is no news send rumors." Without much conscience or principle, he made the *Times* a bold, sensationalist paper.

Although of northern origin, Storey was prosouthern and an ardent champion of states' rights, largely because of his hatred of abolitionists and the antislavery movement. After the issuance of the Emancipation Proclamation in 1862, his partiality toward the Democrats shifted into violent opposition to the administration and to the war.[11] Incensed by what Storey was publishing, Major General Ambrose E. Burnside, commander of the Department of the Ohio, which included Illinois, warned the editor that his virulent "Copperheadism" would not be tolerated forever. On June 1, 1863, Burnside ordered the Chicago *Times* suppressed because of its "repeated expression of disloyal and incendiary sentiments." Ignoring a restraining order by United States District Judge Thomas Drummond, two companies of soldiers seized the office of the *Times* and prevented publication for three days.

Burnside, however, had not counted on the temper of the city and state. A meeting of prominent Chicago citizens, presided over by the mayor, sent Lincoln a request to rescind the general's order. The state legislature in Springfield passed a resolution denouncing the suppression. United States Senator Lyman Trumbull of Illinois also protested. Acting through Secretary of War Edward W. Stanton, Lincoln sent Burnside a tactful message calling upon him to revoke the suppression order against the *Times* and saying that, in the opinion of the president, the "irritation produced by such acts is . . . likely to do more harm than the publication would do." The Stanton letter also informed the general that on "administrative questions such as the arrest of civilians and the suppressions of newspapers not requiring immediate action" the president wanted to be previously consulted. The furor over the Chicago *Times* had the effect of making it for a time the most talked about newspaper in America and of increasing its circulation, thus, according to one of its editors, saving the paper from ruin.[12]

Immediately after the suppression of the *Times* a group of New York journalists, representing fifteen daily and weekly newspapers, met under the chairmanship of Horace Greeley, and adopted a set of resolutions denying the right of the press to uphold treason and rebellion but affirming its right to criticize the acts of government, both military and civil. The Burnside order and its revocation had been widely reported in the press. Horace Greeley's *New York Daily Tribune*, which was erratic in its attitude toward Lincoln, editorially expressed satisfaction over the president's revocation of the Burnside order, although the *Tribune* only four days before had endorsed "war censorship." The president's action, said the *Tribune*,

will doubtless put a stop to 'fantastic tricks' of the latest Military pattern, and enable Gen. Burnside to devote some attention to the armed 'Rebels' in his front as well as to those unarmed ones who subject him to 'a fire in the rear.' We beg leave to assure him that one severe chastisement inflicted on the former will do more than a hundred arrests and suppressions to silence the latter or render their sedition harmless.[13]

The *New York Times*, the leading popular advocate of the administration, was much more prompt and forthright than the *Tribune* in its condemnation of the Burnside order. Referring to General Burnside as a man of "intemperate patriotism" whose "zeal outruns his judgment," the *Times* warned against "injudicious meddling" represented by the exercise of "odious" power over "freedom of speech and of the Press." The general would very speedily find, said the paper, that "he is multiplying ten-fold the very evil he seeks to extirpate." In conclusion, the *Times* declared:

It is very rarely that a military man can be found who is capable of understanding what public opinion is, or who can be made to comprehend that the Press has any other rights than those which he may be pleased to confer upon it. We do not know that we shall gain much on either point by appealing from the camp to the Government; but our interest in the welfare of the country impels us to risk the experiment of counseling President Lincoln to put a check upon Gen. Burnside's superserviceable and dangerous proceedings as speedily as possible.[14]

Four days later the *Times* editorially welcomed Lincoln's revocation of the Burnside order.[15]

In Boston the *Daily Advertiser* voiced "hearty satisfaction" over Lincoln's act in rescinding Burnside's order interfering with the press. The *Advertiser* observed: "Civil liberty has been spared a shock and the government has gained strength from the resolution; in spite of the virulent character of the journal temporarily suppressed by the general, we have no fear that the cause of the country has lost anything." At the beginning of the war, the paper suggested, when even the loyal states stood "apparently on the brink of a horrible revolution" and no one knew "what passions or what desperate designs might be stirred up by artful incitements of partisans," some suppression might have been necessary. But that time, the *Advertiser* continued, "has long since passed by," and "the government no longer stands in danger of subversion or defeat from the attempted incendiaries even of the most abandoned of its opponents."[16]

In Baltimore, the *Sun* reported extensively on the events involving the Chicago *Times*. But the *Sun*, which sympathized with the South, had no editorial comment on the subject, apparently in conformity with a policy of remaining silent on political issues in order to preserve its existence in a military-occupied city.[17] The *Daily Commercial* of Cincinnati, the site of Burnside's headquarters, also maintained a discreet silence on the implications for press freedom of the general's move against the Chicago *Times*, although it published the text of the order.

At the nation's capital the *Daily National Intelligencer* reported the Burnside order, the judge's ruling, the actions of the soldiers and the public protests, but had no comment of its own until Lincoln's act became known, at which time it said "the President has wisely annulled" the general's order.[18] The Washington *Daily Chronicle*, which came closer to being a Lincoln administration organ than any other paper, reported at length on the successive stages of developments in Chicago but withheld comment until the president had countermanded the general's order.

On January 6, the day after publishing news of the revocation, the *Chronicle* carried a long evaluation of the Chicago *Times* and its editor. Storey, according to the *Chronicle*, was "a man of very great ability; cool, sagacious, fearless, and far-seeing, a nervous and powerful writer, and without a superior in the art of managing a newspaper." His paper was characterized as being like most "Copperhead" journals, except that it was "more able and more violent." In nearly every issue, the *Chronicle* said, the *Times* directly or indirectly discouraged enlistments, incited the people to oppose the draft, published forged letters about disaffection in the army and forged accounts of "mutinous disturbances arising out of the negro question." To make matters worse, according to the Washington paper, the *Times* circulated in areas where it would do harm to the Union cause—in southern Illinois and in Paducah, Memphis, Jackson, and other river and railroad towns. It encouraged resistance among southerners in occupied territory by telling them that abolitionists alone were responsible for the war, that people in the North were tired of the conflict but were held in line by a despotic government in Washington, that if the southern armies could resist until March 4, 1865, and a Democratc president succeeded Lincoln at that time, a truce and peace would follow and slavery would be preserved.

In the light of this record, declared the *Chronicle*, General Burnside, being "daily cognizant of the evil" the *Times* was doing in his area, "acted from the highest motives when he suppressed it," and therefore the *Chronicle* found it "hard to censure him." On the other hand, the president, "viewing the subject from a higher stand-point, and being removed from the immediate excitement," acted "on more enlarged principles than those of immediate military necessity." In conclusion, the *Chronicle* said, the president "probably considered the Government too strong and our cause too pure to be injured even by the persistent and malicious assaults of the Chicago *Times*. The one acted as a soldier and the other as a statesman."[19] This comment may well have mirrored the attitude of Lincoln, who did not want to offend Burnside but who was disturbed by the sharp reaction to the suppression in his home state.

Of the various papers examined, none, except the *New York Times*, stood up for freedom of the press for the Chicago *Times* until Lincoln revealed that the administration was willing to tolerate its antiwar stance. This tendency merely to endorse the government's posture hardly indicated a readiness by editors to take a bold and independent position in behalf of freedom of the press.

But most papers showed more sympathy for freedom of expression than did the *Chicago Tribune*. Joseph Medill, its editor, had been an early promoter of Lincoln for president and generally supported him throughout his presidency. Uncompromising in its attitude toward the South from the first, the *Tribune* became a spokesman for the radical wing of the Republican party and urged the president to emancipate the slaves and confiscate southern property. The paper was persistent in demanding more active prosecution of the war.[20]

While the controversy over the suppression of the Chicago *Times* was at its height, the *Tribune* sneered at the "cry of the Copperheads" for " 'Free Speech.' " It sarcastically referred to their "fear" that "the Constitution may be violated" and their "whining about an invasion of their 'constitutional rights' " while they did everything they could to "help the rebels."[21] On June 5 the *Tribune* called Lincoln's revocation of Burnside's order "a most unfortunate blunder," but added that it would not be "just or proper to lay all the blame" on the president, since prominent advisers such as Senator Trumbull had had a hand in persuading him.

As the *Tribune* put it, the Chicago *Times* was "Jeff Davis' organ," a paper that had gone beyond any other, North or South, in its opposition to the war and its devotion to the interests of the rebels. Yet up to the time of Burnside's action, said the *Tribune*, the government not only had "never raised a finger against it" but actually had circulated it through the mails, had transported it on government boats and trains to "all parts of the army of the Mississippi, and gave all possible assistance to place it in the hands of the soldiers," thousands of whom deserted in consequence of "the poison thus distilled into their minds." According to the *Tribune*, the *Times* had "proceeded upon the assumption that nothing can be written or spoken against the Government that is unconstitutional, that the right of free speech covers the utmost license, and that there can be no such thing as written or spoken treason."

But the *Tribune* emphatically disagreed with such a broad interpretation of the First Amendment, and observed that by the time of the revocation a majority of citizens had come to favor Burnside's order and "resolved that it should be enforced against any mob opposition." By the rescission of the Burnside order, the *Tribune* declared, the "minions of Jeff Davis have won a victory by which they will not fail to profit." The lifting of the suppression was called a "triumph of treason."[22]

The second significant case of presidential action with regard to the suppression of newspapers during the war involved the New York *World* and the New York *Journal of Commerce*. Although the *World* early in the war had been a strong Lincoln supporter and an advocate of vigorous military measures and of coercion of the seceding states, it later came under the control of Democratic financiers and politicians and as a result became a severe critic of the president and the more radical members of his cabinet. As a leading organ of the Peace Democrats, it denounced the Emancipation Proclamation as unconstitutional, fanatical, and impossible to execute.

The *Journal of Commerce* was one of a group of papers that in August 1861 was condemned by a New York grand jury for "encouraging the rebels now in arms against the Federal Government by expressing sympathy and agreement with them, the duty of acceding to their demands, and dissatisfaction with the employment of force to overcome them." The *Journal of Commerce* in particular was denounced for its reference to "the present unholy war." The other papers named by the grand jury were the *Daily News*, the *Day-Book*, *Freeman's Journal* (all published in New York City), and the Brooklyn *Eagle*. Although the grand jury asked the court whether these "disloyal" papers were "subject to indictment and condign punishment," its request for prosecution was not granted. Nevertheless, the postmaster general ordered the papers excluded from the mails—an action that put them out of business, at least temporarily.[23] After a change of editors, the *Journal of Commerce* was again admitted to the mails. Although the paper adopted a less aggressive attitude, it remained throughout the war staunchly opposed to the administration.

On May 18, 1864, government officials were shocked to learn that the *Journal of Commerce* and the *World* that day had published a presidential proclamation, purportedly signed by Lincoln and countersigned by Secretary of State William H. Seward, reciting the bleak military outlook, setting a day for public prayer, and ordering a draft of four hundred thousand men. Realizing that the proclamation had been forged and that such an order at this stage of the war would produce serious opposition to the administration, Lincoln, after a conference with cabinet officers where he was pressed hard by Secretary Seward, directed Major General John A. Dix to seize the *World* and the *Journal of Commerce* and to arrest their publishers and others responsible until they could be tried by military commission.

Soldiers took possession of the two newspapers that day. Investigation soon revealed that the *World* and the *Journal of Commerce* although they were antiadministration papers, had not knowingly published a spurious document. They had been victimized by a hoax perpetrated by Joseph Howard, Jr., city editor of the Brooklyn *Eagle*, who expected to profit in the stock market as a result of publication of the fraudulent proclamation. On May 19 editors and publishers of the *New York Tribune*, the New York *Express*, the New York *Herald*, and the New York *Sun* sent Lincoln a telegram saying the fraud might have "succeeded in any daily newspaper establishment in this city," affirming that the event would prompt editors to take "increased vigilance" and requesting that the order suppressing the two papers be rescinded.[24] The New York *Tribune* of May 19 expressed the same view, saying:

> The real facts which led to the publication of this monstrous forgery were not, we presume, known yesterday in Washington, or the suspension of the two journals would not, we suppose, have been ordered. The order, no doubt, will be revoked to-day. We hope it will, for no journal should be punished for a mistake which might have very innocently been committed by the most loyal paper in the land.[25]

The president revoked the suppression order the next day and authorized the two papers to be returned to their proprietors, saying, through Secretary of War Stanton, that he hoped they would exercise more caution in the future.[26]

While the two New York newspapers were allowed to resume publication after two days, the *Picayune* in New Orleans, which also published the bogus proclamation, did not get off so lightly. That paper was suspended for two weeks by General Nathaniel P. Banks as punishment for its offense. Howard, the perpetrator of the fraud, was confined in a military prison for three months and then discharged. (He later became one of the best known writers of the New York press; in 1897 he was elected president of the International League of Press Clubs.)

The closing of the *World* and the *Journal of Commerce* brought an outraged editorial reaction from the *New York Daily News*:

For what military crime have these two journals . . . been arrested in the course of their legitimate business? For what crime have these offices been thronged with soldiers, ingress and egress prohibited, the routine of business interrupted, their affairs thrown into confusion, and a heavy pecuniary loss occasioned? Our sober, justice-loving citizens will hardly credit it when we say it was for publishing, in good faith and without suspicion of wrong, a paper that was represented to them as being a proclamation of Abraham Lincoln, and that they honestly believed was such. The idea *that anyone connected with these journals had anything to do with the forgery of that Proclamation is too preposterous to be entertained by any sane man.*[27]

This outburst of chagrin from the *Daily News* may have been prompted by more than a disinterested belief in freedom of expression. Like the *Journal of Commerce*, the *Daily News* had been among the New York newspapers condemned by the grand jury in 1861 for support of the rebels. In that year the *Daily News* had referred to "the emptiness and folly of this war against brethren," and declared that "the bone, sinew, and intelligence of America utterly repudiate Mr. Lincoln and all his works." Although the denial of mail privileges to the paper in August 1861 caused publication to be suspended for eighteen months, the *News* resumed as an evening paper and continued its opposition to the war and to Lincoln.[28] In its plea for the *Journal of Commerce*, therefore, the *Daily News* was showing sympathy for another antiwar journal.

The next day, May 20, the *New York Tribune* published a portion of the *Daily News* editorial and, after noting that the *Tribune* concurred on the unreasonableness of penalizing the journalistic victims of a forger, went on to condemn the *Daily News* for publishing the same day the letter of a secessionist "scoundrel" attacking Secretary Seward. "We can't quite understand," said the *Tribune*, "how it is that . . . the daily utterance of such villainous, traitorous, and utterly preposterous calumnies, calculated to shake the very pillars of the State, go utterly unrebuked. Can any one explain?"[29]

Although the *New York Times* thought the "summary suppression" of the *World* and the *Journal of Commerce* a matter of "questionable propriety"—"very much like hanging a man charged with crime, in advance of trial"—the *Times* was not so forgiving of the two offending and suppressed journals as were other newspapers. The *Times* chided the *Evening Post* for invoking the constitutional principle of freedom of the press in behalf of the suspended *Journal of Commerce* and the *World*. While insisting that the free press principle was not applicable to the case, the *Times* wanted to make clear that the paper religiously revered freedom of the press and "would be the first to resent and the longest to resist" any "trepsass upon it." The *Times* editorial continued: "We have had such confidence in the strength of the cause that, above all things else, we have desired a fair field for it, both of discussion and of battle."

Fair field for discussion, the paper thought, did not extend either to the forger or to the promulgators of his forgery. "If the press . . . lends itself to crime, its criminality is correspondingly great." This criminality, the *Times* maintained, was not excused by the plea that the editors were not personally involved. "In every responsibility, negligence may constitute unfaithfulness as well as positive misdoing. . . . A discriminating and careful supervisor of night news is, or at least ought to be, an indispensable *attache* of every morning newspaper." The editorial concluded: "Insisting upon the utmost power for the press, we equally insist upon the utmost care in its exercise.[30] Apparently the *Times* thought the *World* and the *Journal of Commerce* should have been prosecuted for their publication of the forgery.[31]

The largely negative reaction to the suppression of the *World* and the *Journal of Commerce* was only one of many episodes indicating that press and public opinion throughout the Civil War was so divided that the government could not easily act against the dissenting press without antagonizing significant segments of the populace. In 1861 the New York *Journal of Commerce* listed 154 "peace papers."[32] Of the seventeen daily papers in New York City at the outbreak of the war, only five, according to the journalistic historian, Frank Luther Mott, could be characterized as measurably loyal to the administration throughout the four years of conflict; nine of the seventeen were proslavery and, of these, five were pro-Confederate. Although New York, which voted twice against Lincoln, was hardly representative of the country, every large city had a proslavery or copperhead newspaper. Press criticism of the conduct of the war and of the administration's political moves was widespread.[33] Obviously, then, numerous suppressions of the press did not prevent published diversity of opinion from flourishing during the Civil War. And freedom of expression found editorial champions, not necessarily because of a principled commitment to the First Amendment but because there were usually substantial numbers of sympathizers with the views that the suppressors found unacceptable.

7

Freedom of the Press
for Political and Labor Radicals

The end of the Civil War brought accelerated change and social turmoil in American society. The era was characterized by mechanization, new waves of immigration, the great expansion of railroads and the organization of big business. Rapid industrialization and the employment of large work forces stimulated the growth of labor unions on a local, state, and national basis. The National Labor Union, founded in 1866, became the first important national labor organization. In 1869 came the formation of the Knights of Labor, which was to exert a strong influence among workers for nearly two decades.

As labor organizations grew in strength, workers began to take concerted action against the arbitrary setting by management of wages and working conditions. The great Railroad Strike of 1877, involving more persons than any labor conflict in the nineteenth century, was precipitated by a 10 percent wage reduction, the latest in a series of wage cuts accompanying the general economic depression after the panic of 1873. Apart from the numbers involved, the railroad strike was significant because in every community railroad workers were aided by sympathizers—coal miners, mill hands, stevedores, and even small businessmen. The united action reflected the

116

bitterness of many people toward the railroads because of their rate discrimination, stock manipulation, bribery, and corruption. One effect of the Railroad Strike of 1877 was the creation among workingmen of class consciousness on a national scale.

Shocked by the vehemence of the upheaval, railroad owners and other propertied elements came to visualize laborers as criminal and began to act accordingly. The railroad strike was crushed by federal troops in some places, by militia and police in others. In its aftermath, to ensure law and order in the future, the militia was strengthened by the building of armories throughout the nation. Many state legislatures enacted conspiracy laws aimed at labor. The strike left on both sides a heritage of distrust that was to lead to a growing number of confrontations.

Chicago in this period was the scene of much labor unrest. In that city, twenty thousand workmen had joined the railroad strikers. Chicago police, reflecting the desperate feeling of the city fathers, had decided on a policy of not firing the customary warning shots over the heads of strikers but firing low instead. This plan was approved by the *Chicago Tribune*, which, along with its rival, the Chicago *Times*, expressed bitter opposition to labor.[1] Large newspapers, which by this time were beginning to entail large investments for presses and other machinery, were taking on the attitudes of big business.[2]

By leading a series of successful strikes in the 1880s against three of Jay Gould's railroad lines, the Knights of Labor became for a time the nation's leading labor organization. In 1886 it boasted 703,000 members. That same year, however, the organization's fortunes were to be dramatically changed by events in Chicago that incidentally demonstrated the attitudes of the press toward labor and toward freedom of speech and press for unorthodox causes.

The movement that brought matters to a head in Chicago in 1886 had started with the launching in 1884 of a national campaign for an eight-hour day. Begun by the Federation of Organized Trades and Labor Unions of the United States and Canada, a rival organization of the Knights, the campaign made no headway in its first year. But in 1885 the F.O.O.T.A.L.U. renewed its efforts and set May 1, 1886, as the day for a general strike if its demand for an eight-hour day had not been granted to all labor. Although the leaders of the Knights did not respond favorably to an invitation to cooperate in the eight-hour day movement, the rank and file did.

In 1886 the average working day, as shown by a study of forty se-lected industries in twenty-eight states, including Illinois, was slightly over 10 hours. The average work week was 61.8 hours. Although the average yearly wage for organized employees in Illi-nois in 1886 came to $566.19, about equal to living expenses for a family, some 24 percent of wage-earning heads of families (accord-ing to a study two years earlier) failed to make enough to support their families, and 9 percent barely made ends meet. These sta-tistics, of course, do not reflect the condition of workers who were unemployed or irregularly employed under a system in which dis-missals or layoffs were far more capricious than today. A not un-common attitude of employers toward their workers was reflected in the comment of one manufacturer, who said: "I regard my em-ployees as I do a machine, to be used to my advantage, and when they are old and of no further use I cast them into the street."

Chicago became a center of eight-hour day activity. On May 1 some eighty thousand men joined the general strike in that city. Leading the effort was the Central Labor Union, an amalgam of twenty-two unions brought together by the persuasion of a small group of anarchists. The anarchists' identification with the eight-hour day objective was enough to give the movement in Chicago an explosive potential.

The volatile nature of the unrest in Chicago was heightened by a labor dispute that had begun weeks before the general strike. At the McCormick Harvester Works employees had been locked out because of unionization efforts. Two days after the general strike began a large group of strikers, including locked-out McCormick employees, held a pep meeting near the McCormick plant, and were addressed by August Spies,[3] editor of the German-language anar-chist publication, the *Arbeiter-Zeitung*. As strike-breakers streamed out of the plant at the end of a shift, locked-out workers confronted them and a melee ensued. Police arrived with guns blazing. One striker was killed and six were seriously wounded.

Having witnessed the action, Spies went home and, fired with indignation, composed what became known as the "Revenge Circu-lar." It denounced the police as "bloodhounds" sent by employers to kill workers who dared to disobey "the supreme will" of their bosses, and called upon workers to take up arms and "destroy the hideous monster" seeking to destroy them. The heading on the circular said: "REVENGE! WORKINGMEN! TO ARMS!" Spies later asserted that he was not the author of the heading and that the word *Revenge*, inserted by a compositor, would have been removed before distribution if he had known about it in time.

The appeal to arms in the so-called Revenge circular might be seen as a rhetorical flourish. But the call was more direct in a second circular announcing a mass meeting of workingmen to be held at Haymarket Square on the evening of May 4 to protest the police shooting of strikers at the McCormick plant. Its message ended with the words, "Workingmen Arm Yourselves and Appear in Full Force!" When Spies, who was to speak at the Haymarket meeting, read the circular, he insisted that the exhortation on arms be removed or he would not only refuse to speak but would not even attend the meeting. As a result, the press was stopped and the offending words removed. Of twenty thousand handbills, two or three hundred with the call to arms in them were, however, distributed. The words "revenge" and "arm yourselves" were to help fuel the future controversy over the Haymarket Square meeting.

That meeting began inauspiciously, with only about twelve to thirteen hundred people showing up in the square, which had been chosen because it could accommodate as many as twenty thousand. Besides Spies, the speakers were Albert Parsons, editor of the anarchist English-language paper, the *Alarm*, and Samuel Fielden, also an anarchist. Spies accused the "capitalistic press" of "misrepresenting the cause of labor." He blamed employers and police for the violence that had occurred. Parsons too condemned police shooting of strikers and hailed socialism as the remedy for the wrongs that workers suffered. Fielden deplored the use of law to advance the interests of large property owners against those of workingmen. Except for harsh general appeals to workers to stand against the oppression of employers, none of the speeches was particularly inflammatory. There were no direct calls for violence.

By about 10:20, with a biting wind sweeping across the square and rain clouds threatening, the crowd had dwindled to about a fourth its original size and the peaceful meeting was about to end. As Fielden was concluding his speech, a police column of 180 men suddenly appeared and marched to the place where Fielden was speaking. A police captain at the head of the column commanded the audience to peaceably disperse. Fielden replied, "we are peaceable"; he and others on the wagon serving as a speaker's stand began to descend. At that moment a dynamite bomb hurtled through the air, struck the ground near the front of the police column and exploded. Stunned members of the crowd began to flee for safety. The police charged, swinging clubs and firing.

The bomb killed Policeman Mathias J. Degan almost instantly; six other policemen died later. Almost seventy policemen were wounded. According to the official report, the police attack killed one member of the crowd and wounded twelve. Other reports placed the number of civilians injured at six times the figure given by the police. One of the wounded spectators died later.

Whipped up by the Chicago press, which lost all semblance of accuracy and objectivity, public opinion was immediately directed against anarchists, socialists, and communists as being responsible for the bomb. Before there was any time for gathering evidence, a cry for vengeance arose. A report in the Chicago *Inter Ocean* the next day, May 5, was typical of the slanted news coverage of the event.

The anarchists of Chicago inaugurated in earnest last night the reign of lawlessness which they have threatened and endeavored to incite for years. They threw a bomb into the midst of a line of 200 police officers, and it exploded with fearful effect, mowing down men like cattle. Almost before the missile of death had exploded the anarchists directed a murderous fire from revolvers upon the police as if their action were prearranged, and as the latter were hemmed in on every side—ambuscaded—the effect of the fire upon the ranks of the officers was fearful. . . . The collision between the police and the anarchists was brought about by the leaders of the latter, August Spies, Sam Fielden, and A. R. Parsons, endeavoring to incite a large mass-meeting to riot and bloodshed.

News reports in the dailies of other cities were equally inaccurate and biased. The *New York Tribune*, for example, reported that three bombs were thrown and that "the mob" had poured "volley after volley" into the midst of the police.

Without waiting to find out whether the bomb-thrower would be identified, the press almost universally condemned anarchists not only for the act of violence at Haymarket Square but for a philosophy of violence that threatened American society. The *Chicago Tribune* said the people of Chicago "must expect an era of anarchy and the loss of their property, if not their lives," if "Anarchism and Communism" were not quickly crushed. The Chicago *Herald*, declaring that the anarchist movement was composed of the "offscourings of Europe," warned that it menaced the very foundations of American society. The *New York Times* on May 6 declared without equivocation: "It is silly to speak of the crime as a riot. All the evidence goes to show that it was concerted, deliberately planned, and coolly executed murder." The *Times* hoped for the death penalty against the anarchists, who, the paper had already decided, were guilty of the bomb-throwing. The *New York Tribune* attributed the crime to foreign anarchists and socialists and asserted that the one cure for this "anarchist illness" was force. The New York *Sun* called for restrictions on immigration and condemned "foreign savages, with their dynamite bombs and anarchic purposes."

The Philadelphia *Press* demanded: "Give the bullet to the disorderly agitators, so long as their hands are uplifted against the law." In Washington, D.C., the *Post* referred to the anarchists as a "horde of foreigners, representing almost the lowest stratum found in humanity's formation." Declaring that America had no room for such "incendiary scum," the Washington *Sunday Herald* urged that they "should be disposed of as quickly as possible." The Cleveland *Leader* trumpeted: "The anarchist wolf—unwisely permitted to take up its abode and propagate its bloodthirsty species in this country—has fastened its hideous, poisonous fangs in the body corporate of the American people." The Columbus, Ohio, *Journal*, proclaimed: "There are too many unhung anarchists and rebels." In St. Louis the *Globe Democrat* announced; "There are no good anarchists except dead anarchists."

How important a force were the violent anarchists, or social revolutionaries, of Chicago who aroused all the excitement? One authority, Henry David, concluded that among Chicago revolutionaries in the 1880s only a handful really contemplated violent action; the others contemplated nothing more dangerous than violent accusation and denunciation. The same authority noted that the activities of the social revolutionaries apparently made little impression upon the labor movement of Chicago. A sign of the labor movement's attitude toward the anarchists was provided by the initial refusal of strikers assembled near the McCormick plant on May 3 to let August Spies speak when they heard he was a socialist. They did not cease their heckling until Spies was vouched for by the secretary of their union. After the Haymarket bombing, most labor leaders denounced the anarchists. In their Chicago organ, the Knights of Labor published a scathing editorial:

> Let it be understood by all the world that the Knights of Labor have no affiliation, association, sympathy or respect for the band of cowardly murderers, cutthroats and robbers, known as anarchists, who sneak through the country like midnight assassins, stirring up the passions of ignorant foreigners, unfurling the red flag of anarchy and causing riot and bloodshed. . . . They are entitled to no more consideration than wild beasts.

Given the hysteria in Chicago and the almost universal condemnation of the anarchists, the events that followed the Haymarket bombing were virtually ordained. August Spies, Samuel Fielden, and Michael Schwab, a member of the editorial staff of the *Arbeiter-Zeitung*, were arrested on May 5. A headline in the Chicago *Inter Ocean* proclaimed: "Peace Reigns. The Howling Assassins of Tuesday Night Captured or in Hiding." Parsons had gone into hiding, but was to surrender him in court on June 21. Adolph Fischer, a young compositor on the *Arbeiter-Zeitung*, was the next to be taken into custody. Thirty-one persons were indicted; only eight actually stood trial for murder. They were Spies, Parsons, Fischer, Schwab, Fielden, George Engel, Louis Lingg, and Oscar Neebe.[4] The first five were all connected with anarchist papers.

The Chicago press had already smoothed the path for the prosecution. On May 1, the day of the general strike over the eight-hour day, the Chicago *Mail* had published an editorial saying:

> There are two dangerous ruffians at large in this city; two sneaking cowards who are trying to create trouble. One of them is named Parsons; the other is named Spies. . . .
> These two fellows have been at work fomenting disorder for the past ten years. They should have been driven out of the city long ago. They would not be tolerated in any other community on earth.

Parsons and Spies have been engaged for the past six months for the precipitation to-day. . . . These fellows do not want any reasonable concession. They are looking for riot and plunder. They haven't got one honest aim nor one honorable end in view.

Mark them for to-day. Keep them in view. Hold them personally responsible for any trouble that occurs. *Make an example of them if trouble does occur.*

Immediately after the bomb-throwing, Melville E. Stone, editor of the Chicago *Daily News*, communicated with William Pinkerton of the Pinkerton Detective Agency, and a number of operatives were put on the trail of the "leading anarchists." On May 5, with the bomb-thrower not identified, Stone suggested to the authorities a way around that difficulty. He proposed that the question of identification be ignored and that prosecution be based on the legal grounds that "Mathias J. Degan had come to his death from a bomb thrown by a person or persons unknown, but acting in conspiracy with August Spies, Albert Parsons, Samuel J. Fielden, and others unknown." The conspiracy charge, requiring less proof than a charge of a specific offense, was to become the favorite technique for prosecuting radicals in the United States.

Accusing Spies, Parsons and Fielden of making "incendiary speeches" on the night of the bombing, the Chicago *Inter Ocean* suggested editorially that they be prosecuted as accessories to murder, and observed: "For months and years these pestiferous fellows have uttered their seditious and dangerous doctrines. Even if they had not opened their lips on Tuesday night, their very presence, with their well-known and destructive views, would have been an invitation to the mob . . . to commit acts of lawlessness." The *Chicago Tribune* also suggested that Spies and others could be punished as accessories.

The anarchists in Chicago were to be prosecuted as accessories to murder under an Illinois statute that made them, if convicted, subject to the same punishment as a principal even if the principal never became amenable to justice. Their role as accessories was to be demonstrated, according to the prosecution, by proof of their participation in a conspiracy.

Despite an objection by the defense that a trial date soon after the event would preclude the possibility of a just verdict, Judge

Joseph E. Gary allowed the prosecution to designate June 21 for the beginning of the trial. Although the choice of a jury consumed twenty-one of the forty-nine days that the trial lasted, the extended process did not mean that the defense was able to secure a fair panel. Jurors were chosen from veniremen picked by Henry L. Ryce, a special bailiff appointed by the court. Ryce admitted his prejudice against the defendants and was quoted as saying: "Those fellows are going to be hanged as certain as death. I am calling such men as the defendants will have to challenge peremptorily and waste their time and challenges. Then they will have to take such men as the prosecution wants." Overruling repeated objections by the defense, Judge Gary allowed the seating of jurors who admitted their prejudice. None of the jurors was an industrial worker; none had an open mind on either the crime or the men they were about to try.

The selection of the jury was completed on July 15, and the trial began on July 16. With the court meeting on week days for two three-hour sessions, the presentation of evidence and the cross-examination of witnesses lasted until August 10. The state's case was based largely on what the defendants said in their speeches and in their writings in the anarchist press, not on what they did. The prosecution presented no proof that any of the defendants actually threw or planted the bomb. In fact only two of them, Spies and Fielden, had definitely been present when the bomb was thrown. Fischer, Lingg, and Engel had not even attended the Haymarket Square meeting. Schwab and Parsons had attended but left before the bombing. No evidence was offered to show that Neebe was present.

No proof was offered that the Haymarket Square speakers had incited violence. An indication that no violence was contemplated was provided by the fact that Parsons had brought his wife and child to the meeting.[5] Mayor Carter H. Harrison of Chicago, who had attended to see that order was maintained, later described the speeches as tame. In fact, Harrison, persuaded that no problems would arise, had left the meeting some time after ten o'clock and on his way home had stopped at the nearest police station, where a riot squad had been assembled, and told Precinct Captain John Bonfield to discharge his reserves for the night. Bonfield, although he agreed with Harrison at the time, had soon afterwards led his squad to the meeting.

Julius S. Grinnell, state's attorney, launched the prosecution's presentation with a word picture of terrible consequences that the eight men in the dock posed for American society. He acknowledged that Americans had long advocated the principles of free speech and complete liberty, including that of making harsh criticisms of our fundamental institutions. But he said citizens were mistaken if they thought American institutions immune from the danger of anarchy. The state now knew, he declared, that the defendants, by the daily preachings of anarchy for years, had been "sapping our institutions." The events of May 4, he asserted, showed that in shouting murder, bloodshed, anarchy, and dynamite, they meant what they said. The existence of American government, according to the state's attorney, had been jeopardized by the defendants, who were ringleaders in an active, widespread revolutionary movement.

The prosecution seemed to be unaffected by the fact that the grand jury, which had indicted the defendants, had found a somewhat less grandiose threat. That body had noted that it had brought in true bills against such persons as had abused the privilege of free speech by causing the riot and bloodshed in Haymarket Square. But the grand jury had also reported that it had been assured that the total number of anarchists in the country from whom danger might be apprehended was less than 100 and probably did not exceed 40 to 50 men. Associated with them and partly subject to "their malign influence," the grand jury said, were perhaps a few hundred others who might be considered dangerous. And finally, said the grand jurors, there were perhaps two to three thousand men "variously classed as socialists, communists, etc." who were not necessarily dangerous to the peace and welfare of society so long as the law was enforced in a manner to entitle it to their wholesome respect. In the eyes of the grand jury, this respect should be exacted by prosecuting the conspiratorial force of anarchist organizers "chiefly under the control of the coterie of men who were connected with the publication of . . . the *Alarm* and *Arbeiter-Zeitung*."

So the anarchist papers and the personal lives of the men who published them became the focus of minute attention. Over the objections of the defense, the state introduced a mass of testimony about the defendants' writings, speeches, correspondence, organizing activities, and personal friendships during the three years prior to 1886. Most of the evidence was not even remotely connected with the bomb-throwing of May 4. The hypothesis of the prosecution was that over a number of years a general conspiracy existed in Cook County, which had as its objectives the overthrow of the existing social order and the destruction of the "legal authorities of the State and county."

Who were these newspaper men whose words aroused such fear? And what were their instruments for conveying the messages of violence? August Spies had been born in central Germany in 1855 and had migrated to the United States at the age of seventeen. The next year he moved to Chicago. Not until 1875 did he acquire any knowledge of socialism. It was not until 1877 that he joined the Socialist Labor party, and the labor struggles of that year led him to accept the doctrine of violence. Since he had run as a candidate for office several times before he adopted revolutionary doctrines, his conversion to radicalism was obviously gradual and was a product of his experiences in the United States. In 1880 he assumed the editorship of the *Arbeiter-Zeitung*, which had been founded in 1876.

Michael Schwab had been a member of the editorial staff of the *Arbeiter-Zeitung* since 1882. Born in 1853, he had come to the United States from Bavaria at the age of twenty-six. When he arrived in Chicago in 1879 he was already an avowed socialist. He then lived briefly in Milwaukee and the West before returning to Chicago in 1882 and becoming a reporter. He made a point at the trial of observing that he was being condemned for writing newspaper articles and making speeches.

Adolph Fischer's connection with a radical newspaper was as a compositor, not a writer. Born in Bremen, he had gone to school in Germany and had become interested in socialism when his teacher attacked it. He had migrated to the United States in 1873 at the age of fifteen and had been setting type for the *Arbeiter-Zeitung* since 1883, the year he arrived in Chicago.

George Engel, born in Germany in 1836, had come to the United States in 1873 after a year's stay in England. From Philadelphia, where he first lived after his arrival in the U.S., he moved to Chicago in 1874. He became acquainted with socialist thought through the columns of the *Vorbote*, one of the Chicago anarchist papers. His shift to more extreme degrees of radicalism was signified by his membership successively in the First International (the Marxist International Workingmen's Association), the Socialist Labor Party, and finally the International Working People's Association, which advocated propaganda by deed along with propaganda by word. He discussed his notions of revolutionary principles in the *Anarchist*, which he helped to establish.

Albert Parsons, as a polished speaker and leader of the revolutionary movement, attracted intense interest at the trial. Although the general circulation press liked to refer to anarchism as an imported ideology, Parsons at least gave the lie to the Chicago *Herald's* characterization of its adherents as being the "offscourings of Europe." Both he and his radicalism were home grown. He could have boasted of his American credentials had he chosen to do so. His ancestors had come over on the second voyage of the Mayflower. His family members included Major General Samuel Parsons of the Revolutionary army; Theophilus Parsons, the American jurist; W. H. Parsons, a brother who was a major general in the Confederate army. Parsons himself had been born in Alabama to parents who were transplanted northerners. Although he was only thirteen at the outbreak of the Civil War, he had joined the Confederate forces. Having been apprenticed earlier as a printer, he went to Texas and founded and edited the Waco *Spectator* in 1868. Because he had become a Republican, however, he was considered a scalawag and lost caste and support, which forced him to give up his newspaper venture. He moved to Chicago in 1873, got a job as a compositor, and joined the typographical union. By 1876 he had joined the Knights of Labor and became a professed socialist. He ran several times for office on the Socialist Labor ticket. Moving steadily to the left, he became increasingly critical of political action as a means of bringing about socialism. By 1884 he had become editor of the anarchist paper, the *Alarm*.

The fierce hostility that these journalists aroused in Chicago cannot be fully understood without considering the anarchist publications with which they were connected. The grand jury had said the alleged conspiracy was chiefly under the control of a group of men connected with the *Alarm* and the *Arbeiter-Zeitung*. Another Chicago publication, the *Anarchist*, the most extremist of the anarchist papers, had been founded in 1886 as a monthly by George Engel with the help of Adolph Fischer, but had lasted for only four or five issues. Of the five official organs of the anarchist movement published in Chicago, the *Alarm* was the only one in English. It was founded on October 4, 1884, and appeared both fortnightly and monthly during its life, with an average edition early in 1886 running to three thousand copies. The *Arbeiter-Zeitung* (Worker News), the first number of which came out on June 1, 1876, was published on week days and had a circulation of between five and six thousand. The other journals were the *Vorbote*, which was begun about 1874 and appeared on Saturday; the *Fackel*, a Sunday publication with a circulation in 1886 of twelve thousand; and *Boudoucnost*, a Bohemian paper.

These then were the publications whose influence the state felt was so dangerous that their operators must be prosecuted. As evidence of the defendants' alleged nefarious schemes, the state's lawyers laid before the court endless citations from the *Alarm*, the *Arbeiter-Zeitung*, the *Fackel*, and the *Anarchist*. Voluminous evidence was offered to show the people of Chicago what they already knew: that the defendants, in speech and in print, had openly and repeatedly expressed their opposition to the existing social order, that they believed it should be replaced by a totally different social system under which property would be expropriated, that they accepted violence as a means of bringing about change, and that some of the defendants and their printed organs had been teaching how to manufacture and use certain instruments of destruction.

The defendants, of course, had made no secret of their aims. Indeed they had sought through anarchist publications to make known to as wide a readership as possible their doctrines and the proposed means of effectuating them. The *Alarm* and the *Arbeiter-Zeitung* reprinted time and again the platform contained in the so-called Pittsburgh Manifesto, which had been adopted at the Congress of the Socialists of North America held at Pittsburgh in October 1883. The manifesto opened with the passage from the Declaration of Independence affirming the right to overthrow despotic government, and went on, borrowing heavily from Marx, to list the objectives to be achieved:

First:—Destruction of the existing class rule, by all means, i.e., by energetic, relentless, revolutionary and international action.

Second:—Establishment of a free society based upon cooperative organization of production.

Third:—Free exchange of equivalent products by and between the productive organizations without commerce and profit-mongery.

Fourth:—Organization of education on a secular, scientific and equal basis for both sexes.

Fifth:—Equal rights for all without distinction of sex or race.

Sixth:—Regulation of all public affairs by free contracts between the autonomous (independent) communes and associations, resting on a federalistic basis.

In the columns of the *Alarm* the attack on private property was constant, and so was the criticism of statutory law, which, the paper argued, enabled special classes to acquire privileges "by force and chicane [*sic*]" and which transformed the means of existence into private property for the privileged few. Because the state, with its laws, was deemed the instrument of economic injustice, coercive force and the denial of liberty, the state was also a target of attack. In an anarchistic society, Parsons wrote in the *Alarm*, "reason and common sense, based upon natural law," would take the place of statute law with its compulsion and arbitrary rules.

The *Arbeiter-Zeitung* declared in one of its issues in 1885 that: "Each workingman ought to have been armed long ago," and continued, "Daggers and revolvers are easily to be gotten. Hand grenades are cheaply . . . produced; explosives, too, can be obtained. . . ." Both the *Arbeiter-Zeitung* and the *Alarm* frequently published articles on the manufacture of dynamite, gun-cotton, nitroglycerine, mercury and silver fulminates, and bombs. They also provided instructions on the use of dangerous explosives.

In offering advice on the use of arms, anarchists often gave as a justification the need to provide for self-defense. Parsons suggested to an audience in a speech in 1885 that they arm themselves because only with force could the working class defend itself against the violence of the police and other governmental agencies. It was true that the Chicago police department had long been used as though it were a private force in the service of employers. As such, it had come to be detested by labor.

Despite the social revolutionaries' propaganda of violence, their rhetoric had usually not been taken with great seriousness by the press at large. Nor did the anarchist rhetoric alarm Chicago Mayor Carter Harrison, who had resisted pressure from propertied classes to take measures of suppression. When he was first inaugurated in 1879, he had referred to the radicals and remarked:

> The constitution of the land guarantees to all citizens the right to peaceably assemble, the petition for redress of grievances. This carries the right to free discussion. It also guarantees the people the right to keep and bear arms. But it does not give to anyone the right to threaten or to resist lawful authority.

A major reason for the tolerance of the radicals' talk of violence until the time of the Haymarket affair may have been that advocacy of lawlessness and violence was hardly peculiar to the anarchist press but a rather common phenomenon. In 1875, Joseph Medill of the *Chicago Tribune* had declared: "Judge Lynch is an American by birth and character. The Vigilance Committee is a peculiarly American institution. . . . Every lamp-post in Chicago will be decorated with a communistic carcass if necessary to prevent wholesale incendiarism."[6]

Two years later, the *Chicago Tribune* was equally unrestrained in its denunciation of the railroad strike. A *Tribune* editorial referred to the strikers as "the scum and filth of the city." Railway men who refused to take pay cuts and dismissal notices, said the *Tribune*, should be made to "step out of the way" by force. According to another *Tribune* editorial a few days later, "Capitalists would offer any sum to see the leaders . . . strung up to a telegraph pole."[7]

Although archrivals in other respects, the *Tribune* and the Chicago *Times* were united in their violent opposition to labor. Both papers opposed the eight-hour day in their editorial columns, the *Tribune* saying it would mean the loss of millions of dollars to employers. Like the Chicago papers, New York papers were vociferous in their denunciations of those who dared to strike for such goals. But few editorial expressions against the underdog matched the venom of an 1884 *Chicago Tribune* editorial: "The simplest plan, probably, when one is not a member of the Humane Society, is to put arsenic in the supplies of food furnished the unemployed or the tramp. This produces death in a short time and is a warning to other tramps to keep out of the neighborhood."[8] That same year the Chicago *Times* suggested that, "Hand-grenades should be thrown among those union sailors who are striving to obtain higher wages, as by such treatment they would be taught a valuable lesson, and other strikers could take warning from their fate."

Thus it is not surprising that labor revolutionaries said that since capitalists recommended the use of violence, they were justified in doing the same. In fact, August Spies contended at the trial that articles in the *Arbeiter-Zeitung* and the *Alarm* dealing with the manufacture and use of explosives were largely modeled upon or translated from articles that had first appeared in the *Chicago Tribune*, the Chicago *Times*, and the Chicago *News*. He referred specifically to items in the *Chicago Tribune* "in which the use of dynamite bombs against striking workingmen is advocated as the most effective weapon against them."

Against this background of a generally prevailing rhetoric of violence, the eight anarchists appear to have been put on trial, not for advocating lawless violence (others had done the same) but for advocating it in a cause unacceptable to the authorities and unacceptable, incidentally, to most of the press. Since none of the eight was ever linked by evidence directly to the Haymarket bombing, they were tried for their spoken and printed words. Although the Haymarket affair occurred during an era of bloody strife during which numerous workers were killed or injured, the fact that the 1886 event exacted an unusually high toll in police casualties provided a pretext for moving to silence the anarchists.

Accusing the defendants of being members of a conspiracy to instigate social revolution, the prosecution said the bomb-throwing was to be merely the first act. As active participants in the alleged conspiracy, the eight were said to be responsible for the violent result at the Haymarket Square meeting regardless of whether any of them actually tossed the explosive. Had not the *Arbeiter-Zeitung*, the state contended, signaled the intended start of a general struggle between capital and labor when it published on May 1 an editorial saying: "Bravely forward. The conflict has begun. . . . Workmen, let your watchword be: No compromise! Men to the front. . . . The first of May is come." This extract and similar sentiments hostile to employers in the same editorial had not the slightest connection with

Degan's death and provided only the flimsiest support for the state's claim of a conspiracy to launch a revolution on May 1. But the court overruled the defense objection on grounds of the irrelevancy of this and a mass of similar evidence.

Defense lawyers responded by offering moderate extracts from the *Alarm*, including quotations from the writing of John Stuart Mill and Victor Hugo. They also showed through cross-examination of state witnesses that no secrecy had accompanied any phase of the revolutionary movement in Chicago, which suggested that it hardly had the elements of a conspiracy.

Although the prosecution had virtually promised at the beginning to offer evidence establishing the identity of the bomb-thrower, no convincing evidence on this point was provided. Testimony suggesting that it was Rudolph Schnaubelt, a young German radical who had been twice arrested and released (and then fled), was thoroughly discredited. Evidence to the effect that the Haymarket bombing stemmed from a conspiratorial meeting of radicals held the night before was riddled with inconsistencies. There were grounds to indicate that two of the state's main witnesses, Harry L. Gilmer and M. M. Thompson, had been coached by the prosecution and offered perjured testimony.

On August 11, the day after the submission of evidence was completed, the state and the defense began their closing arguments. For sheer hyperbole, the prosecution could hardly have been equalled. Its lawyers told the jurors that the question confronting them was "whether organized government shall perish from the face of the earth" and that their responsibility in the case was "greater than any jury in the history of the world ever before undertook." The defense argued, among other things, that the conviction of the defendants was being asked, not because of any proof of their responsibility for the murder of Degan but because of their belief "in the principles of Socialism and Anarchy," because of their advocacy of "doctrines opposed to our ideas of propriety." The defense also contended that if no principal was identified, then "no one could be held as accessory."

Lawyers for the prosecution were extravagantly praised by the Chicago *Inter Ocean* and the *Chicago Tribune*. One defense lawyer's address was said to be enough to put "the jury to sleep," and another's was labeled "sophistry."

Upon the completion of the closing arguments on August 19, the case was ready for Judge Gary's charge to the jury. In this, as in his rulings generally, he was flagrantly partial to the state. He accepted the prosecution's definition of conspiracy and its link to the murder, saying at one point that, if the defendants conspired to excite "the people of this city to sedition, tumult, and riot . . . to take the lives of other persons" as a means of carrying out their designs and if "by print or speech," they advised or encouraged the commission of murder "without designating time, place or occasion at which it should be done," and if, as a result of such encouragement, murder was committed, then all such conspirators were guilty. In the light of such a loose instruction on responsibility for murder, the defense pointed out, Horace Greeley, Wendell Phillips, and William Lloyd Garrison were equally guilty with John Brown of the crime at Harper's Ferry.[9]

The jury's verdict was delivered on August 20. All of the defendants were found guilty, and all but Oscar Neebe were condemned to death. Neebe's penalty was fixed at fifteen years imprisonment. The jury had deliberated only three hours, and two-thirds of this time was spent in discussing Neebe's fate.

Chicago received news of the verdict with overwhelming approval. Cheers went up from a crowd of more than a thousand gathered in front of the Criminal Court Building. No word of criticism either of the conduct of the trial or of the verdict came from a single important newspaper in the country. The Chicago *Inter Ocean* said ". . . such isms as anarchism . . . are of the nature of treason, and . . . in order to secure the public safety, it is necessary that those who seek to propagate them be treated accordingly and summarily." Ignored was the constitutional provision that: "Treason against the United States, shall consist only in levying war against them, or in adhering to their enemies, giving them aid and comfort. No person shall be convicted of treason unless on the testimony of two witnesses to the same overt act, or on confession in open court."

The Chicago *Times* proclaimed with satisfaction that the defendants, instead "of throttling the law," had been throttled by it. The verdict, the *Chicago Tribune* declared,

has killed Anarchism in Chicago, and those who sympathize with its horrible doctrines will speedily emigrate from her borders or at least never again make a sign of their sentiments. It goes still further than this. It is a warning to the whole brood of vipers in the Old World—to the Communists . . ., the Anarchists . . ., the Nihilists . . .—that they cannot come to this country and abuse its hospitality and its right of free speech . . . without encountering the stern decrees of American law. The verdict of the Chicago jury will, therefore, check the emigration of organized assassins in this country.

In New York City the *Sun* said Chicago "deserves the thanks and the gratitude of every community in the country." The New York *Commercial Advertiser* called the verdict "the death blow to anarchy in America," and added that the public owed a vote of thanks to the judge, the prosecuting attorneys, the jury, the police, and the witnesses. The *New York Evening Post* said the verdict constituted "formal notification to all anarchists" in the United States and abroad that they could no longer "carry on their infamous trade" safely in America.[10] The Brooklyn *Eagle* applauded Chicago for "the wholesome example she has set."

The *New York Times* acclaimed the verdict as being "according to the evidence," and saw little danger that an appellate court would grant a new trial. The editorial then went on to say:

The foreigners represented by the six Germans convicted have found, much to their surprise, that in this country a man is not prevented from talking any seditious nonsense that may come into his head at the top of his voice and in public to as many people as he can get to listen to him, or from printing it in a newspaper for as many people to read as he got to buy the paper. . . . It is no wonder that they mistook the easy and contemptuous tolerance which they have found here for pusillanimity and imagined that they had found a country in which they could put their talk and their writing in practice without fear of the police. The dullest of them will be undeceived when their leaders are hanged, and will henceforth understand the distinction drawn by American law and practice between silly and mischievous talk and criminal action.[11]

In New Orleans the *Times-Democrat* saw the Haymarket affair as a tragedy in four acts, in which Act IV will show "a row of gibbetted felons, with haltered throats and fettered hands and feet, swinging slowly to and fro, in the air; then it [the curtain] will be rung down again, and the people will breathe freer, feeling that anarchism, nihilism, socialism, communism are forever dead in America." The Birmingham, Alabama, *Age* pronounced that the "law is equal to the preservation of order." In Atlanta the *Constitution* observed that the conviction "will be received with delight everywhere. . . . no false sympathy must be allowed to interfere with the course of justice. Cranks and philanthropists should be kept off. Silly women with floral tributes should be promptly squelched. The black shadow of the gallows should hang over the prisoners until their final hour."[12]

According to the Louisville *Courier Journal*, the "safety of every home, the well-being of every family, the very existence of social order were involved in these trials, and now . . . there is everywhere a feeling of greater security." The Pittsburgh *Commercial Gazette* declared: "If the hanging of the seven wretched men who have been condemned will rid the country of pestilent anarchists, or hold them in dread regard of the law, their lives will not have been wholly wasted."

In Denver the *Tribune-Republican* expressed the common editorial theme: "This is the greatest victory that the spirit of law and order has achieved in the United States within the past decade."[13] The *Rocky Mountain Daily News* was more imaginative, observing that it has "been clearly demonstrated that the Anarchists stand alone on their bloody platform, and when the weight lifts them up between the heaven they offended and the earth they wronged, no cause but their own will go with them."[14]

Perhaps the most thoughtful editorial analysis of the free speech and free press issue was offered by the *St. Louis Post-Dispatch*, although that paper, like most other general circulation papers, found no reason to question the conduct of the trial or the justice of the verdict on the basis of the evidence. The *Post-Dispatch* editorial said:

It may be stated as a general truth that in America men are allowed to preach any doctrine they please; but when their utterances connect themselves with lawless or murderous deeds in the relation of cause and effect, then the utterances become a part of the crime, and the man who delivers them is an accomplice of the man who violently breaks the law or slays his neighbor. On the same principle mere speculative opinions in opposition to the right of people to own property cannot be punished as crimes in themselves, but when a man uses them to incite robbery or burglary the expression of such opinions become [*sic*] a part of the crime.

The Chicago anarchists doubtless will be punished with special severity because their crime is in the nature of a widely extended conspiracy, and therefore vastly more dangerous. In such a case the accomplices of the chief criminals must be punished more vigorously than the accomplices in ordinary cases.[15]

Like most papers, the *Post-Dispatch* assumed a direct causal relationship between the anarchists' advocacy of violence and the bomb-throwing at the Haymarket meeting—although the evidence fell far short of proving it.

Although the general press view seemed to reflect a widespread feeling that the republic had been saved from imminent social revolution, this attitude was probably not so universally held as press comment implied but was rather the view of the business community. Some labor unions, especially in Chicago, refused to condemn the verdict, fearing no doubt that an expression of sympathy for the defendants would cause them to be tarred with the anarchist brush. But a number of labor periodicals did register dissent from the chorus of approval by the daily press. Despite the pungency of its rhetoric, the *Workmen's Advocate* came closer to expressing the judgment of history than did the general circulation newspapers:

Look at the case in the light of Truth and Reason: 200 policemen raid a peaceable company which had gathered to exercise the right of free assembly and free speech; these policemen are treated to the contents of a bomb thrown by an unknown personage, as likely as not a Pinkerton 'detective'; thereupon begins a reign of terror for the Anarchists; no man or woman whose honest convictions have tended toward Anarchy, and who has expressed those convictions, is safe from arrest. . . . So the play goes on, until the curtain rises upon a new scene—the 'trial.' The prosecution puts upon the stand every professional perjurer in Chicago, with the exception of a few 'journalists'—God save the mark! —who are encouraged to do their share of lying in making reports of the case; [in] spite of all this, it is proven that none of the defendants had any hand in the bomb-throwing; that Parsons, Schwab and Fischer were nowhere near the police at the time . . . and that not a shot was fired except by the police themselves! And the conclusion of the whole matter is that—not for breaking any law, but—for daring to denounce the usurpations of the robber rulers of our Satanic society, these Anarchists must die!

On October 1, 1886, the defense began its argument for a new trial before Judge Gary. The grounds offered were that the jury had not been unprejudiced when it was chosen, that the convicted defendants had not been proven guilty of murder, that there had been no conspiracy to commit the bombing at the Haymarket Square, that those who preached violence had done so only in response to the use of illegal force against workingmen, and that the prosecution had been guilty of serious improprieties. On October 7, Judge Gary denied the motion. Offered a chance to speak before the sentences were pronounced, the defendants spent from October 7 to 9 telling about their lives, analyzing the evidence, castigating the prosecution, denouncing the injustice of the verdict and in various ways making the point that they were being condemned for their beliefs and for exercising their rights of free speech and free press.

As a result of an appeal to the Supreme Court of Illinois, the execution, which had been set for December 3, was stayed. After hearing lengthy arguments in March, the state supreme court, in a unanimous decision on September 14, 1887, affirmed the judgment of the trial court. It offered an analysis of the case totally biased in favor of the state. The daily press paid high tribute to the state appellate court's ruling. An appeal to the United States Supreme Court also was fruitless. The nation's highest tribunal concluded on November 2 that none of the federal questions argued by the defense (the denial of due process and others) was involved in the determination of the case. At this time the First Amendment's guarantees were not considered applicable to the states. The press throughout the country applauded the high court's finding.

Governor Richard J. Oglesby of Illinois was deluged with pleas for clemency, including many from intellectuals and labor leaders. He commuted to life imprisonment the sentences of Fielden and Schwab only. On November 11, 1887, Spies, Parsons, Fischer, and Engel were hanged. Lingg had committed suicide the day before.

Five Haymarket bombing defendants were dead but, despite setbacks, their movement was not. Nor was the case itself closed. The last issue of the *Alarm* had appeared on April 24, 1886, and the paper was not published again until November 5, 1887. The *Arbeiter-Zeitung* ceased publication on May 5, 1886, the day after the bombing. And although its remaining staff was ready to go to press on May 7, no firm in the city was willing to print it. The paper finally was published the next day after an understanding providing that the mayor would suppress it if it carried any inflammatory articles. When the *Alarm* reappeared on November 5, 1887, under the editorship of Dyer D. Lum, it took a more subdued stance on the notions of force and propaganda by deed. The paper declared in a leading editorial that force was not essential "to a revolution, nor its use generally successful." In succeeding issues, the *Alarm* placed its emphasis on the efficacy of social "evolution," and advocated force primarily in response to aggression.

Still Captain Michael J. Schaack of the Chicago police announced that he was carefully reading each issue of the *Alarm*, implying that the police proposed to exercise a censorship function. At the same time the daily press exhibited a thoroughly distrustful attitude toward the radical paper, indicating that it saw no reason to protest police surveillance. Except for a period between April 22 and June 16, 1888, the *Alarm* continued to appear under its new editor, serving as a constant reminder that the Chicago revolutionary movement was not dead. The paper finally ceased publication in February 1889.

With the resumption of large gatherings of Chicago radicals in the spring of 1888, the police threatened to close down their meetings. The Chicago *News* asked, "Shall they again be allowed to preach their radical doctrines?" Encouraged by the daily press, the police shadowed the radicals, raided their places, and disrupted their meetings. In July 1886, Lucy Parsons, widow of the executed Albert Parsons, was arrested for selling a book containing her late husband's writings.

The police hounding of alleged "anarchists" became so intense that some prominent members of the community began to protest. Early in 1889, Judge Murray F. Tuley declared:

. . . the Anarchists have the same rights as other citizens to assemble peaceably for the discussion of their views; . . . the police have no right to presume an intention on their part to break the laws; . . . their meetings must not be prohibited or interfered with until a breach of the law is actually committed; . . . in no other city of the United States except Chicago have the police officials attempted to prevent the right of free speech on such unwarranted pretenses and assumptions of power, and . . . it is time to call a halt.

Police harassment of radicals did subside during the remainder of 1889 and the next year. But in 1891 and 1892 meetings of radicals held to commemorate the hanging of the "four martyrs" brought renewed exertions by the police. On November 12, 1891, the police raided a meeting of the stockholders of the *Arbeiter-Zeitung* on the pretense that the participants were plotting revenge on Chicago for executing their comrades. In January 1892 the Chicago *Herald* reported, on the authority of "an attorney of great prominence, whose only clients are of the wealthy class," that since May 7, 1886, three days after the Haymarket bombing, a group of Chicago business men had contributed several hundred thousand dollars to a secret fund "to aid the municipal government in the suppression of ideas which are antagonistic to those held by good citizens of this country." The money was used to supplement the salaries of the police, who thus had reason to find anarchist plots so that they could continue to collect extra pay. The raid on the *Arbeiter-Zeitung* stockholders' meeting was simply another act in the police drama designed to keep the money flowing. By the end of 1891 the business interests no longer perceived a danger from anarchists, and the books of the fund were closed. Despite the agitation of the police and the accompanying sensationalism of the press, the "anarchist peril" gradually lost its power to stir so-called good citizens.

As the hysteria of the Haymarket affair receded, more and more people came to feel that the trial, conviction, and executions had represented a gross miscarriage of justice. A movement for the pardoning of the still imprisoned defendants, in partial rectification of the wrongs done by the state, began to grow. It included not only representatives of labor but also business and civic leaders. Governor Joseph W. Fifer, Oglesby's successor, was petitioned in behalf of the anarchist prisoners. He considered pardoning Oscar Neebe but was deterred by strong pressure from opposition forces.

With the election in 1892 of John Peter Altgeld, the first Democrat to capture the Illinois governorship in thirty years, the pardon effort was renewed. Clarence Darrow, who joined the petitioners, recalled later: "It was but a very few years after the execution until the bar in general throughout the State, and elsewhere, came to believe that the conviction was brought about through malice and hatred, and that the trial was unfair and the judgment of the court unsound." Shortly after his inauguration in 1893, the new governor received a petition for a pardon bearing sixty thousand signatures. Despite pressure from some citizens to act immediately and warnings from others that granting a pardon would mean the end of his political career, Altgeld stuck to a deliberative course, saying he would be guided by a thorough study of the record and would do what he thought was right regardless of the consequences.

Although the issuance of a pardon as a simple act of mercy, with a minimum of explanation, would have satisfied most of the petitioners, that was not Altgeld's way. He viewed the pardoning power as one to be exercised for the correction of wrongs inseparable from the regular processes of the criminal law. On June 26, 1893, the pardon message was issued with the effect of a thunderbolt from the blue. The governor had determined to free Fielden, Schwab, and Neebe, not because they had been sufficiently punished but because, he asserted, they and the five who were already dead had been "railroaded." They had been tried in effect by a packed jury, he declared. The trial, therefore, was not a legal one. Quoting extensively from the trial record, Altgeld said the proof adduced did not show that the defendants were guilty. The governor observed that the record sustained the charge that the trial was unfair and had been conducted by Judge Gary "with malicious ferocity." He attacked the judge's ruling to the effect that it was not necessary for the state to identify the bomb-thrower or even prove that he came under the advice of or influence of the accused.

The pardon message brought down upon Governor Altgeld a flood of abuse that set a record for vilification in his era.[16] The press called him a "wild-haired demagogue" and an "apologist for murder." In a scorching editorial, the *Chicago Tribune* charged that Altgeld was paying for the votes of "anarchists" and "socialists" with the three pardons. Taking note of the fact that Altgeld was foreign born, the *Tribune* said his act proved that he "was not merely an alien by birth, but an alien by temperament and sympathies." He apparently, said the paper, has "not a drop of true American blood in his veins." (Altgeld had arrived in America when he was three months old.)

The New York *World* published on its front page a cartoon portraying Altgeld on his hands and knees before a black-robed figure of death, carrying a flaming torch in one hand and a bomb with a burning fuse in the other. Around both figures bombs were shown bursting on soil labelled "Illinois." Condemning both the pardons and the message, a *World* editorial said Governor Altgeld's name would be added to the list of men who would be "remembered for something they ought not to have done." The *New York Times* suggested that Altgeld was insane,[17] and that the message revealed him "either as an enemy to the safeguards of society, or as a reckless demagogue . . . incapable of understanding the spirit and the temper of the American people." The *New York Evening Post* opined that the pardon message "reads as if" Altgeld himself were "an anarchist." In New York the *Herald*, the *Tribune* and the *Sun* also denounced the governor.

In Philadelphia the *Press* declared: "A sentence of sweeping and irresistible condemnation will be passed by the American people upon the act of this demagogical governor and upon the Democratic party which placed him in power and gave him this opportunity to show his sympathy with Anarchism." The Louisville *Courier-Journal* asserted that

the Governor's arraignment of the justice of the sentences . . . is a proceeding of the most inopportune kind, to say the very least . . . , and it has inevitably brought upon its author a flood of universal condemnation. . . . it is surely a piece of unwisdom closely resembling culpable indifference to consequences . . . to undertake to reopen and review the action of a court already passed upon by the Supreme tribunals, State and National, and thus to let slip, and . . . to encourage the passions of crazy agitators, already sufficiently inflamed and dangerous.

In Atlanta the *Journal* found the governor's act "outrageous," and went on to observe that the men he released had made it their business "to preach anarchy and assassination. They were sworn and defiant enemies of government and society. They inflamed the passion of their ignorant followers and were as guilty of the murder of the Chicago policemen as if they had shot them down in cold blood." Altgeld, the *Journal* said, "has fired the hearts of demons with fresh courage and fresh hatred of all that we consider sacred."[18]

The *Atlanta Constitution* said the pardon could be viewed "in no other light than a calamitous one." In "their speeches and publications," the paper continued, the anarchists spent months and years in preparing their associates for the Haymarket crime. "Whether the men on trial actually threw a bomb or not at the Haymarket outbreak, they were responsible for the murder. . . . The next time they have a Haymarket affair they should hang all of the guilty parties, and not send any of them to the penitentiary."[19]

In Denver the *Republican* had one of the milder comments from a sampling of press reaction to Altgeld's pardon. The *Republican* said: "By pardoning the three anarchists . . . Altgeld has brought down upon himself the indignation of the thoughtful people of the country." Going on to observe that there was no doubt as to the anarchists' guilt, the editorial declared that if the trial contained technical errors, this matter should have been left to the courts.[20] (The defendants, of course, had already appealed in vain to the United States Supreme Court.)

The *Globe-Democrat* in St. Louis was sure it spoke for the country:

There is practically but one opinion throughout the whole country as to the action of Governor Altgeld. . . . It is condemned everywhere as a gross abuse of the pardoning power, and not a word is said in its defense except by the enemies of society. . . . The use of the pardoning power to defeat the ends of justice in such a case cannot be too severely condemned.

The *St. Louis Post-Dispatch,* expressing a minority viewpoint, seemed to approve the governor's purpose but faulted him for not recognizing the temper of the time (1886).

It was proper that the Governor should clearly and fully set forth the reasons which impelled him to pardon these men, and it must be admitted that he has given reasons for his act, especially in the case of Neebe, sufficient to establish ground for a conscientious exercise of clemency.

But while condemning the extra legal processes which were employed to convict these men, we should not forget the causes which led to their employment. . . .

Gov. Altgeld might have found something besides condemnation for the Chicago authorities and people in the Anarchist trials. He might have found a lesson for the scoundrels. Men who despise law and who either preach or practice the doctrines of assassination are themselves to blame if they suffer the consequences of their own doctrine and deeds. These are the fruits of lawlessness and revolting crime.[21]

In thus arguing that the governor should have excused the Chicago authorities, the *Post-Dispatch* came close to condoning lynch law.

In Chicago the reaction to the governor's pardon was, with the exception of that of the *Chicago Tribune*, more tolerant than in other cities. By 1893, Chicago had perhaps been exposed to enough criticism of the excesses of the Haymarket case to induce in the civic leadership and press alike a chastened sense of their own contribution to injustice. In any event, lawyers and judges in Chicago expressed satisfaction with what had happened, although they did find fault with the language of the pardon message. On the other hand, members of the bench and bar in New York City (who were not likely to have been as familiar with the case) expressed shock and amazement over the pardon and objected vigorously to Altgeld's review of the judicial aspects of the case.

The Chicago *Inter Ocean* recognized that Altgeld had acted within his constitutional rights but attacked his criticism of Judge Gary and the police as "outrageous." The Chicago *Herald* thought the pardons "excusable" because the prisoners had been sufficiently punished, but the paper declared that the pardon should not be regarded as having "removed the stain of guilt from the memories of the Anarchists who sleep at Waldheim." A similar position was taken by the Chicago *Record*.

Perhaps the most favorable reaction came from the Chicago *Times*, which had been purchased by Carter H. Harrison, who had by this time, become mayor again. Harrison personally dictated an editorial that asserted: "Gov. Altgeld has done no more than right in giving them freedom for the rest of their days." While applauding the governor's action, however, the editorial criticized the language of the pardon message.

Chicago was beginning to come to its senses, but the Haymarket bomb had made its mark on history. It produced America's first major "red scare," one which was to have a lasting effect on the popular mind in linking socialism, communism, and anarchism with imaginary threats of social revolution. The pejorative press coverage of the Haymarket affair was to have a continuing impression in identifying an anarchist in the public mind with a long-haired, wild-eyed, unwashed fanatic, armed with a bomb and smoking revolver. In addition to providing a pattern for red-baiting, the campaign against the 1886 Chicago social revolutionaries—because of the tenuous connection of the Haymarket defendants with labor causes —hindered the development of the labor movement for decades.

Henry David, a major authority on the Haymarket affair, studied the record exhaustively and said many years later that for him the precise identity of the bomb-thrower still remained unknown.

A biased jury, a prejudiced judge, perjured evidence, an extraordinary and indefensible theory of conspiracy, and the temper of Chicago led to the conviction. The evidence never proved their guilt. Nor can the conclusion that the bomb was probably thrown by a member of the social-revolutionary movement affect this statement. . . . If the eight men were guilty of [policeman] Degan's death because they had urged the use of force, then William Randolph Hearst should have been tried as an accessory to the murder of McKinley because he wrote in an editorial attacking the President, that "if bad institutions and men can be got rid of by killing, then the killing must be done."

Actually the quoted editorial was only one in a series of Hearst's New York *Journal* that savagely attacked McKinley. After Governor William Goebel of Kentucky was assassinated in 1900, the *Journal* carried the following quatrain:

> The bullet that pierced Goebel's breast
> Can not be found in all the West;
> Good reason, it is speeding here
> To stretch McKinley on his bier.

McKinley's assassin was reported to have had in his pocket at the time he fired the fatal shot a copy of the *Journal* containing an attack on McKinley. In his first message to Congress, Theodore Roosevelt, the new president, said McKinley's killer had probably been inflamed by "reckless utterances of those who, on the stump and in the public press, appeal to dark and evil spirits." The most that Hearst suffered was to be hanged in effigy, to have his paper boycotted, and to experience a temporary loss in circulation.[22]

Considered in the light of history, the Haymarket defendants were not prosecuted as much for advocating violence as for the social doctrines they were preaching and printing.[23] The general circulation press perceived no First Amendment issue of importance, however, and paid little attention to the deeper reasons for the discontent manifested in the radical press. The claim can hardly be made that the opportunity for a balanced judgment was necessarily submerged by the hysteria of the time. The Topeka *Citizen*, in a comment shortly after the bombing, demonstrated that a paper could retain the capacity for reason:

> Now they are using dynamite, these discontented workingmen. For they are workingmen, whether they are foreigners or not. We do not say they are in the right, but are they wholly to blame? Is there not some reason for these outbreaks? To cure an evil it is necessary to eradicate the cause. The killing of a few rioters . . . does little or nothing toward stopping the spread of Anarchist ideas. The proper way would seem to be to lay all prejudice aside and inquire into the cause of this growth of Anarchism. . . . It is not right to condemn ideas without first inquiring into the causes which produced them.

In the case of the Chicago anarchists, the daily press of the nation with virtually one voice not only condemned the ideas they expressed but also condemned their right to express them.

8

A Presidential Big Stick Against Press Freedom

President Theodore Roosevelt may have thought that in diplomacy the best method was to "speak softly and carry a big stick," but with respect to newspapers that offended him, he not only wielded a big stick but spoke loudly about his desire to use it. In 1908 the president's wrath was aroused by newspaper charges of corruption in connection with the purchase of Panama Canal rights. He was so angered by stories in the New York *World* and an editorial in the *Indianapolis News* on the subject that he instituted the first government prosecution of the press for libel since the suits under the Sedition Act of 1798.[1]

But the story of machinations over acquisition of a canal route had begun years before the Roosevelt furor over the press. An incident during the Spanish-American war had sparked new American interest in a canal across the isthmus, an idea that had been talked about since the sixteenth century and that had figured in United States foreign policy since the Polk administration. During the hostilities with the Spanish the United States battleship *Oregon*, ordered to Cuban waters from Puget Sound, had made a long, forced voyage around Cape Horn with national attention riveted on her progress. The event provided a demonstration of a naval need for a canal.

And the acquisition of new island possessions in the Pacific, as a result of the war, added to Americans' perception of the necessity of a canal to facilitate their interests in trade with new areas.

The problem for the United States was to acquire the right to construct a canal in Central America. The isthmus was then a part of Colombia, from which French interests had purchased rights in 1876. By 1889 the construction company under Ferdinand De-Lesseps, who had been the engineer for the Suez Canal, had spent $260 million in a vain effort and had been forced into bankruptcy. A new organization, the Panama Canal Company, was formed for the sole purpose of selling the dubious assets of the French owners to the United States. Competition was provided when an American syndicate, which had purchased a concession from the Republic of Nicaragua, sought construction through a Nicaraguan route.

With the Panama Company asking $109 million for its concession, a commission appointed by President McKinley reported on November 16, 1901, in favor of the Nicaraguan route. The Panama Company responded by lowering its price to $40 million. Meanwhile, Roosevelt, who had assumed the presidency after McKinley's assassination, had come to visualize the digging of the canal as a way of making his own imprint as chief executive. He did not relish the prospect of being known as "His Accidency," a title which had promptly been applied to him. "Making the dirt fly" for the much-talked-about canal, he thought, would redound to the credit of his administration.

Until the canal company dropped its price to $40 million Roosevelt seemed to favor the Nicaraguan route. But when the new price was offered, he persuaded the commission to change its recommendation and support a canal across the isthmus. The commission's about-face came on January 18, 1902, nine days after the House of Representatives had already voted, 308 to 2, in favor of a Nicaraguan canal. The Senate, however, was persuaded to amend the bill to provide that the president was to secure from Colombia a right of way across the Isthmus of Panama, but that if he could not do so "within a reasonable time and upon reasonable terms" he was to turn to Nicaragua. The amended bill became law on June 28, 1902.

This turn of events, so promising for investors in the Panama Canal Company, had not come about without astute behind-the-scenes maneuvering. A key figure in the maneuvering was William Nelson Cromwell, a prominent New York corporation lawyer who had been retained by the Panama Canal Company to represent its interests and who had begun lobbying in 1899. In 1900 the Republican campaign fund received from Cromwell a $60,000 contribution, which may have had some connection with the change in the party platform from its original position in favor of "a Nicaraguan Canal" to one in favor of "an Isthmian Canal."[2]

In his energetic lobbying in behalf of the Panamanian route, Cromwell had the help of Phillippe Bunau-Varilla, an astute Frenchman who had been chief engineer of the original canal company and was a large stockholder in the new firm. Aided by his American connections, Bunau-Varilla was able to see the "right people," including Theodore Roosevelt, Secretary of State John Hay, and Senator Mark Hanna. Bunau-Varilla's imaginative campaign raising the issue of volcanic activity in Nicaragua helped to swing the Senate to a vote in favor of the isthmus canal.

Once the canal bill became law, Hay began negotiating a treaty with General José Concha, the Colombian envoy in Washington. While Concha was absent because of ill health, Hay, by exerting severe pressure, prevailed on Dr. Tomás Herran, the Colombian chargé, to sign a treaty on January 22, 1903. The accord provided that the United States was to obtain a canal zone six miles wide for a cash payment of $10 million and an annuity of $250,000. Herran had acted three days before the arrival of a telegram from Bogotá instructing him not to sign and to await further instructions. When the text of the pact was communicated to the Colombian capital, the government there balked.

Not unreasonably, the Colombians thought the treaty impinged on their country's sovereignty[3] and they objected to the absence of any provision for a payment from the French company. After all, the French concession was to expire in October 1904, at which time Colombia would be able to take over the company's physical assets and dispose of them to the United States. But the treaty stipulated that Colombia could not dicker independently with the canal company. This stricture obviously benefited Cromwell, who by this time had organized an American syndicate, backed by J. P. Morgan and others, whose purpose was to buy up the assets of the company. Cromwell's plans went smoothly in Washington as the Senate, on

March 17, 1903, ratified the treaty. But on August 12 the Colombian Senate rejected the treaty,[4] a setback not only for Cromwell and his associates but also for Roosevelt, who saw expeditious action on the canal as useful to him in getting the Republican nomination in 1904. The president was furious.

Roosevelt, in various utterances, mostly private, referred to the Colombians as the "cutthroats" and "blackmailers of Bogotá," and as "contemptible little creatures." American newspapers—equally outraged that anyone would dare to frustrate United States objectives—applied terms like "thieves of Bogotá," "brigand Senators," and "organized rapacity." Hay sent Colombia a cable amounting to a virtual ultimatum, hinting at the use of force.

Anticipating the rebuff from Colombia, supporters of the Panama route, including agents of the Panama Canal Company, had held an informal meeting in New York in July to plan a course of action. Panama could secede from Colombia. This notion had evidently been entertained for some time. As early as June 14, 1903, the New York *World* had published a dispatch saying Cromwell had had "a long conversation with the President," and that "Panama stands ready to secede . . . and enter into a canal treaty with the United States."[5]

Using agents of the Panama Railroad Company, which was owned by the Panama Canal Company, Bunau-Varilla and other plotters laid the groundwork for a revolt in which Panama would become independent of Colombia. Various bribes were distributed to key people on the scene. General Esteban Huertas, commander of the Colombian garrison, was reported to have been paid $25,000 to lead the rebels.[6] As a result of his conversations with various high officials in Washington, Bunau-Varilla was able to assure the prospective rebels that the United States would not allow the revolt to fail.

On October 19, 1903, three United States war vessels were ordered to the scene of expected hostilities. Upon their arrival on November 2, their commanders were ordered to occupy the Panama railway if a revolution erupted and to prevent Colombian troops from landing. The revolution occurred, as planned, on November 3. The next day the rebels proclaimed Panama an independent republic. Within an hour after receiving the news Roosevelt authorized recognition of the new nation. Afterwards Roosevelt boasted in a speech, "I took the Canal Zone and let Congress debate."[7]

Some press reaction was negative. The New York *American* said it would "rather forego forever the advantage of an interocean waterway than gain one by such means as this."[8] The New York *World* published a cartoon showing a ferocious Roosevelt, sword in teeth and shovel under arm, debarking in Panama from a warship flying the American flag and a pennant emblazoned, "U.S.A./ G.O.P." The caption above read, "THE COUP d'ETAT." American press reaction, however, was by no means weighted against Roosevelt. The *Atlanta Journal*, in a more typical comment than that of the New York *American*, said Colombia was "needlessly obstructing the world's commerce." The *Literary Digest* analyzed the views of some seventy newspapers and found that fifty-three favored the coup, while only seventeen criticized Roosevelt.[9]

With the isthmus in the hands of his purchased friends, Bunau-Varilla, though a French citizen, had himself appointed envoy from the Republic of Panama. On November 13, 1903, he was officially received in Washington. On November 18 he signed with the United States a pact that he had induced his government to approve unseen. The United States Senate, on February 23, 1904, ratified the treaty, 66 to 14. The United States paid to the Panama Republic the $10 million that was to have gone to Colombia, and to the Panama Canal Company the $40 million that its shrewd promoters had bargained for.[10]

Roosevelt's methods in getting the canal construction started were not as immediately effective as his high-handed gunboat diplomacy had been in acquiring the canal zone. After some initial ill-considered appointments to the Canal Zone Commission, he named Colonel George W. Goethals in 1907 to take over as chief engineer and autocrat of the project.[11]

With work on the canal going forward under Goethals, the issue of the earlier behind-the-scenes manipulation in arranging for the project was to arise in 1908, the year when the Republicans were launching another campaign for the presidency. Cromwell, still mindful of his friends, gave $50,000 to the 1908 Republican campaign chest.[12]

Meanwhile, however, Cromwell, who had sent the canal company a bill for $800,000 for his services, was still being besieged by various Panamanians who felt that they had not been adequately rewarded for their role in the revolution. The New York *World*, hearing of the Panamanians' demands, began to make inquiries. Fearing that the Panamanians, whom he called blackmailers, would make use of their claims in the political campaign, Cromwell sent Jonas Whitley, one of his press agents, to the *World* to warn its managing editor, Caleb Van Hamm, not to print falsities about him. Evidently seeking to spike a campaign against himself and the Republicans before it got started, Cromwell authorized Whitley to give certain information to the *World*. Whitley explained that William J. Curtis, a Cromwell partner, had already gone to New York District Attorney William Travers Jerome, to complain about the Panamanian blackmailers. In an article based on Whitley's information and checked by him word for word, the *World*, on October 3, 1908, said in part:

> In brief, Mr. Curtis told Mr. Jerome it had been represented to Mr. Cromwell that the Democratic National Committee was considering the advisability of making public a statement that William Nelson Cromwell, in connection with M. Bunau-Varilla, a French speculator, had formed a syndicate at the time when it was quite evident that the United States would take over the rights of the French bond-holders in the . . . Canal, and that this syndicate included among others Charles P. Taft, brother of William H. Taft, and Douglas Robinson, brother-in-law of President Roosevelt. Other men more prominent in the New York world of finance were also mentioned.
>
> According to the story unfolded by Mr. Curtis, it was said that the men making this charge against Mr. Cromwell had averred that the syndicate thus organized in connection with Bunau-Varilla had gone into the French market and purchased for about $3,500,000 the stocks and bonds of the defunct de Lesseps company, and of the newer concern which had taken over the old company.
>
> These financiers invested their money because of a full knowledge of the intention of the Government to acquire the French property at a price of about $40,000,000, and thus—because of their alleged information from high Government sources—were enabled to reap a rich harvest.[13]

In having the anticipated Democratic charges aired according to his own timing, Cromwell's man was able to have Cromwell's statement denying all the charges in the same issue of the *World*. Before election day the *World* published five articles critical of the canal deal. Although the original information had come from Cromwell's agent, the *World* was imprudent in not checking with Taft and Robinson before publishing the allegations. This weakened the credibility of the rest of the story. Taft later denied any connection with the Panama syndicate; Robinson refused to comment. For most of its critical articles, however, the *World* had enough evidence to justify pointing to the suspicious circumstances.[14]

On November 2, the day before the election, the Indianapolis *News*, which had a special reason for embarrassing Roosevelt, got into the act. Vice-President Charles W. Fairbanks was that paper's owner, although he was not known to the public as such. Fairbanks had been shunted aside by Roosevelt when the president forced the nomination of William Howard Taft as his successor rather than Fairbanks. An election eve editorial in the *News* raised questions about the Panama issue that were designed to be discomforting to Roosevelt but they were nevertheless questions that for the most part deserved to be asked.

The campaign is over and the people will have to vote tomorrow without any official knowledge concerning the Panama Canal deal. It has been charged that the United States bought from American citizens for $40,000,000 property that cost those citizens only $12,000,000 [*sic*]. Mr. Taft was Secretary of War at the time the negotiation was closed. There is no doubt that the government paid $40,000,000 for the property. But who got the money? We are not to know. The administration and Mr. Taft do not think it right that the people should know. The President's brother-in-law is involved in the scandal, but he has nothing to say. The candidate's brother has been charged with being a member of the syndicate. He has, it is true, denied it. But he refuses to appeal to the evidence, all of which is in the possession of the administration, and wholly inaccessible to outsiders. For weeks this scandal has been before the people. The records are in Washington, and they are public records. But the people are not to see them until after the election, if then.[15]

Although the *News* editorial was enclosed in a letter to Roosevelt on November 9 by William Dudley Foulke of Indiana, the president did not reply until December 1. On December 7 newspapers across the nation carried an Associated Press article based on Roosevelt's outraged response to Foulke. The president called Delavan Smith, editor of the *News*, "infamous," and excoriated various newspapers, including the New York *Sun*. Along with the AP story on the Roosevelt letter was an interview with Smith, who said his editorial statements had been based on an account in "a prominent New York newspaper, not the New York *Sun*."[16] Like Smith, Roosevelt did not mention the *World*, although that paper was soon to raise the Panama issue anew in a manner that the president could not ignore. Of the Indianapolis *News* editorial, Roosevelt declared:

> The fact has been officially published again and again that the Government paid $40,000,000 . . . direct to the French Government. . . . The United States Government has not the slightest knowledge as to the particular individuals among whom the French Government distributed the sum. That was the business of the French Government. The mere supposition that any American received from the French Government a "rake-off" is too absurd to be discussed. It is an abominable falsehood, and it is a slander, not against the American Government, but against the French Government. . . . So far as I know there was no syndicate: there certainly was no syndicate in the United States that to my knowledge had any dealings with the Government directly or indirectly. . . .

Denouncing the implication that Douglas Robinson, the president's brother-in-law, and Charles Taft, the president-elect's brother, were involved in a scandal, Roosevelt said the only scandal was in the conduct of Delavan Smith.[17] The reply to the president that galvanized the attention of the nation came, not from Delavan Smith or the Indianapolis *News*, but from the New York *World*. On December 8 the *World* published a long editorial accusing Roosevelt of lying. The *World* called upon Congress "to make immediately a full and impartial investigation of the entire Panama Canal scandal." Observing that an investigation in 1906 by the Senate Committee on Interoceanic Canals had been frustrated by the refusal of Cromwell to answer the most pertinent questions of Senator John Tyler Morgan of Alabama and that, as a result of Senator Morgan's death, the inquiry had not been pursued, the *World* suggested that the time had come for others in Congress to revive Senator Morgan's efforts.

In passing, the editorial noted that Smith's question as to who got the money had been based on the *World's* historical summary and thus the *World* was now accepting Roosevelt's challenge and asking Congress to officially answer the question: "Who got the money?" The paper listed four Roosevelt statements which it said were untrue and which the president must have known to be untrue when he made them: (1) that the United States did not pay a cent of the $40,000,000 to any American citizen; (2) that the money was paid directly to the French government; (3) that the United States government had not the slightest knowledge as to the individuals among whom the French government distributed the money; (4) that there was "no syndicate in the United States that to my knowledge had any dealings with the Government directly, or indirectly."

The *World* asserted that the man who knew all was William Nelson Cromwell and that the two men who were most in Cromwell's confidence were Theodore Roosevelt and Elihu Root, formerly secretary of war and now secretary of state. It was they, according to the editorial, who had aided Cromwell in consummating the Panama revolution, arranged the terms of the purchase of the canal, made the agreement to pay $40 million for the canal properties, and an additional $10 million "for a manufactured Panama republic, every penny of both of which sums was paid by check on the United States Treasury—not to the French Government, as Mr. Roosevelt says, but to J. P. Morgan & Co."

To support its assertions, the *World* cited material from the record of the 1906 Senate investigation. After Cromwell at a Senate hearing had said he could not recall any contract, Senator Morgan had produced a contract under which Cromwell had been "exclusively empowered" by agreement with the board of directors of the New Panama Canal Company of France "to effect with an American syndicate the Americanization of the Panama Canal Company. . . ." The American syndicate, said the *World*, had been "incorporated in New Jersey with dummy directors." Senator Morgan, the paper continued, had unearthed a copy of the syndicate agreement under which subscribers should contract with Cromwell to pay $5 million in cash and to take their several allotments in the enterprise.

Citing the hearing record, the editorial noted that Cromwell had testified that he and two representatives of the attorney general had consummated the transfer and sale to the United States, that the $40 million had been paid to J. P. Morgan & Co., that, of the $40 million, $25 million was paid to the liquidator of the old Panama Canal Company and the remaining $15 million had been paid to the New Panama Canal Company, whose stockholders had already received their shares of $12 million, with the final $3 million being held for final distribution. As further evidence of Cromwell's involvement, the *World* noted that Cromwell had been elected by the Panama Republic as its general counsel and that Cromwell and J. Pierpont Morgan, as "a fiscal commission," had negotiated with Roosevelt an agreement under which the United States was to pay them, as representatives of Panama, the $10 million due that country. But of this money, three-quarters was still being held by the "fiscal commission," the paper said.

In conclusion, the *World* wanted to know to whom the United States had paid $10 million "for bankrupt property whose control could undoubtedly have been bought in the open market for less than $4,000,000." "Who," the paper asked, "bought up the obligations of the old Panama Canal Company for a few cents on the dollar?" And finally: "Among whom was divided the $15,000,000 paid the new Panama Canal Company?"

Whether Robinson or Taft was involved with Cromwell or shared in the profits, the *World* said, was "incidental to the main issue of letting in the light." The last paragraph lashed Roosevelt:

Whether they [Robinson and Taft] did or not, whether all the profits went into William Nelson Cromwell's hands, or whatever became of them, the fact that Theodore Roosevelt as President of the United States issues a public statement about such an important matter full of flagrant untruths, reeking with misstatements, challenging line by line the testimony of his associate Cromwell and the official record, makes it imperative that full publicity come at once through the authority and by the action of Congress.[18]

The *World's* editorial created a nationwide sensation. Roosevelt —always self-righteous and thin-skinned on the Panama issue— wrote the next day to Henry L. Stimson, United States Attorney in New York, saying: "I do not know anything about the law of criminal libel, but I should dearly like to have it invoked against Pulitzer, of the *World*. . . . Would you have his various utterances of the last three or four months . . . looked up?" The president also made inquiries about the possibility of having District Attorney William Travers Jerome of New York prosecute Pulitzer under the state libel law. On December 15, Roosevelt took the highly unusual step of sending Congress a special message on the subject. His jeremiad said in part:

These stories were first brought to my attention as published in a paper in Indianapolis called "The News," edited by Mr. Delavan Smith. The stories were scurrilous and libelous in character and false in every essential particular. Mr. Smith shelters himself behind the excuse that he merely accepted the statments which appeared in a paper published in New York, "The World," owned by Mr. Joseph Pulitzer. It is idle to say that the known character of Mr. Pulitzer and his newspaper are such that the statements in that paper will be believed by nobody; unfortunately, thousands of persons are ill informed. . . . [At this point the President gave a clue as to one of the reasons for his concern.] A member of Congress has actually introduced a resolution in reference to these charges. I therefore lay all the facts before you.

The story repeated at various times by the World and by its followers . . . is substantially as follows: That there was corruption by or on behalf of the Government of the United States in the transaction by which the Panama Canal property was acquired from its French owners; that there were improper dealings of some kind between agents of the Government and outside persons, representing or acting for an American syndicate, who had gotten possession of the French Company; that among these persons, who it was alleged made "huge profits," were Mr. Charles P. Taft, a brother of Mr. William H. Taft, then candidate for the Presidency, and Mr. Douglas Robinson, my brother-in-law; that Mr. Cromwell, the counsel for the Panama Canal Company in the negotiations, was in some way implicated with the United States governmental authorities in these improper transactions; that Mr. W. H. Taft was Secretary of War at the time that by an agreement between the United States Government and the beneficiaries of the deal all traces thereof were "wiped out" by transferring all the archives and "secrets" to the American Government just before the holding of the convention last June at which Mr. Taft was nominated.

These statements . . . are false in every particular from beginning to end. . . . The inventor of the story about Mr. Charles P. Taft, for instance, evidently supposed that at some period of the Panama purchase Mr. W. H. Taft was Secretary of War, whereas in reality Mr. W. H. Taft never became Secretary of War until long after the whole transaction in question had been closed. The inventor of the story about Mr. Douglas Robinson had not taken the trouble to find out that Mr. Robinson had not had the slightest connection, directly or indirectly . . . with any phase of the Panama transaction. . . . The men who attacked Mr. Root in the matter had not taken the trouble to read the public documents which would have informed them that Mr. Root had nothing to do with the purchase, which was entirely arranged through the Department of Justice under the then Attorney-General, Mr. Knox.

Now, these stories as a matter of fact need no investigation whatever. They consist simply of a string of infamous libels. . . . they are . . . a libel upon the United States Government. . . . It should not be left to a private citizen to sue Mr. Pulitzer for libel. He should be prosecuted for that by the governmental authorities. . . . It is . . . a high national duty to bring to justice this vilifier of the American people, this man who wantonly and wickedly and without one shadow of justification seeks to blacken the character of reputable private citizens and to convict the Government of his own country in the eyes of the civilized world of wrongdoing of the basest and foulest kind. . . . The Attorney-General has under consideration the form in which the proceedings against Mr. Pulitzer shall be brought.[19]

In his message to Congress Roosevelt said the records of the liquidation of the French canal company stock, concluded the previous June, were on deposit with the Credit Lyonnaise of Paris. He added that, if Congress desired, he had no doubt that on request of the United States ambassador in Paris, the lists of individuals would be shown to him.[20]

The president's message was disingenuous in the manner in which it dealt with the newspaper charges. It referred to the erroneous newspaper identification of the times when William H. Taft and Elihu Root respectively were secretary of war, although these errors were hardly as egregious as Roosevelt suggested. It was not true, as Roosevelt asserted, that Taft—who was secretary of war from 1904 to 1908—had assumed that office "long after the whole transaction . . . had been closed." Actually Roosevelt, with a view to making Taft secretary of war, had recalled him from the Philippine Islands, where he was civil governor, in January 1904; the Senate had not ratified the treaty with Panama until February 23, 1904. Roosevelt's message exploited another weak point in the *World*'s case by emphasizing alleged libels against Robinson and Charles Taft, about whose role the newspaper at the time admittedly lacked proof and should not have publicized without evidence. But the *World*'s references to Robinson and Charles Taft, based on information supplied by Cromwell's press agent and approved by Cromwell, were apparently not as far off the mark as Roosevelt pretended, although Taft had been given the wrong first name. A *World* editor, Earl Harding, later uncovered and published the text of what he said was a syndicate agreement signed by Robinson and Henry W. Taft. (Cromwell's press agent, Whitley, had at one point in his dealing with the *World* given the name as Henry W. Taft and then had changed it to Charles P. Taft.) In the agreement, Robinson, Henry Taft and others had pledged themselves to buy shares in the new Panama company. Harding also produced a purported bank document containing the names of Henry W. Taft and Douglas Robinson, among others, and listing opposite each name a dollar amount. Since the libel suit was never tried on its merits, these documents were never tested in court. But the *World* had been prepared to use them, if necessary, and to subpoena witnesses to be questioned about them.[21]

Although the apparent newspaper errors as to Root, Robinson, and the Taft brothers may have been journalistically censurable, they were hardly crucial to the main point—whether American investors had profited corruptly from the Panama Canal deal. Roosevelt sloughed off this charge. Whether or not the French records contained the names of American investors is questionable; despite the efforts of Pulitzer's representatives and others, the records were never made public.[22] And Congress, under Republican control during the Roosevelt and Taft administrations, never exhibited any enthusiasm for uncovering the facts.

The astonishing aspect of the Roosevelt message was not that it reflected indignation on the part of a chief executive who felt that his administration had been besmirched but that it categorically equated alleged defamation of high federal officials with "blackening the good name of the American people." Roosevelt was in effect crying, "Lese Majesty," as though he as sovereign stood for the whole people. Although he labeled the offense "criminal libel," Roosevelt's notion that the press should be prosecuted for scandalizing the government and its officers was in effect a reversion to the long discredited doctrine of seditious libel that had been advanced during the administration of John Adams.[23] Ignored was Madison's pertinent maxim that a "free, republican government cannot be libeled"[24]—individuals, yes, but not the government. Roosevelt was also ignoring the advice that he gave at another time:

> If there is one thing we ought to be careful about it is in regard to interfering with the liberty of the press. . . . I think it is a great deal better to err a little bit on the side of having too much discussion and having too virulent language used by the press, rather than to err on the side of having them not say what they ought to say, especially with reference to public men and measures.[25]

The day after Roosevelt's message to Congress, the *World* responded defiantly to what Pulitzer said was the president's attempt to use the power of the government to "stifle the only Democratic newspaper in New York City" for its criticism of his administration.[26]

> Mr. Roosevelt is mistaken. He cannot muzzle The World.
>
> While no amount of billingsgate on his part can alter our determination to treat him with judicial impartiality and scrupulous fairness, we repeat what we have already said—that the Congress of the United States should make a thorough investigation of the whole Panama transaction, that the full truth may be known to the American people.
>
> It is a most extraordinary circumstance that Mr. Roosevelt himself did not demand such an inquiry. . . .
>
> The World fully appreciates the compliment paid to it by Mr. Roosevelt in making it the subject of a special message to the Congress of the United States. In the whole history of American Government no President has ever paid such a tribute to the power and influence of a fearless, independent newspaper. . . .
>
> If The World has libeled anybody we hope it will be punished, but we do not intend to be intimidated by Mr. Roosevelt's threats, or by Mr. Roosevelt's denunciation, or by Mr. Roosevelt's power. . . .
>
> So far as The World is concerned, its proprietor may go to jail . . .

but even in jail The World will not cease to be a fearless champion of free speech, a free press and a free people.

It cannot be muzzled.[27]

Roosevelt's special message to Congress provoked an outpouring of comment from newspapers across the country. In its issue of December 16 and 17, the *St. Louis Post-Dispatch*, also owned by Pulitzer, published a sampling of editorial opinions from thirty-one newspapers. Many of these papers found fault with the intemperateness of the president's language or the wisdom of sending a special message to Congress on such a subject. The extraordinary fact about the editorials from these thirty-one papers, however, was that only five focused directly on the threat to freedom of the press posed by the employment of a criminal libel prosecution against a paper and its editor for raising questions about an important matter of public business.

Of seven New York newspapers quoted, only the New York *Globe* treated the issue of press freedom clearly and in historical perspective. Said the *Globe*:

In 1798 the sensitive Federalists, smarting under unjust attacks, passed the sedition act, providing punishment for uttering false and scandalous charges against Congress or the President. Hamilton begged and pleaded against the enactment of the law, for he foresaw the consequences. And from the day the bill became law, the Federal party went slowly down to ruin.

The notion that the Federal Government could be libeled was repudiated and from the day that the sedition law went off the books no effort has been made to revive it.[28]

By contrast the comment of the *New York Times* was equivalent to a mere tut-tut. While expressing regret that the president "should have thought it necessary to send to Congress a message on such a subject," the *Times* satirically observed:

The public will wait with interest the result of Mr. Bonaparte's [Attorney General Charles J. Bonaparte] search for the constitutional or statutory authority to begin his contemplated action, and men now thought to be learned in the law will add to their knowledge when the form of the proceedings has been determined upon.[29]

Among other big city papers quoted by the *Post-Dispatch*—including papers in Boston, Philadelphia, Pittsburgh, Cleveland, Detroit, and Chicago—only the Chicago *Inter Ocean* saw fit to criticize the president explicitly on the issue of press freedom. The *Inter Ocean* said:

The Constitution defines treason, and neither the Constitution nor the laws recognize the existence of any such crime as "lese majesty."
The President's threats merely show what Mr. Roosevelt would like to do to destroy the liberty of the press—if he could. Fortunately we still have courts which decide according to the law regardless of personal opinions.[30]

(Incidentally, the *St. Louis Post-Dispatch*—although it gave the president's message thorough coverage in its news columns and although it editorially criticized Roosevelt's "abusive and slanderous attacks" and asked what he had to conceal—did not editorially mention Pulitzer or press freedom. Perhaps it was under orders from its owner to let those issues be handled by the *World*.)

The remaining three papers from the sampling that saw an issue of press freedom serious enough to deserve comment were all small papers. Only the Des Moines *Register and Leader* perceived the desirability of concerted action on the part of the press, declaring:

If any serious attempt is to be made to bring a criminal prosecution against Joseph Pulitzer there should be a determined resistance organized by the newspaper press of the entire country.
Mr. Pulitzer may be wholly malicious in what his newspaper has said, but for the national administration to proceed to shut his mouth by a criminal prosecution is merely to revive in the United States the famous controversy over John Wilkes [an English political leader convicted of seditious libel for publishing in his newspaper an article saying speeches by George III were subject to criticism], a controversy of 200 years ago which ended in the discomfiture of the English Government and inspired the letters of Junius.[31]

The *Register and Leader's* editorial reflected a true appreciation of freedom of the press in that the paper was ready to go to Pulitzer's defense even while conceding that he might have been malicious.

Another strong comment on press freedom came from the Columbia, South Carolina, *State.* That paper observed:

Fortunately for Mr. Joseph Pulitzer, and more fortunately for the American people, the Constitution of the United States grants perpetual freedom to the press and the wise men who drafted the instrument doubtless had in mind just such contingencies where the press would need constitutional protection in its efforts to expose corruption, to prevent corruption and to escape the wrath of would-be dictators of tyrannous disposition.[32]

The Auburn, New York, *Citizen,* calling Roosevelt's message "inexcusable and assinine [*sic*]," went on to observe:

That the President of the United States should resort to a special message to Congress to vent his spleen on a newspaper editor seems incredible. That he should call on Congress to attempt to punish the editor for "lese majeste" evidences an alarming mental condition, more than a mere misconception of the Constitution, which guarantees a free and untrammeled press.[33]

Not included in the *Post-Dispatch* roundup of editorials (perhaps because they were published after the press time of the *Post-Dispatch* issue reporting the sampling) were two of the most trenchant comments on the Roosevelt message—one on each side of the question. Castigating Roosevelt for equating criticism of his administration with "TREASON AGAINST THE STATE," the Denver *Rocky Mountain News* said the President's action was,

in effect, a declaration of war on the freedom of the press, and of speech. It is not the first such declaration that Mr. Roosevelt has made, but it is by odds the boldest and most open one. . . . He would use the powers of state to silence the critic. The attorney general of the United States, appointed by Roosevelt, shall draw the prosecution of the publisher who has dared to criticize Roosevelt. The secret service of the United States, controlled by Roosevelt, shall uncover or manufacture such evidence as is needed to make that prosecution effective. The case shall be tried before a federal judge, appointed by Roosevelt, and to make sure that no loophole is left through which the critic may escape, Mr. Roosevelt by public statements from the president's chair seeks to prejudice the jury before the case has begun. . . .

If such a prosecution could be conducted to the end that Mr. Roosevelt plainly wishes, it would mark the end of free speech in the United States. . . . No set of public officials was ever yet elevated to office which did not need the wholesome restraint of public criticism—and the men Mr. Roosevelt has made his agents are certainly no exception to the rule. The News has no intention of standing sponsor for the justice of the criticism the World has made of some of these agents. But the News is prepared to do battle for the right of the World to criticize without fear of any such evil tyranny as Mr. Roosevelt seeks to invoke.[34]

The Denver *Post* had a front page cartoon showing Roosevelt and Pulitzer fighting, with a caption saying, "Having The Time of Their Lives."[35] But in the four days following the delivery of the message, that paper had no written editorial comment. The Denver *Times* carried a news story reporting an editorial by William Jennings Bryan in his weekly paper, the *Commoner*, criticizing Roosevelt on the free press issue and siding with Pulitzer,[36] but the *Times* in the four days after the message had no comment of its own.

Of nearly three dozen newspapers checked, only the *Denver Republican* unequivocally defended Roosevelt and attacked Pulitzer. The *Republican* declared that:

. . . a signal service has been rendered to the nation. The president has called attention anew to the crying evils of the journalism of which Mr. Pulitzer is the high priest.

There is no excuse whatever for the policy adopted by the New York World. Its owner is a very wealthy man. He can afford to loll about the Mediterranean in a palatial yacht and brew his mephitic scandals at long distance. His wealth was gained by ministering to the depraved and degraded. For a long time he has polluted the public mind with just such matter as the president complains of. He is the father of modern yellow journalism . . . who made it a practice to go through Manhattan's back yards and expose for sale the garbage. . . . For years he has been harping on the Panama canal transaction. By insinuation, innuendo and garbled report he has tried to make it falsely appear that the very highest officials in the nation have had their hands in the grabbag. . . . Pulitzer in the defense made by him states that he never accused directly either Mr. Charles Taft or Mr. Douglas Robinson of making profits from the transfer of the Panama property. No, of course not, he simply besmirched them and called upon them with others to appear in the columns of the New York World and defend themselves from the veiled charges and make meat for the Pulitzer readers. . . .

President Roosevelt has done his duty and has rendered a signal service to public morality no matter what congress may do in the matter.[37]

Of the many newspapers that commented on the Roosevelt special message, a number took their cues from the fact that members of Congress had greeted the president's angry outburst with laughter. A news dispatch on the message reported that "every Senator was laughing before the first 14 lines were completed," and that in the House "the President's message was received . . . with a storm of laughter. . . . At the paragraph where the President accused the New York World and its publisher, Joseph Pulitzer, of being of such character that their statements are believed by nobody, the laughter was long and loud."[38]

Like other papers, the *Atlanta Journal* noted that the president had "made himself the butt of ridicule," and added that he had "made this canal inquiry imperative."[39] The Charleston, South Carolina, *Courier* observed that when Roosevelt's message was read in the Senate "there was great hilarity." But that paper wanted Congress to find out "who got the money."[40]

Members of Congress may have found Roosevelt's bombast amusing, but Roosevelt himself was deadly serious—as the government's legal machinery soon demonstrated. A District of Columbia grand jury on February 17, 1909, indicted Joseph Pulitzer, Caleb Van Hamm, and Robert Hunt Lyman of the *World* and the Press Publishing Company, the corporate name of the *World*. The defendants were charged under five counts with criminally libeling Theodore Roosevelt, J. P. Morgan, Douglas Robinson, Charles P. Taft, Elihu Root, and William Nelson Cromwell. Delavan Smith and Charles R. Williams of the Indianapolis *News* were indicted on seven counts.[41]

The *World's* response was an editorial saying: "Mr. Roosevelt is an episode. The World is an institution. Long after Mr. Roosevelt is dead, long after Mr. Pulitzer is dead, long after all the present editors of this paper are dead, The World will still go on as a great independent newspaper, unmuzzled, undaunted and unterrorized."[42] Don C. Seitz, an executive with the *World*, wrote later that the administration "placed an extraordinary number of secret agents upon the World's trail; its mail was opened in the postoffice; the portfolios of its messengers between New York and Washington were examined and the Pulitzer Building itself filled with spies."[43]

On March 4, 1909, the day Roosevelt was to leave office, a federal grand jury in New York indicted the *World* and two of its editors on the ground that twenty-nine copies of an offending issue had been circulated at the military reservation at West Point; others had been routinely sent to the New York post office for examination by postal inspectors. An 1825 federal statute, amended in 1898, entitled: "An Act to Protect the Harbor Defenses from Malicious injury and for other purposes," was used as the basis for the indictment, although the law had never been used before for a libel prosecution. Moreover, according to Stimson's theory, the appearance of the *World* at each of any federal reservation "would constitute a separate offense," thus making the newspaper, or any accused newspaper, subject to repeated prosecutions all over the nation or in other parts of the world. There were then 2,809 government reservations in the United States and many more abroad. Were such a legal concept allowed to stand, the government would indeed have available a big stick against the press.

With Roosevelt out of office and off to Africa on a hunting trip, the case against the *World* was left in the hands of the Taft administration. George W. Wickersham, the new attorney general, continued the prosecution with vigor equal to that of Bonaparte. The cost of the defense would have ruined a publisher of ordinary means.[44]

The first turning point in the government's prosecution efforts came, not in Washington or New York but in Indianapolis, where United States District Judge Albert B. Anderson dismissed the case against the *News* and against Delavan Smith and Charles R. Williams on grounds that, under the Sixth Amendment, the government had no right to require the defendants to stand trial in Washington, D.C.[45] If any offense was committed, it was committed in Indianapolis, Judge Anderson said, and added:

If the prosecuting officers have the authority to select the tribunal, if there be more than one tribunal to select from, if the government has that power, and can drag citizens from distant states to the capital of the nation, there to be tried, then . . . this is a strange result of a revolution where one of the grievances complained of was the assertion of the right to send parties abroad for trial.[46]

Although Judge Anderson based his decision on Sixth Amendment grounds, he included in his opinion a strong dictum on the free press aspects of the case. He asserted that it was the duty of a public newspaper to tell its readers the facts it may find about public questions and to draw inferences from the facts known. He observed that the Panama Canal issue was a great public question and that there were "many very peculiar circumstances about the history" of the business, including the circumstances surrounding the revolution in Panama and the fact that the price was suddenly reduced from over $100 million to $40 million. He noted that there were a number of people who thought "there was something not just exactly right" about the transaction and added that he himself was curious to know what the truth was.

Then came a judicial reference to Cromwell's peculiar role. The judge observed that when the Senate investigating committee asked Cromwell certain pertinent questions, he "stood upon his privilege as an attorney and refused to answer." But, added the judge, "whenever a question was asked which gave him an opportunity to say something in . . . behalf [of his associates], he ostentatiously thanked the examiner for the question and proceeded to answer. To my mind that gave just ground for suspicion." And here, he declared, was a newspaper printing the news, or trying to, about this matter of great public interest and concern.[47]

Reacting to the Anderson decision later, Roosevelt called the judge "a jackass and a crook."[48] But Anderson had done no more than adopt the position of United States Attorney Joseph H. Kealing of Indianapolis, who had resigned rather than represent the government, saying the government was attempting "to put a strained construction on the law." Kealing was opposed to trying to force the defendants to stand trial in Washington, D.C., asserting that there was good and sufficient law in the state court in Indiana.[49] In New York, District Attorney Jerome had declined to prosecute in the state court there.[50]

Judge Anderson's decision, which did not involve Pulitzer and the *World*, had come in October 1909. On January 25, 1910,

United States District Judge Charles M. Hough of the southern district of New York quashed the federal indictment of the *World* and its proprietor and top editors, saying there was no federal statute authorizing the prosecution, that the act relied upon did not apply and that, if construed to cover the acts shown by the evidence, it would be unconstitutional.

Although he had won, Pulitzer was not yet satisfied. He wanted the principle enunciated by Judge Hough to be settled by the highest court in the land so that the press could feel more secure from such prosecutions. Since only the government, as the losing party, could appeal, the *World* kept needling the Justice Department to appeal. The government in due course filed a writ of error, and on October 24, 1910, the Supreme Court heard the arguments in the case.

On January 3, 1911, the Court, with Chief Justice Edward D. White writing for a unanimous bench, ruled in favor of the *World*. He declared that "the lower court was right in quashing the indictment as not authorized" by the federal statute of 1898. So the case ended, after nearly two years of litigation, with a victory for freedom of the press but without an answer ever being provided to the question: Who got the money?[51]

The *World*, in a triumphant editorial with a rather hyperbolic flourish, commented:

> The unanimous decision handed down by the United States Supreme Court yesterday in the Roosevelt-Panama libel case against The World is the most sweeping victory won for freedom of speech and of the press since the American people destroyed the Federalist party more than a century ago for enacting the infamous Sedition law.
> . . . The Supreme Court upholds every contention advanced by the World since the outset of his prosecution. . . . The decision . . . is so sweeping that no other President will be tempted to follow in the footsteps of Theodore Roosevelt, no matter how greedy he may be for power, no matter how resentful of opposition. . . .[52]

The *St. Louis Post-Dispatch* reported the story of the Supreme Court decision on the front page and published more than two full inside pages on the history of the lawsuit and the questions it raised about the Panama transactions. The St. Louis paper also reprinted the *World* editorial, which called again for a congressional investigation. Apparently regarding the issue as one of less significance than the Pulitzer papers, the *New York Times* ran the story of the Supreme Court decision on page six,[53] and during the next four days had not a word to say editorially about the resolution of the great issue of freedom of the press.

Like the *New York Times*, the *Chicago Tribune* reported the Supreme Court decision on page six but ignored the issue editorially during the days immediately following the ruling.[54] The Boston *Evening Transcript*, which did run an editorial on the decision, did not mention freedom of the press and did not seem to regard the ruling as a great vindication of the press.

The ground of this decision was primarily that adequate means are afforded for punishing the circulation of a libel on a United States reservation by State law and in the State courts, without the necessity of resorting to the Federal courts. That being so, suits may apparently still be prosecuted by aggrieved parties but under a different jurisdiction.[55]

The Hartford *Courant*, however, saw long term significance in the decision in the *World* libel case: "No future Attorney General will repeat Mr. Bonaparte's blunder. If the sedition law of President John Adams's time is ever revived—which is most unlikely—it will be by the Congress of the United States and not by the Executive."[56] Actually the Supreme Court had decided the case on the ground that the 1898 statute had been wrongly interpreted by the government as authorizing a federal criminal libel prosecution. Moreover, the court rejected the notion that the paper could be prosecuted in separate suits on any United States reservation where it was circulated. Pulitzer had defeated the president's attempted use of the big stick, but the high court's opinion contained no ringing declaration in support of press freedom. Indeed, there was not even a mention of press freedom. The opinion did suggest that, if there had been a libel offense, New York state law was the applicable law. No further attempt was made by the offended parties to pursue the matter in New York state courts. Roosevelt, when asked by a reporter from the *World* for a comment on the Supreme Court decision, responded: "I have nothing to say."[57]

9

World War I: Pressure for Patriotism Versus Freedom to Dissent

During World War I and its aftermath freedom of expression was subjected to more widespread restriction than at any previous time in United States history. More than 1,900 prosecutions involving speeches, newspaper articles, pamphlets, and books were initiated during the war; well over 800 individuals were convicted. The postmaster general during the war interfered with the distribution of more than 100 publications. Nearly 50 of these were socialist newspapers, including such well-known dailies as the New York *Call* and the Milwaukee *Leader*.[1]

After the war the attorney general launched a mass roundup and deportation of aliens whose political views were deemed dangerous to the nation. During this same period of intense attack on freedom of expression, the Supreme Court for the first time began to provide authoritative interpretation of the First Amendment as to speech and press freedom.[2] The high court's initial rulings on the war cases, however, were hardly a signal that the First Amendment provided a shield for dissenters.

A week after the declaration of war President Wilson named a Committee on Public Information, whose function was to channel information and propaganda to the press and to seek voluntary cen-

169

sorship. The appointment of the committee, with a potential for curbing the flow of information, aroused little editorial comment from the press. The *New York Times* questioned the fitness of the committee's chairman, George Creel, a freelance journalist and editor, saying it was unable to find in his career "any evidence of the ability, the experience, or the judicial temperament required to gain the understanding and cooperation of the press." The *Times-Picayune* of New Orleans, another of the few papers that expressed an opinion on the group, said of the Creel Committee: "It is called a 'velvet glove' censorship, because it is so moderate as compared to the radical and drastic provisions" in other countries.[3] The *Chicago Tribune* welcomed a proposed congressional investigation of Creel because an inquiry might reveal reasons for removing him. The *Tribune* found Creel too much of a propagandist and a partisan, determined to defend all administration officials.[4] But most papers, in their issues during this period, ignored the formation of the committee in their editorial columns.

Creel proved to be a propagandist of imagination and prodigious energy. He saw his job as one of selling the war to the American people and Wilson's ideas of a democratic peace to the world. His committee published over 100 million pieces of literature. Germans were portrayed as barbarians who committed outrageous atrocities. Most newspapers, in a display of patriotic fervor, published all of the six thousand releases that flowed from the committee's News Division, and many donated space for advertising to promote the Liberty Loan campaign.

According to Creel's view, departure from the official line was not to be countenanced. His committee urged citizens to report to the Department of Justice "the man who spreads pessimistic stories." But the various codes devised by the Creel committee for the suppression of military news believed to be helpful to the enemy were reasonable and were followed by most papers.[5] Although the Associated Press refused to comply with Creel's request to kill dispatches telling of the arrival of American troops in France, the AP accepted and observed the rules of proposed voluntary censorship when recommended restrictions were clearly defined.

The *Washington Post*, at that time a Republican paper, was on several occasions at loggerheads with the Creel committee and with military intelligence officers. But apart from German-American and socialist papers, papers in the Hearst chain were the ones most often accused of disloyalty. Having bitterly opposed the United States entry into the war, the Hearst papers continued to be critical of the allies but in general supported the American war effort. Their equivocal attitude, however, caused them to be widely attacked. The *New York Tribune* ran a cartoon showing a snake coiled in the flag, with the snake's body spelling the legend "Hears-ss-ss-t." Former President Roosevelt asked why the mailing privileges of the Hearst papers were not suspended, and some Republicans said Hearst escaped because he was a Democrat. Unlike Hearst—who suffered no long-term consequences, though his papers did temporarily lose circulation because of their carping attitude—Oswald Garrison Villard was forced to sell his *New York Post* in 1918 after his expression of pacifist and civil libertarian views brought a serious decline in its fortunes.[6]

Official and private action against dissenters during the war period was so widespread that an evaluation of the press attitude toward the whole range of efforts at suppression would be a task of formidable magnitude. A check of press reaction to some of the key issues and cases, however, provides an indication of newspaper support, or nonsupport, for freedom of expression on the war. The cases to be considered are: the passage of the Espionage Act of 1917 and the Sedition Act (as an amendment) the next year; the Post Office Department's suspension in 1917 of the second class mail rate of a socialist paper, the Milwaukee *Leader*; the indictment and conviction in 1918 and 1919 of Socialist leaders Victor Berger and Eugene Debs for violating the Espionage Act; the decisions by the Supreme Court in these several cases from 1919 to 1921; and the roundup in 1920 of thousands of alleged radicals by the Justice Department under Attorney General A. Mitchell Palmer.

Only a little more than two months after the declaration of war on Germany, April 6, 1917, Congress debated the bill that was to become the first federal statute since the demise of the Alien and Sedition Acts (in 1801) subjecting citizens to punishment for criticism of the government. The Espionage Act of June 15, 1917, called for imprisonment of up to twenty years and fines up to $10,000 for anyone convicted of obstructing enlistment or recruiting, or attempting to cause insubordination, mutiny, or disloyalty in the armed forces, or conveying false statements with the intent to interfere with the operation of the military or naval forces. Another part of the law authorized the postmaster general to bar from the mails any letter, pamphlet, book, or newspaper containing the previously proscribed kinds of expression or which advocated treason, insurrection, or forcible resistance to any law of the United States.[7] President Woodrow Wilson signed the act, after saying: "I shall not expect or permit any part of this law to apply to me or any of my official acts, or in any way to be used as a shield against criticism."[8]

During the debate on the Espionage Act, many newspapers strongly protested against proposed provisions that would have empowered the president to promulgate regulations prescribing what information might be helpful to the enemy and would have made those publishing such information subject to fine and imprisonment. Although members of Congress disagreed over whether the proposal would have allowed the president actually to prevent the publication of certain information by establishing a board of censors, the bill as drafted unquestionably would have permitted the kind of censorship that is effected by punishment after the fact for the publication of proscribed information.[9]

William Randolph Hearst directed the editor of his New York *American* to launch a vigorous campaign against the espionage bill.[10] The *New York Times* said:

> In preparing this section of the Espionage bill [the so-called censorship section] the authors gave no heed to the necessity of discriminating. They would inflict the penalties of heavy fines and long terms of imprisonment upon friend and foe alike. The newspaper or the individual who publishes or seeks to obtain information about the policies or military operations of the Government with the intent to communicate to the enemy to his benefit and to our harm ought to be made to smart for treason. But the newspaper or the individual who criticizes or points out defects in policies and preparations with the honest purpose of promoting remedial action and warning against danger is not a public enemy.
> It is a Prussian measure. . . .[11]

The Milwaukee *News* declared: "The Censorship bill . . . has aroused such a storm of disapproval that the President seeks to allay popular indignation at this glaring attempt to void Constitutional rights. . . . The whole program to muzzle the press seems to smack of unconstitutionality, tyranny, and deceit."[12]

On May 31, 1917, the House—after weeks of debate and largely because of the opposition of the press—rejected what had come to be labeled the censorship provision, and the administration was reported to have dropped the idea and to have decided to rely on the system of voluntary domestic censorship already being devised by Creel's Committee on Public Information.[13]

With final action still to be taken on the bill, some of the major papers wanted to make sure that the administration stuck with the voluntary censorship plan. The Louisville *Courier Journal* said Wilson "should allow no 'gag' bill to be called 'the Administration measure.' "[14] A week afterward the *Courier Journal* chided the New York *World* for saying that "some form of censorship is both necessary and inevitable."[15] (A few days later, however, the *Courier Journal* advised the administration to censor itself, a suggestion that derived from the fact the officials had put out a statement saying that the draft registration would not equal the Census Bureau's advance estimate.)[16] On June 3 the *St. Louis Post-Dispatch* ran a lengthy article by George Wickersham, who had been attorney general in the Taft administration, questioning the constitutionality of the compulsory censorship proposals.[17]

As a governmental intrusion that would have directly affected all editors' freedom to control the content of their own papers, any kind of legally proscribed information with penalties attached to its use was naturally a matter of concern to the press. But important as it was, censorship did not represent the only prospective intrusion on freedom of expression posed by the Espionage Act. The provisions proscribing statements designed to interfere with the operation of the armed forces and empowering the postmaster general to bar writing of similar kinds from the mails were so broadly drawn as to penalize many forms of innocent criticism. Yet, apart from the compulsory censorship provisions, the press seems to have shown little interest in the potentially repressive aspects of the bill while it was being debated.[18] During the two weeks following the abandonment of the censorship proposal, none of seven major newspapers checked gave any indication in their editorials that they thought the pending legislation might threaten freedom of expression. All of them, in

fact, revealed that they had little sympathy for freedom of expression on the war.

In the time just before and just after final enactment, the *New
York Times* had no editorial dealing directly with the espionage
bill. In an editorial headed, "No Tolerance for Treason," the *Times,*
however, did say:

> The time has come for strict interpretation and prompt enforcement
> of the laws of this country relating to treason, sedition and conspiracy
> against the Government. . . . It is the duty of every good citizen to com-
> municate to the proper authorities any evidence of sedition that comes
> to his notice."[19]

On a matter close to its own interests the *Times,* a little more
than a week later, was not so eager for any involvement by government. A *Times* editorial criticized a proposal to have the government take control of news print.[20] On the day the espionage bill
became law, the *Times* editorially applauded the arrest of the editor
of a German-language paper in Cleveland as a "seditious writer."[21]
The New York *Herald* declared that the internment of the Cleveland
editor "ought to afford a salutary lesson to the editors of other
foreign-language newspapers who are helping the Kaiser by declining to help the United States."[22]

In its only comment on the espionage bill during the first nineteen days of June, the *Boston Evening Transcript* blamed the administration for the sentiment that caused the rejection of the censorship proposal by the House. The *Transcript* noted that the State
Department had gone so far as to say it was dangerous to discuss
differences of opinion between any of the allies. "It is not a question," said the *Transcript*, "of having no censorship at all. It is a
question of reasonable restraint upon the publication of information
which must help the enemy. It is not too late to apply this degree of
restraint." The Boston paper concluded, however, that "it is an
excellent sign that the sentiment of the House of Representatives
is thoroughly and overwhelmingly opposed to the virtual suppression
of all serious discussion."[23] During this same period the *Transcript*
editorially derided the peace cry of Socialists, and, in another comment, exclaimed: "Let there be an end to organized warfare against

us conducted under the mask of radical and pacifist societies and parties." [24]

While editorially ignoring the espionage bill as it moved toward final passage, the *Washington Evening Star* revealed what it thought should be done with critics of the war. In an editorial devoted to the conviction of two men for "distributing seditious literature" at a "peace meeting" in New York, the *Star* noted that one of the two said he was an anarchist. The paper went on to observe that, for "such a creature," convicted of conspiracy to block registration, "the maximum penalty of two years' imprisonment and $10,000 fine is barely sufficient." [25] On the same day that the *Star* reported that the president had signed the espionage bill, the paper editorially asserted that the government must sustain "popular fervor for the war." [26]

The *Atlanta Constitution* had nothing to say editorially about the espionage bill in the final two weeks before it became law. But the paper did turn its attention to a meeting in New York called "The First American Conference on Democracy and the Terms of Peace." The *Constitution* was outraged over a message sent to the conference by former Senator John D. Works of California in which Works had said, "We dishonored ourselves by declaring war without adequate or reasonable cause." This statement, the *Constitution* observed, "constitutes an abuse of the American guarantee of free speech that is as disgraceful as it is unwarranted. . . ." Castigating what it called "a saturnalia of criticism and abuse of their country's attitude" by the conscientious objectors at the meeting, the *Constitution* declared: "It is high time to clamp the lid down on such unpatriotic gatherings as that recently held in New York." [27]

Commenting on the same meeting, the Louisville *Courier Journal* said: "We submit that Mr. Works deserves a jail sentence. . . ." [28] A short time later the *Courier Journal* ridiculed Jane Addams for making an antiwar speech. Taking a lofty stance, the paper said that Addams had gotten way "beyond her depth" and "gave the impression of poll-parrot trying to imitate what she does not comprehend." [29]

In St. Louis the *Post-Dispatch* also failed to editorialize on the Espionage Bill during the period just before and immediately after its enactment. During the same period, however, the *Post-Dispatch* did urge people to join a planned parade in order to show support for the government in war.[30] As the war went on, the *Post-Dispatch* voiced much more insistence on political orthodoxy than it had only a year earlier, in May 1916, when the paper editorially condemned an effort to prevent Margaret Sanger from speaking in St. Louis.[31]

In San Francisco the *Chronicle* found no reason to comment on the espionage bill but during the same period did have occasion to criticize a bill to tax newspaper advertising.[32]

One of the most significant actions against the press under the Espionage Act was the revocation in the fall of 1917 of the second class mail classification of the Milwaukee *Leader*, a Socialist paper edited by Victor Berger, on the grounds that the paper's articles hindered and embarrassed the government in the prosecution of the war. Although many publications were deprived of the second class rate and thus were severely penalized because of their editorial positions, the *Leader* case is appropriate for study because of the prominence of the paper and its editor. The *Leader* had strongly opposed the war from the beginning, but it had done so on the basis of socialist doctrine and opposition to militarism rather than sympathy for the German nation and had not advocated violence or resistance to the draft.[33] Not only did the *Leader* lose its second class rate, but the paper was deprived of the right to receive or send first class mail.[34] The withholding of first class mail caused the *Leader* to lose $70,000 in subscription money and $50,000 in local and national advertising.[35] The paper lost approximately fifteen thousand subscribers.[36]

The *New York Times* on October 4 reported the revocation order.[37] The *Times*, however, had no editorial on the subject during the next several days. The *St. Louis Post-Dispatch* had no news item or editorial on the subject during the same period. But on October 3 the *Post-Dispatch* did carry an editorial page cartoon by Fitzpatrick showing a burly figure labeled, "Treason," climbing onto a platform labeled, "Free Speech."[38] (A few months later the *Post-Dispatch* was objecting editorially to an action by the Post Office Department that presumably affected papers like itself. In an editorial headed, "Interfering With Opinion," the paper protested against a postal zone system that it said "not only taxes the advertising section of great newspapers and periodicals but their circulation. It breaks the country into sections and reduces every periodical and newspaper into a sectional organ."[39])

At the time the postmaster general acted to curb the Milwaukee *Leader*, no editorial on the issue appeared in the *Washington Evening Star*, the *Boston Evening Transcript*, the Chicago *Tribune*, the *Atlanta Constitution*, the Louisville *Courier Journal*, or the *San Francisco Chronicle*. Like the *New York Times*, the *Chicago Tribune* and the *San Francisco Chronicle* at least reported the postmaster general's order, though in inconspicuous places.[40]

Not satisfied with having crippled the Milwaukee *Leader*, the government in February 1918 indicted its editor, Victor Berger (along with four other Socialists) for conspiracy under the Espionage Act. Berger, who had lived in the United States since 1878 when he arrived at the age of eighteen from his native Austria, was one of the most prominent members of the Socialist party in the United States. Generally regarded as a man of ability and integrity in Wisconsin, he had been elected to Congress from Wisconsin and served from 1911 to 1913. In 1918, while under indictment, he was again elected to Congress as a Socialist, defeating the Democratic and Republican candidates in his district.

The indictment of Berger, brought in Chicago because the defendants were alleged to have agreed there on the issuance of publications in various places, was directly related to Berger's work as an editor. He was charged with overt acts said to have consisted of five editorials in the *Leader* that stated in substance that: (1) the United States was at war because the Allies were at the end of their rope, and their obligations would otherwise be worthless; continued fighting would maintain the existing high prices of munitions stock; war meant absolute freedom from labor troubles, since strikes would be put down as treason; the plutocracy and its government in Washington would be able to establish autocracy as a war necessity; war would provide a wonderful chance to establish a large permanent army; the commercial rivalry of Germany would be ended. Submarines, Belgium, invasion, and democracy had nothing to do with it. (2) Many men are driven insane at the front. (3) Young men do not talk as if they considered it an honor to be drafted. (4) Only big business men are enthusiastic about the war, but they do not fight. (5) The Bible contains many passages that are opposed to war and must therefore be considered as treasonable.

On March 10, 1918, the *New York Times* and many other papers reported the indictment of Berger and his four codefendants. Although the indictment had been returned on February 2, the U.S. attorney in Chicago had withheld the news until March 10. Two days later the *Times* had an editorial attack on Socialists in which Berger was condemned for "standing four-square on the disloyal May declaration" of the Socialist party.[41] The Socialists, at a meeting in St. Louis the previous year, had adopted just after the declaration of war a platform in which they urged "continuous, active, and public opposition to the war, through demonstrations, mass petitions, and all other means within our power."[42]

Like most other major papers, the Louisville *Courier Journal* reported the Berger indictment but failed to find in the event any free press implications worthy of editorial comment. The *Courier Journal*'s only comment on the matter at the time was an editorial paragraph chiding the U.S. attorney in Chicago for withholding until March 10 the news of the February 2 indictment for fear, the paper said, of antagonizing "Russian Bolsheviki."[43]

The *Washington Evening Star*, the *Atlanta Constitution*, the *San Francisco Chronicle,* and the *Denver Post* all reported the indictment of Berger but offered no editorial comment. (The *Denver Post*, it should be noted, however, apparently had no editorial page during the World War I era.) The *Boston Evening Transcript* overlooked the charges against Berger in its editorial columns and apparently also in its news columns. That paper, however, had no issue on Sunday, the day the news broke in most papers.

The *St. Louis Post-Dispatch* reported the Berger indictment and, although the paper had no editorial at the time of the matter, the *Post-Dispatch* the previous month had carried an editorial in which it proclaimed that Socialists "must be 100 per cent American and support the President all the way, if they expect their party ever to emerge from . . . odium and discredit. . . ."[44] Eight months previously the *Post-Dispatch* had editorially attacked a Berger speech as "treasonable rant."[45] Newspapers, of course, had every right to condemn what the Socialists were saying. But in recognition of the true spirit of press freedom, they could have denounced the Socialists' opinions while upholding their right to express them.

Berger and his fellow defendants were convicted on January 8, 1919, and the verdict was reported in the *New York Times* the next day. On January 10, the *Times* approved the Berger conviction, saying "All that was necessary for the prosecution was to produce the evidence of his own writings and the anti-war Socialist platform drawn up by him and his colleagues."[44] The conviction was also reported by the *Atlanta Constitution*, the *Atlanta Journal*, the *St. Louis Post-Dispatch*, the *Denver Post*, the *Denver Times*, and the *Rocky Mountain News*. Only the *Rocky Mountain News* saw fit to comment, and its editorial saw no free press issue.

> Victor Berger and his associates have been found guilty of violating the espionage law during the war. The proof was conclusive. The defense was spoiled by pettyfogging. Until the law intervened, the accused were outspoken and took a stand regarding the war . . . wholly unpatriotic. . . .[47]

The Espionage Act was followed on October 6, 1917, by the Trading-with-the-Enemy Act, which authorized the censorship of all messages abroad and required any newspaper or magazine containing articles in a foreign language to file a sworn translation with the local postmaster. This provision was aimed at the German-language press. Still not satisfied with the government's power to control criticism, Attorney General Thomas W. Gregory asked that the Espionage Act be strengthened. He said it had proved an effective instrumentality against deliberate or organized disloyal propaganda but did not reach individual casual or impulsive disloyal utterances. Therefore, he requested that the act be amended to cover attempts to obstruct the recruiting service and to punish efforts intentionally made to discredit and interfere with the flotation of war loans. In drafting the bill, the Senate Committee on the Judiciary decided to go even further and to provide for stamping out all utterances of a disloyal character. The Sedition Act of May 16, 1918, was the result.

The 1918 Sedition Act (repealed in 1921) was extreme enough to give the government virtually unlimited power to punish spoken and written words deemed to be unpatriotic. It not only outlawed "attempts to obstruct" recruiting, as the attorney general had asked, but listed nine other offenses in addition to those specified in the original Espionage Act, including saying or doing anything to obstruct the sale of United States bonds, uttering, writing, printing, or publishing any disloyal, profane, scurrilous, or abusive language, or language intended to cause contempt, scorn, contumely, or disrepute as regards the form of government of the United States, the Constitution, the flag, or the uniform of the army or navy, or any language intended to incite resistance to the United States or promote the cause of its enemies, or language urging any curtailment of production of any things necessary to the prosecution of the war with intent to hinder its prosecution. The powers of the postmaster general were extended to permit him to exclude any written matter of this description from the mails. Moreover, the government now had only to show that the accused person had used disloyal language; it was no longer necessary to prove that some consequence harmful to the war effort had followed or was likely to follow.[48]

As the sedition bill was making its way through Congress, the *Minneapolis Journal* tried manfully to show that any curb on freedom of expression would not be directed at Socialists in particular. In an editorial headed, "Socialism and Sedition," the *Journal* said:

Socialism in its relation to the Nation has no better privilege than any other partisanship. . . .

Socialism in its theories is not guilty of insurrection or treason. But Socialism is to be judged by its acts, exactly: as any other partisanship. . . . And in time of war, be it remembered, utterances often rank as acts and are to be construed as seditious and treasonable. . . .

There are Socialists, plenty of them, who are loyal, patriotic, thoroughly American. There are Socialists who in this time of stress are directly, designatedly, perversely, perniciously, and seditiously the opposite. . . . They are condemned, not because they are Socialists, but because they are anti-American and practically pro-German.

Our people, while their sons are dying in Europe for justice, right, truth, honor, and the future of the United States and civilization, will not much longer tolerate disloyalty, sedition, treason, here at home.[49]

The St. Louis *Republic* (successor to the old *Missouri Republican* of Judge Peck's time) saw no need to equivocate over proposals to curb speech. Referring to objections to the pending bill on the ground that it would violate the First Amendment's guarantee of free speech, the *Republic* said:

This provision of the Constitution has been cited times without number to prove that the Government of the United States is powerless against any loud-mouthed agitator who desires to incite a riot or prevent the enforcement of a law. But the Constitution cannot receive any such interpretation.

There never was any such thing in the United States as freedom to encourage treason. There never was any freedom in this country to aid the enemies of the country by word of mouth or any other way. There can be no law which abridges a freedom that never existed.

Congress has power to punish treasonable utterances because its first duty is to maintain the Government of the United States.[50]

After referring to the most broadly restrictive provision of the bill—that penalizing any language calculated to cast contempt or scorn upon the government—the *New York Tribune* undertook to answer the Hearst papers, which, according to the *Tribune*, had "attacked it [the bill] as an attempt to make mere words treasonable." The Hearst papers, which of course had as much claim as any others to First Amendment protection, were critical of the bill for different motives than the Socialists. While the Socialists wanted freedom to disseminate a broad range of ideological opinions, including their antiwar views, Hearst's interests were personal. The strongly pro-German dispatches from Berlin that were published by the Hearst press, and which presumably might get the Hearst chain in trouble with the government, were prompted by Hearst's own long-standing anti-British feeling. For similar reasons, Hearst had opposed U.S. entry into the European conflict up to the time of the declaration of war.[51]

Noting that the American press had had "very little" to say about the sedition bill, the *New York Tribune* saw little reason for Hearst's alarm.

Nobody seriously believes that a sane government would ever undertake to suppress proper criticism in this country, or that such an attempt, if made, could possibly succeed.

At the end of the amendment it is provided that "nothing in this act shall be construed as limiting the liberty or impairing the right of any individual to publish or speak what is true, with good motives for justifiable ends." And if that clause were not written into the law it would be read into it by the first court called upon to apply it.

The *Tribune* concluded reassuringly that restraints self-imposed by the press would be much more effective than any the government would think of imposing. "It would astonish the government," said the *Tribune*, ". . . to know how much journalistic truth the newspapers, for patriotic reasons, omit to print."[52]

On April 23 the Philadelphia *Evening Telegraph* took note of President Wilson's opposition to the Chamberlain bill, which would have made violators of espionage and sabotage laws subject to court-martial. While conceding that the bill was a radical one of doubtful constitutionality unless the whole country were to be made a military zone with civil law suspended, the *Telegraph* declared that the "provocation" for the measure was great, the Justice Department having failed in so many prosecutions for violation of the Espionage Act. The *Telegraph* was concerned that Socialist candidates in Minnesota, having been convicted of violating the law, were at liberty on bond while their cases were being appealed and were doing the same thing for which they were found guilty. Acknowledging that the Chamberlain bill was deficient in that it did not "appear to discriminate as to the degree of the offense," the *Telegraph* observed that a "more effective law to deal with enemy spies is clearly necessary."[53]

Two weeks later the *Telegraph* was ready to accept the Senate-House conference committee's version of the sedition bill even though the conference report had eliminated the Senate provision that the law should not apply to truthful statements made with good motives. "Any thing," said the *Telegraph*, "which serves to curb sedition and enable the Government to bring spies and traitors to punishment will have the approval of the loyal people of the nation." The paper concluded:

The Department of Justice has complained that it had not sufficient law. With this Act adopted the Attorney General and the Postmaster General will have unprecedented powers. Such powers must be exercised with discretion no less than with vigor.

They are given for the protection of the country against its enemies, alien or native. Healthy public sentiment would never consent to their use to suppress honest and loyal expression of criticism.[54]

On the same day the Washington *Evening Star* found in an event of the day a reason for supporting the proposed law. The *Star* took editorial note of a meeting in New York of the "People's Council" at which a man who had served time in Canada for sedition spoke and at which Scott Nearing urged people to carry propaganda literature in handbags to be distributed, since under the new law it would be impossible to use the mails. "All this sort of thing," the *Star* said, "is the best possible justification for enactment of the law. . . . It is evident that if not curbed by more specific laws the anti-war ultra-bolsheviks and pro-German pacifists will continue their agitation to undermine the popular support of the government."[55]

The New Orleans *States Item* was even more emphatic in its support of the sedition bill.

The law is not intended to curtail liberty of expression by those who are all for the United States and all against the Prussian autocracy. It is only meant to reach and punish the alien or the false citizen who abuses the privileges he enjoys here. . . .

Loyal and patriotic citizens . . . may still form and express opinions regarding proposed policies, and they may even differ with the President before a proposed policy becomes a real policy, provided they express themselves within bounds. . . .

But the disloyal citizen or the enemy alien ought to be muzzled and punished as this law proposes he shall be, and the only matter for regret is that Congress did not pass the law when we entered the war instead of waiting until now.[56]

In the nation's capital the *Washington Post* added its voice to the press chorus in favor of rooting out disloyal utterances. The *Post* declared:

If the Department of Justice carries out the policy it has enunciated for the detection of disloyalty, it will be able to accomplish much toward rooting out the nests of pro-Germans which are known to exist in various parts of the country. . . . The Attorney General has issued instructions to the district attorneys to keep in touch with the newspapers in their districts. . . .

People should take the Attorney General at his word, and whenever they believe they have found information which would assist the prosecuting officers of the government in weeding out sedition they should communicate with the nearest representative of the Department of Justice.[57]

The *Seattle Times*, while admitting that the sedition bill was a drastic measure, observed that a law "had to be passed enabling the courts to deal promptly with cases where individuals openly used abusive, profane, scurrilous or contemptuous language about the United States. . . ." With the statute in effect, the *Times* said, "there will be no excuse for popular action and it is sincerely to be hoped that the law everywhere and under all circumstances will be permitted to take its course."[58]

In Philadelphia the *Press* saw no threat to free speech or a free press from the sedition bill and commented:

The truth is that the new law does not prohibit criticism of public officials. Under this statute, people still have the right to complain of official incompetency or error. As the law was originally contemplated, such criticism would have been made impossible, But, as it finally passed, it prohibited utterances disloyal to the country, but not specific criticisms of official error or malfeasance.[59]

Among the rare press voices raised against the sedition bill were those of the Socialist papers. More than a month before the adoption of the law, the New York *Evening Call* noted that Senator George W. Norris of Nebraska had opposed a provision that would give the postmaster general the power to order nondeliverable all mail to the address of any firm or individual who may be "suspected of disloyalty." The *Evening Call* related that Norris had said, "It will accomplish little if we establish democracy abroad and autocracy at home." The Socialist paper went on to observe sarcastically that "a newspaper that would hint of 'establishing an autocracy at home' would subject itself to the bitter scorn and possible punishment from the powers at Washington. But in the Senate . . . how safe it is to utter words and voice sentiments that are denied to the man in the street or at the editor's desk![60]

Several weeks later the *Call* reminded its readers of the curtailment of freedom of speech in seventeenth-century England and in the United States under the Alien and Sedition Laws of 1798 and recalled Jefferson's remark: "The sedition law is no law and I will not obey it if it comes in the way of my functions." Referring to the provisions of the pending 1918 sedition legislation, the *Call* said: "No such power should be put in the hands of any official in a democracy."[61]

Two days before the bill became law, the Milwaukee *Leader* observed disconsolately that it could not share the view of the *New York Evening Post* that "the author of the New Freedom" [Woodrow Wilson] would not put his signature on the bill. The *Leader* expected the president to sign the measure or allow it to become law without his signature. In any case, the paper thought that the country would later repudiate those responsible for the act. Its editorial concluded that all the observer "has to do is look back a little over a century and see what happened to the men and the party that enacted the similar sedition law in the early days of the republic."[62]

While the sedition amendment to the Espionage Act was making its way through Congress, the *New York Times* again manifested its lack of sympathy for freedom of expression. The particular issue was not the sedition bill but an even harsher measure, introduced by Senator Thomas J. Walsh of Montana, to outlaw any organization that advocated changes in industry, society, or government by the use of force, violence, or physical injury to property. Senator Walsh explained later that he introduced the bill, aimed especially at the Industrial Workers of the World (IWW), to "outlaw the entire organization, to make it a crime to belong to it." The *Christian Science Monitor* called the bill—which, incidentally, did not pass— "more severe and drastic in character than anything hitherto proposed."[63] The *New York Times*, in an editorial headed, "Our Bolsheviks," supported the Walsh legislation.[64]

Although many of the IWW's leaders advocated sabotage and, like the leaders of other radical organizations, engaged in violent rhetoric in the heat of debate, the IWW as an organization never advocated destruction or violence as a means of accomplishing industrial reform. Like other syndicalist organizations, the IWW did advocate strikes as a means of improving working class conditions, and strikes did often lead to violence. But the IWW was probably responsible for far fewer strikes as the nation was gearing for war than other, less damned labor organizations. The IWW did not officially oppose the war, although many of its leaders did, seeing the conflict as a business man's war.[65] Because many of its members were immigrant workers who did not want to become involved in a European military struggle, the IWW became a prime target of sedition legislation.

In addition to supporting the Walsh bill, the *New York Times*, during the time that the Sedition Act was being considered, editorialized against the "seditious talk" of Socialists.[66] On the day the bill became law, the paper favored a proposal of the League for National Unity calling for the election the next fall of a Congress that is "100 per cent loyal."[67] But the *Times* apparently had nothing to say directly on the Sedition Act itself.

In the critical days just before and just after the adoption of the Sedition Act, the harshest law against freedom of speech and freedom of the press ever enacted in the United States, many other papers seemed to think that the legislation raised no issues worthy of comment. No editorials questioning the law during this period could be found in the *Boston Evening Transcript*, the *Atlanta Constitution*, the Louisville *Courier Journal*, the *St. Louis Post-Dispatch*, the *Chicago Tribune*, or the *San Francisco Chronicle*.

On May 26, however, the *Post-Dispatch* editorially praised Nebraska and Texas for adopting disloyalty acts aimed at antiwar speakers and writers.[68] The *San Francisco Chronicle* a few days earlier declared:

> We must get rid of the nonsensical idea that drastic measures which would effectively put an end to the activities of the law-defying element would be an interference with the freedom of speech, or that the suppression of publications advocating the destruction of society would be an invasion of the liberty of the press.[69]

As the Espionage Act went on the statute books, it accentuated the pressure for political orthodoxy on the war. Zechariah Chafee, in his authoritative work on free speech during World War I, described how far the government went in curbing the expression of opinions that were thought to have even the slightest impingement on war policies. Judges, Chafee showed, were swept up in the fervor for conformity on the war. Opinions were treated by the courts as statements of fact and then were condemned as false if they differed with a presidential speech or the resolution of Congress declaring war. Nearly all of the convictions, Chafee determined, were for expressions of opinion about the merits and conduct of the war. Advocacy of heavier taxation instead of bond issues was treated as a crime. Convictions were handed down for saying that conscription was unconstitutional, although the Supreme Court had not yet held it valid; for saying that the sinking of merchant vessels was legal, for urging that a referendum should have preceded the declaration of war, for saying that war was contrary to the teachings of Christ, for criticizing the Red Cross and the Y.M.C.A. Free discussion among civilians, even in the home, as to the justice and wisdom of continuing the war were perilous. Citizens reported each other to the government for alleged disloyal or pro-German utterances.[70]

In the political climate of the time, citizens did not even wait for the Department of Justice to act. On February 12, 1918, in Staunton, Illinois, a mob—stirred by the cry that it was Lincoln's birthday—rushed the homes of suspected pro-German citizens, dragged them into the street and forced them to kiss the flag. Other suspected German sympathizers, if they could play musical instruments, were forced to play "The Star Spangled Banner." Homes of the alleged disloyalists were searched for German flags, but none were found. The police—who, it was reported, had sufficient strength to stop the mob—looked the other way. The next day the *St. Louis Globe-Democrat* commented with evident relish that "it was a Lincoln's birthday celebration, such as Staunton had never before witnessed."[71]

The *Globe-Democrat*'s stance was hardly unusual. Instead of protesting against the curbing of dissent, many newspapers joined the crusade for political orthodoxy. Socialists, many of whom happened to be of German extraction, vehemently opposed the war and were vehemently denounced in the press for doing so. In September 1918, Socialists held a meeting in New York to name candidates for Congress. The *New York Times* editorially proclaimed:

These German Socialists, while to the misfortune of the United States they are technically citizens, are at heart and by their own words irreconcilable aliens, alien enemies. The Department of Justice, which is not averse to harassing patriotic Americans incidentally, might do worse than keep an eye open for the disloyal and treacherous purposes of these accomplices of Germany.[72]

At the same time that the *Times* was suggesting that the Justice Department keep an eye on Socialists, federal prosecutors were in the process of imprisoning Eugene Debs, a leader of the Socialist party who had three times been its candidate for president of the United States. Debs was no transplanted German, having been born in Terre Haute, Indiana. On June 29, 1918, Debs had been indicted under the Espionage Act by a federal grand jury in Cleveland for a speech made earlier to a state Socialist convention in Canton, Ohio. Debs was outraged over the Wilson administration's suppression of Socialists and had gone to Canton with the thought of inviting prosecution. He did not feel that he should be free while others were in prison for saying what he believed.

In the speech Debs reiterated the party's opposition to all capitalistic wars. He praised the Russian Bolsheviki, condemned Prussian militarism and pointed out that Socialists had consistently opposed the Kaiser. Denouncing the treatment of Socialists under the Espionage Act and the double standard in its enforcement, he declared that one of his fellow Socialists, Rose Pastor Stokes, had been sentenced to ten years' imprisonment for expressing in a letter to the *Kansas City Star* criticism of the government far less severe than Theodore Roosevelt had written in the same paper. Socialists, he said, had "come to realize . . . that it is extremely dangerous to exercise the constitutional right of free speech in a country fighting to make democracy safe in the world."[73]

Debs said not a word about enlistment, and his address was not made to soldiers. Nor was any evidence offered to show that anyone had actually resisted the draft as a result of listening to him.[74] But he was indicted for, among other things, attempting to cause insubordination, disloyalty, mutiny, and refusal of duty in the armed forces and attempting to obstruct the recruiting or enlistment service.[75] At his trial in September, Debs and his attorneys admitted the facts but not the charges of law violation presented by the government. Their sole argument was that the Espionage Act violated the First Amendment.[76] Debs pointed out to the court that the Mexican War had been opposed by Abraham Lincoln, Daniel Webster, Charles Sumner, and Henry Clay.[77] (Like some other champions of free speech, however, Debs was not always consistent. The next year he was to argue that the Soviet government, because the Russian Revolution was "a forward step," was right to suppress free speech and a free press, whereas it was wrong to suppress free speech in his own case because American participation in the war was "a reactionary step.")[78] The defense arguments made no impression; Debs was convicted and sentenced to ten years in prison.

Although the conviction of Debs was widely reported, the silencing of this well-known leader of the Socialist party was also widely ignored as a subject worthy of editorial comment. In the several days immediately following the verdict, no editorials on the Debs case appeared in the *New York Times*, the *Boston Evening Transcript*, the *Atlanta Constitution*, the *Atlanta Journal*, the *St. Louis Post-Dispatch*, the Denver *Times*, the *Rocky Mountain News*, or the *San Francisco Chronicle*. In an editorial paragraph, the *Washington Evening Star* confined its comment to the observation: "Eugene Debs is about to make another move in a conspicuously checkered career."[79] The Louisville *Courier Journal* said:

He [Debs] set out to incite disloyalty, by familiar methods, to obstruct recruiting, to encourage every slacker, sulker and skulker in the land, in the aggregate a considerable number in any country in any war. Mr. Debs harangued his audiences with the vigor that was in him. With care that proved futile in that it did not save his bacon, he avoided treason. He did not, as the verdict in Cleveland indicates, oppose "the cause of the United States." He assaulted the Government's methods. Like a wise old rat trying to get the bait without springing the trap, Mr. Debs . . . worked gingerly, but . . . he got his paws in the trap. . . . He is landed. . . .[80]

With the press contributing to the public attitude of intolerance rather than supporting the right to dissent, vigilante groups flourished. Among them were: the Terrible Threateners, the Sedition Slammers, the American Anti-Anarchy Association, the Anti Yellow Dog League, the All-Allied Anti German League, the Liberty

League, the Knights of Liberty, and the American Rights League. The most prominent was the American Protective League, an organization with 250,000 members formed with the approval and operating under the direction of the Department of Justice as a kind of unofficial auxiliary. This group became an enforcer of patriotism, turning citizens into spies against those thought to be engaging in seditious talk and causing the persecution of many who were guilty of nothing more than honest skepticism.[81]

During the hostilities with the Germans, hysteria over the danger from antiwar sentiment remained at fever pitch in the United States despite the protection of three thousand miles of ocean and three allied navies and despite the virtual impossibility of an invasion. The press helped fan the popular opposition to dissent, although, with the national existence unthreatened, the sacrifice of First Amendment rights was by any reasonable measure hardly a justifiable necessity.[82] Despite the encouragement of citizens to become informers and the resulting arrests of thousands, not a single enemy plot was discovered after the nation went to war. Nor was any evidence of sabotage produced.[83]

Yet in 1919, the year after the war ended, the nation was still preoccupied with a perceived threat from foreign sources. In that year the Milwaukee *Journal* was awarded a Pulitzer Prize "for its strong and courageous campaign for Americanism in a constituency where foreign elements made such a policy hazardous from a business point of view."[84] Whether its campaign took courage or not, the *Journal* had enjoyed a great deal of company in upholding patriotism. When Wisconsin editors commented on the Espionage Act and related laws, it was usually to urge their strengthening. Newspapers in the state did little or nothing to discourage the rising mob spirit during the course of the war. The Milwaukee *Sentinel* called free speech "a phony issue" being raised by disloyal elements.[85]

The Denver *Rocky Mountain News* in March 1919, nearly four months after the war ended, still displayed zeal for stamping out disloyalty. A front page headline in that paper said: "Disloyal May / Escape Law's / Full Penalty." The news article reported that Attorney General Gregory had recommended commutation of the sentences of those convicted by juries where the evidence was only circumstantial.[86] In the same issue the *News* editorially welcomed a Senate plan to investigate bolshevism in America.[87]

If wartime fears contributed to the pervasive bias against freedom of expression, one might think that, after the war, when the time came for the Supreme Court to judge the validity of the 1917 Espionage Act and the 1918 Sedition Amendment, the press at least might have seen more clearly the implications of these laws for free speech and a free press. But the immediate postwar period did not become a time of calm reflection. The climactic judicial test of the Espionage Act came in the Schenck case on March 3, 1919, when the Supreme Court unanimously upheld convictions under the 1917 law against a challenge that it violated the First Amendment.

The *Schenck* decision admittedly was not an easy touchstone by which to measure the commitment of the press to freedom. Chafee said this case represented one of the few prosecutions under the 1917 Espionage Act "where there was clearly incitement to resist the draft." The defendants, Charles T. Schenck and Elizabeth Baer, were convicted under the act's provisions for their part in the printing and mailing of circulars to draftees, calling conscription unconstitutional despotism arranged in the interest of Wall Street and urging the recipients in impassioned language to assert their rights. "Such utterances," said Chafee, "could fairly be considered a direct and dangerous interference with the power of Congress to raise armies."[88] The view expressed by Chafee, as will be shown, was later rejected by other authorities.

A circumstance that added credibility to the Supreme Court's position in the *Schenck* case was that the opinion for a unanimous court was written by Justice Oliver Wendell Holmes, a man with a well-deserved reputation as a liberal social philosopher. Holmes, in a passage that was to become famous in American law, said:

We admit that in many places and in ordinary times the defendants in saying all that was said in the circular would have been within their constitutional rights. But the character of every act depends upon the circumstances in which it is done. . . . The question in every case is whether the words used are used in such circumstances and are of such a nature as to create a clear and present danger that they will bring about the substantive evils that Congress has a right to prevent. It is a question of proximity and degree. When a nation is at war many things that might be said in time of peace are such a hindrance to its effort that their utterance will not be endured so long as men fight and no Court could regard them as protected by any constitutional right.[89]

Although Holmes affirmed the *Schenck* conviction, his enunciation of the "clear and present danger" test served the cause of free speech and press in notable ways in relaxing the grip of the so-called bad tendency test by which expression had been measured by the courts for several decades before World War I. Harold L. Nelson in his book, *Freedom of the Press from Hamilton to the Warren Court*, said the *Schenck* decision aided the cause of free speech

in serving as an opening wedge that helped force courts to think out the content of the First Amendment; in evoking, with its elaboration and refinement, some of the noblest thought and language about the democratic ideal that the American judiciary has produced. Expressed in subsequent opinions such as Holmes's dissents in *Abrams* v. *U.S.* and *Gitlow* v. *New York*, and Justice Brandeis' concurrence in *Whitney* v. *California*, it had an impact far beyond the judicial arena, serving as a rallying point for the foes of restraint and giving them a phrase (no doubt at times a catch phrase used as a substitute for thought) for their banner.[90]

Despite its eloquence and its usefulness to free speech, however, Holmes's *Schenck* opinion did not go uncriticized by proponents of greater latitude for expression, nor did it last as a serviceable definitive test. During the thirty-five years after the enunciation of the "clear and present danger" concept, the test was characterized variously as too lenient, too harsh, too vague for use. Over the long term it was used more often perhaps in cases that resulted in convictions for expression than in those in which expression was protected. After the 1951 case of *Dennis* v. *U.S.*, involving the prosecution of the leaders of the Communist party, it underwent a decline in usage.

As Ernest Sutherland Bates pointed out, Holmes's phrase still represented a tendency test—whether the words for which the defendant was being prosecuted would have a tendency to bring about the "clear and present danger." It left the application of the law in any given instance to a matter of conjecture, since, as Bates said, "men's conception of danger is notoriously subjective: a danger clear to one will be laughed at by another." There is a fundamental difference, observed Bates, between the Holmes test and the rule laid down by Thomas Jefferson: "It is time enough for the rightful purposes of civil government for its officers to interfere when principles break out into overt acts against peace and good order."[91]

Professor Thomas I. Emerson of the Yale Law School, an authority on the First Amendment, has also found the "clear and present danger" test "clearly unacceptable."[92] Justice Hugo Black explicitly repudiated the test, saying:

> . . . it is sometimes said that Congress may abridge a constitutional right if there is a clear and present danger that the free exercise of the right will bring about a substantive evil that Congress has authority to prevent. . . . Again, it is sometimes said that the Bill of Rights guarantees must "compete" for survival against general powers expressly granted to Congress, and that the individual's right must, if outweighed by the public interest, be subordinated to the Government's competing interest in denying the right. . . .
> I cannot accept this approach to the Bill of Rights.[93]

But whether the evaluation of the *Schenck* decision is positive or negative, most commentators would agree that the decision was an important one in the literature of free speech. Yet at the time not a single major newspaper among nine checked had any editorial comment on the decision. No editorials on *Schenck* appeared in the *New York Times*, the *Washington Evening Star*, the *Boston Evening Transcript*, the Louisville *Courier Journal*, the *Atlanta Constitution*, the *St. Louis Post-Dispatch*, the Denver *Times*, the *Rocky Mountain News*, or the *San Francisco Chronicle*, although four of these papers had news items on the decision.

During the same week as the *Schenck* decision, however, the *San Francisco Chronicle* editorialized on another freedom of expression issue. The *Chronicle* indicated that it was pleased with the Sacramento *Bee* for its editorial censuring a corporation for bringing suit against the San Francisco paper in several counties of California. The *Chronicle* agreed with the *Bee* that this multicounty litigation was a means of harassing the newspaper and was a threat to freedom of the press.[94] At this time, incidentally, the *Chronicle* was publishing every day over its front page logotype a skyline banner proclaiming: "This Newspaper Is One Hundred Percent American."

A few days after the *Schenck* decision, the Supreme Court unanimously sustained the Debs conviction, saying that the First Amendment issue had been decided by the *Schenck* case. Chafee observed that Debs was probably convicted for the exposition of socialism, a result that was allowed by the wide scope given the jury in the trial judge's charge. Justice Holmes, who again wrote the opinion for the high court, was, according to Chafee, willing to accept the jury's verdict as proof that actual interference with the war was intended and was the proximate effect of the words used.[95] Yet the most extreme statement that Debs had made in his speech was that "you need to know that you are fit for something better than slavery and cannon fodder."[96] The jury was allowed to apply the loose, subjective test that these words had a "tendency" to bring about resistance to the draft.[97] The *Debs* decision was widely reported in the press, but few papers commented on it.

In its editorial on the decision, the *New York Times* at least credited Debs with courage. The *Times* asserted that, "unlike nearly all the rest of his fellow-believers, who were lions on the platform and mice in court, he did not act the baby or seek for loopholes. He had the courage of his convictions. He challenged the law, and the challenge has been met." But the *Times* saw no reason to question whether the Espionage Act was too broad or whether Debs's words posed a real danger to the country. The editorial went on to say:

Debs openly violated the law . . . and rested his case on his own theory of the Constitution. That theory, in a nutshell, was that the Government had no power to defend itself against unbridled speech, even though that speech might lead to the Government's own destruction. . . . His theory amounted simply to the impossible doctrine that he had full liberty to overturn the Constitution, but that the Government had no power to stay him.

. . . So the consequences which Debs invited have now fallen on his head. That is all there is of the case.[98]

The *Washington Evening Star* said simply that the Espionage Act had been upheld in the Debs case and concluded: "The law has proved effective, with teeth in it."[99] In Cleveland the *Plain Dealer* said with evident satisfaction: "Debs's voice is now stilled as it should have been stilled long ago. Doctrines such as he has been pleased to preach are not to be tolerated. The question of free speech is in no wise involved. It is a question of national safety." Commenting on the Debs decision, the Denver *Times* said that "he was condemned, instead of coddled, for violation of the law's express provisions against disloyalty. . . . He made the big mistake, as did La Follette and several others who interpreted the low mumbling of pacificism as the spirit of the American people."[100]

The *Atlanta Constitution* published a news account of the *Debs* decision but had no editorial on the case. However, the Atlanta paper, only two days after the decision, carried a comment on another event in the news that expressed opposition to the concept of a free press. The *Constitution* noted that the solicitor of the Post Office Department had submitted to the Senate a mass of memoranda and a long list of propaganda publications of the I.W.W., radical Socialists, anarchists, and "other malcontents." "Unless the government goes to grips with this thing in earnest and annihilates it," the *Constitution* warned, "sooner or later it is going to get the upper hand on government."

Two years later, when Socialists announced a plan to peacefully picket the White House in favor of clemency for Debs and other political prisoners, the *Constitution* was outraged:

There ought to be a stop put to this whole 'picketing' business.

It is fundamentally wrong both in principle and performance.

It is not democratic, but exactly the opposite. It is nothing more nor less than a species of coercion. . . . if there is no law to prevent this silly, un-American and detrimental practice, one should be enacted and put into operation.[101]

In St. Louis the *Post-Dispatch* reported the *Debs* decision but had no comment at the time. Two years later, however, the *Post-Dispatch* showed some sympathy for Debs and the principle of free speech. Commenting on a Justice Department recommendation of commutation of the Debs sentence, effective February 12, 1922, the St. Louis paper said "Debs violated the espionage act and gloried in his offense. He was justly sentenced." However, the *Post-Dispatch* criticized Wilson for not approving the recommendation for clemency.[102] Three days later the *Post-Dispatch* denounced Debs for criticizing President Wilson but went on to assert that "when neither national honor nor national safety is at stake those whose offenses consisted not of criminal acts, but merely disloyal speech, should be released from prison. The controlling consideration is national safety, not the expression of opinion."[103]

The Supreme Court's 1919 decision upholding the conviction of Debs was editorially ignored at the time by the *Boston Evening Transcript*, the Louisville *Courier Journal*, the *Rocky Mountain News*, and the *San Francisco Chronicle*, although all of them reported the ruling.

In terms of its significance for free speech and a free press at the time, the Supreme Court's 1919 decision in the *Abrams* case was far more important than the Debs decision eight months earlier. As the only case involving the 1918 Sedition Act to come before the high court, *Abrams* gave the tribunal a unique occasion to comment on the act's sweeping restrictions on freedom of expression. Jacob Abrams and four other young Russian immigrants had been arrested for throwing from a factory window in New York City a shower of leaflets denouncing the sending of American troops to Vladivostok and reiterating some typical Socialist admonitions derived from the Communist Manifesto of 1848. They were convicted in October 1918 on all of the four counts of an indictment charging them with conspiracy to violate the act by (1) publishing abusive language about the U.S. form of government, (2) publishing language intended to bring the U.S. form of government into contempt, (3) encouraging resistance to the United States in the war, and (4) inciting curtailment of production of war materials.[104]

Although the defendants had in fact protested against the invasion of their native country, they were actually tried for opposing the war with Germany. An attempt to show that the Russian expedition was not a legitimate part of war had been overruled by United States District Judge Henry De Lamar Clayton with the frivolous comment—typical of many he made during the trial—that the "flowers that bloom in the spring, tra la, have nothing to do with the case."[105] The *New York Times* praised Judge Clayton for his "half-humorous" methods and observed that "Judge Henry D. Clayton deserves the thanks of the city and of the country for the way in which he conducted the trial." [106] The judge's methods were hardly calculated to induce the jury to consider the case on the basis of the evidence, which did not include any showing that one person was led to stop any kind of war work or even that the leaflets had reached a single munitions worker.

On appeal to the Supreme Court the defendants, besides contending that the Sedition Act was unconstitutional, maintained that it was not violated and, in particular, that the criminal intent required by the express terms of the statute did not exist. The high court's majority opinion, upholding the convictions, dismissed in two sentences the defense challenge of the act's constitutionality under the First Amendment. [107] The opinion merely cited decisions on the Espionage Act of 1917 to establish the validity of the much more objectionable provisions of the 1918 law. Speaking for the majority, Justice John H. Clarke explained the court's finding of the required specific intent to hinder the war with Germany by saying:

> It will not do to say . . . that the only intent of these defendants was to prevent injury to the Russian cause. Men must be held to have intended, and to be accountable for, the effects which their acts were likely to produce. Even if their primary purpose and intent was to aid the cause of the Russian Revolution, the plan of action which they adopted necessarily involved, before it could be realized, defeat of the war program of the United States, for the obvious effect of this appeal, if it should become effective, as they hoped it might, would be to persuade persons . . . not to aid government loans and not to work in ammunition factories. . . . [108]

Thus the court construed the act so as to make the remote tendency, the possible incidental consequences, of the leaflets a valid basis for conviction. Besides giving scant weight to the First Amendment, the court ignored the many prejudicial actions of the trial judge that may have led to the conviction. [109] For the first time in the war-related First Amendment cases, Holmes and Justice Louis Brandeis dissented. Writing for himself and Brandeis, Holmes said that the intent required by the statute to hinder the prosecution of the war was not shown. The Holmes opinion, which was to help move a majority of the court to adopt its reasoning in later cases, said in part:

I do not doubt for a moment that by the same reasoning that would justify punishing persuasion to murder, the United States constitutionally may punish speech that produces or is intended to produce a clear and imminent danger that it will bring about forthwith certain substantive evils that the United States constitutionally may seek to prevent. The power undoubtedly is greater in time of war than in time of peace because war opens dangers that do not exist at other times.

But as against dangers peculiar to war, as against others, the principle of the right of free speech is always the same. It is only the present danger of immediate evil or an intent to bring it about that warrants Congress in setting a limit to the expression of opinion where private rights are not concerned. Congress certainly cannot forbid all effort to change the mind of the country. Now nobody can suppose that the surreptitious publishing of a silly leaflet by an unknown man, without more, would present any immediate danger that its opinions would hinder the success of the government arms or have any appreciable tendency to do so. . . .

In this case sentences of twenty years have been imposed for the publishing of two leaflets that I believe the defendants had as much right to publish as the Government has to publish the Constitution of the United States now vainly invoked by them. . . . when men have realized that time has upset many fighting faiths, they may come to believe even more than they believe the very foundations of their own conduct that the ultimate good desired is better reached by free trade in ideas—that the best test of truth is the power of the thought to get itself accepted in the competition of the market. . . . I think that we should be eternally vigilant against attempts to check the expression of opinions that we loathe and believe to be fraught with death, unless they so imminently threaten immediate interference with the lawful and pressing purposes of the law that an immediate check is required to save the country.[110]

Although the *Abrams* decision represented a serious setback for First Amendment protection, the case received scant notice in the press at the time. Holmes's passionate defense of freedom of expression—a dissent that was to become a classic in First Amendment legal literature—was in the process also ignored. Of seven major newspapers checked—the *New York Times*, the *Washington*

Evening Star, the *Boston Evening Transcript*, the *Louisville Courier Journal*, the *Atlanta Constitution*, the *St. Louis Post-Dispatch*, and the *San Francisco Chronicle*—none had an editorial on *Abrams* immediately following the decision. Only four—the *New York Times*, the *Washington Evening Star*, the *Boston Evening Transcript*, and the *Atlanta Constitution*—appear to have had news reports on the decision, and these were brief and inconspicuous.

During the same period as the *Abrams* decision six of the seven papers had editorials on other subjects that were insensitive to First Amendment rights. Commenting on a decision of the House of Representatives to exclude Victor Berger from the seat to which he had been elected, the *New York Times* said Berger "had no case at all" in his plea to be seated. The *Times* blamed Berger for the "treasonable Socialist platform of 1917" denouncing the war.[111] Berger had been barred from the House because of his alleged disloyalty in opposing the war. The House ignored the precedent of the Civil War when, at that conflict's very height in 1864, the Democratic party had elected members on a platform in opposition to the war, and those members were duly seated.[112] The lawmakers also disregarded Berger's argument that honored Americans of the past—Daniel Webster, Henry Clay, and Charles Sumner—had suffered no reprisals for vigorously denouncing the Mexican War.[113]

Like the *Times*, the *Washington Evening Star*, the *Boston Evening Transcript*, and the *San Francisco Chronicle* approved the exclusion of Berger. The *Star* commented: "Any other action would have shocked and astounded the country."[114] The *Transcript* went even further by endorsing an American Legion resolution that called on Congress to pass legislation punishing Victor Berger by deporting him.[115]

Two days after the *Abrams* decision, the Louisville *Courier Journal* noted a Justice Department seizure of an anarchist manifesto calling for revolution. The editorial declared: "It is high time to take drastic measures against the anarchists."[116] The *St. Louis Post-Dispatch* said the "administration's determination to deport radical aliens who are preaching and campaigning for the violent overthrow of our government will be endorsed by public opinion." The editorial went on to say that "the leaders should be gotten rid of."[117]

Editorializing against anarchist societies, the *San Francisco*

Chronicle said the "first step is to define illegal associations and penalize membership in them"—in the case of the foreign-born, by deporting all of them; in the case of native Americans, by "permanent disfranchisement and deprivation of all civil rights."[118]

A half a century after the *Abrams* decision historian Henry Steele Commager made the ironic comment that, if Abrams were still alive, he "might have the dubious consolation of knowing that almost everyone agrees with his argument" that the Wilson administration should not have sent troops to Russia.[119]

Not long after the Supreme Court affirmed the convictions of the defendants in the *Abrams* case, the Justice Department launched one of that period's most sweeping actions against radical opinion. Under the direction of Attorney General A. Mitchell Palmer, in January 1920 federal agents raided hundreds of places where radicals were known to meet. The dragnet arrests swept up everyone in or near the premises, including chance passers-by—in all, four thousand persons. Without the authority of arrest warrants, the agents hauled their victims to jail, where many of them were held incommunicado. Books, papers, and pictures in the raided places were seized without search warrants. Hundreds of aliens were summarily deported without even having the chance to notify their families. The press generally approved the deportation of the alleged radicals, having already reported the discovery by the Justice Department of a great conspiracy against the government evidenced by the reputed uncovering of a quantity of bombs in New Jersey. Later reports revealed, however, that only three pistols had been found in the countrywide raids and no explosives at all. Many of the raided meetings had actually been held at the behest of government agents who had infiltrated the radical groups as members in order to facilitate the planned arrests.[120]

In the midst of the Red Scare, fanned by Attorney General Palmer, a score of sedition bills were introduced in the Senate and House. To gain support for the legislation to authorize suppression of left-wing pamphlets, Palmer declared:

The continual spread of the seeds of evil thought, the continual inoculation of poison virus of social sedition, poisonous to every fiber and root, to every bone and sinew, to the very heart and soul of all that by our standards is integrity in citizenship or personal character cannot help but foster frightfully the revolutionary disease. Is there . . . no Government policy . . . that can stand effectively for social sanitation? [121]

Although the nation was no longer at war in 1920, press comment still reflected a sense of danger in the air that overshadowed any latent squeamishness about First Amendment rights. Commenting on the Palmer raids, the *New York Times* said:

If some or any of us . . . have ever questioned the alacrity, resolute will, and fruitful, intelligent vigor of the Department of Justice in hunting down these enemies of the United States, the questioners and the doubters have now cause to approve and applaud. . . . The more of these dangerous anarchists are arrested, the more of them are sent back to Europe, the better for the United States.[122]

The *Washington Evening Star*, going beyond approval of the arrest of the alleged radicals, wanted no demonstrations in their behalf. On January 2 the *Star* declared:

Those who are marching in the open and who are proclaiming a purpose to come to Washington to petition for the release of the jailed seditionists and propagandists of disorder and revolt are just as malevolent, though their methods are different, as those who meet in secret and plot with bombs . . . and who print the vile leaflets they are now circulating surreptitiously through the very mails.[123]

In the national capital also the *Washington Post* spoke with equal vehemence, saying:

The time has come when foreign enemy propaganda must be prevented from utilizing freedom of speaking and printing in America for the purpose of destroying America itself. The abuse of free speaking and printing must be defined and punishment provided. . . . The right of free speech, printing and assembly in the United States should not include the right to preach bolshevism directly or indirectly.[124]

In St. Louis the *Globe-Democrat* saw no need to make excuses for what was being done. That paper said:

Free speech is as open to them [immigrants] as to all others. Here is given all the personal freedom that is consistent with the protection of society. America demands no more of the stranger within its gates than obedience to its laws and respect for its institutions. But these strangers, these uninvited intruders . . . are a public menace, an intolerable nuisance, and our self respect, as well as the safety of our people demands their expulsion from the country.[125]

The *St. Louis Post-Dispatch* was among the few papers to question the methods being used. In an editorial on the Palmer raids, the *Post-Dispatch* observed:

The right and duty of our government to protect itself and to guard our institutions against revolution and unlawful action and propaganda are unquestioned. . . . But the dragnet is not a good police device. . . . Let us clean up the revolutionists and the propagandists of disorder, lawlessness, and violence. But let us do it in a sane, legal, orderly manner. Let the government proceed to arrest by warrant those against whom there is evidence of guilt and punish those who are proved guilty. Free government cannot be saved by the destruction of the pillars upon which it stands—free speech, free assemblage, and freedom from official oppression in any form.[126]

A few days later the *Post-Dispatch* was even more emphatic. The arbitrariness of the methods being applied had become more apparent. The *Post-Dispatch* expressed displeasure, declaring:

We do not object to sedition laws as a means of defense against disorder, but as a mainstay of free government, founded upon the consent of the people and controlled by the will of the majority, registered through the ballot box, they are jokes. . . . The last governments which depended upon sedition laws and bureaucratic police for their maintenance were the imperial governments of the Czar, the Kaiser, and the Austrian Emperor. Where are these governments now?[127]

In questioning the proposed new sedition laws, the *San Francisco Examiner* showed a rare perception among major daily papers of the meaning of the First Amendment, even though its position was qualified.

It is right to deport trouble making aliens who come to war upon American institutions. It is well to send them back to their own country. The first duty of a government is to repel a foreign invasion. This duty extends, we think, to the invasion of a foreign disease or of alien germs that menace the welfare of the nation.

But we do not think the obnoxious aliens are more dangerous than the tendencies of some American statesmen. These officials are trying to change our laws so that any American citizen who DISAGREES WITH THEIR IDEAS or advocates a change in government may be sent to jail for twenty years.[128]

No such doubts about the trend against free speech were exhibited in Denver, where the Denver *Times* ran an editorial entitled, "Stern Rule for Anarchists," which called for their deportation.[129] The *Rocky Mountain News* foresaw positive good emerging from the raids: "the lasting benefits which will come from these 'red' raids will be the awakening of the nation to the necessity of guarding . . . against . . . the snapping of our American ideals in favor of exotic doctrines, discontent with the orderly processes of government and political truckling to the alien vote."[130]

Among the important free press cases that arose during the war, two of the last to be decided by the Supreme Court involved Victor Berger. The decisions were handed down early in 1921. On January 31 the court reversed Berger's conviction under the Espionage Act on the ground that the trial judge had been prejudiced, not that the law was defective. Derogatory remarks about German Americans made by Judge K. M. Landis before the trial caused the high court to say they showed an "objectionable inclination or disposition of the judge" that disqualified him from sitting.[131] After the trial, Landis had said he regretted that the law did not allow him "to have Berger lined up against a wall and shot."[132]

The *New York Times*, however, saw no reason for upsetting Berger's conviction. Its editorial on the Supreme Court's action said that "so far as can be discovered, the 'prejudice' attributed to Judge Landis was shared at the time and is now shared by all patriotic Americans. It was a prejudice in favor of the United States as against Germany, in favor of the law and against the breakers of the law."[133] In the same editorial, the *Times* hailed President Wilson's "refusal in the face of great pressure to commute the sentence of Eugene V. Debs" as a "triumph of justice."

On March 7, 1921, the Supreme Court upheld Postmaster General Burleson's order of October 1917 denying second class mail rates to Berger's Milwaukee *Leader*. Writing for the majority, Justice Clarke curtly dismissed the *Leader's* claim that it had been deprived of the rights of a free press. Clarke noted that the Espionage Act, under which the postmaster general had acted, had been held valid in *Schenck*. He argued, moreover, that the postmaster general had withdrawn the *Leader's* second class privilege but had not excluded it from other classes of mail. All the petitioner had to do, said Clarke, was to mend its ways, publish a paper conforming to the law, and apply again for its second class privilege.[134] This was equivalent to saying, however, that the postmaster general was the ultimate editor of all publications wishing to benefit from the second class rate.

Justices Brandeis and Holmes dissented, Brandeis saying the decision could "determine in large measure whether in times of peace our press shall be free." Brandeis denied that, under the law, the postmaster general had the power, as exercised in this case, to deny the second class rate to a newspaper on the grounds that it violated the Espionage Act; it might be held not mailable but not denied a favorable rate. Moreover, said Brandeis, the postmaster general could not, on the basis of a judgment of some issues of a newspaper, exclude future issues of the paper from the mail as a preventive measure or as a punishment. If such power were possessed, the dissenter said, the postmaster general "would, in view of the practical finality of his decisions, become the universal censor of publications." Brandeis, with Holmes agreeing, said that the government might decline altogether to distribute newspapers or decline to carry any at less than the cost of the service, but it could not, without violating freedom of the press, single out as unqualified for the second class rate those newspapers whose views were deemed to be against public policy.[135]

No decision of the Supreme Court had gone so far in upholding governmental powers over the press as that in the Milwaukee *Leader* case. Yet not one of the nine great newspapers across the country that were checked had an editorial protest against the decision. Most of the papers reported the decision in their news pages but ignored it on their editorial pages. The *Boston Evening Transcript* declared editorially that Holmes and Brandeis were wrong in dissenting. This case is one, the *Transcript* said, "where the judgment of the court coincides not only with the general opinion but with plain common sense and public necessity." The paper saw the issue as a simple one in which Berger could have gone on using the mails if he had cut out false reports and false statements in his paper.[136]

During the week of the Milwaukee *Leader* decision, the *St. Louis Post-Dispatch* had nothing to say on that subject but did print an editorial on a free speech issue further removed from newspapers. The *Post-Dispatch* opposed movie censorship in a sharply worded editorial which said in part: "Have we not had enough of moral prigs clothed with authority and armed with legal bludgeons to dragoon us into their pinched standards of life and conduct, art and literature?"[137] The *New York Times*, the *Washington Evening Star*, the *Atlanta Constitution*, the *Atlanta Journal*, the *Chicago Tribune*, the Louisville *Courier Journal*, and the *San Francisco Chronicle*, like the *Post-Dispatch*, editorially ignored the Milwaukee *Leader* decision even though the Brandeis and Holmes dissents should have alerted the press to its threatening import.

Twenty-five years later, in 1946, the Supreme Court was to take a different view when it overruled the postmaster general's revocation of the second class mail rate of *Esquire* magazine. Justice Douglas, writing for the majority, cited the Holmes and Brandeis dissents in the Milwaukee *Leader* case. But in *Hannegan* v. *Esquire* the Court did not explicitly reverse the decision in the *Leader* case.[138]

In the vigorous dissents of Holmes and Brandeis during the immediate postwar years came the first murmurings of a judicial inclination to uphold the First Amendment as a barrier against intrusion by the government into the domain of press freedom. But the press at the time—except for Socialist papers and an occasional outcry from other publications—can hardly be said to have been in sympathy with the cause of protecting minority press opinion from governmental suppression. Indeed, many newspapers were little more than cheerleaders for the prosecutors of the unorthodox press.

10

The Supreme Court Applies the First Amendment

In the years following World War I, when the Supreme Court began making pronouncements on what the First Amendment meant for press freedom, a convenient touchstone for evaluating the attitude of the press toward its own special guarantee became available. If a litigant took an issue as far as the Supreme Court, and if the tribunal undertook to rule on it, the matter was presumably one of significance for the nation. Moreover, the requirement that two sides formulate their positions in arguments before the court helped to define and sharpen the freedom of expression issue and to give it the kind of prominence that should have commanded the attention of the institution—namely, the press—most likely to be affected by an authoritative judicial pronouncement. Whether the high court was sympathetic or not toward the claimed First Amendment right, its judgment should have provided an obvious basis for press comment.

Press reaction to some of the Supreme Court's first decisions involving the First Amendment—in the *Schenck*, *Abrams*, *Debs*, Milwaukee *Leader*, and *Berger* cases—has already been noted. In none of them did the high court uphold the claimed right of First Amendment protection. The justices, having for generations not hesitated to uphold property rights of the wealthy,[1] seemed reluctant to venture into the unfamiliar legal waters of freedom of expression protection for dissenters who often challenged the prevailing economic and social order.

In the 1920 case of *Gilbert* v. *Minnesota* the Supreme Court upheld a Minnesota sedition law and the sentence of a Non-Partisan League speaker convicted under it for saying the United States had been stampeded into the war "by newspaper rot to pull England's chestnuts out of the fire for her." Justice Brandeis, in dissent, described the statute as "an act to prevent teaching that the abolition of war is possible." Five years later, in 1925, the Supreme Court upheld the conviction under a New York criminal anarchy law of Benjamin Gitlow, a leader of the left wing of the Socialist party, for publishing in the party's newspaper, *Revolutionary Age*, a tedious justification of a dictatorship of the proletariat and an appeal for a general strike.[2] In dissent, Justice Holmes advanced a boldly permissive doctrine: "If in the long run the beliefs expressed in proletarian dictatorship are destined to be accepted by the dominant forces of the community, the only meaning of free speech is that they should be given their chance and have their way."[3]

Although the Court in the *Gitlow* case upheld the New York law, the majority opinion by Justice Edward T. Sanford was significant in that it proclaimed: ". . . we may and do assume that freedom of speech and of the press—which are protected by the First Amendment from abridgement by congress—are among the fundamental personal rights and 'liberties' protected by the due process clause of the Fourteenth Amendment from impairment by the States."[4] Having never invalidated an act of Congress for being in conflict with the First Amendment, the Supreme Court was hinting that it might overthrow state laws. Gitlow's lawyer, Walter Pollak, although he lost the case for his client, had won what was to prove an important principle of law.[5]

The *New York Times*, still committed to orthodoxy, saw no need, in commenting about the case, to be concerned about freedom of speech or press.

Yesterday's decision of the Supreme Court in the Gitlow case is, in its essence, simply a reaffirmation of an old principle of law and government. Any constituted Government is entitled to protect itself against overthrow by violence. It can make the use of force against it-self a crime. . . . Two dissenting justices argue that the utterances of Benjamin Gitlow did not involve an "immediate danger" to the Government of New York. Doubtless this is true. . . . But there is such a thing as a moral peril in addition to one merely physical. And the Supreme Court is of the opinion that an open incitement to violence against the State is a moral peril against which the State may lawfully protect itself by a stringent statute.

There is no denial of free speech.[6]

But some major newspapers were beginning to concede that freedom of expression should not be just for the social pillars of the community. In St. Louis the *Post-Dispatch* declared that

the wisdom of such acts as the New York Statute and the Supreme Court's validating opinion is questionable. The danger of soap-box vehemence is imaginary. Justice Holmes' dissenting opinion is . . . that of a philosopher. . . . He would let the fire alarm clang, serenely con-fident there would be no blaze. . . . Justice Holmes knows that our Government cannot be protected from verbal assaults by suppression, nor can our institutions be secured by jailing their critics. . . . The permanency of our Governments rests on the faith and intelligent loyalty of the people. If that faith falters and that loyalty withers the Government is doomed and statutes and court judgments will not avail to save it.[7]

Even the *St. Louis Globe-Democrat*, which was inclined to be more alarmist on such subjects than the *Post-Dispatch*, questioned the *Gitlow* decision, observing that:

The right of free speech vested in the individual is to be exercised in conformity with the right to protect itself and to preserve public order vested in the government. The danger under such laws is that mean-ings not so intended may be attached to certain terms of our flexible language and that phrases and figures of speech may be unfairly construed as advocating the use of arms against the government and so be made an occasion of political harassment and oppression es-pecially under war stress or at other times of high feeling. That, in even Gitlow's case, not only Justice Brandeis, but as clear a thinker as Justice Holmes, while upholding the statute, declared the language he used had been wrongfully interpreted and constituted no offense whatever, is at least worthy of attention.[8]

Six years after the *Gitlow* decision the Supreme Court had under review a Minnesota statute that empowered courts in that state to enjoin as a public nuisance the publication of newspapers or periodicals judged to be "malicious, scandalous and defamatory." Truth was a defense only if "published with good motives and for justifiable ends." The *Saturday Press* of Minneapolis had published articles stating that a Jewish gangster was in control of gambling, bootlegging, and racketeering in the area and charging that law enforcement officials, including the county attorney, were guilty of gross neglect in allowing such conditions to exist. The accused county attorney sued under the gag law to have the newspaper suppressed. The trial judge granted a permanent injunction against the *Saturday Press*. J. M. Near, publisher of the paper, appealed to the Minnesota Supreme Court for relief and was turned down, whereupon he appealed to the United States Supreme Court.[9]

Chief Justice Charles Evans Hughes, speaking for a five-member majority of the Court, ruled the Minnesota law, so far as it authorized the proceedings in the *Near* case, to be an "infringement of the liberty of the press guaranteed by the Fourteenth Amendment." In thus invalidating a state law for the first time on grounds that it infringed press freedom, Hughes said:

> If such a statute, authorizing suppression and injunction on such a basis, is constitutional, it would be equally permissible for the legislature to provide that at any time the publisher of any newspaper could be brought before a court . . . and required to produce proof of the truth of his publication . . . and of his motives, or stand enjoined. If this can be done, the legislature may provide machinery for determining in the complex exercise of its discretion what are justifiable ends and restrain publication accordingly. And it would be but a step to a complete system of censorship.

Hughes also observed that the fact that the liberty of the press may be abused by miscreant purveyors of scandal does not make any the less necessary the immunity of the press from previous restraint in dealing with official misconduct.[10]

But the chief justice noted that protection as to "previous restraint is not absolutely unlimited," and went on to suggest that the government might prevent the publication of military information in wartime and might even restrain "obscene publications."[11] (This qualification was to trouble the press in the Pentagon Papers case in 1971.)

Among the leading newspapers checked, those that commented all welcomed the *Near* decision. Like the rest, the *New York Times* had a positive reaction: "Its [the Court's] decision will amply reward those who saw from the first the peril that lay in the Minnesota law." But true to its position—maintained at least since World War I—that sedition (the excitement of discontent against the government) was outside the limits of press freedom, the *Times* noted that sedition, as well as other excesses, was not covered by the protection afforded by the *Near* decision. Under the heading, "Free But Responsible," the *Times* editorial said that "if they [irresponsible persons] flaunt obscenity, the police can come down upon them. If they preach sedition or advocate overthrow of this Government, the appropriate statutes can be snapped upon them like handcuffs. . . ."[12] The *Washington Post* declared:

In making void the Minnesota law attempting to abridge the liberty of the press the United States Supreme Court has swept aside a subtle and dangerous innovation which, if not thus stopped, might have worked great mischief in that State. . . .

The power to suppress a periodical, if lodged in public officers, would lead to irremediable wrong, whereas abuse of liberty of the press is a wrong that can be remedied. The Supreme Court has decided this case on the solid ground of public interest.[13]

In a strong editorial entitled, "A Decision Against Press Censorship," the *Boston Evening Transcript* said: "The court we are sure did a good day's work for liberty and justice in invalidating the Minnesota law."[14] The Louisville *Courier Journal* saw in the decision a protection of the courts as well as other institutions.

If it [the law] had been held constitutional, Minnesota's example would have been emulated by political machines throughout the country, resulting not only in press censorship, but in the corruption of the judiciary to control the censorship. . . .

The integrity of the courts is the ultimate reliance of a free people, but their freedom from political molestation must rely ultimately on freedom of speech and of the press. . . .[15]

The *St. Louis Post-Dispatch*, in an editorial quoting favorable reactions to the *Near* decision by the *New York Herald Tribune*, the *Kansas City Star*, and the Houston *Post-Dispatch*, observed that, by "holding unconstitutional the Minnesota newspaper gag law, the United States Supreme Court reaffirmed the great democratic principle of freedom of the press."[16]

In Denver the *Rocky Mountain News* noted the narrowness of the majority on the high court. Its editorial, headed, "End of Gag Law," said:

Freedom of the press was upheld Monday by the U.S. Supreme Court. But the margin was dangerously close.

In the 5-to-4 decision, the new liberal majority . . . saved one of America's basic rights. The Minnesota press gag law was declared unconstitutional. . . .

It should be obvious . . . that the laws of libel give necessary and adequate protection. . . .[17]

The *San Francisco Chronicle* called attention to the importance of the case for the press in general by recalling that it had been taken up by the American Newspaper Publishers' Association. The *Chronicle* declared that the Minnesota law "erected an authority by which any newspaper could be suppressed by the dictum of a pliant judge on the mere complaint of a corrupt official. . . . Happily the Supreme Court has put an end to that danger."[18]

After the Supreme Court decision, Robert R. McCormick, publisher of the *Chicago Tribune*, was widely acclaimed by newspaper publishers for having seen to it that their collective interests were defended. The *Tribune* had entered the controversy over the *Saturday Press* in 1928, had brought the case to the attention of the Publishers' Association and had led the move to appeal the decision of the Minnesota Supreme Court.[19]

Not all major newspapers, however, considered the *Near* decision so significant as to require comment. In Atlanta the *Journal* and the *Constitution* both reported the decision in their news columns, but neither paper saw fit to editorialize on the case in the days immediately after the ruling, although editors holding a national convention in Atlanta at the time were reported as applauding the decision.[20]

The *Near* decision came in a year when the Supreme Court, with a changing membership, took the first step of a twenty-year trend toward a more liberal position on freedom of expression.[21] In a series of cases in the 1930s the high court upset the convictions of a young woman for raising a red flag at a California children's camp,[22] of a Communist speaker in Oregon,[23] and of a distributor of Communist literature in Georgia.[24] It held that peaceful picketing was a form of free speech and threw First Amendment safeguards around meetings in public parks, parades, and pamphlet peddling.[24] All of these decisions were important for freedom of expression.

During this period the Supreme Court followed the doctrine that First Amendment rights had a "preferred position" against state regulation. The next significant ruling after *Near* that affected newspapers came in 1936 in *Grosjean* v. *American Press Co.* The case arose as a result of an act of the Louisiana legislature imposing a special 2 percent tax on the gross advertising receipts of newspapers with twenty thousand or more circulation a week. Approved at the behest of the political machine of Governor Huey Long, which controlled the legislature, the tax fell on only 13 of 163 newspapers in the state, 12 of which were outspoken critics of Long. The nine publishers of the affected newspapers brought suit in the United States District Court to enjoin enforcement of the tax law. A permanent injunction was granted, and this lower court decision was unanimously affirmed by the Supreme Court.[26]

After reviewing the history of newspaper tax laws as a form of restraint on the press in Great Britain and in Massachusetts in 1785, Justice George Sutherland declared the Louisiana tax law an abridgement of the liberty of the press as guaranteed by the due process clause of the Fourteenth Amendment—not because newspapers should be immune from ordinary forms of taxation for the support of government but because this tax was imposed "with the plain purpose of penalizing the publishers and curtailing the circulation of a selected group of newspapers." Sutherland made clear that the protection against the federal government provided by the First Amendment and against the states provided by the Fourteenth Amendment was not limited to immunity from previous restraints on publication. In summarizing the purposes behind the decision, Sutherland wrote:

> The predominant purpose of the grant of immunity here invoked was to preserve an untrammeled press as a vital source of public information. The newspapers, magazines, and other journals of the country, it is safe to say, have shed and continue to shed, more light on the public and business affairs of the nation than any other instrumentality of publicity; and since informed public opinion is the most potent of all restraints upon misgovernment, the suppression or abridgement of the publicity afforded by a free press cannot be regarded otherwise than with grave concern.[27]

Press reaction to the *Grosjean* decision among those newspapers checked was universally laudatory. Quoting a passage from the Supreme Court's opinion saying that to "allow the press to be fettered is to fetter ourselves," the *New York Times* added simply: "Here is a precedent set up for the protection of the press in this country."[28] The *Boston Evening Transcript* used a superlative in its assessment of the danger that had been averted, saying the Louisiana tax, "now happily thrown into the discard, constituted the worst threat to a free press that this country has so far experienced. . . . The Supreme Court, rightly and by unanimous judgment, refuses to countenance any legislation of this sort."[29]

The *Washington Evening Star* saw national ramifications, observing:

> No free press could exist under such a law. If a statute of that character were held to be constitutional in one State it would be equally constitutional in the other forty-seven. If a State law making such provisions were constitutional, then a Federal law of similar design would be constitutional. There is no free press under a dictatorship. And without a free press the people hear only one side of a

a controversy, one set of alleged facts. The rest is suppressed. They are denied an opportunity to judge for themselves the wisdom or value of the government imposed upon them. . . .

In this opinion no effort was made to deny the right of government to tax the owners of newspapers for the support of government. . . . But the right of government to force, through devastating taxation, newspapers to publish only what government desires published or to cease publication is a vastly different thing.[30]

A similar theme was expressed by the *Washington Post*: ". . . the importance of the decision extends far beyond the confines of Louisiana. If the law had been permitted to stand, it would have jeopardized the freedom of the press in every State of the Union."[31]

In Atlanta the *Journal* congratulated the Louisiana newspapers that had challenged the advertising tax law, which the *Journal* said had obviously been "designed to punish and intimidate that portion of the State's press" that had criticized the "tyrannous regime" of the late Huey Long. After quoting the Supreme Court decision at length, the *Journal* asserted that "every friend of democracy and lover of freedom will rejoice that so deadly a weapon has been struck, once and for all, from the hand of an unscrupulous tyranny, and will hope that the time is not distant when its last shameful relics will be swept away."[32] The *Atlanta Constitution* had nothing to say about the decision; nor did the Louisville *Courier Journal*.

The *St. Louis Post-Dispatch* printed the text of the Supreme Court decision in its news columns and in its editorial columns said:

Had there been no court to invalidate this law, the people of Louisiana would be confronted with a statute seriously threatening the fundamental constitutional guaranty of freedom of the press. . . . The Post-Dispatch has said repeatedly that the guaranties of the Bill of Rights need the protection afforded by judicial review of the acts of legislative bodies. Huey Long's attempted gag rule in Louisiana is a striking case in point.[33]

The previous day the *Post-Dispatch* had editorially supported the right of Earl Browder, secretary of the American Communist party, to speak at a meeting of the American Civil Liberties Union in a Springfield, Illinois, high school.[34]

In San Francisco the *Chronicle* made a point of noting that newspapers were subject to ordinary forms of taxation in their business character, and went on to observe:

> It is the special, arbitrary and discriminating tax, obviously designed to cripple their purely press function, that is banned. . . .
>
> The decision means that the Constitutional guarantee of freedom of the press cannot be nullified by codes, licenses, censorship, taxation or any other device.[35]

In the *Bridges* case in 1941 the Supreme Court imposed a curb on the long-asserted power of the courts to punish for contempt those who voiced or printed remarks held likely to prejudice the outcome of pending cases or otherwise to harm the administration of justice. The case arose as a result of California state court contempt convictions of labor leader Harry Bridges and of the publisher and editor of the *Los Angeles Times*. The two cases were joined before the high court.[36]

The struggle by the press over the power of the courts to limit press freedom had been going on since the beginning of the republic. A period of ascendancy for the press had been reached when Congress, following the 1831 impeachment trial of Judge Peck, had enacted a law providing that the contempt power of federal judges should extend only to misbehavior of persons in the presence of the courts or "so near thereto as to obstruct the administration of justice."[37] By 1860 twenty-three of the thirty-three states had adopted similar acts limiting the courts' summary contempt power.[38] Clearly federal and state lawmakers had intended judges' power to punish for contempt to be restricted to contemptuous behavior in their immediate presence or very near the court in a geographical sense.

In 1855, however, the Arkansas Supreme Court had ignored the prevailing trend by upholding the conviction of a newspaper for publishing an account suggesting that the Arkansas Supreme Court itself had accepted bribery in a murder case. In so doing, the state high court rejected an Arkansas statute limiting the courts' power to cite for out-of-court, or so-called constructive contempt.[39]

More than forty years after the Peck impeachment trial, the United States Supreme Court sustained the 1831 federal act that grew out of it. Speaking for the Court in *Ex parte Robinson* in 1873,

Justice Stephen J. Field recognized the power of Congress to restrict the reach of federal judges. In state courts, meanwhile, a trend toward adoption of the Arkansas doctrine had begun, with many tribunals holding that, regardless of legislative enactments, courts had an inherent power to punish for contempt those publications having a "reasonable tendency" to interfere with the orderly administration of justice.

By 1907 in a case originating in Colorado (*Patterson* v. *Colorado*), the United States Supreme Court lent its support to the power of state courts to cite as contemptuous publications those that "would tend to obstruct the administration of justice" while a case was pending. Pendency was the essential criterion, according to Justice Oliver Wendell Holmes, who observed that once the case was closed, courts were subject to the same criticism as other institutions, but until then they should not be denied the power to prevent interference with the course of justice by "premature statement, argument or intimidation."[40] The Court ruling ignored the possibility that, by the time press criticism was allowed, an injustice that might otherwise have been checked or corrected by criticism, might be irreversible.

As complaints against the press in United States courts became more pointed through the years, judges took a more expansive view of the federal contempt power despite the supposedly restrictive legislation of 1831. By 1918 the judicial reversal of the contempt doctrine of the 1831 statute was complete, although the act had never been repealed. In that year the Supreme Court considered a case in which a judge had cited the Toledo, Ohio, *News-Bee*[41] for contempt for publishing a series of articles involving a transit company dispute, then before the federal court, in which the paper concluded that there could be but one decision by the judge (one against the streetcar company) and that any other would evoke suspicion of the judge's integrity and fairness and would prompt public resistance. The high tribunal upheld the lower court's contempt action and, in interpreting the 1831 act, construed in a causal rather than a geographical sense its authorization of punishment of contemptuous behavior "so near" to the court "as to obstruct the administration of justice."

Chief Justice Edward D. White, speaking for a majority of five, said the act of 1831 "conferred no power not already granted and imposed no limitation not already existing"—a statement so para-doxical as to confound the drafters of any statute. On the constitu-tional issue, White declared:

... however complete is the right of the press to state public things and discuss them, that right, as every other right enjoyed in human society, is subject to the restraints which separate right from wrong-doing. . . . Not the influence upon the mind of the particular judge is the criterion but the reasonable tendency of the acts done to influence or bring about the baleful result is the test.

In making the criterion a "reasonable tendency" to bring about a baleful result, the Court left contempt proceedings against the press, regardless of where the offense occurred, largely to the discretion of the trial judge, with the implication that his discretion would not be questioned unless greatly misused. Holmes and Justice Louis Brandeis dissented; two other justices took no part.[42]

For more than two decades after the Toledo *News-Bee* decision, the doctrine of contempt by publication seemed to be firmly rooted in American law. Then in 1941 came the Supreme Court's ruling in *Nye* v. *United States*[43] that effectively overruled the *News-Bee* de-cision, rejected the "reasonable tendency" test, and once more con-strued the words "so near thereto" in a geographical sense so that as the 1831 act required, the cited misbehavior must occur in the vicinity of the court. Although the high court's reversal of the con-tempt conviction in the *Nye* case did not involve misconduct by a newspaper, the fact that alleged persuasion or coercion of a litigant occurred more than 100 miles from the site of the district court was taken by the Supreme Court as a reason for returning to the geo-graphical rule. This in turn had a bearing on the law respecting con-temptuous publications.[44]

Having discarded the "reasonable tendency" criterion in the *Nye* case, the Supreme Court in *Bridges* v. *California*,[45] decided the same year, felt obliged to refine the test for deciding when miscon-duct in the proximity of the court constituted contempt. The *Bridges* case, however, did not involve an interpretation of the federal con-tempt law, since the two contempt actions before the high court were taken in a California state court. One was the conviction of labor leader Harry Bridges for his publication of a telegram to the secretary of labor criticizing the decision of the judge in a case involving a labor dispute and threatening a strike if the decision was enforced. The other was the conviction of the publisher and editor of the *Los Angeles Times* for the publication of editorials commenting on a pending case in a state court.

Both convictions were reversed. The Supreme Court indicated that "neither 'inherent tendency' nor 'reasonable tendency' [to interfere with justice] is enough to justify a restriction of free expression." Instead the court prescribed as a test the concept that there must be a "clear and present danger," that "the substantive evil must be extremely serious and the degree of imminence extremely high before utterances can be punished."

The Supreme Court's decision in *Bridges* was announced on the day after the Japanese attack on Pearl Harbor. Evidently the *New York Times* and the *Washington Post* were editorially too preoccupied with the war to comment on the ruling. Although both papers reported the decision, neither had an editorial on it during the days immediately following the issuance of the opinion.

Other major newspapers, however, thought the *Bridges* case worthy of comment; of those papers checked, all welcomed the decision. The *Atlanta Constitution* said: "Another challenge to one of the inherent freedoms of this country, one of the freedoms which the young men of this country are again taking up arms to defend, has been met and put down."[46] In an editorial headed, "A Notable Decision," the *Atlanta Journal* said: "For this clarification of the rights of the press, we believe the people of America will have cause to be grateful to the majority of the Supreme Court."[47]

The Louisville *Courier Journal* clearly articulated the risks inherent in the broad contempt power that had been sanctioned prior to the *Nye* and *Bridges* decisions. The Louisville paper observed:

Freedom of the press received a substantial guarantee Monday from the United States Supreme Court that the Bill of Rights shall not be whittled away by judicial construction. . . .

The five justices concurring in the opinion, of course, could conceive the possibility of a powerful press actually overawing a judge on occasion; but that danger would not be as great as the continuing danger of unrestrained judicial power to overawe the press by the arbitrary authority of a judge to punish for any criticism he chooses to regard as having an inherent or reasonable tendency to interfere with his idea of the administration of justice. Such latitude of personal discretion could be used effectually to muzzle the press and leave the "corrosion of power" without any antidote.[48]

In St. Louis the *Post-Dispatch* declared:

In rebuffing the argument that comment on a judicial decision is not to be tolerated until the very last legal technicality has been met, Justice Black . . . took a practical working view of the constitutional guarantee against infringement on free speech. . . .

. . . he held it to be the duty of the courts not to see how, by lawyers' logic, they may narrow a provision of the Bill of Rights . . . but, on the contrary, to see how far the horizons of our liberty can be pushed.[49]

The *San Francisco Chronicle,* although it approved the *Bridges* decision, was not entirely satisfied:

No real guidance is set up by the decisions of the Supreme Court in the Los Angeles Times and Harry Bridges contempt cases. . . .

All we get, then, is a "working principle" that the evil must be "extremely serious and the degree of imminence extremely high before utterances can be punished." With this principle we can agree; unless there is real damage there is no real contempt.[50]

As in earlier periods of conflict, the approach of World War II brought demands to curb criticism of the government. More than forty sedition bills were introduced in the seventy-sixth Congress, which sat just prior to United States entry into the war. From these was distilled the Alien Registration Act (known as the Smith Act), Section 2 of which was modeled on the 1902 New York Criminal Anarchy Law. It became law on June 28, 1940, as the first national peacetime sedition statute since the Alien and Sedition Laws of 1798.[51] Part of Section 2 read:

It shall be unlawful for any person. . . . with the intent to cause the overthrow or destruction of any government in the United States, to print, publish, edit, issue, circulate, sell, distribute, or publicly display any written or printed matter advocating, advising, or teaching the duty, necessity, desirability, or propriety of overthrowing or destroying any government in the United States by force or violence.[52]

The law was similar to one that had been sought unsuccessfully by Attorney General A. Mitchell Palmer in 1920[53] and, according to Thomas Emerson, was an anachronism at the time it was passed, since internal security problems in the United States in 1940 were hardly likely to arise from public advocacy that the government be overthrown by force and violence. At the time the Communist party, against which the measure was most particularly directed, was in its united front phase calling for cooperation between the United States and the Soviet Union. Needless as the act was, it still posed a threat, by its explicit terms, to freedom of the press. Its restrictions on freedom of the press should have called forth protest from newspapers. Yet one study of sixteen newspapers across the nation, which were examined for the period that the Alien Registration Act was under consideration, found that only three papers in the sample carried editorials on the subject, and one of these supported the measure. The lack of editorial comment may have been due, however, to the haste with which the act was passed after Section 2 (pertaining to the press) was written into it.[54]

Whatever the reason for newspaper inattention to the Smith Act, the sixteen papers that were analyzed for the period when the act was under consideration were found nevertheless to be supportive of freedom of expression in 69.5 percent of their editorials dealing with a variety of subjects in which such freedom was an issue.[55] But in allowing the Smith Act to become law with little opposition, the press was to leave the government, as will be shown later, with a weapon designed to curb freedom of expression.[56]

The Smith Act was invoked only twice during the war—once, in a case in which eighteen members of the Socialist Workers party were convicted of conspiracy to violate the law. The Court of Appeals upheld the convictions, relying on the *Gitlow* decision; the Supreme Court declined to review the appellate court ruling. The second wartime use of the Smith Act occurred with the 1942 indictment of twenty-eight alleged pro-Nazis in the District of Columbia. The judge died during the course of the trial of these defendants, and the case was later dismissed.[57] Not until 1948 was the act to be invoked again, this time against the leaders of the Communist party of the United States. In this case the Smith Act was finally to be tested in the Supreme Court and held constitutional.

With the onset of World War II a system of voluntary domestic self-censorship for the press was established as it had been in World War I. The army and navy announced almost immediately their intention to invoke the Espionage Act of 1917 when necessary to protect military information of value to the enemy.[58] The Post Office Department undertook to keep suspect publications from using the mails. Although the department moved against Father Charles Edward Coughlin's *Social Justice* and against the Trotskyite *Militant*, no case involving postal restrictions of this kind reached the Supreme Court during the war. During World War II—except for the relocation and detention of Japanese Americans—the excesses against civil liberties of the World War I period were not repeated. There were, according to Zechariah Chafee, only seven reported criminal prosecutions for antiwar speeches and publications. The Supreme Court in 1943, in *Taylor* v. *Mississippi*, reversed the conviction of two defendants under a Mississippi sedition law for preaching that all modern nations, including the United States, were in the grip of demons. In *Hartzel* v. *United States* in 1944 the Court reversed the conviction under the Espionage Act of a defendant for distributing pro-Nazi, anti-British, and anti-Roosevelt material.[59]

The Supreme Court decision of the World War II period that probably attracted more editorial attention from the press than any other was the ruling on the government's antitrust action against the Associated Press. As a result of a complaint by Marshall Field, whose newly launched Chicago *Sun* had been barred from membership in the Associated Press and denied the right to purchase AP service, the United States attorney general had filed a civil action in 1942 charging the AP under the Sherman Antitrust Act with being a combination and conspiracy in restraint of trade and commerce in news among the states and with attempting to monopolize a part of that trade.

The heart of the government's charge was that the AP was operated under a system of by-laws which, by concerted action, had been written to prohibit all AP members from selling news to nonmembers and to grant each member the power to block its nonmember competitors from membership. The AP contended that extension of the Sherman Act to the press would violate the First Amendment, a claim that was echoed in much of the press of the nation.[60]

Because the Chicago *Sun* supported President Franklin D. Roosevelt against the Roosevelt-hating *Chicago Tribune*, the suit was seen as politically inspired. The *New York Daily News* said: "In the event of a government victory, the press services of the United States will be under the thumb of the White House." The *Detroit News* trumpeted: "We see in this, not the end perhaps, but surely the greatest peril to a free press in America." From its monopoly position in Kansas City, the *Kansas City Star* declared: "This is the sort of thing that belongs in the totalitarian states, not in a free democracy."[61]

Robert Lasch—who then worked for the Chicago *Sun* but who nevertheless was a reliable observer of press reaction to the AP suit—concluded that the above-quoted comments "were not extremist positions" but were in fact a fair sample of opinions handed down by the press long before the government brought its case to trial. The AP sought to buttress its position by publishing a large collection of editorials viewing the case with alarm.[62]

At the AP's annual membership meeting in 1942 the vote on Field's application for membership was 684 against and 287 in favor. McCormick, publisher of the *Chicago Tribune*, against which the *Sun* was competing, said: "It is not at all a question between Mr. Field and myself, but one between a free press and government coercion." With no attempt to disguise its editorial slant, the *Tribune* ran a news article saying the suit proposes to reduce the AP to the level of a public utility, subject to government regulation and control."[63] The Cincinnati *Enquirer* declared that the "government's remarkable suit against the Associated Press, on the grounds of monopoly, is a threat to the freedom of the press itself."[64]

Despite outcries from the press, a federal district court held that the by-laws unlawfully restricted admission to AP membership and violated the Sherman Act insofar as they clothed a member with powers to impose or dispense with conditions upon the admission of his business competitor. The Supreme Court, by a five-to-three vote (Justice Jackson did not participate) affirmed the judgment of the lower court. In his opinion for the majority, Justice Black noted that the court below had found that, out of 1,803 daily news-papers published in the United States, with a total circulation of 42,080,391, 1,179 of them, with a circulation of 34,762,180 were under a joint contractual obligation not to supply either AP or their own "spontaneous" news to any nonmember of AP.[65] Black observed:

It would be strange indeed . . . if the grave concern for freedom of the press which prompted adoption of the First Amendment should be read as a command that the government was without power to protect that freedom. The First Amendment, far from providing an argument against application of the Sherman Act, here provides powerful reasons to the contrary. That Amendment rests on the assumption that the widest possible dissemination of information from diverse and antagonistic sources is essential to the welfare of the public, that a free press is a condition of a free society. Surely a command that the government itself shall not impede the free flow of ideas does not afford non-governmental combinations a refuge if they impose restraints upon that constitutionally guaranteed freedom. Freedom to publish means freedom for all and not for some. Freedom to publish is guaranteed by the Constitution, but freedom to combine to keep others from publishing is not. . . . The First Amendment affords not the slightest support for the contention that a combination to restrain trade in news and views has any constitutional immunity.[66]

Justice Owen J. Roberts, one of the three dissenters, wrote:

The decree here approved may well be, and I think threatens to be, but a first step in the shackling of the press, which will subvert the constitutional freedom to print or to withhold, to print as and how one's reason or one's interest dictates. When that time comes, the state will be supreme and freedom of the state will have superseded freedom of the individual to print, being responsible before the law for the abuse of the high privilege.

It is not protecting a freedom but confining it to prescribe where and how and under what conditions one must impart the literary product of his thought and research. This is fettering the press, not striking off its chains.[67]

Contrary to the dire predictions of some papers, the AP did not become a regulated public utility. The news service was allowed to frame new rules of admission so long as they did not relate to the applicant's competitive status. As a result of the court decision, AP membership in a very few years did expand considerably, from 1,274 in 1943 (when the injunction was first granted) to 1,708 in 1949.[68] This obviously contributed to greater variety in the channels of information available to newspapers and, through them, to the public. The AP continued to flourish and to expand its services without any apparent outside restrictions on its freedom to cover and edit the news.

Wilbur Schramm in *Responsibility in Mass Communication* later wrote:

In retrospect, the press outcry seems a bit silly . . . the White House did *not* put its thumb on the wire services, no newspaper was restrained or censored. The question was commercial: whether a news service could be withheld from some newspapers for competitive reasons.

The dangerous element in all this is that the press puts itself in the position of crying "Wolf!" when it is threatened by a rabbit. It helps neither public understanding of freedom of the press nor public respect for the First Amendment to associate them with . . . restrictive membership in a news service.[69]

Government intervention to change the structure of the media (as in the AP case) so as to promote diversity offers a less risky way to protect freedom than intervention in matters of content, which poses the threat of censorship or control.[70]

Eight months later the Supreme Court acted in a case involving a government curb based on content. The postmaster general had revoked the second class mail permit of *Esquire* magazine on the ground that the magazine did not meet an 1879 law's requirement that a publication must be "for the dissemination of information of a public character, or devoted to literature, the sciences, arts, or some special industry," and have a legitimate list of subscribers. Although *Esquire* might not be technically obscene, the postmaster general suggested, there was ample proof that its writings and pictures were "morally improper and not for the public welfare and the public good." Certain regular features of the magazine, although a small percentage of the total bulk, were said "to reflect a smoking room type of humor, featuring in the main, sex."

In response to a suit by *Esquire*, a federal district court refused to grant an injunction against the postmaster general. The Court of Appeals reversed the district court, and the postmaster general appealed to the Supreme Court, which upheld the appellate court judgment. Writing for the Supreme Court, Justice Douglas said the controversy plainly was not over whether the magazine published information of a public character or was devoted to literature or the arts but over whether its contents were "good" or "bad." To uphold the order of revocation would, he said, "therefore, grant the postmaster general a power of censorship. Such a power is so abhorrent to our tradition that a purpose to grant it should not be easily inferred."[71] After reviewing the development of the postal laws, Douglas continued:

. . . a requirement that literature or art conform to some norm prescribed by an official smacks of an ideology foreign to our system. . . . What seems to one to be trash may have for others fleeting or even enduring values. But to withdraw the second-class mailing rate for this publication today because its contents seemed to one official not good for the public would sanction withdrawal of the second-class rate tomorrow from another periodical whose social or economic views seemed harmful to another official. . . . Congress has left the Postmaster General no power to prescribe standards for the literature or the art which a mailable periodical disseminates.[72]

While acknowledging that Congress could constitutionally make it a crime to send fraudulent or obscene material through the mail, Douglas said "grave constitutional questions are immediately raised once it is said that the use of the mails is a privilege which may be extended or withheld on any grounds whatsoever." He cited the dissenting opinions of Holmes and Brandeis in the 1921 Milwaukee *Leader* case, thus implying that the court was repudiating the rationale of that case, if not expressly overruling the decision.

Press reaction was far more sympathetic to the protection of *Esquire*'s mailing privileges than it had been to the same claim for the Milwaukee *Leader* twenty-five years earlier. Then the issue had involved the allegedly seditious nature of the social and economic doctrines of the accused publication rather than allegedly salacious material. Even before the Supreme Court ruling, *Esquire* itself had published a sampling of editorials from eighteen newspapers, all taking issue with the postmaster general and some strongly protesting his order as a violation of freedom of the press.

The *New York Times*—which evidently had not considered the Milwaukee *Leader* decision important enough to comment on— said of the *Esquire* ruling:

The exhibits in the case . . . did convince it [the Court] that to censor Esquire now would sanction the withdrawal of the second-class rate tomorrow from another periodical whose social or economic views seemed harmful to another official. Certainly neither the makers of the Constitution nor any Congress intended to create a postal or any other kind of peacetime censorship.[73]

The key word in the *Times* editorial, entitled, "Defeat For Censorship," seems to have been "peacetime." Presumably the *Times* would have viewed the issue differently in wartime.

The *St. Louis Post-Dispatch*—which, like the *Times*, had editorially ignored the Milwaukee *Leader* decision—went even further than the court on the issue in the *Esquire* case. Observing that the court had denied the postmaster general's authority to withhold the second-class rate from a publication on the basis of the quality of its contents, the *Post-Dispatch* noted that the decision still left the postmaster general with the power to determine whether or not a publication was fit to enter the mails—that is, whether it was mailable at any rate. The St. Louis paper went on:

This, too, is a form of censorship involving danger to freedom of the press. In fact, the Postoffice's continued right to bar a periodical from the mails is an even greater power than the now abolished right to penalize it with higher rates.

Bills now pending in both houses of Congress would remove this power from the hands of the Postoffice and give it to the courts, where it obviously belongs. . . . Now that the Supreme Court has unanimously taken its stand against one-man censorship, as far as the Esquire case permitted it to go, Congress can finish the job by promptly passing the bills.[74]

In Denver the *Rocky Mountain News* declared: "It is no part of a postmaster general's business to penalize a publication for not conforming to his notion of what's good for the public. Justice Douglas, who wrote the Supreme Court decision, made that clear."[75]

The *San Francisco Chronicle* supported the Supreme Court decision but did not want to be understood as supporting obscenity. "The use of the mails, the Court found, is not a privilege which may be extended or withheld on capricious grounds. If it were, the Post Office might bar the mails to economic or political ideas it did not approve. . . . [But] obscenity is no shadowy matter. . . . If the Post Office sees the offense in the public prints it can proceed legally and after getting a conviction it will have warrant for barring the offenders from the mails."[76] The *Washington Post*, the *Atlanta Constitution*, and the Louisville *Courier Journal* all reported the decision in their news columns but had no editorial comment during the week of the decision.

Although the *Esquire* decision provided substantial protection for United States newspapers and periodicals, it did not protect periodicals mailed to the United States from overseas. In 1948, under a 1938 law aimed at Nazi literature, the government began intercepting unsealed mail from overseas containing alleged communist propaganda. Unless the addressee made a special request to the post office to receive the mail, it was destroyed. The practice was intended to cut the flow of communist tracts into the United States at cut-rate bulk prices. Persons with an interest in seeing the material felt that the screening interfered with First Amendment rights. Most recipients would fear that in acknowledging an interest in the officially disapproved reading matter, they would subject themselves to job discrimination or other forms of retaliation.

Acting on this rationale, President Kennedy in 1961 stopped the interception, only to have Congress a year later enact a law to authorize the practice. In June 1965 the Supreme Court in *Lamont* v. *Postmaster General*, for the first time in its 175-year history, struck down an act of Congress on the explicit ground that it violated the free speech and free press guarantees of the First Amendment.[77] Justice Douglas wrote: "We rest on the narrow ground that the addressee in order to receive his mail must request in writing that it be delivered. This amounts in our judgment to an unconstitutional abridgement of the addressee's First Amendment rights."[78]

A few months after the *Esquire* decision, the Supreme Court dealt again with the judiciary's use of its contempt power to curb criticism of the courts. A Florida trial court had found the publisher and associate editor of the Miami *Herald* guilty of contempt for criticizing local judges as being too lenient toward criminal defendants and saying the courts were being "subverted into refuges for lawbreakers." The contempt citation had charged that the publications impugned the integrity of the court, tended to create a distrust for the court, suppressed the truth and tended to obstruct the impartial administration of justice in pending cases. On appeal from the Florida Supreme Court, which upheld the convictions, the United States Supreme Court in *Pennekamp* v. *Florida* reversed the judgment.[79]

Justice Stanley Reed wrote for the Court: "We conclude that the danger under this record to fair judicial administration has not the clearness and immediacy necessary to close the door of permissible public comment. When that door is closed it closes all doors behind it."[80]

Commenting on the Supreme Court decision in *Pennekamp*, the *New York Times* said: "The courts ought to be, and will be protected against disorder and libel, but they ought also to recognize that the Bill of Rights is part of the basic law of the land, and that it permits criticism of public officials, judges not excepted.[81] The *Atlanta Journal* praised the decision, but added:

In granting so wide a latitude to journalistic censure the Supreme Court goes further than conscientious newspapers would wish to tread, though by no means would we intimate that the action of the Miami Herald was not fully conscientious as well as courageous. . . . A newspaper that is wilfully false to the truth is false to its readers who are its ultimate and inexorable judges.[82]

The *Atlanta Constitution* had no comment.

In the nation's capital the *Washington Post*, while welcoming the decision, took the occasion to lecture the press:

If it [the Supreme Court decision] warrants rejoicing, it calls no less for some sober reflection. For freedom of the press, like any other freedom, may be menaced not only by control from without but also by irresponsibility from within. In the exercise of any right, restraint is an inescapable corollary.

. . . restraint was scarcely evident in the Miami *Herald* editorials under consideration. These editorials impugned the motives of Florida judges on grounds which were, to say the least, unsubstantial.[83]

On the other hand, the Louisville *Courier Journal* saw the decision itself as encouraging responsibility: "The precious quality of free speech was described anew in a unanimous ruling. . . . Far from encouraging irresponsibility of expression, we have an idea that here is a very challenge to moderation."[84] In St. Louis the *Post-Dispatch* declared:

Justice [Frank] Murphy went further than any of his colleagues. "The freedom of the press," he affirmed, ". . . also includes the right to criticize and disparage, even though the terms be vitriolic, scurrilous and erroneous."

No respectable editor, of course, desires to be "scurrilous and erroneous," but he would certainly like to define the terms for himself rather than have them defined for him by a pompous, stupid or corrupt court possessed of the power to fine and imprison for "constructive contempt of court."[85]

In Denver the *Rocky Mountain News* and the *Denver Post* editorially ignored the *Pennekamp* decision, although it was in a Colorado case that the Supreme Court in 1907 had upheld the kind of state court contempt power that it was now diminishing in *Pennekamp*.[86]

The *San Francisco Chronicle* foresaw that the rationale of the Florida court's action could have gone a long way toward stemming criticism of the courts. Noting that the contempt citation had held that newspaper comment on a case while it was being tried contained the danger of influencing the courts toward improper decision, the *Chronicle* observed:

Improper comment admittedly contains such danger. But to enfold this theory into a general ruling would mean barring proper comment as

well as improper, and, since the Appellate courts would be identically
involved it would mean outlawing all comment until after decision by
the United States Supreme Court. Thus the courts would be insulated
against all criticism.

The Supreme Court wisely refused to accept such blanket theory. . . .[87]

In 1947 in *Craig* v. *Harney*, the Supreme Court reversed a Texas
state court contempt conviction of the editor of the Corpus Christi
Caller-Times for saying, among other things, that a judge's action
represented a "travesty on justice." Justice Douglas said for the
Court that "the law of contempt is not made for protection of
judges who may be sensitive to the winds of public opinion. Judges
are supposed to be men of fortitude, able to thrive in a hardy climate." This case—which, unlike *Bridges* and *Pennekamp*, involved
only private litigants—signaled the growing unwillingness of the
Supreme Court to sanction the use of the contempt power to curb
criticism of the courts or prejudicial publicity.[88]

The Supreme Court exhibited a continuing concern over the prejudicial impact of the press by reversing convictions that appeared
to have resulted in part from unfair publicity. Trial courts were in
effect being told to turn to other remedies than contempt citations,
such as granting motions for change of venue or postponement of
the trial.

Increased protection against the contempt weapon was clearly
pleasing to editors and publishers. In *Craig* v. *Harney* the American Newspapers Publishers Association had filed an *amicus curiae*
brief on the side of the Texas paper in which it noted that its membership embraced more than 700 newspapers whose publications
represented more than 80 percent of the total daily and Sunday
circulation of newspapers published in the United States.[89]

Although the issue of freedom of the press versus fair trial was
to be the focus of many Supreme Court cases in the twenty years
after *Craig*, those cases—including the leading 1966 decision in
Sheppard v. *Maxwell*—involved a judicial search for ways to dilute
the effects of prejudicial publicity rather than direct assaults on the
press. Not until the 1970s was the contempt citation to be significantly revived as judges again attempted to control the press by
issuing restrictions against printing what they perceived would interfere with the administration of justice.

11

Freedom of Expression Since World War II

Although the Supreme Court was generally support-
ive of the values of freedom of expression during the period from
1931 (the year of the decision in *Near* v. *Minnesota*) to 1951, its
rulings were by no means all favorable to unfettered expression.
In *Chaplinsky* v. *New Hampshire* (1942), for example, the court
upheld the municipal court conviction of a Jehovah's Witness who
during the course of distributing literature on the street had addressed a city marshal as "a God damned racketeer" and "a damned
Fascist."[1] speaking for a unanimous Supreme Court, Justice Frank
Murphy said:

. . . it is well understood that the right of free speech is not absolute at
all times and under all circumstances. There are certain well-defined
and narrowly limited classes of speech, the prevention and punishment
of which have never been thought to raise any constitutional problems.
These include the lewd and obscene, the profane, the libelous, and the
insulting or "fighting" words—those which by their very utterance inflict injury or tend to incite an immediate breach of the peace. . . . such
utterances are no essential part of any exposition of ideas, and are of
such slight social value as a step to truth that any benefit that may be

derived from them is clearly outweighed by the social interest in order and morality. . . .[2]

Despite its focus on a seemingly minor matter, this decision, by dictum at least, carved large chunks out of the First Amendment and was prophetic of the equivocal way in which the court would deal with such issues as libel and obscenity. In 1948 the Court, dividing four to four (Justice Felix Frankfurter disqualified himself), let stand a New York ban on grounds of obscenity of Edmund Wilson's highly acclaimed novel, *Memoirs of Hecate County*.[3] In 1952 the Court upheld an Illinois "group libel" law making it illegal to expose "the citizens of any race, color, creed, or religion to contempt, derision or obloquy. . . ." Joseph Beauharnais had been convicted of violating the law for publishing and distributing on the downtown streets of Chicago leaflets calling on his fellow Chicagoans "to prevent the white race from becoming mongrelized by the negro." Black and Douglas dissented from the decision affirming the conviction.[4]

The Court's ambivalence in dealing with the exceptions to First Amendment protection mentioned in *Chaplinsky* was evident in two other cases of this period. In 1949 the Court overturned the breach-of-the-peace conviction of Father Terminiello, a suspended Catholic priest, who had harangued a Chicago audience of sympathizers with a message of religious and racial hate while a mob of demonstrators outside hurled bricks and bottles. Although the police maintained sufficient control to allow Terminiello to deliver his entire speech—in which he hurled such epithets as "Communistic Zionistic Jews," "slimy scum," "snakes," and "bedbugs"—he was arrested afterward. Justice Douglas, writing for a five-member majority, declared that the

function of free speech under our system of government is to invite dispute. It may indeed best serve its high purpose when it induces a condition of unrest, creates dissatisfaction with conditions as they are, or even stirs people to anger. Speech is often provocative and challenging. It may strike at prejudices and preconceptions and have profound unsettling effects as it presses for acceptance of an idea. That is why freedom of speech, though not absolute, . . . is nevertheless protected against censorship or punishment, unless shown to produce a clear and present danger of a serious substantive evil that arises far above public inconvenience, annoyance, or unrest. . . .[5]

But in 1951, in *Feiner* v. *New York*, the court reverted to the "fighting words" doctrine of *Chaplinsky* when it upheld the disorderly conduct conviction of Irving Feiner, a young college student who had mounted a sidewalk soapbox in Syracuse and addressed an interracial crowd, some apparently hostile and some sympathetic, and called President Truman a "bum" during the course of a speech in which he urged Negroes to "rise up in arms and fight for their rights."[6]

Justice Black—who, along with Justices Douglas and Murphy, favored a preferred position for First Amendment rights and tended to view the protection of freedom of expression in absolutist terms —dissented.[7] With the deaths of Justices Murphy and Wiley Rutledge (who also often sided with Black and Douglas) in 1949, the Court had begun to retreat from its general stance of according a preferred position to the rights of free speech, press, assembly, and petition. Following a rationale espoused by Justices Frankfurter and Robert H. Jackson, the Court in the next few years tended to balance the guarantees of freedom against the wisdom and reasonableness of the social regulation.[8] (This was a tendency against which Black was to protest repeatedly.)

In viewing the various freedom of expression issues with which the Supreme Court continued to wrestle, it should be useful to think of them in terms of the three broad categories into which, according to Professor Franklyn S. Haiman of Northwestern University, most major cases of the twentieth century fall: (1) expression involving provocation to anger and the problem of preserving the peace (fighting words), (2) expression involving political heresy and the problem of national survival (national security), (3) artistic expression and the problem of public morality (obscenity).[9] As we have seen, the Court in *Chaplinsky* had already indicated that obscenity, libel, and fighting words were excluded from any certainty of protection.

In a 1951 case involving an alleged threat to the national security (*Dennis* v. *United States*),[10] the Court was to register its most precipitous retreat from the protection of political heresy since its affirmations of the convictions of World War I dissenters. But the decision in *Dennis* did not arise in a social vacuum; it can be better understood after a review of the years leading up to the ruling. Antagonism toward Communists and other radical minorities, although always present, had been somewhat blunted during the early days of the New Deal. At the height of the Depression many liberals and left-wing idealists had found reasons to challenge the fundamentals of the American social order. Some of them manifested an interest in and sympathy with the Soviet Union and with Marxist theory. The New Deal itself had promoted social experimentation and rapid social change similar in some respects to proposals made long before by political radicals. After strong initial resistance to the Roosevelt administration's proposed expansion of federal power, the Supreme Court upheld the New Deal laws and during the same period expanded the protection of civil liberties.[11] Incidentally, in all four elections in which Franklin Roosevelt ran, a majority of newspapers in the United States exercised their freedom by opposing his candidacy.

The gains for First Amendment freedoms during the 1930s and 1940s, however, were by no means universal and constant. Although the Supreme Court (which is the focus of this study) was generally supportive of rights, the political climate for free expression, it must be remembered, was affected also by other centers of governmental and private power. Many states during the period enacted or strengthened laws aimed at curbing radical speech.[12] State legislative bodies conducted inquiries into Communist infiltration of labor unions and colleges. Congress created the House Committee on Un-American Activities in 1938. This committee conducted sweeping investigations, without procedural safeguards, of allegedly subversive individuals and groups, thus chilling the atmosphere for free discussion. Aided and abetted by official action, businesses penalized unorthodox expression by black-listing and the denial of jobs.[13] Congress passed the Smith Act in 1940, prohibiting the advocacy of violent overthrow of the government.

Two and a half months after Pearl Harbor, Roosevelt, under the claim of military necessity, ordered the removal from their communities and detention of 112,000 Japanese-Americans, two-thirds of whom were citizens. The detention of these people behind barbed wire—which, incidentally, was approved by the Supreme Court—

was called by the American Civil Liberties Union "the worst single wholesale violation of civil rights of American citizens in our history."[14] The evacuees' liberty of speech was, of course, also affected[15]

By constant baiting of the Japanese, some West Coast newspapers, particularly those in the Hearst chain, had contributed to a demand for relocation.[16] Some California papers called for fair treatment of the Japanese-Americans even during the first weeks after the war started. But most papers—including those that initially proclaimed the loyalty of resident Japanese—later demanded evacuation or, at least, approved the program once it was announced.[17] The *San Francisco Chronicle*, even though it questioned the legality of summary treatment of citizens, said that "we have to be tough, even if civil rights do take a beating for a time."[18]

Public attitudes, which may reflect or reinforce press attitudes (the cause and effect process is not always clear), are an integral part of the environment for freedom of discussion. Public intolerance may inhibit freedom just as prosecution or the threat of it may exert a deterrent effect on free discussion. Thus, the period of the German-Russian nonaggression pact contributed to a revival of antiradicalism in the American public and heightened official repressive moves during that time. The climate then shifted toward one of greater toleration during four years of anti-Nazi combat when the Communist party line and United States policy coincided.

With the end of the war, another outbreak of anti-Communist fear led to new measures of repression that were to culminate in McCarthyism and the *Dennis* decision. In March 1947, President Harry Truman issued an executive order establishing a comprehensive loyalty program for federal employees. Similar programs were instituted at state and local levels of government. In 1948 the federal government began a series of prosecutions of Communist party leaders under the Smith Act. Congress in 1950 enacted the Internal Security Act providing for the registration of "Communist-action" and "Communist-front" organizations and for emergency detention of alleged subversives.[19]

Seeking to assure his reelection by taking advantage of the mood of the time, Senator Joseph McCarthy of Wisconsin made a speech in Wheeling, West Virginia, on February 9, 1950, in which he charged that the State Department was "thoroughly infested with Communists." He waved what he said was a list of 205 names of persons who had been made known to the secretary of state as members of the Communist party but who were still working and making policy in the State Department. Despite pressure to produce documentation of his charges, he never provided proof.[20] But the continuing technique of disseminating unsubstantiated charges served to make the Wisconsin senator a national phenomenon, to blacken the names of many in and out of government, and to generate a wave of public hostility to unorthodox views.

The press, by its handling of the news of McCarthy and his investigating committee, played a part in the process of extralegal punishment of many who were McCarthy's targets. As Alan Barth of the *Washington Post* observed in his book, *The Loyalty of Free Men*:

Allegations which would otherwise be ignored because they would be recognized as groundless and libelous are blown up on front pages and given a significance out of all relation to their intrinsic merit after they have been made before a committee of Congress. Thus, what is one day regarded as unpublishable gossip is treated the next day as news of great moment because it has been uttered under official auspices. Refutation, no matter how compelling, never catches up with charges of disloyalty and never erases their imprint.[21]

In a speech expressing revulsion against McCarthy's name-calling tactics, Senator Margaret Chase Smith said: "Freedom of speech is not what it used to be in America. It has been so abused by some that it is not exercised by others."[22]

Many leading newspapers, having themselves been subjected by McCarthy to the ridiculous charge of being Communist voices, in time denounced his tactics on their editorial pages. Among the great number of papers that excoriated the Wisconsin senator were the *New York Times*, the *New York Post*, the *Washington Post*, the *Pittsburgh Post-Gazette*, the Louisville *Courier-Journal*, the Milwaukee *Journal*, and the *St. Louis Post-Dispatch*.[23] Like the McCarthy committee in the Senate, the House Committee on Un-American Activities, which under various chairmen used similar tactics, eventually came under widespread press condemnation.[24] But the House committee, later known as the Internal Security Committee, was not abolished until 1975.

With respect to the press and the congressional committees that sought to police thought and speech, it should be noted, however, that McCarthy, at least during the first part of his anti-Communist crusade, had the support of a substantial number of newspapers, including such big papers as the *Chicago Tribune* and the New York *Journal-American*.[25] So did the witch-hunters on the Un-American Activities Committee. Papers that lent support to the House committee included the *New York Daily News*, the New York *Mirror*, the Buffalo *Evening News*, the *Chicago Tribune*, Miami *Daily News*, and the Cincinnati *Enquirer*.[26]

While the country was going through the recriminations and loyalty purges of the McCarthy era, the case of *Dennis* v. *United States* was working its way toward the Supreme Court. After a nine-month trial in 1949, Eugene Dennis, general secretary of the Communist party, and ten of his fellow Communist leaders had been convicted under the 1940 Smith Act for advocating and conspiring to advocate the forcible overthrow of the United States government.[27]

At the trial Judge Harold Medina, who presided, was disingenuous in telling the jury that books and pamphlets were not on trial, that the *Daily Worker* and the *Communist Manifesto* would not be salted away for five years in a stuffy jail cell. The indictment, however, had charged the defendants with publishing and circulating books, magazines, and newspapers advocating the principles of Marxism-Leninism. The government introduced more than 100 books, pamphlets, brochures, and newspapers, including many issues of the *Daily Worker*, as prosecution exhibits to prove that the Communists did indeed advocate and teach the violent overthrow of the government. Many of the books and articles, however, were scholarly studies of economics, government, and law—hardly manuals for would-be revolutionaries.[28]

The Court of Appeals for the Second Circuit had upheld the conviction, noting that there was abundant evidence that the Communist party printed and circulated the revolutionary classics of communism, which were dangerous.[29] Speaking for the Court of Appeals, Judge Learned Hand stretched the Holmes "clear and present danger" test virtually beyond recognition and substituted a kind of sliding scale for sedition cases. "In each case," he wrote, "Courts must ask whether the gravity of the 'evil,' discounted by its improbability, justified such invasion of free speech as is necessary to avoid the danger."[30] Hand was saying in effect that if the threatened evil posed by the objectionable speech was very great, government action could come at a more remote stage from the anticipated arrival of the evil. Although it was still labeled the "clear and present danger" doctrine, the Hand theory hardly required government action to await the imminence of the danger envisaged by the author of the doctrine. The Hand doctrine came close to measuring speech by its "bad tendency," as was done in World War I days.[31]

In its six-to-two majority opinion (Justice Tom Clark, who had been attorney general when the case was initiated, did not participate), the Supreme Court sustained the conviction and adopted in full Hand's revised version of the Holmes test.[32] Writing for himself and Justices Stanley Reed, Harold Burton, and Sherman Minton (Justices Robert Jackson and Felix Frankfurter wrote lengthy concurring opinions), Chief Justice Fred Vinson upheld the constitutionality of the Smith Act and observed that

the Smith Act . . . is directed at advocacy, not discussion. . . . the basis of the First Amendment is the hypothesis that speech can rebut speech, propaganda will answer propaganda, free debate of ideas will result in the wisest governmental policies. It is for this reason that this Court has recognized the inherent value of free discourse. An analysis of the leading cases in this Court which have involved direct limitations on speech, however, will demonstrate that both the majority of the Court and the dissenters in particular cases have recognized that this is not an unlimited, unqualified right, but that the social value of speech must, on occasion, be subordinated to other values and considerations. . . .

. . . Overthrow of the Government by force and violence is certainly a substantial enough interest for the Government to limit speech. . . .

If, then, this interest may be protected, the literal problem which is presented is what has been meant by the use of the phrase "clear and present danger" of the utterances bringing about the evil within the power of Congress to punish. . . .

. . . Certainly an attempt to overthrow the Government by force, even though doomed from the outset because of inadequate numbers or power of the revolutionists, is a sufficient evil for Congress to prevent. . . .

We agree that the standard as defined is not a neat mathematical formulary. Like all verbalizations it is subject to criticism on the score of indefiniteness. . . . We have shown the indeterminate standard the phrase [clear and present danger] necessarily connotes.[33]

Perhaps no other case illustrates better than *Dennis* that the Supreme Court does not sit in serene judgment interpreting the law evenly without regard for the temper of the people.

Justices Black and Douglas both wrote passionate dissents. Black argued:

These petitioners were not charged with an attempt to overthrow the Government. They were not charged with overt acts of any kind designed to overthrow the Government. They were not even charged with saying anything or with writing anything designed to overthrow the Government. . . . The indictment is that they conspired to organize the Communist Party and to use speech or newspapers and other publications in the future to teach and advocate the forcible overthrow of the Government.

. . . No matter how it is worded, this is a virulent form of prior censorship of speech and press, which I believe the First Amendment forbids. I would hold Section 3 of the Smith Act authorizing this prior restraint unconstitutional on its face and as applied.

. . . the other opinions in this case show that the only way to affirm these convictions is to repudiate directly or indirectly the established "clear and present danger" rule. This the Court does in a way which greatly restricts the protections afforded by the First Amendment. . . .

. . . I cannot agree that the First Amendment permits us to sustain laws suppressing freedom of speech and press on the basis of Congress' or our own notions of mere "reasonableness." Such a doctrine waters down the First Amendment so that it amounts to little more than an admonition to Congress.[34]

Like Black, Justice Douglas made a distinction between overt acts and speech that posed a danger, and then offered a cogent factual analysis of the status of Communists in the nation—a matter which the majority had given no critical examination. Douglas wrote:

If this were a case where those who claimed protection under the First Amendment were teaching the techniques of sabotage, the assassination of the President . . . the planting of bombs, the art of street warfare, and the like, I would have no doubts. The freedom to speak is not absolute; the teaching of methods of terror and other seditious conduct should be beyond the pale. . . . This case was argued as if those were the facts. . . . There is a statute which makes seditious conspiracy unlawful. Petitioners, however, were not charged with a "conspiracy to overthrow" the Government. They were charged with a conspiracy to form a party and groups and assemblies of people who teach and advocate the overthrow of our Government by force and violence. . . .

. . . This record, however, contains no evidence whatsoever showing that the acts charged, viz., the teaching of the Soviet theory of revolution with the hope that it will be realized, have created any clear and present danger to the Nation. The Court, however, rules to the contrary. . . .

. . . If we are to take judicial notice of the threat of Communists within the nation, it should not be difficult to conclude that *as a political party* they are of little consequence. . . . Free speech—the glory of our system of government—should not be sacrificed on anything less than plain and objective proof of danger that the evil advocated is imminent. On this record no one can say that petitioners and their converts are in such a strategic position as to have even the slightest chance of achieving their aims. . . .[35]

The reaction of the press to the *Dennis* decision was overwhelmingly favorable to the majority view. A survey of editorial comments by twenty-three papers from virtually every section of the country showed that nineteen endorsed the decision with varying degrees of enthusiasm, two took an ambiguous position, and two strongly criticized the decision.

The *New York Times* said, "What is important . . . is . . . the establishment of a principle. The principle is that liberty shall not be abused to its own destruction."[36] The *Atlanta Constitution* declared: "It is a welcome decision. . . ."[37] The *Washington Post* commented:

We do not think the decision belittles the great principle of freedom of speech. The court has said only that individuals engaged in a conspiracy to teach and advocate the overthrow of the Government by force and violence cannot use freedom of speech as a shield for their plot. . . . Freedom of speech for all legitimate purposes remains."[38]

In Denver the *Rocky Mountain News* scoffed: "The 11 Red traitors are now at the end of their legal rope, and will go to jail. In the Russia they love they would have been at the end of hempen ropes long ago, without even benefit of trials and appeals lasting over two years."[39] The *Denver Post* observed: "The decision, as we understand it, does not prohibit a man from thinking Communist thoughts." Then, reflecting a misreading of the issue in the case, the *Post* went on: "It does make it illegal for him to take part in the Communist conspiracy to overthrow this government by force and violence."[40] The case, of course, did not deal with a conspiracy to overthrow the government, but with a conspiracy to teach the overthrow.

The *San Francisco Chronicle* said that "the United States Supreme Court has cleared up a king-sized quibble. . . . The American people knew full well that the Communists were quibbling. . . . The reason why, until now, the country has had to put up with it have been difficult to boil down to a few words, but they have been valid and important. The due process of law is a right guaranteed by our system. . . ."

In Indianapolis, the *Star* said the Supreme Court "makes possible the protection of the people's liberties without endangering the constitutional rights of free speech and free press. . . ."[41] The *Indianapolis News*, equally untroubled, declared: "Neither the challenged act nor the present decision in any way infringes on the traditional American rights of freedom of opinion and expression."[42]

The Minneapolis *Star* was not so unconcerned: "The Star believes —despite deep misgivings about its consequences for the free speech principle—that Chief Justice Vinson made the only possible decision."[43] The *Oregon Journal* of Portland declared: "How the dissenting justices can argue the Smith Act violates the Constitution baffles a mind not versed in 'liberal' legal quibbles." In Texas the *Fort Worth Star-Telegram* observed: "We cannot feel that the Supreme Court's decision endangers any of the fundamental American rights."[44] The *New York Daily News*, the Baltimore *Sun*, the

Philadelphia *Bulletin*, the *Philadelphia Inquirer*, the New Orleans *Times-Picayune*, the *Kansas City Star*, the Memphis *Commercial Appeal* and the Nashville *Tennessean* also supported the decision.[45]

The two papers that did not clearly signal a position for or against the decision were the *Christian Science Monitor* of Boston and the *Arkansas Gazette* of Little Rock. The *Monitor* commented that "if a balance has needed restoring in favor of governmental powers to deal with subversive teachings the Supreme Court has restored it. But the basic problem remains still poised on the knife edge between liberty and security."[46] The *Arkansas Gazette* said:

> The kind of despotism which they [the defendants] support makes them peculiarly undeserving applicants for the protection of our Bill of Rights. Yet Americans should be on notice that the Supreme Court's latest interpretation of the Bill of Rights is narrower than the one Thomas Jefferson envisaged when he said: "If there be any among us who wish to dissolve this union, or to change its republican form, let them stand undisturbed, as monuments to the safety with which error of opinion may be tolerated where reason is left free to combat it."[47]

Only two newspapers among the twenty-three condemned the *Dennis* decision in unequivocal terms. They were the *St. Louis Post-Dispatch* and the Louisville *Courier-Journal*. In an editorial headed, "Six Men Amend the Constitution," the *Post-Dispatch* declared:

> These six justices say that the Communists by organizing "*to teach and advocate* the overthrow of the Government of the United States by force and violence *created* a 'clear and present danger' of an attempt to overthrow the Government by force and violence."
>
> They cite no overt acts of force.
>
> They present no record of violence.
>
> They find danger both clear and present through teaching and advocacy alone.
>
> Never before has such a restriction been placed on the right to hold opinions and to express them in the United States of America. . . .
>
> Six men have amended the United States Constitution without submitting their amendment to the states for ratification. That is the nub of this decision.[48]

After noting its own opposition to Communist doctrine, the Louisville *Courier-Journal* observed:

> When we say . . . that by its decision upholding the Smith Act the Supreme Court has set this nation's feet on a difficult and dangerous path, we know that we invite protests and name-calling. . . .
>
> This law undoubtedly restricts and modifies the First Amendment. . . . It is now a criminal offense . . . to advocate, print or distribute the doctrines of Marx and Lenin. . . .
>
> Under the act as now confirmed all the members of the Communist party may be arrested, tried and found guilty.
>
> And what then? Suppose this were done, are we thus all preserved from some overhanging threat, some clear and present danger, as the court's majority opinion implies?
>
> It is doubtful, for not even the most timid among us really feel that this despised and fanatic handful of bitterly unpopular men . . . has any real chance of overthrowing the government by force. . . .
>
> . . . Our best defense against tyranny or oppression from any source is free discussion of all that it involves.[49]

With the *Dennis* case having brought about the affirmation of the Smith Act by the highest court, other prosecutions followed in the same pattern. Communist writers and editors, including the editor and executive editor of the *Daily People's World* in Los Angeles, were indicted.[50] In all, more than 100 persons were convicted under the Smith Act.[51] Clearly the act was used, for the most part with the approval of general circulation newspapers, for restriction of freedom of speech and of the press.[52]

Six years after *Dennis* in *Yates* v. *United States*,[53] the Supreme Court was called upon to deal with the conviction under the Smith Act of fourteen secondary leaders of the Communist party. In reversing the convictions, the Court dealt with subtleties of language and found fault with the trial court for not having made clear to the jury the distinction between advocacy of action to overthrow the government by force and violence and advocacy of abstract doctrine on this subject. "The essential difference," said Justice John Marshall Harlan for the majority, "is that those to whom the advocacy is addressed must be urged to *do* something, now or in the future, rather than merely to *believe* in something." The outcome in *Yates* may have been due as much to the change in membership and outlook on the high bench as to the tenuous difference between advocacy of action and advocacy of abstract doctrine. Vinson and Minton, who had voted with the majority in *Dennis*, were no longer on the Court. Chief Justice Earl Warren and Justice Harlan, who had joined the Court after *Dennis*, voted with the majority in *Yates*. Justices Harold Burton and Felix Frankfurter voted to affirm in *Dennis* and to reverse in *Yates*. Black and Douglas concurred in the outcome as far as it went but would have gone further by ordering the acquittal of all of the defendants on the ground that they had been convicted under an unconstitutional act. Justices William Brennan and Charles Whittaker, who were new to the Court, did not participate. Clark dissented.[54]

Other Supreme Court cases in the 1950s dealt with important freedom of expression issues that did not directly touch newspapers. In *Burstyn* v. *Wilson*[55] in 1952 the Court decided unanimously that New York state's suppression of the film, *The Miracle*, on grounds that it was "sacrilegious," was a violation of the guarantees of the First Amendment. In thus bringing motion pictures under the protection of the First Amendment, the court reversed a thirty-seven-year-old decision, in which it had suggested that movies, as a form of commercial entertainment, were not protected.[56]

Five years after *Burstyn* the Supreme Court—in the 1957 companion cases of *Roth* v. *United States* and *Alberts* v. *California*[57]— was again concerned with expression as it affected public morality, this time on grounds of alleged obscenity rather than sacrilegiousness. Samuel Roth, a New York bookseller, was convicted under a federal obscenity statute of mailing an obscene book; David Alberts, a California bookseller, was convicted under the California penal code for keeping obscene and indecent books for sale and writing and publishing an obscene advertisement. In a majority opinion, written by Justice Brennan, the Court for the first time explicitly placed obscenity beyond the protection of the First and Fourteenth Amendments. "We hold," said Brennan, "that obscenity is not within the area of constitutionally protected speech or press." The Court thus upheld the censorious aspects of both the federal and California statutes. Black and Douglas dissented.

Roth was significant as a constriction of First Amendment coverage. (Judge Jerome Frank of the United States Court of Appeals for the Second Circuit, in an opinion on the same case, had urged the Supreme Court to liberate speech and press entirely from laws against obscenity.)[58] But *Roth* was also significant for offering for the first time Supreme Court standards for judging obscenity. Although he did not present the definition in concise form, Brennan suggested that obscenity was material that "deals with sex in a manner appealing to prurient interest," that has a "dominant theme" that taken "as a whole" is judged to be such by "the average person applying contemporary community standards," and that is "utterly without redeeming social importance." Douglas, speaking in dissent for himself and Black, said: "Government should be concerned with antisocial conduct, not with utterances. Thus, if the First Amendment guarantee of freedom of speech and press is to mean anything in this field, it must allow protests even against the moral code that the standard of the day sets for the community. In other words, literature should not be suppressed merely because it offends the moral code of the censor."

Despite Justice Brennan's attempt to define obscenity, his definition obviously did not satisfy his fellow justices or provide clear guidance for lower courts. In obscenity cases during the next decade, the court swung one way and then the other in upholding or striking down censorship,[59] although the trend was toward an increasingly narrow boundary around what might be legally proscribed as obscene. In a 1964 case, *Jacobellis* v. *Ohio*,[60] Justice Brennan suggested that material proscribed on obscenity grounds must be judged to be obscene by "society at large," not by a local or state community. (In a 1965 case, *Freedman* v. *Maryland*,[61] the Supreme Court in effect abolished movie censorship, although not in an obscenity case.) The vacillation of the court on obscenity cases continued into the 1970s, as will be shown later.

During the 1960s, however, there were other cases that had a more direct bearing on newspapers. The most important such case involved libel—an area which the court had several times suggested was not constitutionally protected.[62] On March 29, 1960, the *New York Times* had published a full-page advertisement, signed by a number of northern supporters of civil rights and (without their knowledge) by four black ministers in the South. The ad criticized the conduct of public officials, especially the police, during racial demonstrations in Montgomery, Alabama. Although no officials were named, L. B. Sullivan, police commissioner of Montgomery, brought a libel action against the *Times* and the four ministers, and was awarded a $500,000 judgment in a Montgomery circuit court— a judgment that was upheld by the Alabama Supreme Court, but unanimously reversed by the United States Supreme Court.

Justice Brennan, writing for the Court, noted that "for the first time" the Court was required "to determine the extent to which the constitutional protections for speech and press limit a state's power to award damages in a libel action brought by a public official against critics of his official conduct." Until 1964, when *New York Times* v. *Sullivan*[63] was decided, libel suits were a matter of state law, with each state following different rules—although many states, but not all, provided a qualified privilege (a limited defense against libel suits) for citizens criticizing their public officials. The suit against the *Times* came against a background of an increasing number of civil libel suits by public officials seeking heavy damages for criticism by press and public. During April 1963, for example, at least seventeen libel actions by public officials in three southern states were pending in the courts, with the damages being sought exceeding $288 million.

The Court's *Sullivan* decision placed a federal limitation on such libel suits under the First Amendment. Brennan noted the occasions on which the Court had said that libel was not constitutionally protected and went on to observe: "Those statements do not foreclose our inquiry here. None of the cases sustained the use of libel laws to impose sanctions upon expression critical of the official conduct of public officials." He referred to the Sedition Act of 1798, which imposed criminal penalties for seditious libel of public officials, and noted that, although that act had never been tested in the Supreme Court, "the attack upon its validity has carried the day in the court of history."

Brennan declined to accept the plaintiff's argument that the free press guarantee was inapplicable to the *Times* in the case of a paid, "commercial" advertisement, noting first that the ad was not really commercial but rather "communicated information, expressed opinion, recited grievances, protested claimed abuses, and sought financial support on behalf of a movement whose existence and objectives are matters of the highest public interest and concern." Therefore, said Brennan, the fact that the *Times* was paid for the ad was immaterial:

> Any other conclusion would discourage newspapers from carrying "editorial advertisements" of this type, and so might shut off an important outlet for the promulgation of information and ideas by persons who do not themselves have access to publishing facilities—who wish to exercise their freedom of speech even though they are not members of the press. . . . The effect would be to shackle the First Amendment in its attempt to secure "the widest possible dissemination of information from diverse and antagonistic sources." [64]

Although there were some admitted misstatements of fact in the ad—such as that Dr. Martin Luther King had been arrested seven times, when he had only been arrested four times—Brennan asserted: "The constitutional guarantees require, we think, a federal rule that prohibits a public official from recovering damages for a defamatory falsehood relating to his official conduct unless he proves that the statement was made with actual malice—that is, with knowledge that it was false or with reckless disregard of whether it was false or not." [65] In the course of his opinion, Brennan made one curious allusion to past attempts to curb freedom of expression without seeming to recognize the irony of his observation. He said the Court was not compelled to give any more weight "to the epithet 'libel' than we have to other 'mere labels' of state law." Noting such labels as "insurrection, contempt, advocacy of unlawful acts, breach of the peace, obscenity . . . and the various other formulae for the repression of expression," Brennan suggested that, like these, "libel can claim no talismanic immunity from constitutional limitations. It must be measured by standards that satisfy the First Amendment." But the fact was that on many occasions the Supreme Court had allowed such formulae to be used to curb freedom of expression under standards held to satisfy the First Amendment.

Justices Black, Douglas, and Arthur Goldberg concurred in the result in *Sullivan* but would have enunciated a different rule. Speaking for himself and Douglas, Goldberg said he thought the First and Fourteenth amendments afforded citizens and the press "an absolute unconditional privilege to criticize official conduct," but not to make defamatory statements on "the private conduct of a public official." He foresaw difficulty in protecting free speech under a rule that allowed the imposition of liability for malice—a matter that called on a jury to evaluate a "speaker's state of mind."[66] Black said he believed that the First and Fourteenth amendments "not merely 'delimit' a state's power to award damages to 'a public official against critics of his official conduct' but completely prohibit a state from exercising such a power." Several years earlier Black had taken the position that all libel suits were absolutely forbidden by the First Amendment.[67]

The *Sullivan* decision was widely hailed by the newspapers and by spokesmen for the press, including the president of the American Society of Newspaper Editors and the chairman of the society's Freedom of Information Committee.[68] The *New York Times* said:

> It is an increasingly important function of the press—and must be, if the press is to live up to its proper responsibilities—to encourage the free give-and-take of ideas and, above all, to be free to express criticism of public officials and public policies. This is all part of the lifeblood of a democracy. In its landmark decision yesterday, the Supreme Court of the United States has struck a solid blow not only for freedom of the press but for the prerogatives of a free people.[69]

The *Washington Post* observed:

> Citizens would receive very little information about or opinion on the conduct of government officials in a society where the reprisals for expressions alleged to be wrongful were so sanguinary as to destroy accused publications. Where the punishment for allegations admitted to be in error amounts to confiscation, little will be said about government by prudent publishers.
> . . . As the area for freedom of public utterance, in our society, is great, so is the responsibility to use that freedom with care and discretion.[70]

In Atlanta the *Constitution* hailed the ruling as upholding the "fundamental rights of the press and the people," and went on to observe: "In recent years we have witnessed a rash of harassments and intimidations, mainly under state libel laws to silence the press. In many instances these have been aimed at newspapers and other media which have dared to champion unpopular causes."[71] The Louisville *Courier-Journal* declared:

> The Supreme Court's unanimous decision . . . adds new luster to the First Amendment.
> . . . the court did much more than consider the reporting of racial matters in its ruling. It held that freedom of comment on official conduct would be endangered by unlimited libel awards. . . . It sanctions even inaccurate or false statements about public officials, so long as malice is not proved.[72]

The *Pittsburgh Post-Gazette* said the ruling would stand "as a historic judicial vindication of the First Amendment," and concluded that, considering "the harassing and costly effect of successive libel suits, the Brennan opinion erects an essential bulwark for freedom of the press."[73]

In St. Louis the *Post-Dispatch's* editorial conclusion was that:

> If this libel case had been allowed to stand, government would have been left with a powerful if indirect weapon of attack upon criticism of policies which officialdom might think to be above criticism. But the Alabama decisions do not stand. The Supreme Court has affirmed and strengthened the "profound national commitment" to free debate on public issues.[74]

The *Denver Post* welcomed the decision by saying that "the right of newspapers to engage in non-malicious criticism of public officials received important reinforcement from the U.S. Supreme Court. . . ." But the paper made a point of differing with the Goldberg-Douglas-Black view that would "have established an absolute privilege for criticism of officials, even when the criticism is prompted by malice. . . . It is probably well that the majority did not go that far."[75]

Also in Denver the *Rocky Mountain News*, a Scripps Howard paper, quoted E. W. Scripps as saying: "We shall tell no lies about persons or policies for love, malice or money," and went on to observe: "The court thus gives legal voice to the creed by which the Scripps Howard newspapers have lived and will continue to live. . . ."[76]

The *San Francisco Chronicle*, after summarizing the decision, said:

The Supreme Court, throwing it [the libel claim] out, said that "debate on public issues should be uninhibited, robust and wide open and that may well include vehement, caustic and sometimes unpleasantly sharp attacks on government." This is surely wise doctrine and useful instruction to public officials everywhere.[77]

The New Orleans *Times-Picayune* had nothing to say about the *Sullivan* decision during the week it was announced.

In the same year as the *Sullivan* decision, the Supreme Court, in the case of *Garrison* v. *Louisiana*[78] reversed the criminal libel conviction of a Louisiana district attorney who had said a backlog of criminal cases was caused by the laziness and inefficiency of judges and who had criticized the judges for not authorizing expenses for a vice investigation, thus indicating clearly where the judges' sympathies lay. The Court held that the Louisiana criminal libel statute contained constitutionally invalid standards in that, contrary to the *Sullivan* rule, which absolutely forbade punishment of truthful criticism, it directed punishment for true statements made with "actual malice." The Supreme Court thus limited state power to impose criminal sanctions for criticism of official conduct just as it had, in *Sullivan*, restricted the right of an individual to collect civil damages. Justice Douglas, in a concurring opinion, noted the parallel between criminal libel and the notorious doctrine of seditious libel that was used when the "libeler . . . outraged the sentiments of the dominant party."[79]

The standards for libel cases were further refined in two 1967 decisions—*Curtis Publishing Co.* v. *Butts* and *Associated Press* v. *Walker*.[80] In the *Curtis* case the Supreme Court upheld a $460,000 federal court libel judgment against the *Saturday Evening Post* based on an article in which the magazine had charged that Wally Butts, athletic director of the University of Georgia, had conspired with the University of Alabama coach to "fix" a football game between the two universities. In *Associated Press* v. *Walker* the Supreme Court reversed a $500,000 Texas court libel judgment against the Associated Press that had been based on a dispatch about events connected with the racial integration of the University of Mississippi in which it was reported that a resigned army general, Edwin A. Walker, had personally led a charge of students against federal marshals. All of the justices seemed to agree that some measure of constitutional protection for the press, as provided in *Sullivan*, should be extended when libel plaintiffs were "public figures" or were involved in issues of public interest. But the Court, dividing five to four, upheld the judgment for Butts on the grounds that the *Post* article was not "hot news," and that the magazine ignored "elementary precautions" to make sure of the truth of its assertions.

In *Walker*, however, the Court held unanimously that the plaintiff, because he was a public figure, was not entitled to collect damages since the AP was dealing with news that required immediate dissemination and had received its information from a trustworthy and competent correspondent. Consistent with their absolutist rejection of all libel actions against the press, Black and Douglas dissented in the Butts case and concurred in the Walker case.

In another case decided the same year, 1967, the Supreme Court for the first time decided a question involving privacy law and the mass media. The Court reversed a judgment for damages against Time, Inc., awarded under a New York privacy statute, for a 1955 article in *Life* magazine describing a play based in part on the ordeal of the James J. Hill family when it was held captive by a group of escaped convicts.[81] In an application of the rule in *New York Times* v. *Sullivan*, Justice Brennan said for a five-member majority that the trial court had erroneously failed to require the plaintiff to prove actual malice.

While all of these cases calling for further application of the *Sullivan* rule were still making their way toward the Supreme Court, the justices in 1966 had decided an issue other than libel in which Alabama officials were again involved in a head-on collision with the press, this time an Alabama newspaper.[82] The Alabama Corrupt Practices Act made it a crime "to do any electioneering or to solicit any votes . . . in support of or in opposition to any proposition that is being voted on on the day on which the election affecting such candidates or proposition is being held." On November 6, 1962, Birmingham held an election for the people to decide whether they preferred to keep their existing city commission form of government or replace it with a mayor-council form of government. The

Birmingham *Post-Herald* in 1962 had begun a campaign against the city's two most prominent segregationist politicians, Mayor Art Hanes and Police Commissioner Eugene T. Connor. The paper pressed for a change to the mayor-council form of government, which would have eliminated the positions held by Hanes and Connor and, it was thought, set Birmingham on a more moderate racial course.

On election day the *Post-Herald* carried an editorial, written by its editor, James E. Mills, strongly urging the people to adopt the mayor-council form of government. Mills was later arrested on a complaint charging that, in publishing the editorial, he had violated the Corrupt Practices Law. Although the law had been on the books for fifty-one years, it had never before been invoked in a recorded case. Writing for the Supreme Court, Justice Black held the Alabama law invalid under the First Amendment. He observed that the law "by providing criminal penalties for publishing editorials such as the one here silences the press at a time when it can be most effective. It is difficult to conceive of a more obvious and flagrant abridgement of the constitutionally guaranteed freedom of the press."

The interest of the press in the case was indicated by the fact that the Alabama and Southern Press Associations had filed friend-of-the-court briefs on behalf of Mills[83] and many newspapers across the country had editorially supported Mills during the course of the litigation. In welcoming the Supreme Court decision, the *Washington Post* said:

There are considerations of fairness and propriety that make most newspapers reluctant, as a general rule, to publish any material for or against the election of political candidates on Election Day. The fact that there is no opportunity to verify or refute such last-minute arguments makes this sort of self-restraint seem desirable in the public interest. . . .

It is a very different matter, however, to forbid the publication of such material by law. Self-restraint is a newspaper's responsibility. Legal restraint is a frustration of the newspaper's function.[84]

The *Pittsburgh Post-Gazette* declared: "One of the most arrogant recent attempts at official suppression of freedom of the press was checked this week by the U.S. Supreme Court."[85] The *St. Louis*

Post-Dispatch, like all other papers whose editorials were read, was pleased with the decision. In its comment, the *Post-Dispatch* said of the press: ". . . no other institution . . . is now so well equipped to alert the public to public issues or to inspire public discussion of them. In this area silence is the enemy of good government, and government cannot silence the press on election day or any other day."[86] During the week of the Supreme Court decision in the *Mills* case the *New York Times*, the *Atlanta Constitution*, the *Denver Post*, and the *San Francisco Chronicle* had no editorial comment on the ruling.

While the courts and newspaper editors seemed to have little trouble in reaching general agreement in their respective spheres on cases involving restrictions on newspapers themselves, such as in the *Mills* case, issues of obscenity in 1966 were still leading to sharp divisions. Only two months before the *Mills* decision, the Supreme Court had ruled on three obscenity cases that produced fourteen separate opinions by seven justices. Those decisions also led to markedly diffferent editorial reactions from the press.

In the three decisions, announced on the same day, March 21, 1966, the Supreme Court: (1) held that the eighteenth-century novel, *Fanny Hill*, was not "utterly without redeeming social value" and thus had been improperly held obscene by a Massachusetts court,[87] (2) affirmed the New York conviction of Edward Mishkin, who published admittedly "sadistic and masochistic" tracts,[88] and (3) affirmed the federal conviction, under the mail obscenity statute, of Ralph Ginzburg, a publisher, for sending through the mails three erotic publications—*Eros*, a hard-cover magazine; *Liaison*, a biweekly newsletter; and *The Housewife's Handbook on Selective Promiscuity*, a short book.[89]

The *Ginzburg* decision attracted the most attention because in it the Court added a new test for obscenity—the publisher's intent, as evidenced by the marketing technique of "pandering." Writing for the majority, Justice Brennan said:

. . . there was abundant evidence to show that each of the accused publications was originated or sold as stock in trade of the sordid business of pandering. . . . *Eros* early sought mailing privileges from the post-masters of Intercourse and Blue Ball, Pennsylvania. . . .

The "leer of the sensualist" also permeates the advertising for the three publications. . . .

We perceive no threat to First Amendment guarantees in thus holding that in close cases evidence of pandering may be probative with respect to the nature of the material in question and thus satisfy the *Roth* test.[90]

Vigorous dissents were written by Justices Black, Douglas, Harlan, and Potter Stewart. All four objected to the addition of the "pandering" test to the *Roth* standards. Stewart said:

. . . Neither the statute under which Ginzburg was convicted nor any other federal statute I know of makes "commercial exploitation" or "pandering" or "titillation" a criminal offense. And any criminal law that sought to do so in terms so elusively defined by the Court would, of course, be unconstitutionally vague and therefore void.[91]

Black wrote: ". . . as I have said many times, I believe the Federal Government is without any power whatever under the Constitution to put any type of burden on speech and expression of ideas of any kind (as distinguished from conduct). . . ."[92]

In his dissent, Douglas called attention to advertising techniques universally observable in the magazine and other supplements of newspapers. He observed:

The use of sex symbols to sell literature, today condemned by the Court, engrafts another exception on First Amendment rights that is as unwarranted as the judge-made exception concerning obscenity. . . . The advertisements of our best magazines are chock full of thighs, ankles, calves, bosoms, eyes, and hair, to draw the potential buyer's attention to lotions, tires, food, liquor, clothing, autos, and even insurance policies. The sexy advertisement neither adds to nor detracts from the quality of the merchandise being offered for sale. . . . A book should stand on its own, irrespective of the reasons why it was written or the wiles used in selling it. I cannot imagine any promotional effort that would make chapters 7 and 8 of the Song of Solomon any the less or more worthy of First Amendment protection than does its unostentatious inclusion in the average edition of the Bible.[93]

Considering the prurient appeal, albeit subtle, of some of the advertising in its own pages, the *New York Times* moralizing on the *Ginzburg* and other decisions was just a bit hypocritical. That paper's editorial said:

Mr. Justice Brennan and his majority colleagues have shown wisdom and moral courage in the subtle and arduous task of upholding the law against obscenity while still protecting liberty of expression. . . .

In the "Fanny Hill" case, the Court permitted publication because the book has at least some slight historical and literary interest. . . .

The Court inescapably concluded that Ginzburg had no scholarly, literary, or scientific interests; he was strictly an entrepreneur in a disreputable business who took his chances on the borderline of the law and lost. He is no different from Edward Mishkin, the defendant in the third case. . . .

. . . so swiftly has the revolution in law and public opinion moved that freedom of the creative writer and publisher has turned into license for the merchants of pornography.

The public clearly has the right through the enforcement of laws to curb this "sordid business of pandering." [94]

The *Washington Post* found it "disquieting" that Ginzburg was to be sent to prison for five years "for the mere publication of words and pictures which, however offensive to some, seem to have redeeming value to others of comparable decency and taste." The *Post* editorial entitled, "Literary Fog," continued:

The country is left without any clear standards as to what is permissible and what is impermissible in artistic or literary expression. The inevitable result is to put a damper on publication. . . .

People have been arguing for two centuries about whether *Fanny Hill* is art or obscenity. It could be both. . . . It should constitute a warning of a sort that this widely circulated, much-discussed book, now cleared by the Court, was the first literary work ever to be banned in the United States. . . . There is, we think, much shrewd common sense behind an observation made by Mr. Justice Douglas in the *Fanny Hill* case:

"Perhaps the most frequently assigned justification for censorship is the belief that erotica produces antisocial conduct. But that relationship is yet to be proven. Indeed, if one were to make judgments on the basis of speculation, one might guess that literature of the most pornographic sort would, in many cases, provide a substitute—not a stimulus—for antisocial conduct."

. . . He [Douglas] spoke as an interpreter of the Constitution should speak, for the rights of minorities. And he pointed out that books which seem vulgar, worthless and odious to some, may have utility and significance for others.[95]

The Louisville *Courier-Journal* seemed unable to come to any firm conclusions on the obscenity rulings. Its editorial ended with the observation that "in an ideal society censorship would be neither tolerated nor needed. But in an ideal society, probably such exhausting distinctions as now have to be made between pornography with some social merit and pornography without any merit would also never rise to plague us."[96]

In Pittsburgh the *Post-Gazette*, in commenting on the three cases, concentrated on the new test enunciated in *Ginzburg*:

. . . the high court said that publications may be judged not only by their contents but also by the manner in which they are promoted and advertised. . . . Obviously a comprehensive application of the new rule would require subtle judgments of a vast volume of printed material designed solely for purposes of commercial exploitation.

The Supreme Court would have been wiser if it had avoided trying to judge a publication on any other basis than the merit of its contents.[97]

The comment of the *St. Louis Post-Dispatch* on the three cases was terse:

The 14 separate opinions in three obscenity cases just decided by the Supreme Court appear to confuse an already confused area of the law. . . .

The [Brennan] rule makes little sense. Conceivably such advertising might reflect the intent of the seller, but how can it be "decisive" in determining the nature of the product? . . . The decisive test should be whether the publications themselves were obscene. If that is not to be the test, a good deal of innocent material will be open to prosecution.[98]

The *Denver Post*, without offering a judgment on whether stricter or more lenient standards were needed, declared: "The need for a clear public policy regarding obscenity and pornography and for clear standards for judging suspect material remains great and the latest decisions, instead of helping to meet that need, may have merely introduced new complications in an already complex area of law. . . ."[99]

In San Francisco the *Chronicle* commented:

The rulings, and the unusual number of dissenting and independent opinions, confirmed the difficulty of defining obscenity to everybody's satisfaction. They testified also that since 1957, no measuring stick has been devised that serves better than the three criteria of the Roth case.[100]

The *Atlanta Constitution*, among the eight newspapers across the country that were checked, was the only one that had no comment on *Ginzburg* during the week of the decision.

As divisions in the Supreme Court over obscenity standards continued and as the Court found itself spending an inordinate amount of its time adjudicating cases in this area, the Court—under the influence of conservative members appointed by President Richard Nixon—sought again in 1973 to enunciate rules that would make judging easier but would at the same time give greater discretion to local authorities for censoring. In *Miller* v. *California*,[101] one of five obscenity rulings announced on June 21, 1973, the Court, with Chief Justice Warren Burger speaking for the majority in all five cases, held for the first time that obscenity could be judged by state rather than national standards and added a new twist to the *Roth* rule. Instead of being judged as to whether it was "utterly without redeeming social value," a work could be judged by whether, taken as a whole, it lacked "serious literary, artistic, political, or scientific value"—obviously a standard making suppression easier.[102]

Of the numerous freedom of expression decisions since the Supreme Court began to rule on First Amendment issues more than fifty years ago, probably none involved more drama or excited more public interest than the so-called Pentagon Papers case in 1971 in which the Nixon administration sought to bar the *New York Times*, the *Washington Post,* and other papers from publishing the government's classified history of U.S. decision-making in the Vietnam war.[103] For the first time in United States history general circulation newspapers had been restrained by court order from publishing material that the government claimed would endanger national security.[104] After fifteen days of litigation—during part of which the *Times* was subjected to prior restraint by judicial decree—the Supreme Court, on June 30, 1971, in a six-to-three decision, freed the *Times,* the *Post,* and other papers to publish articles based on the Pentagon documents. Because no opinion by a single justice commanded a majority, the Court issued its ruling in an unsigned order that offered little authoritative exposition of the law[105]—saying little more than: "Any system of prior restraints of expression comes to this court bearing a heavy presumption against its constitutional validity."[106]

All nine justices wrote opinions—Douglas, Brennan, Stewart, Marshall, Black, and White writing in favor of lifting the injunction; Burger, Harlan, and Blackmun, dissenting. As might have been expected from their previous decisions, the opinions of Douglas and Black offered the strongest support for the positions of the newspapers. Douglas asserted that "the dominant purpose of the First Amendment was to prohibit the widespread practice of governmental suppression of embarrassing information" and "was adopted against the widespread use of the common law of seditious libel to punish the dissemination of material that is embarrassing to the powers-that-be."[107] Black adhered to the view that the government's case against the *Washington Post* should have been dismissed and the injunction against the *New York Times* vacated without oral argument when the cases were presented to the Court. "I believe that every moment's continuance of the injunction against these newspapers amounts to a flagrant, indefensible and continuing violation of the First Amendment."[108]

Justice Harlan stated a view that was reflected in varying phrases by his fellow dissenters:

Pending further hearings in each case conducted under the appropriate ground rules, I would continue the restraints on publication. I cannot believe that the doctrine prohibiting prior restraints reaches to the point of preventing courts from maintaining the status quo long enough to act responsibly in matters of such national importance as those involved here.[109]

Few examples in history demonstrate more vividly than the Pentagon Papers case the justification for the freedom of the press guaranteed by the First Amendment. Publication of information based on the Pentagon documents revealed to the American people how their governmental leaders over a period of more than twenty years had misled and deceived them, had authorized clandestine warfare, possibly violated treaties, and made gross misjudgments that led the nation ever deeper into a bloody and costly morass in Vietnam. Such information provided by the press would obviously be useful to the electorate in making political judgments. Its publication was barred by no statute,[110] and a statute's validity, even had there been one, would have been questionable under the First Amendment. Yet in the classic confrontation between the press and the government over the right to publish, the government insisted on its power to prohibit publication; the press was less than heroic in its defense of its rights; and the Supreme Court, as a result of its internal quibbling, failed to fully vindicate the First Amendment.

In its presentation before the Supreme Court, the press offered narrow and timid arguments[111] and no lofty appeal to the grand design of the First Amendment. Professor Alexander Bickel, speaking for the *Times*, conceded that the president had an inherent power to establish a classification system and to protect it perhaps with criminal sanctions; he concentrated on the First Amendment's barrier against prior restraint rather than its support for the right to publish—period.[112] With the argument cast in these terms, the Court put the case in terms of a question of prior restraint rather than freedom to publish. And most of the justices spoke of possible criminal liability of the newspapers, although no facts were presented and no legal arguments made on the issue of whether a crime had been committed. Neither the lawyers' arguments nor the opinions seemed to recognize that, even in the absence of prior restraint, the threat of subsequent punishment might exert a drastically chilling effect on the exercise of First Amendment rights.[113]

John S. Knight, publisher of the Knight newspapers, seemed to recognize the situation when, writing in the Detroit *Free Press*, he offered only two cheers for the Supreme Court victory:

For the first time in our history except for wartime censorship, the Government prevented for 15 days publications of articles under the plea of national security. Therefore, the press in its euphoria may not be giving sufficient thought to the possibility that actually a precedent has been set for further restraints upon the right to publish.[114]

In its own editorial, the *Times* too said in effect that the Supreme Court decision was a limited victory—but for a different reason than that given by Knight. The *Times* noted that the Supreme Court had not held that the First Amendment "gave an absolute right to publish anything under all circumstances." What the *Times* sought, said the editorial, "was the right to publish these particular documents at this particular time without prior Governmental restraint." That, the editorial noted, was what the Supreme Court granted. The *Times* also took the occasion to lecture the Nixon administration on a penchant for secrecy and on the excessive classification of government documents. Still, the *Times* could not resist the temptation to exult over what it called "a ringing victory for freedom under law"[115]—despite the deeply divided Court and the thinly disguised judicial warnings.

Like the *Times*, the *Washington Post* recognized the qualified nature of the outcome, saying the decision "does not resolve the dilemma posed by the First Amendment's protections of the press, on the one hand, and the government's undoubted right to protect security on the other." While deploring the great extent of classification and calling for a reexamination of the system, the *Post*, like much of the press, still paid obeisance to the great god, secrecy, by saying that "the government has a very broad grant of authority to conduct its activities in secret. . . ." What authority? Most classification has been imposed, not by statutory grant but by executive fiat under executive orders stemming from a claimed inherent authority undefined by the Constitution. The *Post*'s concession of such secrecy authority to the government under questionable circumstances seemed inconsistent with its own emphasis, and that of many other papers, on the right of the public, under the First Amendment, to be informed.

Nevertheless, the *Post* found sufficient reason to express gratification in majestic terms:

> That we are again free to print this material is an undoubted gain if only because to have remained under restraint would have been an immeasurable loss not for us alone, nor for the press alone, but for the public, and for the country, and for the democratic processes: *It is the purpose and effect of the First Amendment to expose to the public the maximum amount of information on which sound judgment can be made by the electorate.* [Italicized portion quoted from the decision by U.S. District Judge Gerhard Gesell in favor of the Post.][116]

In Atlanta the *Constitution* declared:

> The decision . . . was a profound one for the very democratic process of this nation. . . .
>
> We hold that the efforts to suppress the stories was [*sic*] simply wrong headed. Publication of the Pentagon papers simply did not pose "grave and irreparable harm" to the United States, as the government contended, and the court refused to buy that contention.[117]

To a greater extent than most papers, the Louisville *Courier-Journal* expressed misgivings about the way the Supreme Court dealt with the case. After noting that the decision was "of course a victory for freedom of the press and the people's right to know," the paper went on to observe that "the Court decided merely that a gadfly press may not be swatted by the government before it stings—this time." The editorial continued: "the 180–word formal order . . . does not condemn the government's effort to muzzle the press, nor does it clarify the boundary line between the government's right to secrecy and the public's right to information." The paper also deplored the fact that none of the justices "commented on the propriety of the judicial hearings on a newspaper's right to publish." Taking issue with the view of the minority justices that the Court needed more time to study the issues, the *Courier-Journal* said: "Had the minority prevailed, an unsympathetic court could keep vital information out of print for months on the ground that speed would mean irresponsibility." In a direct challenge to Blackmun's suggestion that the press would be to blame if the war were prolonged, the paper said:

Could not one say with greater justification that if the American people had not been kept in the dark all these years about Vietnam they might have ended the war a long time ago, or never joined it in the first place? If there are "sad consequences" still to come, shall we blame those who expose how decisions are made in Washington; or shall we blame the fact that decisions are made by men too well shielded by secrecy from any kind of public accountability?[118]

The *St. Louis Post-Dispatch* stressed the weakness of the government's case:

. . . there is little evidence that the principle of a free press was colliding with or endangering the operation of a complex government in any way whatsoever. The Pentagon papers . . . reveal history, not military secrets. . . .

It is remarkable that this first big claim to precensorship should be made on so flimsy a basis, concerning old documents about a war never declared. . . .

Freedom of the press, we firmly believe, was bound to win against so unprecedented and irrational an attack.[119]

Although the *Denver Post* welcomed the decision, that paper conceded that there might be an occasion for prior restraint.

We do not take the position, as Justices Black and Douglas did, that the First Amendment does not allow *any* previous restraint on newspapers, no matter how great the peril to American lives and the national safety.

But we say that the danger must be so vast, so specific and so clear that the courts can recognize it immediately or else the press ought not to be restrained at all. Despite Wednesday's decision, we do not consider that freedom of the press is secure when the government can prevent publication for 15 days.

By keeping information out of the marketplace of ideas at a crucial stage in decision-making, the government can steer the country down a path that might be spurned if the information were available at the right time.[120]

In an editorial that was remarkably bland for the subject, the *San Francisco Chronicle* merely summarized the positions of various justices and concluded with a note of warning:

... despite the flat declaration of Justice Brennan that the First Amendment "stands as an absolute bar against the imposition of judicial restraints" in the matters here involved, a reading of the opinions, concurring and dissenting, leaves the layman with a feeling that the newspapers, while left free to print the Pentagon Papers, have been silently warned to avoid printing any that might indeed imperil national security, if by any lapse of editorial judgment, they might decide to do so.[121]

The *New York Times* was probably accurate when it said editorially that, in deciding that publication of the Pentagon papers would not harm the national security, the *Times* was supported by "the overwhelming majority of the American press."[122] Most papers welcomed the outcome as necessary to a free press, but many agonized over the conflict between press freedom and national security. Of eighty-two first- and second-day editorials from across the nation, reprinted by *Editorials on File*, only three might be said to have concluded that the Supreme Court decision was unwise,[123] and only three straddled the issues to such an extent that their conclusions were unclear.[124]

The *San Diego Union*'s position typified the views of those papers that reacted with entirely negative comments.

Certainly the real issue in yesterday's ruling was not freedom of the press. . . .

It is plain now that the federal government took the wrong case before the bar. It permitted the issue to be argued on the fuzzy grounds of how secret a secret is rather than on the basis of whether the laws involving theft and receipt of stolen property apply to everyone.[125]

(Herbert Klein, former editor of the *San Diego Union* and in 1971 White House director of communications, said a few months after the Pentagon Papers controversy that, were the decision his to make, he would still prosecute the *New York Times* and the *Washington Post* for publishing the Pentagon Papers.)[126]

The *Nashville Banner* (which was not among the eighty-two papers whose editorials were reprinted by *Editorials on File*) expressed an even more bitter attitude than the *San Diego Union*.

It is a shocking ruling. . . . The nation will live to regret a decision validating an act of recklessness unmatched in U.S. history. The issue in this case . . . was not the merit or demerit of what had been published but the essential guardianship of privileged information. . . . With this as a precedent, what assured protection is there of Government-secret documents?[127]

Despite the outpouring of editorials about the Pentagon Papers case and its significance for freedom of the press, most newspapers lost interest once the confrontation between government and press had receded into the past. The government continued to classify thousands of documents each year, and the press mounted no widespread crusade to end the system of excessive secrecy that many papers had said impaired the people's right to know and interfered with the freedom of the press to inform them.

Among the many issues each year that affect freedom of the press, none usually hit a raw nerve in editors as much as did a case involving a so-called right to reply law in Florida, which was challenged in the Supreme Court and decided in 1974.[128] Florida's law, adopted in 1913, provided that:

If any newspaper in its columns assails the personal character of any candidate . . . or charges said candidate with malfeasance or misfeasance in office, or otherwise attacks his official record, or gives to another free space for such purpose, such newspaper shall upon request of such candidate immediately publish free of cost any reply he may make thereto. . . .

The case arose when the Miami *Herald* published two editorials attacking the integrity of Pat Tornillo, who was a teacher's union official and a candidate for the Florida House of Representatives in 1972. When the *Herald* refused to publish Tornillo's proposed replies, he brought suit under the right of reply statute. Although the Dade County circuit court ruled against the candidate and held the law unconstitutional, the Florida Supreme Court reversed the circuit judgment; the *Herald* then appealed the case to the United States Supreme Court, which found the Florida act unconstitutional.

Writing for a unanimous Court, Chief Justice Warren Burger said that, under the First Amendment, government could not compel "a newspaper to print that which it would not otherwise print," for to do so would be the constitutional equivalent of censorship. He said the Florida law exacted a penalty from newspapers by requiring expenditures to print the reply that would take space that could be devoted to other material the newspaper may have preferred to print. He pointed out that the law might actually limit "the vigor and variety of public debate" rather than increase it, because editors might choose "the safe course" of reducing or moderating their coverage of election campaigns. Because the law authorized a governmental "intrusion into the function of editors," the court found it invalid.

The reaction of the press was predictably strong in support of the decision in the Miami *Herald* case. Editors naturally didn't want to be answerable to government for what went into their papers. Although Mississippi was the only other state to have a right of reply law on its statute books at the time of the 1974 decision, a Supreme Court ruling validating the Florida law would surely have given new encouragement to the ever-present disposition among legislators to introduce such legislation.[129]

Of the seven editorials on the Miami *Herald* decision reprinted by *Editorials on File*, all praised the ruling.[130] Many editorials from other papers also expressed opposition to right of reply laws both before and after the decision. The *New York Times*, while commending the decision, also said that it "points up more strongly than ever the importance of voluntary action by newspapers to insure hospitality to opposite viewpoints and to permit access by those whom the press attack."[131]

In its editorial, the *St. Louis Post-Dispatch* observed that: "The substitution of political or official judgment for an editor's judgment does nothing to guarantee fairness; it only guarantees that the free press is no longer free, and cannot contribute to the free discussion of ideas essential to political health."[132]

The *Oregon Journal* in Portland commented that "while the [Florida] law and others like it are unconstitutional, the principle behind them is sound. A newspaper does owe a reasonable right of reply to persons with whom it may disagree, and not just to political candidates either."[133] Although the *Oregon Journal*'s perception might be that it offers a right of reply "to anyone," many of its readers probably think differently—as no doubt would the readers of most newspapers. The existence of a perceived problem of inadequate response opportunities in the media for the targets of criticism has been testified to: by (1) recurring attempts to enact laws to enforce a right of reply, (2) by the Federal Communication Commission's "fairness doctrine" (upheld by the Supreme Court in the *Red Lion* case, 395 U.S. 367, 1969) under which broadcasters are required to provide balanced treatment of controversial issues, and (3) by respectable legal opinion in favor of an enforceable right against newspapers.[134] This widespread attitude is reflected in a paraphrase of a rather cynical comment by the late A. J. Liebling: "Freedom of the press is great for those who own one." Despite the Supreme Court decision in the Miami *Herald* case, the public is not likely to feel that the First Amendment truly promotes robust and wide-open discussion unless the press moves voluntarily to provide easier and more comprehensive access than it does now to citizens who feel that they have been shut out.

Among various Court decisions critically affecting freedom of the press in recent years, perhaps none received so little sustained press attention as the rulings on a book that the Central Intelligence Agency undertook to censor. The case arose in 1972 when the CIA went into federal court in Virginia and got an injunction against Victor Marchetti, a former CIA official, ordering him not to disclose any information about the CIA and requiring him to submit any manuscript about the agency for clearance by the CIA. Marchetti thus became the first American writer to be served with an official censorship order by a United States court.[135] The order by United States District Judge Albert V. Bryan, Jr., was upheld by the United States Court of Appeals for the Fourth Circuit, and the Supreme Court refused to hear the case.[136]

In 1973, in compliance with the Bryan order, the manuscript of a book, *The CIA and the Cult of Intelligence*, by Marchetti and a coauthor, John D. Marks, a former State Department employee, was submitted to the CIA for censorship. The agency designated 339 portions of the book that were to be deleted. As a result of hard-fought objections from the authors, the CIA finally reduced its demanded deletions to 168. Following a suit by the authors and Alfred A. Knopf, the publisher, Judge Bryan found only 27 of the 168 disputed items to be excludable from the manuscript as classified material, but he postponed enforcement of the decision pending an appeal by the government.[137] In an astonishing display of insensitivity to the First Amendment in this second round of litigation, the court of appeals in 1975 upheld the government's right to censor a book before publication—to delete not just the 27 items designated by Judge Bryan but all 168 items designated by the CIA, the rationale being that the CIA's security classifications must be presumed correct and that judges were not qualified to rule on such matters.[138]

The basis for the decision advanced by the government and accepted by the court was that Marchetti and Marks had waived their First Amendment rights when they signed agreements with their respective agencies not to reveal classified information they had learned during their employment. Government lawyers had argued that this was not a First Amendment case but merely an action to enforce a contract with former employees.[139] So secrecy agreements signed by government employees handling classified material became a vehicle for arbitrary censorship of the writing of Marchetti and Marks and presumably for that of many present and former government employees if the government chooses to use it. The potential of this censorship tool for use in a capricious manner is apparent in that thousands of government employees routinely sign secrecy agreements and just as routinely break them. Are some favored employees to have freedom and others to be suppressed? High level officials from presidents down have revealed "secrets" when they wrote their memoirs.[140] Prior to the *Marchetti* case, the government had never sought to enforce the secrecy pledges, apparently for the simple reason that disclosures from all levels were commonplace and served official purposes just as often as they did the purposes of the "leaker" of material.

No law penalizes the release of classified information, except for the original Atomic Energy Act, with respect to information classified under it, and the Espionage Act, with respect to certain information transmitted to a foreign power with intent to injure the United

States.[141] Hence the government devised the novel "contract doctrine." And the Supreme Court on May 27, 1975, by refusing to review the Marchetti case, let stand the court of appeals decision upholding the doctrine.

As a result of the government's successful litigation, *The CIA and the Cult of Intelligence* was published with 168 blank spaces in its pages, the first such book ever to appear in the United States.[142] Only a few years after the government failed to restrain the *New York Times* for more than fifteen days, lawyers for the Nixon administration succeeded in imposing prior restraint on a book that exposed the excesses and blunders of the CIA. The suit left the government with a method for preventing the disclosure of official misjudgment or misconduct that might be revealed in some of the millions of classified documents, 99 percent of which, according to expert testimony, should never have been classified in the first place.[143] A lifetime injunction against further writing by Marchetti, without CIA clearance, was imposed as a part of the litigation over the book. Although the legal battle over the Marchetti-Marks book received considerable coverage from the press, there was nothing like the outpouring of editorial protest over censorship that occurred in the Pentagon Papers case.[144] Of the 140 newspapers monitored by *Editorials on File*, only seven had editorials in response to the court of appeals and the Supreme Court rulings on the *Marchetti* case, even though they involved unprecedented restraint on freedom of the press.[145]

In contrast to their crusade on the Pentagon Papers case, the *New York Times* and the *Washington Post* mounted no editorial campaign on the *Marchetti* case, although it also involved a matter of excessive classification and although the court decisions in Marchetti were more ominous in principle for press freedom.

The Providence *Journal*, one of the few papers to comment on the Supreme Court action in *Marchetti*, said:

> The United States Supreme Court, by upholding a lower court's open-ended censorship order against an author who is a former intelligence agent, has set an unhealthy precedent that nibbles away at the First Amendment. . . .
>
> By refusing to review the Marchetti case, the Supreme Court upheld the lower court's censorship of sections of the book. Also left untouched,

however, was a more significant order, requiring Mr. Marchetti to submit all his future writing about the CIA to the agency for pre-publication censorship. . . .

Such a blanket restriction . . . will tend to reverse the trend away from excessive government secrecy and over-classification of documents.[146]

In its editorial the *Philadelphia Inquirer* sought to show the frivolous nature of the CIA censorship by quoting from the Marchetti-Marks book one of the passages that had originally been deleted by the agency and then restored in negotiations with the authors. It revealed only that Richard Helms, then director of the CIA, had mispronounced Malagasy. After further comment, the *Inquirer* concluded:

. . . there is the question of whether any citizen can be required to sign away his constitutional rights as a condition of government employment. . . . the case . . . fundamentally . . . comes down to the right of a free people to know what their government is doing. It is a pity that the Supreme Court seems itself to have succumbed to the "cult of intelligence" and come out on the wrong side.[147]

In Pittsburgh the *Post-Gazette* observed:

Almost casually, a near-unanimous U.S. Supreme Court has compromised freedom of the press and free speech by allowing the Central Intelligence Agency to censor a critical book by a former CIA employee. . . .

The court . . . sanctioned . . . the prior restraint long considered anathema to the Bill of Rights. The effect of the decision is to encourage government agencies unhappy about proposed books by former employes to suppress such writings—on the pretext of their choice.[148]

The *St. Louis Post-Dispatch* declared:

By declining to review a lower court decision allowing the first prior restraint on the publication of a book in the history of the nation, the Supreme Court has let stand—at least for the area covered by the Fourth Circuit Court of Appeals—an appalling precedent for freedom of the press. . . .

The only encouragement to be derived from the high court's action is that the justices did not take the case and uphold the circuit court on the merits of its decision. In another case posing similar issues the high court may see the havoc that can be wrought with the First Amendment by allowing the Government to have virtually unreviewable censorship authority over egregiously over-classified material; and it may rule differently.[149]

In contrast to the paucity of newspaper editorial comment on the *Marchetti* case, which did not directly concern newspapers but which nevertheless was highly significant for freedom of the press, the comment by newspapers on a gag order decision by the Supreme Court (*Nebraska Press Association* v. *Stuart*) two years later (1976) was nationwide and came from papers large and small.

The case originated in Nebraska, where a Lincoln County district judge, Hugh Stuart, had ordered the press not to report any of the details in the arrest of a murder suspect, or the suspect's confession and other facts that had been presented in open court at the pretrial stage. He even forbade the press to report his gag order. The Stuart order, which was upheld by the Nebraska Supreme Court, aroused intense press interest because judges, with the objective of ensuring an impartial jury, had been issuing gag orders in increasing numbers despite the U.S. Supreme Court's advice in the 1966 case, *Sheppard* v. *Maxwell*,[150] to use means other than press restraint to provide for a fair trial. According to the Reporters Committee for Freedom of the Press, 174 judicial gag orders had been issued in the United States from 1967 through 1975, with the number growing each year[151]

Thus when the Nebraska case was appealed to the United States Supreme Court, no fewer than twenty-five newspapers and broadcasters from across the nation filed a friend-of-the-court brief in support of the Nebraska Press Association, one of the parties in the litigation. Although the Court ruled unanimously that the Nebraska judge's order was improper[152] and that a judge may never restrain the press from reporting what happens in public, Chief Justice Burger, joined by four other justices, suggested that under the most unusual circumstances and with clear justification a judge may limit criminal case reporting. Justice Brennan, in a concurring opinion joined in by Justices Thurgood Marshall and Potter Stewart, argued that "resort to prior restraints on the freedom of the press is a constitutionally impermissible method" of ensuring a person's right to a fair trial.

All of the twenty-two papers whose editorials on the decision were reprinted by *Editorials on File* greeted the ruling affirmatively, although many did not think it went far enough.[153] The *St. Louis Post-Dispatch* exemplified the expressed reservations of the press when it said:

> Although the decision in the Nebraska case is an important victory for freedom of the press when viewed against the gravity of the threat, the ruling cannot be regarded as an augury for freedom from all improper judicial restraint in the future. . . . Justice Brennan expressed the historical—and to the press, more acceptable—view . . . when he said: "The press may be arrogant, tyrannical, abusive and sensationalist, just as it may be incisive, probing and informative. But at least in the context of prior restraints on publication, the decision on what, when and how to publish, is for editors, not judges."[154]

Decisions such as *Nebraska Press Association* v. *Stuart* and a few others in recent years have upheld in a limited fashion press claims of protection. But the general trend of Supreme Court rulings on the First Amendment during the years that Nixon appointees have been able to influence decision-making has been negative for press freedom. In 1972, in *Banzburg* v. *Hays*,[155] the Supreme Court, in a five-to-four decision, declined to confer First Amendment protection for the right of reporters to withhold from a grand jury the names of confidential news sources—although the majority opinion explicitly noted that news gathering qualified for the First Amendment protection. Of the eighteen newspapers whose editorial reactions were reprinted in *Editorials on File*, fifteen found fault with the *Branzburg* decision on free press grounds. Only three papers agreed in general with the ruling.[156]

In 1973 the Court let stand a United States Fifth Circuit Court of Appeals decision that reporters, under pain of punishment for contempt, are bound to obey a judicial order banning publication even if the order is unconstitutional. A Baton Rouge, Louisiana, judge had enjoined two reporters from reporting an open court hearing, an order that violated the First Amendment, according to the court of appeals, but that the reporters were nevertheless required to abide by until its validity was adjudicated. This could delay the publication of news for years unless provision is made for immediate appeal.

In a 1974 libel case, *Gertz* v. *Robert Welch, Inc.*,[157] the Supreme Court reevaluated its holding in a case only three years before (*Rosenbloom* v. *Metromedia., Inc.*[158]) and, contrary to that decision, held that although public figures and public officials must prove recklessness to recover in defamation suits against the news media, private individuals need prove only negligence even though matters of public interest were being discussed in the allegedly libelous publication. Two years later, in *Time, Inc.* v. *Mary Alice Firestone*,[159] the Court again put the press in jeopardy in a ruling involving the fields of libel and privacy. As a result of an erroneous report of a judge's divorce order in a complex case in which the opinion was far from a model of clarity, *Time* magazine was required to pay a libel judgment to Mrs. Firestone on the grounds that she was not a "public figure" and need only prove negligence rather than malice. Yet Mrs. Firestone had sought public attention by holding press conferences during the litigation.[160] The decision holds the press to a standard of accuracy and understanding of legal niceties of such strictness that it is bound to have a chilling effect on the discussion of cases of public interest.

The prospect is that, faced with possible huge libel judgments in complex cases, the press will apply self-censorship in this field, as it already does in dubious "national security" cases. Self-imposed censorship in such cases, as in the treatment of possibly libelous material, stems no doubt from feared litigation. After all, most of the Supreme Court justices did refer to the possible criminal liability of the press in the Pentagon Papers case. But it should be noted that much of the self-censorship in the reputed "national security" area stems not from a fear of penalties but from a natural affinity between establishment journalists and establishment figures in government whose judgments the journalists accept. Take as an example the press failure for months, as a result of CIA pleas, to report the American effort to raise a Soviet submarine from the bottom of the Pacific Ocean.[161]

In 1977–1978, with few exceptions, the Supreme Court continued to exhibit an anti-press bias in its decisions. One of the exceptions was the Court's 1977 decision overturning on First Amendment grounds an Oklahoma judge's order barring three Oklahoma City newspapers from publishing the name and picture of an eleven-year-old boy charged in a killing—information that had been obtained in a public hearing.[162] Another exception was the Court's 1978 ruling that invalidated on narrow grounds a Virginia statute under which the Norfolk *Virginian-Pilot* had been convicted and fined for revealing the name of a judge who was under what was supposed to be a confidential investigation by the state's Judicial Inquiry and Review Commission.[163] A sampling of editorial reaction indicated unanimous press support for the decision among the twenty-two papers involved.[164]

In three other significant 1978 decisions the Supreme Court was the source of bad news for a free press and for the people, in whose behalf the First Amendment was adopted. In *Houchins* v. *KQED*,[165] the Court flatly rejected the idea that there is a "right to know" about government action and policy. The decision came in a suit by a San Francisco public television station that had been denied access to the Alameda County jail to investigate conditions after an inmate had committed suicide. Rejecting two lower federal court decisions holding that, under the First Amendment, journalists have broader rights of access to prisons that the general public, Chief Justice Burger said the news media had no more right than others to interview inmates and make photographs and recordings. "There is an undoubted right to 'gather news from any source by means within the law,' " the chief justice wrote, citing *Branzburg*, "but that affords no basis for the claim that the First Amendment compels others— private persons or governments—to supply information." Since members of the public were not permitted to use cameras or recording devices or to interview inmates at the Alameda County facility, the chief justice was saying in effect that the First Amendment gives the press no right to serve as the eyes and ears of the public in scrutinizing a closed government institution where abuses can be most easily hidden.[166]

Despite this judicial blow against the public's right of access through the press to information about public institutions, the press seemed rather lukewarm in its defense of the right. Although all of the thirteen editorials reprinted by *Editorials on File* favored the notion of public access, only six of the thirteen challenged the Supreme Court's position with vigor.[167]

Another 1978 ruling that held ominous implications for the press was *Zurcher* v. *Stanford Daily*,[168] in which the Supreme Court upheld the power of the police, using a search warrant, to make a surprise visit to a newspaper's offices and to ransack the premises even when no one there is suspected of a crime. In affirming the reasonableness of such searches, the Court also weakened the Fourth Amendment, which has been held to allow the issuance of search warrants only when there is probable cause to believe that a crime has been committed.

The case arose when police in Palo Alto, California, in 1971 got a warrant and combed through the files of the *Stanford Daily*, a student newspaper, in search of photographs of a student demonstration, hoping that such photographs might help them identify demonstrators who might have been responsible for violence that had occurred. The student paper, supported by much of the nation's media, argued that the search had been a violation of the Constitution's free press guarantee and that a more acceptable procedure would have been to seek evidence by subpoena, which would have required a hearing and given the paper a chance to defend its rights in court. But the Supreme Court, overturning decisions in the paper's favor by both a federal district court and the court of appeals, took the naive position—in a majority opinion written by Justice White—that such unannounced searches would not interfere with "the press's ability to gather, analyze and disseminate news." Justice Potter Stewart, one of three dissenters, emphasized the "serious burden on a free press imposed by an unannounced police search of a newspaper office: the possibility of disclosure of information received from confidential sources or of the identity of the sources themselves."[169]

By permitting the police to arm themselves with warrants and make surprise raids on newspaper offices, the Supreme Court in effect sanctioned the use of the press as a vehicle for police investigations and gravely jeopardized its intended role as independent watchdog of the police and other government agencies. If the sanctity of its files cannot be protected from surprise government examination or seizure, the press will hardly be in a position to gather and publish news from confidential sources about official incompetence or corruption.

Although editorial reaction to the *Stanford Daily* case was overwhelmingly critical of the Supreme Court decision, adverse press reaction was not unanimous. A sampling of editorials from twenty-two newspapers reprinted by *Editorials on File* showed that nineteen found fault with the decision, two waffled on the issues, and one, the Birmingham, Alabama, *News*, actually supported the decision,[170] saying: "Some suggest that the opinion . . . is a clear violation of the First Amendment guarantees of freedom of the press and threatens all Americans. Of course the fear is unfounded. . . ."[171]

One of the mildly concerned papers, the *Oklahoma City Times*, concluded its straddling editorial by saying: "A far greater danger of government interference with the press is the vast power wielded by such regulatory agencies as the Occupational Safety and Health Agency (OSHA), the Equal Employment Commission (EEOC) and the Internal Revenue Service (IRS)."[172]

In a much-publicized case toward the end of 1978,[173] the Supreme Court, as in the *Stanford Daily* case, again showed its inclination to side with government against the press in the matter of compulsory disclosure of confidential information. The refusal of the Court to review the New Jersey contempt convictions of the *New York Times* and its reporter, Myron Farber, indicated that when journalists are confronted with sweeping orders from state judges, they had better not rely on so-called state shield laws or on the First Amendment's free press guarantee to protect them from summary punishment if they refuse to comply.

In New Jersey, Farber was jailed for nearly six weeks and the *Times* was fined $285,000 when the reporter and the newspaper refused to comply with a trial judge's subpoena ordering the surrender to the judge of all the documents on which Farber had based his news articles about Dr. Mario E. Jascalevich. The doctor's trial for murder in connection with drug-related deaths in a hospital where he practiced had stemmed from Farber's investigative reports. Although Farber had taken the stand and answered almost all questions put to him, he refused to disclose confidential sources on which his articles were based or to respond to a dragnet subpoena that might have disclosed such sources by requiring him to turn over to the judge "statements, pictures, memoranda, recordings and notes of interviews with witnesses." Some commentators made much of the point that the required disclosure would have been to the judge in private.[174] But this did not change the obvious fact that a source who had been promised confidentiality would still feel compromised by the revelation of his name to a public official (the judge) with power to make public disclosure and to compel appearance in court. Moreover, the indiscriminate subpoena served, at the request of the defendant, on Farber and the *Times* and requiring them to deliver unpublished notes and other journalistic raw material represented an intolerable government intrusion into the editing processes of the press.

For their refusal to comply, the reporter and the newspaper were cited for contempt and summarily sentenced without ever being given an opportunity to present in court their legal arguments in support of their contention that they were protected by the First Amendment and by a broad New Jersey statute designed to safeguard the press against just such compulsory disclosure of confidential material. New Jersey courts, including that state's supreme court, held that the New Jersey shield law and the First Amendment were outweighed by the Sixth Amendment, which guarantees a defendant the right to have compulsory process to obtain witnesses in his favor. Although for years, often without statutory mandate, the courts have exempted from compulsory process testimony that would violate the confidentiality of lawyer-client, doctor-patient, priest-penitent and husband-wife relationships, the New Jersey high court (with the implicit approval of the U.S. Supreme Court) declined to recognize a similar privilege of confidentiality between a journalist and his sources—although a strong argument can be made that this would serve as high a social purpose as the other forms of protected confidentiality.

No one knew—and the defense lawyers did not specify—how Farber's documents would serve as evidence in Jascalevich's favor. In fact, Jascalevich was eventually acquitted without the benefit of Farber's documents. Yet the contempt convictions of Farber and the *Times* stood, with no recognition by the nation's highest court of the serious implications for press freedom implicit in the New Jersey court decisions. If the Supreme Court had required that at least a subpoena must stipulate what documents were needed and why, the relative importance of Sixth and First Amendment rights could have been argued and perhaps a reasonable rule promulgated. As matters stood, a defendant was acquitted, the press was convicted, and the New Jersey courts, with no interference from the U.S. Supreme Court, said in effect that the Sixth Amendment authorizes judges to make arbitrary demands on the press regardless of the deleterious effect on news-gathering, much of which depends on the protection of confidential sources.[175]

The implications of all this for press freedom were well put by Justice Stewart, dissenting in the *Branzburg* case in 1972 when the Court first refused to recognize a journalistic privilege to protect confidential sources. At that time Stewart said:

The Court's crabbed view of the First Amendment reflects a disturbing insensitivity to the critical role of an independent press in our society. . . . The Court thus invites state and federal authorities to undermine the historic independence of the press by attempting to annex the journalistic profession as an investigative arm of government.

. . . It is obvious that informants are necessary to the newsgathering process. . . . If it is to perform its constitutional mission, the press must do far more than merely print public statements or publish prepared handouts. . . . The First Amendment concern must not be with the motives of any particular news source, but rather with the conditions in which informants of all shades of the spectrum may make information available through the press to the public.[176]

The *New Yorker* magazine, referring to the *Farber* case, succinctly summed up the situation:

Even from the standpoint of law enforcement, the results [of compulsory disclosure] will be ironic, because reporters who can be compelled to identify their sources in court aren't going to learn anything that the courts want to know. As soon as the courts start fishing for evidence in this pond, the pond will dry up. The courts will then lose not only any confidential information that the reporters may have possessed but also the articles based on that information—articles that on many occasions in the past have brought the very existence of crimes to the government's attention in the first place. Thus, at a single stroke the judicial system will defeat both the First Amendment and itself.[177]

Press reaction to the *Farber* case indicated support for the *Times* and its reporter by a big majority of newspapers. Of forty-three editorials reprinted by *Editorials on File*, thirty-six backed the free press position of the *Times*, although with varying degrees of enthusiasm.[178]

In 1979 a case with potential disastrous consequences for freedom of the press arose when, at the request of the U.S. Department of Justice, *The Progressive* magazine of Madison, Wisconsin, was judicially enjoined for six months from publishing an article about the hydrogen bomb that was alleged by the government to contain restricted information, even though all of the author's sources were public. U.S. District Judge Robert Warren accepted the government's argument that, under the Atomic Energy Act of 1954, certain information about weapons was classified "at birth" even if it was the product of an author's own thoughts or was assembled by the author from public sources. Although appellate judicial support for such flagrant censorial power would pose an unprecedented threat to First Amendment rights, the press nationally was ambivalent about the case. The *New York Times* (at the beginning) and the *Washington Post*, those supposed preeminent champions of press freedom, equivocated on the grounds that *The Progressive* might be endangering national security by giving other nations secret bomb data, even though similar information had been available on library shelves for years. The government finally was forced to drop its censorship effort when a small daily, the *Press Connection*, of Madison, Wisconsin, boldly published much of the same material that *The Progressive* had been barred from printing. Thus was the point made that the press must be free to publish information needed for democratic decision making on arms control, although an ominous precedent was set by six months of prior restraint.[179]

As the nation approached the 190th anniversary (June 15, 1980) of the adoption of the Bill of Rights—with the Supreme Court often expressing a narrow view of the First Amendment in obscenity, national security, and criminal trial contexts—the press was faced with a growing challenge to defend its freedom. The fact that Justice Brennan spoke for a minority of the Court in his concurring opinion in the *Nebraska* case was indicative of the problem. The Supreme Court apparently was not ready, in Brennan's phrase, to leave the "decision on what, when and how to publish . . . for editors, not judges."

12

The Press: How Faithful to Freedom?

One clear impression emerges from this survey of more than 175 years of press reaction to various freedom of expression issues in the United States. It is that, except when their own freedom was discernibly at stake, established general circulation newspapers have tended to go along with efforts to suppress deviations from the prevailing political and social orthodoxies of their time and place rather than to support the right to dissent. Strong support of the First Amendment's role in protecting the right to dissent from prevailing public opinion has been left largely to dissenting publications themselves, although they were often too weak to make themselves heard.

During the presidential term of John Adams, when fear of the radicalism of the French Revolution was the prevailing sentiment and when war fever against France was running high, Federalist papers, then dominant, were as eager as the government to put down press voices that supported the French revolutionaries. Since they still felt an obligation to pay homage to the First Amendment, Federalist papers justified their call for suppression by accusing their party opponents of sedition or treason, which were said to be outside the bounds of constitutional protection. So it has been ever since. Even though the First Amendment's command is categorical, those who have perceived danger in one or another form of speech or publication have found a way to rationalize exceptions to the command. They have been unwilling to abide by Jefferson's axiom that "it is time enough for the rightful purposes of civil government for its officers to interfere when principles break out into overt acts against peace and good order."

In practice, Jefferson himself did not fully subscribe to his axiom. But in his day, once the era of the Alien and Sedition Laws had passed, the power of the federal government was never used to crush dissent. In Jefferson's time, too, the character of the press was different. Newspapers were personal or party organs and diversity stemmed naturally from the individuality of editors and proprietors. Editorial positions changed. Jeffersonian, or Republican, papers—which for a time were in the minority position and vigorously defended their right to be protected in dissent—eventually came to represent the majority view.

When the abolitionist movement emerged, general circulation newspapers, even in the North, tended to be hostile to the abolitionists' right to disseminate their views. Abolitionists, like dissenters of other times, defended their right to publish and to be circulated without impediment; they demonstrated their commitment to free expression by providing space in their columns for their sharpest critics. Only when the abolitionist movement gained in strength and when mob outrages and proposed government strictures against abolitionist organs could be perceived as a threat to their own interests did general circulation papers take up the cause of press freedom that the abolitionists had raised. But there was no press crusade for freedom vigorous enough to offset the extralegal devices that continued in use as a means of curbing the abolitionist press, especially in the South, as long as slavery existed.

When the nation was engaged in wars in which popular opinion was sharply divided—as was the case in the War of 1812, the Mexican War, and the Civil War—the antiadministration or antiwar press formed a faction strong enough to command grudging respect for its right to publish. There were exceptions, of course, as in cases in which an antiwar paper sought to exist in a community where public opinion was overwhelmingly against its position. The experience of the *Federal Republican* in Baltimore in 1812 was such an example.

When war engendered united public support, however, as in World War I and World War II, newspapers were as hostile to the expression of antiwar sentiment as was the general public. World War I provided an especially flagrant example of the press joining the popular hue and cry for restricting expression against the war. There was an almost total abdication by the general circulation press of any responsibility to uphold freedom for dissent.

In analyzing intolerance, it is not possible to define cause and effect. Do the media (newspapers for most of our history, and now broadcasting) initiate the mood? Or do they merely follow the political leadership in stirring the passions of war or witch-hunting and then succumb to those passions themselves? Although antiwar expression in World War II was not altogether free of restraint, it was not in as much need of defense, since neither the government nor vigilante groups mounted the kinds of campaigns for suppression that had been launched during the First World War.

On ideological issues, such as labor radicalism in the late nineteenth century and socialism and communism in the twentieth century, leading newspapers have spoken almost with one voice in denying the applicability of the First Amendment to the protection of freedom for such views in times of perceived crisis. The First Amendment rights of such groups as anarchists, wobblies (members of the Industrial Workers of the World), Socialists and Communists were undermined by Draconian measures with little protest from the press. These radicals of more recent time have hardly ever gained the privilege of support for their freedom from established political figures and from established organs of information as did French sympathizers during the time of Jefferson and as did abolitionists later. By the time labor radicals came on the scene, ownership of a large newspaper required a big financial investment, and control of the press was lodged in well-to-do business entrepreneurs who had little or no interest in defending freedom of expression for those who seemed to threaten the economic order of which they were a part.

In the matter of alleged obscenity, as in war and political ideology, the press has been reluctant to defend freedom of expression when the challeged material offended the dominant views of its own con-

stituency. The Supreme Court's exclusion of so-called obscenity—
a category of expression never satisfactorily defined—from the
protection of the First Amendment has brought no outpouring of
editorial protest, although the press has become somewhat more
favorable to freedom as the public has become more permissive in
its acceptance of sexually oriented material.

When the issue did not involve material that was unpopular on
ideological or moral grounds (radicalism and obscenity) but instead
involved the right of the press to be free of official restraint against
publishing material of general public acceptability, newspapers have
been much more disposed to defend freedom of expression. Thus
newspapers generally welcomed the attempted punishment of Judge
Peck for his abusive treatment of a lawyer-writer. In later times
newspapers almost universally supported the New York *World*'s
fight against a federal criminal libel action—although few of them
focused on the dispute as an issue of press freedom. Still later, the
press generally commended Supreme Court decisions invalidating
a Minnesota press gag law and a Louisiana tax on newspaper advertising (*Near* v. *Minnesota* and *Grosjean* v. *American Press Co.*),
decisions curbing the contempt power of judges (*Bridges* v. *California, Pennekamp* v. *Florida*, and *Craig* v. *Harney*), a decision
limiting the libel accountability of the press (*New York Times* v.
Sullivan), a ruling checking the authority of public officials to penalize election-day editorializing (*Mills* v. *Alabama*), and a decision
denying the government power to prevent publication of the ques-
tionably classified Pentagon Papers (*New York Times* v. *United
States*).

The attitude of the press toward freedom to publish material covered by the so-called national security label, as in the Pentagon
Papers case, deserves special mention. Although newspapers overwhelmingly supported the right of the press to publish the Pentagon
Papers despite the government's claim that publication would endanger national security, the press over the long term has not shown
itself eager to challenge the national security barrier. The prestige
of the *New York Times* and the evident excessive secrecy surrounding the three-year-old history of the Vietnam War helped the press to
overcome its reluctance in the Pentagon Papers case. More often
than not, however, the challenging of a national security claim has
been treated by the press like criticism of the nation in wartime—

a practice not to be welcomed. The national security label has for the most part retained a sanctified status and a capacity to check press freedom to report on many areas of government. Yet knowledgeable classifiers themselves have admitted that the label has been unjustifiably used to keep secret millions of public documents, and the misuse of the secrecy stamp to merely avoid embarrassment or to shield incompetence or worse has been repeatedly demonstrated.

National security has become the modern equivalent of seditious libel in the government's legal arsenal for keeping the press at bay. And the press, despite its frequent emphasis on the right to know, has been timid about risking the government's fire unless one of the powerful members of its own fraternity is threatened, as in the Pentagon Papers case. Thus, most newspapers showed little sympathy for Victor Marchetti, when he disclosed CIA secrets that shed light on the agency's weaknesses, or initially for Columbia Broadcasting System correspondent Daniel Schorr, when he leaked for publication a secret report by the House Intelligence Committee on the failures and abuses of intelligence agencies.[1]

Press submissiveness toward government claims of the need for secrecy in the national interest was far less habitual in 1795 when editor Benjamin Franklin Bache of the Philadelphia *Aurora*—ignoring the secrecy label attached to the Jay Treaty by the Washington administration and the Senate—published first a summary and then the full contents of the treaty. Other papers widely reprinted the document. Despite a public outcry and the administration's fear that U.S. relations with other countries would be irreparably harmed and the security of the nation undermined, no court injunction to stop the presses was sought.

Viewed in historical perspective and in the context of many issues, then, the record of the press in defending First Amendment rights has been a mixed one. Leading newspapers have seldom committed themselves unequivocally to the defense of freedom of expression for unpopular materials or views espoused by weak special-interest publications. They have usually taken clearcut stands against government restraint on the press when the material involved was of general public interest or, at least, was not violative of political or moral convictions. Championship of the First Amendment by that portion of the press in the strongest position to make freedom of expression effective appears, therefore, to have been based more on self-interest than on principle. Such narrowly focused support for freedom of the press is better than no support, but it hardly fosters the dissemination of the diverse viewpoints and information on public affairs and the other broad objectives envisaged by First Amendment philosophers.

From Jefferson and Madison in the eighteenth century to Holmes, Brandeis, Black, and Douglas in the twentieth, First Amendment interpreters in official positions have, in their most libertarian promulgations, proclaimed a freer role for speech and press than have editors of leading newspapers when uninhibited expression was being challenged. Jefferson would have left "undisturbed" those who would dissolve the Union. Madison said the freedom guaranteed by the First Amendment was absolute so far as the federal government was concerned. Holmes, joined by Brandeis, said in his *Abrams* dissent that "we should be eternally vigilant against attempts to check the expression of opinions that we loathe and believe to be fraught with death, unless they so imminently threaten immediate interference with the lawful and pressing purposes of the law that an immediate check is required to save the country."

Black and Douglas espoused the view that *any* restriction on free communication, regardless of the apparent worthlessness of the "speech," presents an inherent danger to a free society. In his Pentagon Papers opinion, Black said the press "was protected so that it could bare the secrets of government. . . ."

Academic philosophers of the First Amendment have also been more libertarian in their views than editors of the establishment press. Alexander Meiklejohn—although he applied his absolutist theory only to communication having to do with the process of self-government—wrote: "Shall we give a hearing to those who hate and despise freedom, to those who, if they had the power, would destroy our institutions? Certainly, yes! Our action must be guided, not by their principles, but by ours. We listen, not because they desire to speak, but because we need to hear. . . ."[2]

Thomas Emerson has expounded a "full protection" theory for expression that is broader than those of Holmes, Black, or Meiklejohn. For Emerson, freedom of expression functions in a democratic society as: (1) "a means of assuring individual self-fulfillment," (2) "an essential process for advancing knowledge and discovering truth," (3) a mode for "participation in decision making by all members of society," and (4) a "method of achieving a more adaptable and hence a more stable community, of maintaining the precarious balance between healthy cleavage and necessary consensus." Under the first function, Emerson would protect an individual's right of self-expression regardless of the social value of what is expressed. He would also extend protection to such physical acts as picketing, the public burning or turning in of draft cards, and flag desecration (as forms of symbolic speech), all of which Black, in his later years, had excluded. Still, Emerson would set limits on expression he classifies as "action," such as obscene telephone calls, threatening gestures, disruptive heckling, sit-ins, commands or instructions related to immediate lawless acts, and wartime broadcasts for an enemy.[3]

Emerson has raised an ideal doctrinal standard to which the press must repair if it is to fulfill its proper role in helping to maintain the efficacy of the First Amendment. But while an orderly philosophical system with maximum latitude for freedom of expression provides useful validation for those inclined to support freedom, we must recognize that the legal system of the real world does not function in a calculable way for most litigants, including the press. Despite academic and judicial attempts to make the law appear logical and predictable, it is not a discipline like the physical sciences in which order is imposed by natural phenomena. It is more like a form of theology, in which the guiding principles are not immutable but vary according to what each theologian (judge) in the last analysis finds personally revealed in his/her scriptural (legal) authority.

Being mindful of this and of the resulting historical fluctuations in interpretation of the law and being mindful of changes in Supreme Court membership and of periodic swings from greater to lesser protection of free expression and back again, editors should be aware that they cannot leave championship of the First Amendment to dissident minorities or to a group of nine jurists. Even if they differ widely on political and social philosophy, editors and publishers should be able to unite in recognizing their responsibility to plead for the widest possible scope for the constitutional guarantee that was extended to the press alone among private enterprises, not simply to enable it to make money but also to enable it to carry out a public trust.[4]

Although the Supreme Court has the final word on the legal

meaning of the First Amendment, most cases involving freedom of expression do not reach the Supreme Court. The day-to-day acceptance or rejection of free expression depends on the mood of the public, which the press can help to sway in favor of greater tolerance. A 1970 survey, based on face-to-face interviews with a sample of 2,486 adults living in the forty-eight contiguous states, found that a majority of the adult population of the United States rejects the free exercise of speech and press when it is directed at criticism of basic popular dogma. Majorities of those questioned opposed allowing people to make speeches against God and allowing the publication of books attacking our system of government.[5] Obviously there was a serious lack of understanding of one of the basic tenets of the American constitutional system for which the press must bear some of the blame and which it should feel some obligation to correct.

The press can also help to shape the attitudes of public officials, from the local to the Supreme Court level, whose actions in turn have a bearing on the climate of freedom. Despite their isolated and politically immunized positions, Supreme Court members are themselves not unaffected by the public mood. Note Mr. Dooley's folk wisdom about the Supreme Court following the election returns.[6]

The press itself, through its business decisions, has been directly responsible for one kind of weakening of the system for free expression. Limitations on the diversity of sources of information and ideas, as envisioned under the First Amendment, have resulted not only from the failure of the press to support freedom for unorthodox publications but also from the trend toward economic monopoly in the structure of the media. The trend is signified by the growth of media conglomerates, such as RCA, CBS, and Time, Inc., with interests in magazines and book publishing as well as broadcasting.

An example of how conglomerate growth practices might affect press freedom was provided in 1979 by the move on the part of American Express, a financial conglomerate, to take over McGraw-Hill, a communications conglomerate. As the publisher of books, sixty trade magazines and newsletters, Standard and Poor's rating service, and *Business Week* magazine and as the owner of four television stations, McGraw-Hill has interests that obviously conflict with those of American Express. Louis H. Young, the editor of *Business Week*, warned that "American Express might taboo certain story subjects" and might not "support the editors after they had written unpopular ideas or critical stories that unleashed corporate or government complaints."

Fred W. Friendly, professor of journalism at Columbia University, raised the question, in connection with the American Express–McGraw-Hill battle, whether "four centuries of press struggles to break the licensing bonds of censorial governments could end with a new variety of restraints, where the gatekeepers of information are a handful of superconglomerates not steeped in the ethos of the news business." He asked also whether some means might be found to insulate the editors of conglomerate-owned publications against arbitrary dismissal by corporate overlords.[7]

The independence of the daily press itself has been affected by the growth of newspaper groups such as Gannett and Knight-Ridder, with controlling interests in dozens of newspapers.[8] While groups have gobbled up papers, competition at the local level has diminished. Of the 1,500 cities in the United States with daily newspapers, 97 percent, as of early 1977, had no local daily competition. One observer noted that, although the ownership structure of various communications facilities is fragmented, most of the news and entertainment received by the American public is produced by five organizations: the Associated Press, United Press International, the Columbia Broadcasting System, the National Broadcasting Co., and the American Broadcasting Co.[9] Similarity in content is fostered not only by concentrated ownership and control but by the herd instinct among journalists, especially in the Washington press corps, who cover the same events in the same way, talk to each other, and reinforce each other's perceptions.

Because of press dependence on very limited sources of supply for news, such as the major wire services, and because of editors' tendency to trust the judgments projected in the news budgets of such suppliers, the image of social and political reality conveyed to the public may be greatly skewed. It is usually shaped by a focus on crisis, drama, and sensation rather than by a study of trends and an evaluation of what is socially important. This impression is reinforced by the findings of a research project at Sonoma State College in California in which a panel of nationally prominent people was asked to name the "ten best censored stories of 1976"—that is, significant stories that were largely neglected by the media. Leading the list was the largely untold story of Jimmy Carter's relationship with the Trilateral Commission, a private international group headed by David Rockefeller and assembled for the purpose of discussing politics related to Rockefeller interests. The panel also selected other significant subjects that for the most part were unreported by the media.

Whatever the choice of events for coverage may be, some people, of course, would disagree; but an evident fact is that many segments of American society feel that their concerns are not adequately covered. The National Advisory Commission on Civil Disorders reported in 1968 that most blacks distrusted what they referred to as the "white press" and that many black residents in several cities felt the media to be unfair in reporting civil disturbances. The commission itself was concerned over the failure of the media to report adequately on race relations and ghetto problems.[10] Recognizing media preoccupation with visual excitement, many groups, ranging from blacks to students to farmers, have planned varying kinds of demonstrations with calculated dramatic impact in order to gain media attention for minority causes. Whether the dissatisfaction of different minorities adds up to general public dissatisfaction is not clear. But there should be cause for concern in the press as a result of a 1977 Harris poll showing that *only the press*, among the country's major institutions and professions, suffered a drop in public confidence—from an already low 20 percent in 1976 (in comparison to confidence in other institutions) to 19 percent in 1977.[11]

The discontent of various groups who feel that they have been slighted or ignored by the media is another manifestation of the access problem exemplified by the *Tornillo* case. Although the Supreme Court properly decided in that case that freedom of the press would not be served by an enforceable right of reply, the fact remains that a great many people feel that the First Amendment does not adequately serve them. Moreover, such feelings are not a newly discerned phenomenon. As long ago as 1939, William Allen White, editor and publisher of the Emporia, Kansas, *Gazette*, recognized it when he made some caustic comments on distorted press coverage in an essay on "The Obvious Anxiety of Rich Publishers About Freedom of the Press."[12]

If government interference with press content is not an acceptable remedy for complaints about press omissions and distortions, as is clearly the case, the obvious answer is voluntary affirmative support by the press of diversity and comprehensiveness in the coverage of public affairs and of fuller freedom for individual and group dissent. Otherwise publishers should be haunted by Mark Twain's cynical comment: "It is by the goodness of God that in our country we have those three unspeakably precious things: freedom of speech, freedom of conscience, and the prudence never to practice either of them."

True freedom of expression depends as much on positive implementation by the press as it does on enforcement of the First Amendment's guarantee against official abridgement of press freedom. Without both kinds of liberation for expression, greater credence would be given to the postulation of a kind of imagined freedom offered by the Marxist philosopher, Herbert Marcuse. Freedom of speech, as practiced in the United States today, he said, is an opiate of the people. The First Amendment provides us with no more than a catharsis, he observed. It is used by those in power to create the illusion that we are free and equal. It is a distraction, letting us say what we want to say while making sure that the most disturbing ideas fall on deaf ears and have no real impact on the nation's decision makers.[13]

History suggests that the exercise of First Amendment rights has been far more effective in enabling the public, including dissident minorities, to influence events than the Marcuse doctrine recognizes. Yet the Marcuse postulation contains enough troubling truth to challenge the press and citizens alike to devise a system that provides for, even encourages, communication to the public from a multitude of sources. Some evidence of an effort on the part of the press to widen the spectrum of published views is apparent in the form of so-called op ed pages that provide space for a variety of columns and articles by authors whose opinions do not necessarily coincide with those of the paper in which they appear. But with rare exceptions, such pages do not provide a forum for writers whose views would be regarded as heretical; nor do letters columns, which are usually restricted to communications of a stipulated modest length.

A more meaningful opportunity for those who do not own a press to exercise their freedom of expression could be provided if newspapers expanded their letters columns and their op ed pages to give readier and more complete access both to persons who feel they have been hurt by news articles or editorials and to individuals and groups who request space to reply because they disagree with something published. For those who feel they have been generally shut out, newspapers could help to fulfill the vision of First Amendment philosophers by allotting a regular given space—a half page or a page per week or month (depending on circumstances)—to dissident individuals or groups who demonstrably do not normally get coverage of their views. Such critics—whether they are Marxists or black liberationists or homosexuals—would be free to use the space as they saw fit, subject only to certain ground rules as to libel and taste. Finally, the effort to broaden the spectrum could include a conscious move by mass circulation newspapers to reprint material from small, offbeat publications whose words seldom reach the general public.

Such suggestions, of course, are predicated on the assumption that editors and publishers are committed to freedom of expression, which is probably unrealistic, given their often demonstrated lack of commitment. Yet some public-spirited editors and publishers would surely be responsive to a call to give greater scope to the democratic concept of free speech. And more editors in the future might be committed to freedom of expression if journalism schools, as a part of the regular curriculum, offered courses in First Amendment history and theory.

Even though the press generally has not, in times of crisis, stood in the forefront of the fight for freedom of expression, history offers some admirable examples in which editors and newspapers, by extension, put principle above expediency or business interest—Elijah Lovejoy defending his press to the death, the *St. Louis Post-Dispatch* and the Louisville *Courier-Journal* braving the tide of national opinion to condemn the *Dennis* decision. Lovejoy showed that one editor can make a difference. He showed the importance of upholding a minority point of view, such as the advocacy of abolition. In his own day, Lovejoy was looked upon by most of his fellow citizens as a zealot and a stubborn, dangerous radical. Yet who now would dispute that he simply recognized many truths before his contemporaries did? There is as much reason today for upholding freedom of expression for unpopular people who may have insights on truth ahead of their time.

Still the nation cannot afford to rely on editors or newspapers, even committed ones, to be the only custodians of freedom of expression. Just as the press was given its constitutionally protected role in order that it might serve as a check against government, so the press, under the constitutionally designed system of checks and balances, should be countered by other nongovernmental institutions. Citizens' press councils, without enforcement powers, can appropriately serve that function. The National News Council—created to monitor the national news media, to criticize unfairness, and to support freedom of expression—is a suitable model, although its effectiveness has been limited by the stubborn resistance of much of the media. Useful services in monitoring and commenting on the shortcomings of the media can also be performed by journalism reviews and by internal ombudsmen now established in some newspapers to receive complaints from aggrieved parties and to intercede for them.

But the ultimate reality, regardless of the safeguarding institutions that may be devised, was recognized long ago by Alexander Hamilton when he said that the "liberty of the press . . . whatever fine declarations may be inserted in any constitution respecting it, must altogether depend on public opinion, and on the general spirit of the people and the government." The efficacy of the First Amendment depends on the people's acceptance of the validity of the philosophical premise on which it is based—that, without scrutiny and criticism of government and even the disclosure of official secrets by the press, the people will be more vulnerable to misrule and abuse of power. The press is being constantly challenged to earn the people's acceptance.

Justice Holmes said the theory of our Constitution was "that the ultimate good desired is better reached by free trade in ideas—that the best test of truth is the power of the thought to get itself accepted in the competition of the market."[14] Many critics of First Amendment theory today—not only Herbert Marcuse but also conservative constitutional scholars who advocate enforced access—argue that the market in ideas is not open. The press is also being challenged to open up the market.

John Stuart Mill, in his essay, "On Liberty," wrote:

Men are not more zealous for truth than they often are for error, and a sufficient application of legal or even social penalties will generally succeed in stopping the propagation of either. The real advantage which truth has consists in this, that when an opinion is true, it may be extinguished once, twice, or many times, but in the course of ages there will generally be found persons to rediscover it, until some one of its reappearances falls on a time when from favorable circumstances it escapes persecution until it has made such a head as to withstand all subsequent attempts to suppress it.

The value of freedom of expression is a *truth* that has been discovered and put down at least since the time of Socrates. The framers of the First Amendment were so sure of the value of freedom of expression that for the first time in history they made its protection an article in a written national constitution. Yet the value of freedom of expression, as a *truth* that the framers sought to ensure against all subsequent attempts at suppression, must still be rediscovered and defended by each generation.

Bibliographical Comments

For general historical narrative, the authority used most was the two-volume work, *Growth of the American Republic*, by Samuel Eliot Morison and Henry Steele Commager (1937). The sources relied on most for the history of freedom of speech and freedom of the press in the United States were: Thomas I. Emerson, David Haber, and Norman Dorsen, *Political and Civil Rights in the United States*, vol. 1 (1967); Harold L. Nelson, ed., *Freedom of the Press from Hamilton to the Warren Court* (1967); Mauritz Hallgren, *Landscape of Freedom: The Story of American Liberty and Bigotry* (1941); Ernest Sutherland Bates, *This Land of Liberty* (1930); Frank Thayer, *Legal Control of the Press* (1962); James R. Mock, *Censorship—1917* (1941); Frank Luther Mott, *American Journalism: A History of Newspapers in the United States Through 250 Years—1690–1940* (1949); Edwin Emery and Henry Ladd Smith, *The Press and America* (1954); and for the twentieth century, United States Supreme Court Reports.

Although no studies known to me have been addressed specifically to my objective of a long-term historical survey of press response to attacks on freedom of expression, a number of excellent treatises contain material that is adaptable to such a survey. Leonard W. Levy's books, *Legacy of Suppression* (1960), *Freedom of the Press from Zenger to Jefferson* (1966), and *Jefferson and Civil Liberties: The Darker Side* (1973), provided a wealth of material on the colonial period and the early years of the republic. James Morton Smith's *Freedom's Fetters: The Alien and Sedition Laws and American Civil Liberties* (1956), thoroughly covered the battle over the Alien and Sedition

293

Laws. Russell B. Nye's study, *Fettered Freedom* (1972), was an invaluable source on attacks on press freedom during the abolitionist controversies. Henry David's work, *The History of the Haymarket Affair* (1958), was a rich source of information on attacks on the radical labor press and the response thereto. For a few segments of my study, as indicated in the chapter notes, I made extensive use of such secondary sources. But in most instances this study was supported by additional material from primary sources. That part dealing with the twentieth century, for which newspaper files are readily available, is based largely on primary materials.

For more limited studies of press response to free press issues, see: F. Dennis Hale, "A Comparison of Speech and Press Verdicts of Supreme Court," *Journalism Quarterly* 56(1979):43, and John D. Stevens, "Freedom of Expression: New Dimensions," in *Mass Media and the National Experience*, ed. Ronald T. Farrar and John D. Stevens (1971).

Notes

1. The *New York Times*, July 18, 1975, p. 28, reported that new research had established that the Declaration was first printed on Dunlap's press, although it had long been thought that the *Pennsylvania Evening Post* (Philadelphia) was first in publishing the document; see Edwin Emery and Henry Ladd Smith, *The Press and America*, 119. Dunlap is identified as publisher of the *Pennsylvania Packet* in Frank Luther Mott, *American Journalism*, 88.
2. Emery and Smith, *Press and America*, 87, 89; Mott, *American Journalism*, 71–72.
3. Adams quoted in Mott, *American Journalism*, 76.
4. Arthur M. Schlesinger, *Prelude to Independence*, 126–127, 238; Mott, *American Journalism*, 93–94; David Duncan Wallace, *South Carolina—A Short History*, 231.
5. Harry Hayden Clark, ed., *Poems of Freneau*, xix.
6. Emery and Smith, *Press and America*, 126–127.
7. Ibid., 131.
8. Edward Mead Earle, ed., *The Federalist*, x. Note at the beginning of each essay shows the identity of the newspaper that published it.
9. Leonard W. Levy, *Legacy of Suppression*, 129, 135, 136; Leonard W. Levy, ed., *Freedom of the Press from Zenger to Jefferson*, 62, 66.
10. Levy, *Legacy*, 25–29.
11. Levy, ed., *Zenger to Jefferson*, 5, 9; Levy, *Legacy*, 141–142, 215.
12. Schlesinger, *Prelude to Independence*, viii, 189, 261, 285, 295, 297;

Levy, *Legacy*, 64, 69, 176, 183; Leonard W. Levy, *Jefferson and Civil Liberties*, 25.

13. Levy, *Legacy*, 80–81, 177.
14. Ibid., 179–180; Schlesinger, *Prelude to Independence*, 297–298.
15. Richard L. Perry, ed., *Sources of Our Liberties*, 285.
16. Levy, *Legacy*, 181.
17. Charles C. Tansill, ed., *Documents Illustrative of the Formation of the Union of the American States*, 18.
18. [James Madison], *Journal of the Constitutional Convention*, 3, 58; Mott, *American Journalism*, 119.
19. [Madison], *Journal*, 69, 559, 717, 728; Irving Brant, *The Bill of Rights*, 228.
20. Levy, *Legacy*, 16–17, 184–185, 281.
21. Ibid., 190–191, 202–207; Levy, ed., *Zenger to Jefferson*, 130–142. Perry, ed., *Sources of Our Liberties*, 301–386.
22. Bennett B. Patterson, *The Forgotten Ninth Amendment*, 100–101, 104–105. This work contains a record of the debates in the House of Representatives on proposals for a bill of rights.
23. Ibid., 110, 111, 112–114, 117, 162, 187.
24. Ibid., 119, 177.
25. Ibid., 187–188, 210.
26. Ibid., 169. For a discussion of the first Congress and the Bill of Rights, see also Brant, *Bill of Rights*, 48–57, 60–62, 69–74.
27. Zechariah Chafee, Jr., *Free Speech in the United States*, 29.
28. Brant, *Bill of Rights*, 223.
29. Chafee, *Free Speech*, 16; Levy, *Legacy*, 215, 234, 238, 247.
30. Levy, *Legacy*, viii, 258–309; Levy, ed., *Zenger to Jefferson*, lxx–lxxvii.
31. Chafee, *Free Speech*, 14–15.
32. Many of the papers started between 1783 and 1800 were short-lived; on Jan. 1, 1801, 202 papers were being published. Mott, *American Journalism*, 113, 115.
33. Samuel Eliot Morison and Henry Steele Commager, *The Growth of the American Republic*, 1:219–222.
34. Ibid., 242, 243, 251–252.
35. Clarence S. Brigham, *Journals and Journeymen*, 61. For the partisan affiliations of various editors and newspapers of this period, see Mott, *American Journalism*, 122–134; Emery and Smith, *Press and America*, 136–148.
36. An account of Philip Freneau's activities as an editor is contained in the introduction to *Poems of Freneau*, edited by Harry Hayden Clark.

37. In a sedition trial in Great Britain, focused on the rights of a free press, Paine was convicted in absentia for his publication of the *Rights of Man*. Levy, *Legacy*, 253.
38. Alexander De Conde, *Entangling Alliance*, 112–113, 115, 116.
39. Morison and Commager, *American Republic*, 1:225.
40. Mott, *American Journalism*, 108, 127.

CHAPTER 2

James Morton Smith, in *Freedom's Fetters*, has written probably the most comprehensive study of the passage of the Alien and Sedition Laws of 1798 and of the prosecutions under them. This chapter relies substantially on that study, especially pages 94–155, on passage of the Sedition Law, and pages 176–220, 247–257, 277–328, 338–359, 361–417, on prosecutions. Unless otherwise indicated, quotations from newspapers and individuals were taken from these pages.

1. Irving Brant, *The Bill of Rights*, 234–235.
2. Leonard W. Levy, *Legacy of Suppression*, 241–242; Brant, *Bill of Rights*, 246–247.
3. Quoted in Frank Luther Mott, *American Journalism*, 147.
4. Quoted in Brant, *Bill of Rights*, 249.
5. Mott, *American Journalism*, 147–148; Brant, *Bill of Rights*, 248.
6. Brant, *Bill of Rights*, 249.
7. Samuel Eliot Morison and Henry Steele Commager, *The Growth of the American Republic*, 1:270–271; Brant, *Bill of Rights*, 271–272.
8. Brant, *Bill of Rights*, 249–250.
9. Boston *Columbian Centinel*, July 4, 1798, p. 2, col. 4.
10. Boston *Independent Chronicle*, July 5 to July 9, 1798, p. 3, col. 2.
11. Ibid., July 9 to July 12, 1798, pp. 1, 2.
12. Brant, *Bill of Rights*, 251–252.
13. Mott, *American Journalism*, 122. Brant, *Bill of Rights*, 251, says the Federalists had a five- or ten-to-one advantage in the number of papers on their side.
14. Quoted in Levy, *Legacy*, 261.
15. Ibid., 258–259.
16. Ibid., 262.
17. For a summary of the debate, see Brant, *Bill of Rights*, 251–265.
18. For text of the act, see James Morton Smith, *Freedom's Fetters*, 441–442.
19. Allan Nevins, *Times of Trial*, 50.
20. Boston *Columbian Centinel*, July 18, 1798, p. 2, col. 1.
21. Levy, *Legacy*, 246, 292. For perhaps obvious reasons, no case

under the Sedition Law was ever appealed to the U.S. Supreme Court; Mott, *American Journalism*, 152. Nevertheless, it has been pronounced unconstitutional as a violation of the First Amendment by various authorities, including Zechariah Chafee, Jr., *Free Speech in the United States*, 174; and Mott, *American Journalism*, 152. In his majority opinion in *New York Times* v. *Sullivan*, Justice Brennan remarked that the attack on the validity of the Sedition Act of 1798 "has carried the day in the court of history." (376 U.S. at 276).

22. Mott, *American Journalism*, 149; Smith, *Freedom's Fetters*, 185–186; Morison and Commager, *American Republic*, 1:273.
23. Quoted in Mott, *American Journalism*, 146.
24. Alfred Owen Aldridge, *Man of Reason: The Life of Thomas Paine*, 183–184.
25. Brant, *Bill of Rights*, 275.
26. Leonard W. Levy, ed., *Freedom of the Press from Zenger to Jefferson*, 197–198.
27. Levy, *Legacy*, 273; Levy, ed., *Zenger to Jefferson*, 197–229.
28. Levy, *Legacy*, 268–269, 282–296.
29. Ibid., 297–302.
30. Hartford *Connecticut Courant*, Jan. 5, 1801, p. 1.
31. Worthington Chauncey Ford, ed., *Thomas Jefferson Correspondence Printed from the Originals in the Collection of William K. Bixby*, 139.
32. Ibid., 138.
33. Andrew A. Lipscomb and Albert Ellery Bergh, eds., *The Writings of Thomas Jefferson*, 11:155.

CHAPTER 3

1. Frank Luther Mott, *American Journalism*, 174.
2. Quoted in Thomas A. Bailey, *A Diplomatic History of the American People*, 141.
3. Edwin Emery and Henry Ladd Smith, *The Press and America*, 184.
4. Quoted in Thomas Boyd, *Light-Horse Harry Lee*, 308.
5. Ibid., 308–309; Mauritz Hallgren, *Landscape of Freedom*, 164.
6. Baltimore *Federal Gazette*, quoted in New York *Commercial Advertiser*, June 27, 1812, p. 2, col. 4.
7. New York *Commercial American*, June 25, 1812, p. 2.
8. Ibid., June 26, 1812, p. 2, col. 4.
9. Charleston *City Gazette and Commercial Daily Advertiser*, July 3, 1812, p. 2, col. 2.

10. "A Mobocracy," reprinted in New York *Commercial Advertiser*, Aug. 7, 1812, p. 2, cols. 2, 3, 4.
11. Boyd, *Light-Horse Harry Lee*, 309–310, 314, 315, 329; Noel B. Gerson, *Light-Horse Harry—A Biography of Washington's Great Cavalryman, General Henry Lee*, 232.
12. Hallgren, *Landscape of Freedom*, 163.
13. Salem *Gazette*, quoted in New York *Commercial Advertiser*, Aug. 7, 1812, p. 2, col. 4.
14. Baltimore *Whig*, quoted in the *Weekly Aurora* (a Philadelphia Republican paper), Aug. 4, 1812.
15. Washington *National Intelligencer*, Aug. 1, 1812, quoted in Philadelphia *Weekly Aurora*, Aug. 11, 1812.
16. Washington *National Intelligencer*, Aug. 13, 1812, p. 2, cols, 1, 2.
17. Ibid., Aug. 13, 1812, p. 2, col. 3.
18. Ibid., Aug. 15, 1812, p. 3, cols. 2, 3.
19. New York *Columbian* quoted in *New York Evening Post*, Aug. 6, 1812, p. 2, col. 4.
20. *New York Evening Post*, Aug. 6, 1812, p. 2, cols. 4, 5.
21. Ibid., Aug. 3, 1812, p. 2, col. 5.
22. Boston *Independent Chronicle*, Aug. 6, 1812, p. 2, col. 5.
23. Ibid., Aug. 8, 1812, p. 2, col. 3.
24. Boston *Columbian Centinel*, Aug. 5, 1812, p. 2, col. 3.
25. Hartford *Connecticut Courant*, Aug. 4, 1812, p. 2, col. 3.
26. Quoted in Boyd, *Light-Horse Harry Lee*, 328–329.
27. Charleston *City Gazette and Commercial Daily Advertiser*, Aug. 8, 1812, p. 2, col. 2.
28. *Charleston Courier*, Aug. 8, 1812, p. 1, cols. 4, 5.
29. Quoted in John Allen Krout and Dixon Ryan Fox, *The Completion of Independence, 1790–1830*, 202.
30. Quoted in Frank Thayer, *Legal Control of the Press*, 46.
31. Marquis James, *The Life of Andrew Jackson*, 255–256.
32. Quoted in A. S. Colyar, *Life and Times of Andrew Jackson*, 1:351.
33. *New York Evening Post*, Mar. 27, 1815, p. 2, col. 1.
34. Washington *National Intelligencer*, Mar. 25, 1815, p. 3, col. 1.
35. David Karsner, *Andrew Jackson—The Gentle Savage*, 245; John Spencer Bassett, ed., *Correspondence of Andrew Jackson*, 2:224.
36. Quoted in Colyar, *Jackson*, 1:353, 355.
37. Bassett, ed., *Jackson Correspondence*, 2:183.
38. Augustus C. Buell, *History of Andrew Jackson*, 2:56; Bassett, ed., *Jackson Correspondence*, 2:225.
39. Bassett, ed., *Jackson Correspondence*, 2:226.

40. Ibid., 2:226–227.
41. James Parton, *Life of Andrew Jackson*, 2:313–314, 315; Karsner, *Jackson*, 247; Bassett, ed., *Jackson Correspondence*, 2:227, 289–290.
42. *New York Evening Post*, Apr. 11, 1815, p. 2, col. 3.
43. Ibid., Apr. 17, 1815, p. 2, col. 2.
44. *Charleston Courier*, Apr. 6, 1815, p. 2, col. 2.
45. James, *Jackson*, 748, 760.

CHAPTER 4

1. Floyd Calvin Shoemaker, *Missouri and Missourians*, 1:256, 679; William Nisbet Chambers, *Old Bullion Benton—Senator From the New West*, 71, 81.
2. Perry McCandless, *A History of Missouri*, 2:2; Chambers, *Benton*, 87–88, 89.
3. Chambers, *Benton*, 67, 82, 85.
4. McCandless, *Missouri*, 2:13, 17; Chambers, *Benton*, 70, 71, 89.
5. U.S. Congress, *Impeachment—Selected Materials*, 136.
6. Ibid., 136–137.
7. Shoemaker, *Missouri*, 1:265; Harry Krantz, "Landmark Impeachment," *St. Louis Post-Dispatch*, Nov. 18, 1973, p. 20.
8. Arthur J. Stansbury, ed., *Report of the Trial of James H. Peck*, 5; Walter B. Stevens, *Centennial History of Missouri*, 1:223; Louis Houck, *A History of Missouri*, 3:20; William E. Foley, *A History of Missouri*, 1:199.
9. Stansbury, ed., *Trial Report*, 15.
10. Quoted, ibid., 39.
11. *Impeachment—Selected Materials*, 138.
12. Russell B. Nye, *Fettered Freedom*, 138, 154.
13. Stansbury, ed., *Trial Report*, 105.
14. Ibid., 425.
15. Nye, *Fettered Freedom*, 78.
16. Stansbury, ed., *Trial Report*, 479, 482.
17. Harold L. Nelson, ed., *Freedom of the Press from Hamilton to the Warren Court*, 140.
18. Irving Brant, *Impeachment: Trials and Errors*, 126–127.
19. Washington *National Intelligencer*, Feb. 1, 1831, p. 2, col. 3.
20. Buchanan and Wirt quoted in McCune Gill, *The St. Louis Story*, 1:103.
21. Washington *National Intelligencer*, Feb. 1, 1831, p. 3, col. 1.
22. Ibid., Mar. 4, 1831, p. 3, col. 1.
23. See, for example, St. Louis *Beacon*, Jan. 27, 1831, p. 2, and St. Louis

Missouri Republican, Feb. 15, 1831, p. 2, col. 5.

24. St. Louis *Beacon*, Feb. 3, 1831, p. 1, col. 4.

25. St. Louis *Missouri Republican*, Feb. 15, 1831, p. 2, col. 5.

26. Charleston *Mercury*, Feb. 9, 1831, p. 2, col. 4.

27. Washington *National Intelligencer*, Feb. 1, 1831, p. 2, col. 6; p. 3, cols. 1, 4.

28. Ibid., Feb. 8, 1831, p. 1, col. 1.

29. New York *Courier and Enquirer, Richmond Whig*, Washington *Globe*, and Boston *Courier* quoted in St. Louis *Beacon*, Mar. 10, 1831, p. 2, col. 3.

30. Charleston *Mercury*, Feb. 9, 1831, p. 2, col. 4, and *Charleston Courier*, Feb. 9, 1831, p. 2, col. 2, reported the acquittal without comment.

31. Washington *National Intelligencer*, Feb. 3, 1831, p. 1, col. 3.

32. Nelson, ed., *Freedom of the Press*, 140.

33. Washington *National Intelligencer*, Mar. 3, 1831, p. 3, col. 1.

34. Richmond *Enquirer*, semiweekly, Mar. 8, 1831, p. 1, col. 4, reported the House action on the bill but offered no comment on that date or immediately afterward.

35. Frank Thayer, *Legal Control of the Press*, 555.

36. Gill, *St. Louis Story*, 1:103.

37. J. Thomas Scharf, *History of St. Louis City and County*, 1:907.

CHAPTER 5

On the difficulties of the abolitionist press and the reaction of other newspapers, two major sources are: Harold L. Nelson's *Freedom of the Press From Hamilton to the Warren Court*, which reprints many contemporary documents; see especially 167–220; and Russell B. Nye's *Fettered Freedom*, a study of "Civil Liberties and the Slavery Controversy, 1830–1860"; see especially, pages 69–85, 117–173. Unless otherwise indicated, quotations of individuals and newspapers were taken from Nye's study.

1. Frank Luther Mott, *American Journalism*, 307.

2. Charles M. Wiltse, ed., *David Walker's Appeal*, ix, xi.

3. Nelson, ed., *Freedom of the Press*, 174–176.

4. Frank Luther Mott, *American Journalism*, 322.

5. Ibid., 306.

6. Nelson, ed., *Freedom of the Press*, 212–213.

7. *Richmond Whig* quoted in *Niles Weekly Register*, Baltimore, Aug. 22, 1835, XIL, 448.

8. Baltimore *Republican and Commercial Advertiser*, Aug. 8, 1835, p. 2, col. 1,

9. *Daily Albany Argus*, Aug. 12, 1835, p. 2, col. 3, and Aug. 13, 1835, p. 2, col. 3.
10. *Albany Daily Advertiser* quoted in *Daily Albany Argus*, Aug. 13, 1835, p. 2.
11. Boston *Daily Advertiser*, Aug. 20, 1835, p. 2, col. 2.
12. *Boston Evening Transcript*, Aug. 22, 1835, p. 2, cols. 1, 2.
13. *Boston Atlas* quoted in *Niles Weekly Register*, Aug. 22, 1835, XIL, 448.
14. Philadelphia *National Gazette*, Aug. 11, 1835, p. 2, col. 2.
15. Quoted in Nelson, ed., *Freedom of the Press*, 215.
16. Ibid., 216–217.
17. *Charleston Courier*, Dec. 15, 1835, p. 3, col. 3.
18. Baltimore *Republican and Commercial Advertiser*, Dec. 9, 1835, p. 3, col. 4.
19. *Daily Albany Argus*, Dec. 18, 1835, p. 2, col. 5.
20. Philadelphia *National Gazette*, Dec. 15, 1835, p. 3, col. 1.
21. *Boston Daily Evening Transcript*, Dec. 10, 1835, pp. 1, 2.
22. Nelson, ed., *Freedom of the Press*, 210–211.
23. Ibid., 179–193.
24. Cincinnati *Daily Gazette*, Aug. 15, 1836, p. 2, col. 1.
25. *Pittsburgh Gazette*, Cleveland *Advertiser*, and Dayton *Journal* quoted in Cincinnati *Philanthropist*, Oct. 21, 1836, p. 2.
26. Nye, *Fettered Freedom*, 136.
27. John Gill, *Tide Without Turning*, 34, 35.
28. St. Louis *Missouri Argus*, Sept. 11, 1835.
29. Quoted in Gill, *Tide Without Turning*, 46.
30. St. Louis *Observer*, Oct. 11, 1835.
31. Quoted in [Henry Tanner], *An Eye-Witness*, 55.
32. Merton L. Dillon, *Elijah P. Lovejoy, Abolitionist Editor*, 63.
33. Gill, *Tide Without Turning*, 52–55; Dillon, *Lovejoy*, 69–72.
34. Quoted in [Tanner], *An Eye-Witness*, 60–61; Gill, *Tide Without Turning*, 55.
35. Gill, *Tide Without Turning*, 59.
36. For details on Lovejoy's quarrel with Judge Lawless, see Dillon, *Lovejoy*, 86–88; Gill, *Tide Without Turning*, 60–72.
37. Quoted in Gill, *Tide Without Turning*, 73–74.
38. Quoted in Dillon, *Lovejoy*, 112.
39. Alton *Spectator*, quoted in Gill, *Tide Without Turning*, 129; St. Louis *Missouri Republican* referred to in Dillon, *Lovejoy*, 107.
40. *Louisville Gazette*, Sept. 10, 1837.
41. Lexington *Intelligencer*, Sept. 15, 1837.
42. Quoted in Mauritz Hallgren, *Landscape of Freedom*, 249.

43. Quoted in [Tanner], *An Eye-Witness*, 158–159.
44. Quoted ibid., 161–162.
45. Quoted ibid., 164–165.
46. Quoted ibid., 164.
47. Quoted ibid., 165.
48. Hallgren, *Landscape of Freedom*, 250; Mott, *American Journalism*, 307.

CHAPTER 6

1. Samuel Eliot Morison and Henry Steele Commager, *The Growth of the American Republic*, 1:482–483; Thomas A. Bailey, *A Diplomatic History of the American People*, 270, 276–277; Philip Van Doren Stern, ed., *The Life and Writings of Abraham Lincoln*, 297–299; Mauritz Hallgren, *Landscape of Freedom*, 257.
2. Quoted in Bailey, *Diplomatic History*, 271–272.
3. Quoted in Frank Luther Mott, *American Journalism*, 255; Morison and Commager, *American Republic*, 1:489.
4. Quoted in Bailey, *Diplomatic History*, 276n36.
5. Mott, *American Journalism*, 255, 308; James R. Mock, *Censorship—1917*, 10.
6. Tom Reilly, "Newspaper Suppression During the Mexican War, 1846–48," *Journalism Quarterly* 54(1977):262.
7. Thomas I. Emerson, David Haber, and Norman Dorsen, *Political and Civil Rights in the United States*, 1:45–47; Hallgren, *Landscape of Freedom*, 257–258, 259–260; Mott, *American Journalism*, 336.
8. Harold L. Nelson, ed., *Freedom of the Press from Hamilton to the Warren Court*, 221–222; Mott, *American Journalism*, 337.
9. Mott, *American Journalism*, 338, 352, 356, 357, 358; Frank Thayer, *Legal Control of the Press*, 46; Nelson, ed., *Freedom of the Press*, 222, 223; Hallgren, *Landscape of Freedom*, 259.
10. Nelson, ed., *Freedom of the Press*, 229; Mott, *American Journalism*, 225.
11. Mott, *American Journalism*, 357, 358; J. Cutler Andrews, *The North Reports the Civil War*, 29, 30.
12. Nelson, ed., *Freedom of the Press*, 230–232; Hallgren, *Landscape of Freedom*, 260–261; Mock, *Censorship*, 13.
13. *New York Daily Tribune*, June 2, 1863, p. 4, col. 4; June 6, 1863, p. 4, col. 2.
14. *New York Times*, June 4, 1863, p. 4, col. 4.
15. Ibid., June 8, 1863, p. 4, col. 5.
16. Boston *Daily Advertiser*, June 6, 1863, p. 2, col. 1.
17. Mott, *American Journalism*, 360.

18. Washington *Daily National Intelligencer*, June 6, 1863, p. 3, col. 1.
19. Washington *Daily Chronicle*, June 6, 1863, p. 2, col. 2.
20. Mott, *American Journalism*, 347–348.
21. *Chicago Tribune*, June 4, 1863, p. 2, col. 2.
22. Ibid., June 5, 1863, p. 1, col. 1.
23. Nelson, ed., *Freedom of the Press*, 223–225.
24. Ibid., 232–236, 243–245; Mock, *Censorship*, 14; Mott, *American Journalism*, 351.
25. *New York Daily Tribune*, May 19, 1864, p. 4, col. 3.
26. Nelson, ed., *Freedom of the Press*, 246–247.
27. *New York Daily News* quoted in *New York Tribune*, May 20, 1864, p. 4, col. 4.
28. Mott, *American Journalism*, 353.
29. *New York Tribune*, May 20, 1864, p. 4, col. 4.
30. *New York Times*, May 21, 1864, p. 4, cols. 4, 5.
31. See Curtis D. MacDougall, *Hoaxes*, 13, 23, 268, 306. This rather self-righteous attitude on the part of the *Times* did not anticipate that the *Times* itself in future years was to be taken in by a number of hoaxes.
32. Mott, *American Journalism*, 355.
33. Ibid., 339–340.

CHAPTER 7

On the development of American society immediately after the Civil War, the principal source was Samuel Eliot Morison and Henry Steele Commager, *The Growth of the American Republic*, 2:105–173. For the background of labor radicalism of the period, a major source was Joseph G. Rayback, *A History of American Labor*, 129–168. The authoritative source on the Haymarket affair and press reaction to it was Henry David, *The History of the Haymarket Affair*. Quotations from newspapers and individuals, unless otherwise indicated, were taken from David's work.

1. John Tebbel, *An American Dynasty*, 53.
2. Frank Luther Mott, *American Journalism*, 497–505.
3. Rayback, *American Labor*, 166.
4. Ibid., 167.
5. Ibid., 167–168.
6. Quoted in Harvey Goldberg, ed., *American Radicals*, 129.
7. Quoted in Tebbel, *Dynasty*, 53.
8. Quoted ibid., 54.
9. John Brown, whose 1859 raid on Harper's Ferry had caused more deaths than the Haymarket bomb, had drawn inspiration from Gar-

rison's frenzied abolitionist paper, the *Liberator*, and from Greeley's *New York Tribune*. After the Bible, these papers were his favorite readings. As good a case could have been made for a charge that Garrison and Phillips, if not Greeley, were responsible for Brown's violence as was made for the charge against the Chicago anarchists. For Garrison's and Greeley's reported influence on John Brown, see J. C. Furnas, *The Road to Harper's Ferry*, 20, 301, 311. Richard Hofstadter, *The American Political Tradition and the Men Who Made It*, 150, says Phillips would defend the murder of a slave-catcher by a slave.

10. New York *Sun*, New York *Commercial Advertiser*, *New York Evening Post* quoted in *St. Louis Post-Dispatch*, Aug. 20, 1886, p. 1, cols. 5, 6.
11. *New York Times*, Aug. 21, 1886, editorial page, cols. 3, 4.
12. *Atlanta Constitution*, Aug. 21, 1886, p. 4, cols. 1, 2.
13. Denver *Tribune-Republican*, Aug. 21, 1886, p. 4, col. 2.
14. Denver *Rocky Mountain Daily News*, Aug. 21, 1886, p. 4, col. 2.
15. *St. Louis Post-Dispatch*, Aug. 21, 1886, p. 4, col. 2.
16. Goldberg, ed., *American Radicals*, 134.
17. Ibid., 134.
18. *Atlanta Journal*, June 28, 1893, p. 4, col. 1.
19. *Atlanta Constitution*, June 28, 1893, p. 4, col. 3.
20. *Denver Republican*, June 29, 1893, p. 4, col. 2.
21. *St. Louis Post-Dispatch*, June 27, 1893, p. 4, cols. 2, 3.
22. Mott, *American Journalism*, 541.
23. Mauritz Hallgren, *Landscape of Freedom*, 295.

CHAPTER 8

1. Frank Luther Mott, *American Journalism*, 606.
2. W. A. Swanberg, *Pulitzer*, 413.
3. Ibid., 414.
4. Ibid., 413, 415.
5. Quoted in Swanberg, *Pulitzer*, 415.
6. Ibid., 416.
7. Quoted in Thomas A. Bailey, *A Diplomatic History of the American People*, 545.
8. Quoted ibid., 542.
9. Ibid., 543.
10. Swanberg, *Pulitzer*, 416–417.
11. The canal was completed in 1913 and opened to commercial traffic in Aug. 1914. Not until 1921, after Roosevelt was dead and after the whole affair had rankled in the minds of Colombians for years,

did the United States pay Colombia $25 million as partial recompense for its earlier unscrupulous treatment. Samuel E. Morison and Henry Steele Commager, *The Growth of the American Republic*, 2:405; Bailey, *Diplomatic History*, 546.

12. Swanberg, *Pulitzer*, 412.
13. Quoted ibid., 417–418.
14. Don C. Seitz, *Joseph Pulitzer: His Life and Letters*, 358–362.
15. Quoted in Swanberg, *Pulitzer*, 418.
16. Ibid., 419; Seitz, *Pulitzer*, 355, 356.
17. Roosevelt quoted in Swanberg, *Pulitzer*, 419.
18. Seitz, *Pulitzer*, 357–363; Swanberg, *Pulitzer*, 420–421.
19. Quoted in Harold L. Nelson, ed., *Freedom of the Press from Hamilton to the Warren Court*, 122–124.
20. Seitz, *Pulitzer*, 365.
21. Ibid., 353; Earl Harding, *The Untold Story of Panama*, 49, 58–60, 61; David Howarth, *Panama: 400 Years of Drama and Cruelty*, 243.
22. Swanberg, *Pulitzer*, 431; Seitz, *Pulitzer*, 366.
23. Nelson, ed., *Freedom of the Press*, 120–121.
24. Quoted in Leonard W. Levy, *Legacy of Suppression*, 273.
25. Quoted in "Speaking of a Free Press," ANPA Foundation pamphlet, 1970, p. 20.
26. Seitz, *Pulitzer*, 371.
27. Reprinted in *St. Louis Post-Dispatch*, Dec. 16, 1908, p. 4.
28. Quoted ibid., Dec. 17, 1908, p. 6.
29. Quoted ibid., Dec. 16, 1908, p. 1, col. 8.
30. Quoted ibid., Dec. 17, 1908, p. 6, col. 3.
31. Quoted ibid., Dec. 16, 1908, p. 4, col. 2.
32. Quoted ibid., p. 4, col. 1.
33. Quoted ibid., Dec. 17, 1908, p. 6, col. 4.
34. Denver *Rocky Mountain News*, Dec. 17, 1908, p. 14.
35. *Denver Post*, Dec. 17, 1908, p. 1.
36. Denver *Times*, Dec. 18, 1908, p. 9.
37. Denver *Republican*, Dec. 17, 1908, p. 6.
38. *St. Louis Post-Dispatch*, Dec. 16, 1908, p. 4, cols. 6, 7.
39. Quoted ibid., Dec. 17, 1908, p. 6, col. 3.
40. Quoted ibid., Dec. 16, 1908, p. 4, col. 2.
41. Swanberg, *Pulitzer*, 425–426; Seitz, *Pulitzer*, 367–368.
42. Quoted in Swanberg, *Pulitzer*, 426.
43. Seitz, *Pulitzer*, 373.
44. Ibid., 370–371, 373, 377; Swanberg, *Pulitzer*, 428, 430.
45. Seitz, *Pulitzer*, 378.
46. Nelson, ed., *Freedom of the Press*, 131, 132.

47. Ibid., 126, 127–128. Case, *U.S.* v. *Smith*, reported in 173 Federal Reporter 227. See also Mott, *American Journalism*, 605–606.
48. Quoted in Swanberg, *Pulitzer*, 437.
49. Seitz, *Pulitzer*, 378; Harding, *Panama*, 51–52.
50. Swanberg, *Pulitzer*, 425.
51. Ibid., 439, 448; Seitz, *Pulitzer*, 381, 383, 384, 385. For Supreme Court opinion, see *U.S.* v. *The Press Publishing Co.*, 219 U.S. 1 (1911).
52. New York *World* editorial of Jan. 4, 1911, reprinted in *St. Louis Post-Dispatch*, Jan. 4, 1911, editorial page.
53. *New York Times*, Jan. 4, 1911, p. 6.
54. *Chicago Tribune*, Jan. 4, 1911, p. 6, col. 5.
55. *Boston Evening Transcript*, Jan. 4, 1911, p. 16, col. 4.
56. Hartford *Courant* quoted in *Boston Evening Transcript*, Jan. 5, 1911, p. 11.
57. Harding, *Panama*, 100.

CHAPTER 9

1. There seems to be no dispute among authorities that the period of World War I and its aftermath brought an unparalleled degree of suppression of freedom of expression. Since the figures on arrests, prosecutions, convictions, and withdrawals of mail privileges vary from one authority to the next, I have used round numbers. See Zechariah Chafee, Jr., *Free Speech in the United States*, 3, 50; Zechariah Chafee, Jr., *The Blessings of Liberty*, 70; Thomas I. Emerson, David Haber, and Norman Dorsen, *Political and Civil Rights in the United States*, 1:52; Samuel Eliot Morison and Henry Steele Commager, *The Growth of the American Republic*, 2:478; Harold L. Nelson, ed., *Freedom of the Press from Hamilton to the Warren Court*, 248, 254; Frank Luther Mott, *American Journalism*, 624; John D. Stevens, "Press and Community Toleration: Wisconsin in World War I," *Journalism Quarterly* 46(1969): 256.
2. Chafee, *Free Speech*, 14–15; Chafee, *Blessings of Liberty*, 70, 71.
3. Oscar Theodore Barck, Jr., and Nelson Manfred Blake, *Since 1900*, 225–226; James R. Mock, *Censorship—1917*, 45–47; Mott, *American Journalism*, 625–626.
4. *Chicago Tribune*, May 16, 1917, p. 6, col. 1.
5. Nelson, ed., *Freedom of the Press*, 250–253, 255.
6. Mott, *American Journalism*, 627; W. A. Swanberg, *Citizen Hearst*, 312; Edwin Emery and Henry Ladd Smith, *The Press and America*, 594, 595.

7. Emerson, Haber, and Dorsen, *Political and Civil Rights*, 1:53–54; Nelson, ed., *Freedom of the Press*, 248–250; Barck and Blake, *Since 1900*, 223.

8. Quoted in Chafee, *Free Speech*, 38.

9. Emery and Smith, *Press and America*, 593; Mott, *American Journalism*, 623; Thomas F. Carroll, "Freedom of Speech and of the Press in War Time: The Espionage Act," *Michigan Law Review* 17:623, 625–626. See also Neil Sheehan et al., *Pentagon Papers*, 666.

10 John K. Winkler, *W. R. Hearst*, 272, 276.

11. *New York Times*, Apr. 13, 1917, p. 12, col. 2. For debate on the espionage bill and other press reaction to the censorship proposal, see Carroll, "Freedom of Speech," 621, 622, 624, 627, 628, 663.

12. Quoted in Carroll, "Freedom of Speech," 624.

13. Frank Thayer, *Legal Control of the Press*, 47.

14. Louisville *Courier Journal*, June 1, 1917, p. 4, cols. 2, 3.

15. Ibid., June 7, 1917, p. 4, col. 2.

16. Ibid., June 10, 1917, p. 4 of editorial section.

17. *St. Louis Post-Dispatch*, June 3, 1917, p. 1 of editorial section.

18. Carroll, "Freedom of Speech," 628.

19. *New York Times*, June 6, 1917, p. 10, cols. 2, 3.

20. Ibid., June 14, 1917, p. 10, col. 2.

21. Ibid., June 15, 1917, p. 8, col. 3.

22. New York *Herald* quoted in *Boston Evening Transcript*, June 16, 1917, part 3, p. 3, col. 3.

23. *Boston Evening Transcript*, June 1, 1917, p. 10, col. 2.

24. Ibid., June 11, 1917, p. 10, cols. 3, 4.

25. *Washington Evening Star*, June 14, 1917, p. 6, col. 3.

26. Ibid., June 16, 1917, p. 4, col. 1.

27. *Atlanta Constitution*, June 2, 1917, p. 6, col. 2.

28. Louisville *Courier Journal*, June 2, 1917, p. 4, col. 3.

29. Ibid., June 16, 1917, p. 4, col. 1.

30. *St. Louis Post-Dispatch*, June 1, 1917, p. 14.

31. Ibid., May 24, 1916, p. 14, col. 2.

32. *San Francisco Chronicle*, June 13, 1917, p. 18, col. 2.

33. Chafee, *Free Speech*, 248–250; Donald M. Gillmor and Jerome A. Barron, *Mass Communication Law*, 89; Ernest Sutherland Bates, *This Land of Liberty*, 117.

34. U.S. Congress, [House] Special Committee on Right of Victor Berger to Be Sworn In, *Hearings*, 1:719.

35. Berger *Hearings*, 1:535, 681.

36. Chafee, *Free Speech*, 248.

37. *New York Times*, Oct. 4, 1917, p. 8.
38. *St. Louis Post-Dispatch*, Oct. 3, 1917, editorial page.
39. Ibid., Mar. 10, 1918, editorial page.
40. *Chicago Tribune*, Oct. 4, 1917, p. 3, col. 5; *San Francisco Chronicle*, Oct. 4, 1917, p. 3, col. 6.
41. *New York Times*, Mar. 12, 1918, p. 12, col. 2.
42. See Chafee, *Free Speech*, 142; Ray Ginger, *The Bending Cross—A Biography of Eugene Victor Debs*, 341; Berger *Hearings*, 2:19.
43. Louisville *Courier Journal*, Mar. 12, 1918, p. 4, col. 4.
44. *St. Louis Post-Dispatch*, Feb. 23, 1918, p. 10.
45. Ibid., June 14, 1917, p. 14.
46. *New York Times*, Jan. 10, 1919, p. 12, col. 3.
47. Denver *Rocky Mountain News*, Jan. 10, 1919, p. 6, col. 2.
48. Chafee, *Free Speech*, 39–41; Barck and Blake, *Since 1900*, 223–224; Mott, *American Journalism*, 623–624.
49. *Minneapolis Journal*, Apr. 5, 1918, photocopy in American Civil Liberties Union Papers, vol. 53, at Princeton University Library (hereafter cited as ACLU Papers).
50. St. Louis *Republic*, Apr. 5, 1918, in ACLU Papers.
51. The Hearst newspapers were by no means the only ones to express anti-British sentiments; Mott, *American Journalism*, 616. Several biographers of Hearst agree as to his hatred of the British and his opposition to the war, though not for reasons of pacifism; Mott, *American Journalism*, 617. But their judgments differ as to his motives. One biography says: "Hearst's treatment of the war news published in his papers was motivated, first by his personal hatred of Great Britain, and, second, by the fact that the bulk of his readers were Irish-Americans and German-Americans." Oliver Carlson and Ernest Sutherland Bates, *Hearst*, 186. Another says: "Hearst's efforts to embarrass the United States government after war was declared in 1917 cast a curious light on his *own* definition of patriotism, which is, the unquestioning support of the government and its policies by all citizens no matter what those policies may be." Ferdinand Lundberg, *Imperial Hearst*, 228. W. A. Swanberg says: "Hearst sincerely believed that the United States should stay out of the war." Swanberg, *Citizen Hearst*, 294. "Many who knew him best, even though they might disagree with his opinions or methods, never doubted his fundamental patriotism." Swanberg, *Citizen Hearst*, 302.
52. *New York Tribune*, Apr. 11, 1918, in ACLU Papers.
53. Philadelphia *Evening Telegraph*, Apr. 23, 1918, in ACLU Papers.
54. Ibid., May 6, 1918, in ACLU Papers.

55. *Washington Evening Star*, May 6, 1918, p. 6, col. 2.
56. New Orleans *States Item*, May 10, 1918, in ACLU Papers.
57. *Washington Post*, May 14, 1918, in ACLU Papers.
58. *Seattle Times*, May 22, 1918, in ACLU Papers.
59. Philadelphia *Press*, June 11, 1918, in ACLU Papers.
60. New York *Evening Call*, Apr. 6, 1918, in ACLU Papers.
61. Ibid., Apr. 30, 1918, in ACLU Papers.
62. Milwaukee *Leader*, May 14, 1918, in ACLU Papers.
63. Quoted in Donald Johnson, *The Challenge to American Freedoms*, 97–98.
64. *New York Times*, May 2, 1918, p. 12, col. 4.
65. Johnson, *Challenge to Freedoms*, 87, 88, 94, 95; Bates, *Land of Liberty*, 133.
66. *New York Times*, May 7, 1918, p. 12, col. 2.
67. Ibid., May 16, 1918, p. 12, col. 2.
68. *St. Louis Post-Dispatch*, May 26, 1918, p. 2, col. 3. For Nebraska and Texas laws, see Chafee, *Free Speech*, 587–594.
69. *San Francisco Chronicle*, May 22, 1918, p. 20, col. 2.
70. Chafee, *Free Speech*, 51–52, 54. See also Barck and Blake, *Since 1900*, 224–225; Morison and Commager, *American Republic*, 2:479.
71. Quoted in Mock, *Censorship*, 35.
72. *New York Times*, Sept. 13, 1918, p. 10, col. 2.
73. McAlister Coleman, *Eugene V. Debs*, 284; Ginger, *Bending Cross*, 353, 356; Floy Ruth Painter, *That Man Debs and His Life Work*, 116–117.
74. Bates, *Land of Liberty*, 156, 157.
75. Mock, *Censorship*, 211.
76. Ginger, *Bending Cross*, 562.
77. Ibid., 370.
78. *Dictionary of American Biography*, 1930 ed., s.v. "Debs, Eugene Victor."
79. *Washington Evening Star*, Sept. 14, 1918, p. 6, col. 4.
80. Louisville *Courier Journal*, Sept. 14, 1918, p. 4, col. 1.
81. Bates, *Land of Liberty*, 98, 99; Johnson, *Challenge to Freedoms*, 65; Chafee, *Free Speech*, 65–66.
82. Bates, *Land of Liberty*, 152.
83. Mauritz Hallgren, *Landscape of Freedom*, 365.
84. John Hohenberg, ed., *The Pulitzer Prize Story*, 336.
85. Stevens, "Press and Community Toleration," 257.
86. Denver *Rocky Mountain News*, Mar. 3, 1919, p. 1, col. 3.
87. Ibid., Mar. 3, 1919, p. 6.

88. Chafee, *Free Speech*, 81.
89. Quoted in Nelson, ed., *Freedom of the Press*, 64–65.
90. Nelson, ed., *Freedom of the Press*, 61–62. On cases involving the "clear and present danger" test, see Don R. Pember, "The Smith Act as a Restraint on the Press," *Journalism Monographs*, 13–15.
91. Bates, *Land of Liberty*, 159.
92. Thomas I. Emerson, "Legal Foundations of the Right to Know," (Lecture given at Washington University School of Law, Mar. 3, 1976), 7.
93. Hugo L. Black, "The Bill of Rights," (James Madison Lecture, New York University School of Law, Feb. 17, 1960), 3.
94. *San Francisco Chronicle*, Mar. 7, 1919, p. 18, cols. 1, 2.
95. Chafee, *Free Speech*, 84.
96. Emerson, Haber, and Dorsen, *Political and Civil Rights*, 1:74.
97. Chafee, *Free Speech*, 84–85; Bates, *Land of Liberty*, 157.
98. *New York Times*, Mar. 12, 1919, p. 10, cols. 3, 4.
99. *Washington Evening Star*, Mar. 11, 1919, p. 6, col. 1.
100. Denver *Times*, Mar. 13, 1919, p. 6.
101. *Atlanta Constitution*, Mar. 12, 1921, p. 8, col. 2.
102. *St. Louis Post-Dispatch*, Feb. 1, 1921, p. 28, col. 2.
103. Ibid., Feb. 4, 1921, p. 20, col. 2.
104. James Morton Smith and Paul L. Murphy, eds., *Liberty and Justice*, 361–363; Emerson, Haber, and Dorsen, *Political and Civil Rights*, 1:74; Chafee, *Free Speech*, 113, 114; Bates, *Land of Liberty*, 160.
105. Quoted in Chafee, *Free Speech*, 118.
106. Quoted in Chafee, *Free Speech*, 126n19.
107. 250 U.S. at 619.
108. 250 U.S. at 621.
109. See Chafee, *Free Speech*, 119, 121, 123, 125, 126, 127.
110. 250 U.S. at 627–628, 629, 630.
111. *New York Times*, Nov. 12, 1919, p. 12, col. 3.
112. Bates, *Land of Liberty*, 118.
113. Berger *Hearings*, 1:410.
114. *Washington Evening Star,* Nov. 11, 1919, p. 6, col. 2.
115. *Boston Evening Transcript*, Nov. 12, 1919, p. 2 of editorial section, col. 1.
116. Louisville *Courier Journal*, Nov. 12, 1919, p. 4, col. 4.
117. *St. Louis Post-Dispatch*, Nov. 10, 1919, p. 22, col. 3.
118. *San Francisco Chronicle*, Nov. 14, 1919, editorial page.
119. Henry Steele Commager, "The Misuse of Power," *New Republic* (Apr. 17, 1971), 19.
120. John Lofton, *Justice and the Press*, 27; Stanley Coben, *A. Mitchell*

Palmer: Politician, 221; Chafee, *Free Speech*, 204–215; Emerson, Haber, and Dorsen, *Political and Civil Rights*, 1:58; Bates, *Land of Liberty*, 124–129; Max Lowenthal, *The Federal Bureau of Investigation*, 147–155; Hallgren, *Landscape of Freedom*, 371–372.

121. Quoted in Chafee, *Blessings of Liberty*, 67.
122. *New York Times*, Jan. 5, 1920, editorial page. For editorial reactions to the Palmer raids by the *New York Times*, the *Washington Evening Star*, the *Washington Post*, the *St. Louis Globe-Democrat*, the *St. Louis Post-Dispatch*, and the *San Francisco Examiner*, I am indebted for research to Greg Hauptman, a student at Washington University in 1972.
123. *Washington Evening Star*, Jan. 2, 1920, p. 6.
124. *Washington Post*, Jan. 4, 1920, p. 4, section 2.
125. *St. Louis Globe-Democrat*, Jan. 4, 1920, p. 2B.
126. *St. Louis Post-Dispatch*, Jan. 4, 1920, p. 2, section 2. Dorothy Bowles, in "Newspaper Support for Free Expression in Times of Alarm," *Journalism Quarterly* 54(1977):278, says the *Philadelphia Inquirer*, the New Orleans *Times-Picayune*, the Baltimore *Sun*, and the *Chicago Tribune* took the position that the Palmer raids were an infringement on constitutional rights.
127. *St. Louis Post-Dispatch*, Jan. 7, 1920, p. 24.
128. *San Francisco Examiner*, Jan. 6, 1920, editorial page.
129. Denver *Times*, Jan. 3, 1920, p. 6. A few days later the Denver *Times* was editorially noting the sacrifices of publishers during the war and defending an increase in the price of newspapers. Denver *Times*, Jan. 7, 1920, p. 6.
130. Denver *Rocky Mountain News*, Jan. 5, 1920, p. 6, col. 1.
131. Chafee, *Free Speech*, 76n74.
132. Quoted in Hallgren, *Landscape of Freedom*, 364.
133. *New York Times*, Feb. 2, 1921, p. 10, col. 3.
134. Chafee, *Free Speech*, 298–299; Gillmor and Barron, *Mass Communication Law*, pp. 89, 92.
135. Gillmor and Barron, *Mass Communication Law*, 93, 95, 97, 99.
136. *Boston Evening Transcript*, Mar. 8, 1921, part 2, p. 2, cols. 2, 3.
137. *St. Louis Post-Dispatch*, Mar. 11, 1921, p. 22, col. 2.
138. Gillmor and Barron, *Mass Communication Law*, 99, 103, 105.

CHAPTER 10

1. See Arthur S. Miller, "The Court Turns Back the Clock," *The Progressive* (October 1976), 22.
2. Ernest Sutherland Bates, *This Land of Liberty*, 164; Ernest Sutherland Bates, *The Story of the Supreme Court*, 256; Zechariah

Chafee, Jr., *Free Speech in the United States*, 285n1, 290, 318; Thomas I. Emerson, David Haber, and Norman Dorsen, *Political and Civil Rights in the United States*, 1:79.

3. Quoted in Bates, *Supreme Court*, 256.
4. Emerson, Haber, and Dorsen, *Political and Civil Rights*, 1:82.
5. Zechariah Chafee, Jr., *The Blessings of Liberty*, 73.
6. *New York Times*, June 9, 1925, p. 20, col. 1.
7. *St. Louis Post-Dispatch*, June 10, 1925, p. 18.
8. *St. Louis Globe-Democrat*, June 10, 1925, p. 16, cols. 1, 2.
9. Emerson, Haber, and Dorsen, *Political and Civil Rights*, 1:674; Chafee, *Free Speech*, 376; Frank Thayer, *Legal Control of the Press*, 108.
10. Emerson, Haber, and Dorsen, *Political and Civil Rights*, 1:677–678.
11. Ibid., 676; Chafee, *Free Speech*, 379; Donald M. Gillmor and Jerome A. Barron, *Mass Communication Law*, 80.
12. *New York Times*, June 3, 1931, p. 24, cols. 1, 2.
13. *Washington Post*, June 3, 1931, p. 6, col. 2.
14. *Boston Evening Transcript*, June 2, 1931, part 2, p. 2, col. 3.
15. Louisville *Courier Journal*, June 3, 1931, p. 6, cols. 1, 2.
16. *St. Louis Post-Dispatch*, June 3, 1931, p. 2C, col. 2.
17. Denver *Rocky Mountain News*, June 3, 1931, p. 6, col. 1.
18. *San Francisco Chronicle*, June 3, 1931, p. 24, cols. 1, 2.
19. John Tebbel, *An American Dynasty*, 325–326.
20. *Atlanta Journal*, June 2, 1931, p. 3, col. 7.
21. Chafee, *Free Speech*, 357–358, 362; Chafee, *Blessings of Liberty*, 77–79.
22. Chafee, *Free Speech*, 362.
23. Ibid., 384.
24. Ibid., 388.
25. Alfred H. Kelly and Winfred A. Harbison, *The American Constitution*, 792, 793.
26. Chafee, *Free Speech*, 382; William A. Hachten, *The Supreme Court on Freedom of the Press*, 76–77; Gillmor and Barron, *Mass Communication Law*, 105–106.
27. Gillmor and Barron, *Mass Communication Law*, 109.
28. *New York Times*, Feb. 11, 1936, p. 22, col. 1.
29. *Boston Evening Transcript*, Feb. 11, 1936, part 2, p. 2, col. 3.
30. *Washington Evening Star*, Feb. 11, 1936, p. A–8, col. 1.
31. *Washington Post*, Feb. 11, 1936, p. 8, col. 2.
32. *Atlanta Journal*, Feb. 11, 1936, p. 4, col. 2.
33. *St. Louis Post-Dispatch*, Feb. 11, 1936, p. 2C, col. 3.

34. Ibid., Feb. 10, 1936, p. 2C, col. 3.
35. *San Francisco Chronicle*, Feb. 11, 1936, p. 10, col. 1.
36. Hachten, *Supreme Court*, 90.
37. John Lofton, *Justice and the Press*, 113–115; Harold L. Nelson, ed., *Freedom of the Press from Hamilton to the Warren Court*, 140–141.
38. Gillmor and Barron, *Mass Communication Law*, 426.
39. Thayer, *Legal Control*, 555–556; Nelson, ed., *Freedom of the Press*, 141–153.
40. Lofton, *Justice and the Press*, 117.
41. Gillmor and Barron, *Mass Communication Law*, 427.
42. Lofton, *Justice and the Press*, 119–120.
43. Gillmor and Barron, *Mass Communication Law*, 428.
44. Lofton, *Justice and the Press*, 126.
45. Gillmor and Barron, *Mass Communication Law*, 431.
46. *Atlanta Constitution*, Dec. 12, 1941, p. 16, col. 2.
47. *Atlanta Journal*, Dec. 13, 1941, p. 4, col. 1.
48. Louisville *Courier Journal*, Dec. 10, 1941, p. 6, cols. 1, 2.
49. *St. Louis Post-Dispatch*, Dec. 9, 1941, p. 20, col. 2.
50. *San Francisco Chronicle*, Dec. 9, 1941, p. 20, cols. 1, 2.
51. Dorothy Bowles, "Newspaper Support for Free Expression in Times of Alarm," *Journalism Quarterly* 54(Summer 1977):273; Don R. Pember, "The Smith Act as a Restraint on the Press," *Journalism Monographs—Number Ten*, 1, 2, 7; Nelson, ed., *Freedom of the Press*, 320.
52. Nelson, ed., *Freedom of the Press*, 321–322.
53. Ibid., 320–321; Pember, "Smith Act," 4.
54. Bowles, "Newspaper Support for Free Expression," 271, 274, 276, 277.
55. Ibid., 275, 278.
56. Pember, "Smith Act," 3, 24–25.
57. Ibid., p. 10; Emerson, Haber, and Dorsen, *Political and Civil Rights*, 1:78, 100.
58. *Washington Post*, Dec. 9, 1941, p. 17, col. 1.
59. Lofton, *Justice and the Press*, 30, 31; Chafee, *Blessings of Liberty*, 79; Emerson, Haber, and Dorsen, *Political and Civil Rights*, 1:61.
60. Marshall Field, *Freedom Is More Than a Word*, 140–141; Gillmor and Barron, *Mass Communication Law*, 533–534; Hachten, *Supreme Court*, 289, 290.
61. Quoted in Robert Lasch, "For a Free Press," *Atlantic* (July 1944), 39.
62. Ibid., 39; Field, *Freedom*, 140–141.

63. Tebbel, *Dynasty*, 327, 329, 330, 331.
64. Quoted in Field, *Freedom*, 141. For other newspaper comments on the case, see ibid., 144.
65. *Associated Press* v. *U.S.*, 326 U.S. 1, 9n4.
66. 326 U.S. at 20.
67. Hachten, *Supreme Court*, 294–295.
68. Keith Roberts, "Antitrust Problems in the Newspaper Industry," *Harvard Law Review* 82 (1968):332.
69. William L. Rivers and Wilbur Schramm, *Responsibility in Mass Communication*, 58.
70. See John De J. Pemberton, Jr., "The Right of Access to Mass Media," in *The Rights of Americans*, ed., Norman Dorsen, 294–295.
71. Gillmor and Barron, *Mass Communication Law*, 99–100, 101.
72. Ibid., 102–103. See also Hachten, *Supreme Court*, 186; Emerson, Haber, and Dorsen, *Political and Civil Rights*, 1:697.
73. *New York Times*, Feb. 5, 1946, p. 22, col. 3.
74. *St. Louis Post-Dispatch*, Feb. 5, 1946, p. 2B, cols. 1, 2.
75. Denver *Rocky Mountain News*, Feb. 6, 1946, p. 14.
76. *San Francisco Chronicle*, Feb. 5, 1946, p. 14, col. 2.
77. Hachten, *Supreme Court*, 188–189.
78. Ibid., 190.
79. Gillmor and Barron, *Mass Communication Law*, 438; Hachten, *Supreme Court*, 95; Lofton, *Justice and the Press*, 159.
80. Gillmor and Barron, *Mass Communication Law*, 439.
81. *New York Times*, June 5, 1946, p. 22, col. 3.
82. *Atlanta Journal*, June 5, 1946, p. 10, col. 1.
83. *Washington Post*, June 9, 1946, p. 4B, col. 2.
84. Louisville *Courier Journal*, June 5, 1946, p. 6, col. 2.
85. *St. Louis Post-Dispatch*, June 5, 1946, p. 2B, col. 3.
86. Lofton, *Justice and the Press*, 117.
87. *San Francisco Chronicle*, June 4, 1946, p. 10, col. 2.
88. Gillmor and Barron, *Mass Communication Law*, 442; Hachten, *Supreme Court*, 101; Lofton, *Justice and the Press*, 127.
89. Gillmor and Barron, *Mass Communication Law*, 442–443.

CHAPTER 11

1. 315 U.S. 568.
2. 315 U.S. at 571–572.
3. 355 U.S. 848.
4. *Beauharnais* v. *Illinois*, 343 U.S. 250, 267.
5. *Terminiello* v. *City of Chicago*, 337 U.S. 1, 4–5.

6. 340 U.S. 315; Franklyn S. Haiman, *Freedom of Speech: Issues and Cases*, 30. For "fighting words" cases in the 1970s, see Franklyn S. Haiman, "How Much of Our Speech Is Free?" *Civil Liberties Review* (Winter 1975), 111.
7. 340 U.S. at 32.
8. Alfred H. Kelly and Winfred A. Harbison, *The American Constitution*, 792–793.
9. Haiman, *Freedom of Speech*, xiii, xvi.
10. 341 U.S. 494.
11. Kelly and Harbison, *American Constitution*, 790, 817.
12. See Zechariah Chafee, Jr., *Free Speech in the United States*, 577–597, esp. 585, 588, 589, 591, 592, 593.
13. Alan Reitman, ed., *The Pulse of Freedom*, 71–72, 115.
14. Ibid., 112–113.
15. See John D. Stevens, "From Behind Barbed Wire: Freedom of the Press in World War II Japanese Centers," *Journalism Quarterly* 48(1971):279.
16. Leo Katcher, *Earl Warren*, 140; Audrie Girdner and Anne Loftis, *The Evacuation of Japanese-Americans During World War II*, 66–67; Carey McWilliams, *Prejudice—Japanese-Americans*, 234, 248.
17. Martin Grodzins, *Americans Betrayed*, 383.
18. Allan R. Bosworth, *America's Concentration Camps*, 56; Grodzins, *Americans Betrayed*, 382.
19. Thomas I. Emerson, David Haber, and Norman Dorsen, *Political and Civil Rights*, 1:62.
20. Reitman, ed., *Pulse of Freedom*, 159–160.
21. Alan Barth, *The Loyalty of Free Men*, 12. For the role of the press, see also *Progressive* (April 1954), 33.
22. Quoted in Barth, *Loyalty of Free Men*, 13.
23. *Progressive* (April 1954), 59–62; James Rorty and Moshe Decter, *McCarthy and the Communists*, 74, 77.
24. John Cogley, *Report on Blacklisting*, 1:147. For the role of the press in connection with the Un-American Activities Committee, see Frank J. Donner, *The Un-Americans*, 147–162, 303–304.
25. *Progressive* (April 1954), 58.
26. Donner, *The Un-Americans*, 150. For public attitudes toward McCarthy, see Daniel Bell, ed., *The Radical Right*, 327–348; for newspaper publishers' attitudes toward the internal Communist threat, see Samuel A. Stouffer, *Communism, Conformity and Civil Liberties*, 194.

27. Don R. Pember, "The Smith Act as a Restraint on the Press," *Journalism Monographs—Number Ten*, 10, 11.
28. Ibid., 23–24, 25, 26.
29. Ibid., 28.
30. William A. Hachten, *The Supreme Court on Freedom of the Press*, 27; Haiman, *Freedom of Speech*, 67.
31. Kelly and Harbison, *American Constitution*, 892.
32. 341 U.S. 494, 510.
33. 341 U.S. at 502, 503, 509, 515, 516.
34. 341 U.S. at 579–581.
35. 341 U.S. at 581, 582, 587, 589, 590.
36. Quoted in *St. Louis Post-Dispatch*, June 5, 1951, p. 6A.
37. *Atlanta Constitution*, June 5, 1951, p. 12, cols. 1, 2.
38. *Washington Post*, June 6, 1951, p. 12, cols. 2, 3.
39. Denver *Rocky Mountain News*, June 6, 1951, p. 28.
40. *Denver Post*, June 5, 1951, p. 12, cols. 1, 2.
41. *San Francisco Chronicle* and *Indianapolis Star* quoted in *St. Louis Post-Dispatch*, June 5, 1951, p. 6A.
42. *Indianapolis News* quoted in *St. Louis Post-Dispatch*, June 6, 1951, p. 1C.
43. Minneapolis *Star* quoted in *St. Louis Post-Dispatch*, June 5, 1951, p. 6A.
44. *Oregon Journal* and *Fort Worth Star-Telegram* quoted in *St. Louis Post-Dispatch*, June 6, 1951, p. 5C.
45. Favorable comments on Supreme Court decision by *New York Daily News*, Philadelphia *Bulletin*, *Philadelphia Inquirer*, New Orleans *Times-Picayune*, *Kansas City Star*, Memphis *Commercial Appeal*, and the Nashville *Tennessean* quoted in *St. Louis Post-Dispatch*, June 5, 1951, p. 6A.
46. Quoted in *St. Louis Post-Dispatch*, June 6, 1951, p. 1C.
47. Little Rock *Arkansas Gazette*, June 6, 1951, editorial page.
48. *St. Louis Post-Dispatch*, June 5, 1951, p. 2C.
49. Quoted ibid., June 10, 1951, p. 2B.
50. Pember, "The Smith Act," 26, 27.
51. Emerson, Haber, and Dorsen, *Political and Civil Rights*, 1:121.
52. Pember, "The Smith Act," 3.
53. 354 U.S. 298.
54. Emerson, Haber, and Dorsen, *Political and Civil Rights*, 1:123, 132, 133; Haiman, *Freedom of Speech*, 73, 74.
55. 343 U.S. 495.
56. Haiman, *Freedom of Speech*, 96–97.

57. 354 U.S. 476.
58. For Judge Frank's comment, see Haiman, *Freedom of Speech,* 107–108. Judge Curtis Bok in an earlier Pennsylvania case had also taken a more liberal view than the Supreme Court. See Haiman, *Freedom of Speech,* 99–100.
59. Ibid., 113–128.
60. 378 U.S. 184.
61. 380 U.S. 51.
62. Emerson, Haber, and Dorsen, *Political and Civil Rights,* 1:583n6.
63. 376 U.S. 254.
64. 376 U.S. at 266.
65. 376 U.S. at 279–280.
66. Haiman, *Freedom of Speech,* 81–82.
67. Hachten, *Supreme Court,* 139.
68. *Editor and Publisher,* Mar. 21, 1964, p. 54.
69. *New York Times,* Mar. 10, 1964, editorial page.
70. *Washington Post,* Mar. 10, 1964, editorial page.
71. *Atlanta Constitution,* Mar. 11, 1964, p. 4, cols. 1, 2.
72. Louisville *Courier Journal,* Mar. 10, 1964, cols. 2, 3.
73. *Pittsburgh Post-Gazette,* Mar. 11, 1964, editorial page.
74. *St. Louis Post-Dispatch,* Mar. 12, 1964, editorial page.
75. *Denver Post,* Mar. 10, 1964, p. 22, cols. 1, 2.
76. Denver *Rocky Mountain News,* Mar. 12, 1964, p. 60.
77. *San Francisco Chronicle,* Mar. 11, 1964, editorial page.
78. 379 U.S. 64.
79. Hachten, *Supreme Court,* 145–146.
80. 388 U.S. 130.
81. *Time, Inc.* v. *Hill,* 385 U.S. 374.
82. *Mills* v. *Alabama,* 384 U.S. 214.
83. Hachten, *Supreme Court,* 68–69.
84. *Washington Post,* May 25, 1966, p. A24.
85. *Pittsburgh Post-Gazette,* May 25, 1966, editorial page.
86. *St. Louis Post-Dispatch,* May 24, 1966, p. 2C.
87. *A Book Named "John Cleland's Memoirs of a Woman of Pleasure"* v. *Attorney General of Massachusetts,* 383 U.S. 413.
88. *Mishkin* v. *New York,* 383 U.S. 502.
89. *Ginzburg* v. *U.S.,* 383 U.S. 463.
90. 383 U.S. at 467, 468, 474.
91. 383 U.S. at 500.
92. 383 U.S. at 476.
93. 383 U.S. at 482–483.

94. *New York Times,* Mar. 24, 1966, editorial page.
95. *Washington Post,* Mar. 23, 1966, p. A20, col. 1.
96. Louisville *Courier-Journal,* Mar. 23, 1966, p. A6, cols. 3, 4.
97. *Pittsburgh Post-Gazette,* Mar. 23, 1966, p. 8, col. 1.
98. *St. Louis Post-Dispatch,* Mar. 23, 1966, p. 2B.
99. *Denver Post,* Mar. 23, 1966, p. 24, cols. 1, 2.
100. *San Francisco Chronicle,* Mar. 22, 1966, p. 38, col. 1.
101. 413 U.S. 15.
102. See Nathan Lewin, "Sex at High Noon in Times Square," *New Republic* (July 7–14, 1973), 19; Mel Friedman, "The Supreme Court and 'Obscenity'" *Nation* (Aug. 6, 1977), 110.
103. *New York Times Co.* v. *U.S.,* 403 U.S. 713.
104. *New York Times,* June 20, 1971, p. 1E, col. 4.
105. Ibid., July 1, 1971, p. 1, col. 8.
106. Neil Sheehan et al., *The Pentagon Papers as Published by The New York Times,* 652.
107. Ibid., 654–655.
108. Ibid., 662.
109. Ibid., 674.
110. See Douglas comment in Sheehan et al., *Pentagon Papers,* 653.
111. See Charles Rembar, "Paper Victory," *Atlantic* (November 1971), 61, 63.
112. *New York Times,* June 27, 1971, p. 25.
113. Rembar, "Paper Victory," 62, 65, 66.
114. Quoted in *St. Louis Post-Dispatch,* July 16, 1971, editorial page, "Mirror of Public Opinion."
115. *Editorials on File,* 1971, p. 799.
116. Ibid., 801.
117. Ibid., 803.
118. Ibid., 821.
119. *St. Louis Post-Dispatch,* July 1, 1971, editorial page.
120. *Editorials on File,* 1971, p. 809.
121. Ibid., 811.
122. Ibid., 799.
123. The *San Diego Union* (*Editorials on File,* 1971, p. 807); the *Burlington* (Vt.) *Free Press* (*Editorials on File,* 1971, p. 808); the Norfolk, Va., *Ledger-Star* (*Editorials on File,* 1971, p. 810).
124. The *Tulsa Daily World* (*Editorials on File,* 1971, p. 828); the *Dallas Morning News* (*Editorials on File,* 1971, p. 836); the *Richmond Times-Dispatch* (*Editorials on File,* 1971, p. 871).
125. *Editorials on File,* 1971, p. 807.

126. *Boston Globe*, Dec. 2, 1971.
127. *Nashville Banner* quoted in *St. Louis Post-Dispatch,* July 4, 1971, "Mirror of Public Opinion."
128. *Miami Herald* v. *Tornillo*, 418 U.S. 241.
129. For examples of legislator support for an enforced right to reply, see *The Masthead* [publication of the National Conference of Editorial Writers] (Spring 1974), 16; *Detroit News* editorial, June 22, 1974, in *Editorials on File*, 1974, p. 761.
130. *Editorials on File*, 1974, pp. 759–763.
131. *New York Times*, June 27, 1974, p. 44, col. 1.
132. *St. Louis Post-Dispatch*, June 26, 1974, editorial page.
133. *Editorials on File*, 1974, p. 763.
134. See Jerome A. Barron, "Access to the Press—A New First Amendment Right," *Harvard Law Review* 80(June 1967):1641–1678; Jerome A. Barron, *Freedom of the Press for Whom?*; Arthur S. Miller, "The Right of Reply," *New York Times*, Apr. 24, 1974, op ed page; Roger J. Traynor (former chief justice of the California Supreme Court), quoted in *The Masthead* (Spring 1974), 35.
135. Victor Marchetti and John D. Marks, *The CIA and the Cult of Intelligence*, 19.
136. Ibid., 21.
137. Ibid., 25, 26.
138. *Knopf, Inc.* v. *Colby*, 509 F. 2d 1362, 1368, 1370 (4th Cir., 1975).
139. Marchetti and Marks, *CIA*, 22.
140. Ibid., 24.
141. Ibid., 23.
142. Ibid., 24. Obviously encouraged by its victory in the *Marchetti* case, the government in 1978 brought suit against Frank Snepp, an ex-CIA agent who had published without CIA clearance a book entitled, *Decent Interval*, in which he exposed the agency's blunders during the 1975 American evacuation of Saigon. Even though the agency acknowledged that Snepp had divulged no important classified information, a federal district court ruled that Snepp's secrecy oath required him to submit to the CIA for prior review anything he wrote about the agency. The U.S. Court of Appeals for the Fourth Circuit and the Supreme Court upheld the district court's order and also allowed the government to seek civil damages. *Washington Post*, Sept. 15, 1978; *New York Times*, Mar. 22, 1979, A15.
143. Marchetti and Marks, *CIA*, 24.

144. Statement to author by Melvin Wulf, counsel for Victor Marchetti. On the *Marchetti* case, see also Taylor Branch, "The Censors of Bumbledom," *Harper's* (Jan. 1974), 56–63.

145. Statement to author by Judith Buncher, editor, *Editorials on File*.

146. Providence *Journal*, June 1, 1975, editorial page.

147. *Philadelphia Inquirer*, June 2, 1975, editorial page.

148. *Pittsburgh Post-Gazette*, June 4, 1975, editorial page.

149. *St. Louis Post-Dispatch*, June 2, 1975, editorial page.

150. 384 U.S. 333.

151. Robert Trager and Harry W. Stonecipher, "Gag Orders: An Unresolved Dilemma," *Journalism Quarterly* 55(1978):231.

152. *Nebraska Press Association* v. *Stuart*, 96 S.Ct. 291.

153. *Editorials on File*, 1976, pp. 873–880.

154. *St. Louis Post-Dispatch*, July 1, 1976, editorial page.

155. 408 U.S. 665.

156. *Editorials on File*, 1976, pp. 884–889. Those papers that found the decision acceptable were the Norfolk, Va., *Ledger-Star*, the *Tulsa World*, and the *Wisconsin State Journal*.

157. 418 U.S. 323.

158. 403 U.S. 29.

159. 424 U.S. 448.

160. Alan U. Schwartz, "Danger: Pendulum Swinging," *Atlantic* (Feb. 1977), 31–32.

161. Wicker, "The Submarine Story," *St. Louis Post-Dispatch*, Mar. 24, 1975, op ed page; *Washington Post*, Oct. 23, 1977, p. 1. See also John D. Marks, "The Story That Never Was," *More* (June 1974), 20 (on press self-censorship of plans for invasion of Cambodia); Ben Bagdikian, "The Story Beneath the Non-Story," *New York Times*, Sept. 2, 1975, op ed page.

162. *Oklahoma Publishing Co.* v. *District Court of Oklahoma County*, 45 U.S. Law Week 3596.

163. *Landmark Communications* v. *Virginia*, 46 U.S. Law Week 4389 (5–1–78).

164. *Editorials on File*, 1978, pp. 587–592.

165. *Houchins* v. *KQED*, 46 U.S. Law Week 4830 (6–29–78).

166. 46 U.S. Law Week at 4832.

167. *Editorials on File*, 1978, pp. 916–920.

168. *Zurcher* v. *Stanford Daily*, 46 U.S. Law Week 4546 (5–31–78).

169. For White comment, see 46 U.S. Law Week at 4550, 4551; for Stewart comment, see 46 U.S. Law Week at 4552.

170. *Editorials on File*, 1978, pp. 691–699.

171. Ibid., 691.

172. Ibid., 693.
173. *New York Times* v. *New Jersey*, 47 U.S. Law Week 3365 (11–28–78).
174. Anthony Lewis, "The Farber Case," *New York Times*, Aug. 7, 1978, op ed page.
175. Theodore White, "Why the Jailing of Farber 'Terrifies Me,'" *New York Times Magazine* (Nov. 26, 1978), 27; *Los Angeles Times* editorial, Aug. 20, 1978; Jonathan Kwitny, "A Judicial War on the Press," *Wall Street Journal*, Aug. 23, 1978, editorial page. See also dissent by Justice Morris Pasham of the New Jersey Supreme Court, reprinted in "Mirror of Public Opinion," *St. Louis Post-Dispatch*, Sept. 27, 1978, editorial page.
176. Stewart dissent, 408 U.S. at 725, 729, 730.
177. "Talk of the Town," *New Yorker* (Aug. 14, 1978), 23.
178. *Editorials on File*, Sept. 1–15, 1978, pp. 1101–1111; Nov. 16–30, 1978, pp. 1427–1433.
179. *U.S.* v. *The Progressive*, 47 U.S. Law Week 2636 (1979); *New York Times* editorial, Mar. 11, 1979; *Washington Post* editorial, Mar. 11, 1979; "Born Secret," *Progressive*, May 1979.

CHAPTER 12

1. *Editorials on File*, 1976, pp. 298–306.
2. Franklyn S. Haiman, *Freedom of Speech*, 149; Franklyn S. Haiman, "How Much of Our Speech Is Free?" *Civil Liberties Review* (Winter 1975): 112. See also John Rawls, *A Theory of Justice*, 223–225.
3. Haiman, "How Much of Our Speech Is Free?" 113.
4. See Douglas dissent in *Branzburg* v. *Hays*, 408 U.S. at 721.
5. W. Cody Wilson, "Belief in Freedom of Speech and Press," *Journal of Social Issues* 31, no. 2(1975):69, 71, 74.
6. Edward J. Bander, *Mr. Dooley*, 52.
7. *Wall Street Journal*, Jan. 26, 1979, editorial page.
8. Kevin Phillips, "Busting the Media Trusts," *Harper's* (July 1977), 28, 29.
9. Martin H. Seiden, *Who Controls the Mass Media?* 46.
10. National Advisory Commission, *Report on Civil Disorders*, 374, 375, 382.
11. *New York Times*, Jan. 8, 1978, p. 15, col. 1.
12. Harold L. Nelson, ed., *Freedom of the Press from Hamilton to the Warren Court*, 122.
13. Haiman, "How Much of Our Speech Is Free?" 135.
14. *Abrams* v. *United States*, 250 U.S. at 630 (1919).

Bibliography

ARTICLES:

Bagdikian, Ben. "The Story Beneath the Non-Story." *New York Times.* (Sept. 2, 1975), op ed page.

Barron, Jerome A., "Access to the Press—A New First Amendment Right." *Harvard Law Review* 80(June 1967):1641.

Black, Hugo L., "The Bill of Rights." *New York University Law Review* 35(1960):865.

Bowles, Dorothy. "Newspaper Support for Free Expression in Times of Alarm." *Journalism Quarterly* 54(Summer 1977):271.

Branch, Taylor. "The Censors of Bumbledom." *Harper's* (Jan. 1974), 56.

Carroll, Thomas F. "Freedom of Speech and of the Press in War Time: The Espionage Act," *Michigan Law Review* 17(June 1919):621.

Emerson, Thomas I. "Communication and Freedom of Expression." *Scientific American* (Sept. 1972), 163.

Friedman, Mel. "The Supreme Court and 'Obscenity'." *Nation* (Aug. 6, 1977), 110.

Haiman, Franklyn S. "How Much of Our Speech Is Free?" *Civil Liberties Review* (Winter 1975), 111.

Hale, F. Dennis. "A Comparison of Coverage of Speech and Press Verdicts of Supreme Court." *Journalism Quarterly* 56(Spring 1979): 43.

Krantz, Harry. "Landmark Impeachment." *St. Louis Post-Dispatch* (Nov. 18, 1973), 26.

323

Kwitny, Jonathan. "A Judicial War on the Press." *Wall Street Journal* (Aug. 23, 1978), editorial page.

Lasch, Robert. "For a Free Press." *Atlantic Monthly* (July 1944), 39.

Lewin, Nathan. "Sex at High Noon in Times Square." *New Republic* (July 7–14, 1973), 19.

"McCarthy: A Documented Record." *Progressive* (Apr. 1954).

Marks, John D. "The Story That Never Was." *More* (June 1975), 20.

Miller, Arthur S. "The Court Turns Back the Clock." *Progressive* (Oct. 1976), 22.

Phillips, Kevin. "Busting the Media Trusts." *Harper's* (July 1977), 23.

Reilly, Tom. "Newspaper Suppression During the Mexican War, 1846–1848." *Journalism Quarterly* 54(Summer 1977):262.

Rembar, Charles. "Paper Victory—The United States v. The New York Times and the Washington Post." *Atlantic* (Nov. 1971), 61.

Roberts, Keith. "Antitrust Problems in the Newspaper Industry." *Harvard Law Review* 82(Dec. 1968):319.

Schwartz, Alan U. "Danger: Pendulum Swinging." *Atlantic* (Feb. 1977), 31–32.

Stevens, John D. "From Behind Barbed Wire: Freedom of the Press in World War II Japanese Centers." *Journalism Quarterly* 48(Summer 1971):279.

Trager, Robert, and Stonecipher, Harry W. "Gag Orders: An Unresolved Dilemma." *Journalism Quarterly* 55(Summer 1978):231.

White, Theodore. "Why the Jailing of Farber 'Terrifies Me'." *New York Times Magazine* (Nov. 26, 1978), 27.

Wilson, W. Cody. "Belief in Freedom of Speech and Press." *Journal of Social Issues* 31, no. 2(1975):69.

BOOKS AND PAMPHLETS:

Aldridge, Alfred Owen. *Man of Reason: The Life of Thomas Paine.* Philadelphia: J. B. Lippincott Co., 1959.

Andrews, J. Cutler. *The North Reports the Civil War.* Pittsburgh: University of Pittsburgh Press, 1955.

Bailey, Thomas A. *A Diplomatic History of the American People.* New York: Appleton-Century Crofts, 1950.

Bander, Edward J. *Mr. Dooley on the Choice of Law.* Charlottesville, Va.: Michie Co., 1963.

Barck, Oscar Theodore, Jr., and Blake, Nelson Manfred. *Since 1900: A History of the United States in Our Times.* New York: Macmillan Co., 1947.

Barron, Jerome A. *Freedom of the Press for Whom? The Right of*

Access to Mass Media. Bloomington: Indiana University Press, 1973.

Barth, Alan. *The Loyalty of Free Men.* New York: Pocket Books, 1952.

Bassett, John Spencer, ed. *Correspondence of Andrew Jackson.* 7 vols. Washington, D.C.: Carnegie Institution of Washington, 1927.

Bates, Ernest Sutherland. *This Land of Liberty.* New York: Harper and Brothers, 1930.

————. *The Story of the Supreme Court.* Indianapolis: Bobbs-Merrill Charter Books, 1963.

Bell, Daniel, ed. *The Radical Right: The New American Right.* Garden City, N.Y.: Doubleday and Co., 1963.

Bosworth, Allan R. *America's Concentration Camps.* New York: W. W. Norton and Co., 1967.

Boyd, Thomas. *Light-Horse Harry Lee.* New York: Charles Scribner's Sons, 1931.

Brant, Irving. *The Bill of Rights.* New York: New American Library, 1967.

————. *Impeachment: Trials and Errors.* New York: Alfred A. Knopf, 1972.

Brigham, Clarence S. *Journals and Journeymen: A Contribution to the History of Early American Newspapers.* Philadelphia: University of Pennsylvania Press, 1950.

Buell, Augustus C. *History of Andrew Jackson.* 2 vols. New York: Charles Scribner's Sons, 1904.

Carlson, Oliver, and Bates, Ernest Sutherland. *Hearst: Lord of San Simeon.* New York: Viking Press, 1936.

Chafee, Zechariah, Jr. *The Blessings of Liberty.* Philadelphia: J. B. Lippincott, 1956.

————. *Free Speech in the United States.* Cambridge: Harvard University Press, 1967.

Chambers, William Nisbet. *Old Bullion Benton, Senator from the New West: Thomas Hart Benton.* Boston: Little, Brown and Co., 1956.

Clark, Henry Hayden, ed. *Poems of Freneau.* New York: Hafner Publishing Co., 1960.

Coben, Stanley. *A. Mitchell Palmer: Politician.* New York: Columbia University Press, 1963.

Cogley, John. *Report on Blacklisting.* 2 vols. New York: Fund for the Republic, 1956.

Coleman, McAlister. *Eugene V. Debs—A Man Unafraid.* New York: Greenberg Publishers, 1930.

Colyar, A. S. *Life and Times of Andrew Jackson.* 2 vols. Nashville: Marshall and Bruce Co., 1904.

David, Henry. *The History of the Haymarket Affair.* 2d ed. New York: Russell and Russell, 1958.

De Conde, Alexander. *Entangling Alliance: Politics and Diplomacy Under George Washington.* Duke University Press, 1958.

Dillon, Merton L. *Elijah P. Lovejoy, Abolitionist Editor.* Urbana: University of Illinois Press, 1961.

Donner, Frank J. *The Un-Americans.* New York: Ballantine Books, 1961.

Dorsen, Norman, ed. *The Rights of Americans—What They Are, What They Should Be.* New York: Vantage Books, 1970.

Earle, Edward Meade, ed. *The Federalist.* New York: Modern Library, 1937.

Editorials on File. New York: Facts on File, 1971, 1974, 1976, 1978.

Emerson, Thomas I., Haber, David, and Dorsen, Norman. *Political and Civil Rights in the United States.* 2 vols. Boston: Little, Brown and Co., 1967. Revised 1976 and 1979.

Emery, Edwin, and Smith, Henry Ladd. *The Press and America.* New York: Prentice-Hall, 1954.

Field, Marshall. *Freedom Is More Than a Word.* Chicago: University of Chicago Press, 1945.

Foley, William E. *A History of Missouri, 1673–1820.* Columbia: University of Missouri Press, 1971.

Ford, Worthington Chauncey, ed. *Thomas Jefferson Correspondence Printed from the Originals in the Collection of William K. Bixby.* Boston, 1916.

Furnas, J. C. *The Road to Harpers Ferry.* New York: William Sloane Associates, 1959.

Gerson, Noel B. *Light-Horse Harry—A Biography of Washington's Great Cavalryman, General Henry Lee.* New York: Doubleday and Co., 1966.

Gill, John. *Tide Without Turning: Elijah P. Lovejoy and Freedom of the Press.* Boston: Starr King Press, [1958].

Gill, McCune. *The St. Louis Story.* 3 vols. St. Louis: Historical Record Association, 1952.

Gillmor, Donald M., and Barron, Jerome A. *Mass Communication Law.* St. Paul, Minn.: West Publishing Co., 1969.

Ginger, Ray. *The Bending Cross—A Biography of Eugene Victor Debs.* New Brunswick, N.J.: Rutgers University Press, 1949.

Girdner, Audrie, and Loftis, Anne. *The Evacuation of Japanese-Americans During World War II.* New York: Macmillan Co., 1969.

Goldberg, Harvey, ed. *American Radicals.* New York: Monthly Review Press, 1957.

Grodzins, Martin. *Americans Betrayed: Politics and the Japanese Evacuation.* Chicago: University of Chicago Press, 1949.

Haiman, Franklyn S. *Freedom of Speech: Issues and Cases.* New York: Random House, 1967.

Hachten, William A. *The Supreme Court on Freedom of the Press.* Ames: Iowa State University Press, 1968.

Hallgren, Mauritz. *Landscape of Freedom: The Story of American Liberty and Bigotry.* New York: Howell, Soskin and Co., 1941.

Harding, Earl. *The Untold Story of Panama.* New York: Athene Press, 1959.

Hofstadter, Richard. *The American Political Tradition and the Men Who Made It.* New York: Vintage Books, 1954.

Hohenberg, John, ed. *The Pulitzer Prize Story.* New York: Columbia University Press, 1959.

Houck, Louis. *A History of Missouri.* 3 vols. Chicago: R. R. Donnelly and Sons Co., 1908.

Howarth, David. *Panama: 400 Years of Drama and Cruelty.* New York: McGraw-Hill Book Co., 1961.

James, Marquis. *The Life of Andrew Jackson.* New York: Bobbs-Merrill Co., 1938.

Johnson, Donald. *The Challenge to American Freedoms—World War I and the Rise of the American Civil Liberties Union.* Lexington: University of Kentucky Press, 1963.

Karsner, David. *Andrew Jackson—The Gentle Savage.* New York: Brentano's, 1927.

Katcher, Leo. *Earl Warren: A Political Biography.* New York: McGraw-Hill Book Co., 1967.

Kelly, Alfred H., and Harbison, Winfred A. *The American Constitution: Its Origins and Development.* New York: W. W. Norton and Co., 1955.

Krout, John Allen, and Fox, Dixon Ryan. *The Completion of Independence, 1790–1830.* Vol. 5 of *A History of American Life.* Edited by Arthur M. Schlesinger and Dixon Ryan Fox. 12 vols. New York: Macmillan Co., 1944.

Levy, Leonard W., ed. *Freedom of the Press from Zenger to Jefferson.* New York: Bobbs-Merrill Co., 1966.

————. *Jefferson and Civil Liberties: The Darker Side.* New York: New York Times Book Co., 1973.

————. *Legacy of Suppression.* Cambridge: Harvard University Press, 1960.

Lipscomb, Andrew A., and Bergh, Albert Ellery, eds. *The Writings of Thomas Jefferson.* 20 vols. in 10. Washington, D.C.: Thomas Jefferson Memorial Association of the United States, 1905.

Lofton, John. *Justice and the Press.* Boston: Beacon Press, 1966.

Lowenthal, Max. *The Federal Bureau of Investigation.* New York: William Sloane Associates, 1950.

Lundberg, Ferdinand. *Imperial Hearst—A Social Biography.* New York: Equinox Cooperative Press, 1936.

MacDougall, Curtis D. *Hoaxes.* New York: Dover Publications, 1958.

McCandless, Perry. *A History of Missouri, 1820–1860.* Columbia: University of Missouri Press, 1972.

McWilliams, Carey. *Prejudice—Japanese-Americans: Symbol of Racial Intolerance.* Boston: Little, Brown and Co., 1944.

Mack, Gerstle. *The Land Divided: A History of the Panama Canal and Other Isthmian Canal Projects.* New York: Alfred A. Knopf, 1944.

[Madison, James]. *Journal of the Constitutional Convention.* New York: Scott, Foresman and Co., 1893.

Marchetti, Victor, and Marks, John D. *The CIA and the Cult of Intelligence.* New York: Dell Publishing Co., 1974.

Miner, Dwight Carroll. *The Fight for the Panama Route.* New York: Columbia University Press, 1940.

Mock, James R. *Censorship—1917.* Princeton, N.J.: Princeton University Press, 1941.

Morison, Samuel Eliot, and Commager, Henry Steele. *The Growth of the American Republic.* 2 vols. New York: Oxford University Press, 1937.

Mott, Frank Luther. *American Journalism: A History of Newspapers in the United States Through 250 Years—1690–1940.* New York: Macmillan Co., 1949.

National Advisory Commission on Civil Disorders. *Report Of: What Happened? Why Did It Happen? What Can Be Done?* New York: Bantam Books, 1968.

Nelson, Harold L., ed. *Freedom of the Press from Hamilton to the Warren Court.* New York: Bobbs-Merrill Co., 1967.

Nevins, Allan. *Times of Trial.* New York: Alfred A. Knopf, 1958.

Nye, Russell B. *Fettered Freedom.* Urbana: University of Illinois Press, 1972.

Padover, Saul K., ed. *The Complete Madison: His Basic Writings.* New York: Harper and Brothers, 1953.

Painter, Floy Ruth. *That Man Debs and His Life Work.* Bloomington: Indiana University Graduate Council, 1929.

Parton, James. *Life of Andrew Jackson.* 3 vols. New York: Mason Brothers, 1860.

Patterson, Bennett B. *The Forgotten Ninth Amendment.* Indianapolis: Bobbs-Merrill Co., 1955.

Pember, Don R. "The Smith Act as a Restraint on the Press," *Journalism Monographs—Number Ten.* Austin, Tex.: Association for Education in Journalism, 1969.

Perry, Richard L., ed. *Sources of Our Liberties.* Chicago: American Bar Foundation, 1959.

Pritchett, C. Herman. *The American Constitution.* New York: McGraw-Hill Book Co., 1959.

Rawls, John. *A Theory of Justice.* Cambridge: Belknap Press of Harvard University Press, 1971.

Rayback, Joseph G. *A History of American Labor.* New York: Macmillan Co., 1959.

Reitman, Alan, ed. *The Pulse of Freedom—American Liberties: 1920s–1970s.* New York: W. W. Norton and Co., 1975.

Rivers, William L., and Schramm, Wilbur. *Responsibility in Mass Communication.* New York: Harper and Row, 1969.

Rorty, James, and Decter, Moshe. *McCarthy and the Communists.* Boston: Beacon Press, 1954.

Scharf, J. Thomas. *History of St. Louis City and County.* 2 vols. Philadelphia: Louis H. Everts and Co., 1883.

Schlesinger, Arthur M. *Prelude to Independence: The Newspaper War on Britain, 1764–1776.* New York: Alfred A. Knopf, 1958.

Seiden, Martin H. *Who Controls the Mass Media?* New York: Basic Books, 1974.

Seitz, Don C. *Joseph Pulitzer: His Life and Letters.* New York: Simon and Schuster, 1924.

Sheehan, Neil, et al. *The Pentagon Papers as Published by the New York Times.* New York: Bantam Books, 1971.

Shoemaker, Floyd Calvin. *Missouri and Missourians.* 5 vols. Chicago: Lewis Publishing Co., 1943.

Smith, James Morton. *Freedom's Fetters: The Alien and Sedition Laws and American Civil Liberties.* Ithaca, N.Y.: Cornell University Press, 1956.

Smith, James Morton, and Murphy, Paul L., eds. *Liberty and Justice: A Historical Record of American Constitutional Development.* New York: Alfred A. Knopf, 1958.

Stansbury, Arthur Jr., ed. *Report of the Trial of James H. Peck.* Boston: Hilliard, Gray and Co., 1833.

Stern, Philip Van Doren, ed. *The Life and Writings of Abraham Lincoln*. New York, Modern Library, 1940.

Stevens, John D. "Freedom of Expression: New Dimensions," in *Mass Media and the National Experience*. Edited by Ronald T. Farrar and John D. Stevens. New York: Harper and Row, 1971.

Stevens, Walter B. *Centennial History of Missouri*. 6 vols. St. Louis: S. J. Clarke Publishing Co., 1921.

Stouffer, Samuel A. *Communism, Conformity and Civil Liberties*. Garden City, N.Y.: Doubleday and Co., 1955.

Swanberg, W. A. *Citizen Hearst*. New York: Charles Scribner's Sons, 1961.

————. *Pulitzer*. New York: Charles Scribner's Sons, 1957.

[Tanner, Henry]. *An Eye-Witness: An Account of the Life, Trials and Perils of Rev. Elijah P. Lovejoy*. 1881. Reprint. New York: Augustus M. Kelley, 1971.

Tebbel, John. *An American Dynasty*. Garden City, N.Y.: Doubleday and Co., 1947.

Thayer, Frank. *Legal Control of the Press*. 4th ed. Brooklyn: Foundation Press, 1962.

Wallace, David Duncan. *South Carolina—A Short History: 1520–1948*. Chapel Hill: University of North Carolina Press, 1951.

Wiltse, Charles M., ed. *David Walker's Appeal*. New York: Hill and Wang, 1965.

Winkler, John K. *W. R. Hearst*. New York: Simon and Schuster, 1928.

PUBLIC DOCUMENTS:

Tansill, Charles C., ed. *Documents Illustrative of the Formation of the Union of the American States*. Washington, D.C., 1917.

U.S. Congress, House Committee on the Judiciary. *Impeachment: Selected Materials*. 93d Congress, 1st session. October 1973.

————, [House] Special Committee Appointed Under the Authority of House Resolution No. 6 Concerning the Right of Victor L. Berger to Be Sworn in as a Member of the Sixty-Sixth Congress. *Hearings*. 2 vols. 1919.

————. *Senate Documents* (1911–1912). Vol. 32, p. 61.

SPECIAL COLLECTION:

American Civil Liberties Union Archives. Princeton University Library. Princeton, N.J.

Table of Cases

Index

Buffalo *Evening News*: Un-American Committee supported by, 237
Burger, Warren, 257, 258, 270, 273; *Tornillo* opinion of quoted, 265
Burk, John, 29; editor of New York *Time Piece*, 38; editor of *Polar Star and Boston Daily Advertiser*, 37; prosecuted under common law, 35, 37–40; sedition law attacked by, 39–40; target of 1798 acts of Congress, 23
Burke, Edanus, 8
Burleson, A. R., 204
Burnside, Ambrose E., 104, 109–110, 111; ordered seizure of Chicago *Times*, 106; seizure order revoked by Lincoln, 107
Burr, Aaron, 40
Burstyn v. *Wilson*, 244
Burton, Harold, 238, 244
Business Week, 286
Butler, Pierce: "licentious publications" opposed by, 6

Cabell, Samuel J.: indicted for seditious libel, 21; indictment of denounced by Virginia House of Delegates, 22
Calhoun, John C.: author of bill to declare war in 1812, 51; presides over Peck impeachment trial, 69; proposes giving states regulatory power over mails, 86; roll on impeachment verdict called by, 73
California, 212
Callendar, James Thomas: convicted under Sedition Act, 44; writing of leads to prosecution of Harry Croswell, 45
Canada, 44
Carter, Jimmy, xii, 288
Caucus Club: organization of Revolutionary propagandists, 2
Central Intelligence Agency, 272; injunction won by, xiv, 266–268
Central Labor Union of Chicago, 118
Chafee, Zechariah, 191, 194, 221; on freedom of speech in World War I, 186–187; on press protection intended by framers, 9
Chamberlain bill, 182

Chambers, Ezekiel F.: absent at Peck trial conclusion, 73
Chaplinsky v. *New Hampshire*, 231–232, 233
Charles, Joseph: editor of *Missouri Gazette*, chides Thomas Hart Benton, 65
Charles X of France, 75
Charleston (S.C.) *City Gazette*: implies approval of mob action against press, 51, 56; Jay Treaty attacked by, 17
Charleston (S.C.) *Courier*: abolitionist press curb approved by, 85; Baltimore mob effect on press freedom lamented by, 56; on jailings by Jackson, 61; Panama Canal inquiry urged by, 164
Charleston (S.C.) *Mercury*, 76
Charleston (S.C.) *Patriot*: on abolitionist press curb, 92; "lynch law" proposal of quoted, 83
Charleston, S.C., 3, 51, 55–56, 61, 80, 95; abolitionist literature burned at, 82; citizens of condemn abolitionists' use of mails, 84; Edmond Charles Genêt arrives at, 16
Chicago, 117, 121, 122, 126, 127, 130, 138, 144, 161, 177, 178; businessmen of reported to finance suppression of radical ideas, 139; lawyers of satisfied with pardon of anarchists, 143
Chicago *Daily News*: editor of pushes prosecution in Haymarket affair, 123
Chicago *Herald*, 127, 139; on pardon of anarchists, 143
Chicago *Inter Ocean*: Haymarket affair distorted by, 120; incendiary speeches blamed by for bombing, 123; guilty verdict in Haymarket bombing trial cheered by, 133; pardon of anarchists accepted by, 143; prosecution presentation praised by, 132; on Roosevelt attack on New York *World*, 16
Chicago *Mail*: denounces anarchists, 122–123
Chicago *News*: police curb on anarchist meetings encouraged by, 138

Haswell, Anthony (editor of *Vermont Gazette*): convicted under Sedition Act, 43
Hay, George: writes in favor of press freedom, 45
Haymarket affair, 119–120, 131, 139, 142, 144, 145; indictments in, 122; newspapers denounce, 120–121; newspapers urge prosecution for, 122–123
Haymarket bombing trial: appellate courts uphold judgment in, 137; begins, 124; freedom of press and speech involved in, 125, 131, 133; guilty verdict in cheered by press, 133–136
Hayne, Robert Y.: and burning of abolitionist material, 84
Hearst newspapers: accused of disloyalty, 171; on Japanese-Americans, 235; sedition bill attacked by, 181
Hearst, William Randolph, 144, 145; espionage bill opposed by, 172; Roosevelt attacks, 171
Hendricks, William: votes for acquittal in Peck case, 76
Higginson, Thomas W., 15
Hobart, John Sloss: judge in sedition cases, 39
Holmes, Oliver Wendell, 204, 205, 207, 216, 217, 237, 284, 291; *Abrams* dissent of quoted, 198; "clear and present danger" test enunciated by, 192; *Debs* case opinion written by, 194; *Gitlow* dissent of quoted, 207; *Schenck* opinion of quoted, 191–192
Holt, Charles (editor of New London [Conn.] *Bee*), 55; convicted under Sedition Act, 43
Hough, Charles M.: indictment of New York *World* quashed by, 167
Houchins v. *KQED*: press reaction to, 273; right to know rejected in, 273
House of Representatives: reporting of debates allowed by, 26; votes for impeachment of Judge Peck, 69
Houston *Post-Dispatch*, 211
Howard, Joseph, Jr.: author of bogus presidential proclamation, 112

Hudson, Brazillai (editor of *Connecticut Courant*): indicted for seditious libel, 46; Supreme Court decision in case of, 47
Huger, Alfred (postmaster at Charleston, S.C.): and abolitionist mail, 82
Hughes, Charles Evans: *Near* opinion of quoted, 209

Illinois Anti Slavery Convention: press freedom upheld by, 97
Illinois Legislature: Chicago *Times* seizure denounced by, 106
Illinois Supreme Court: Haymarket bombing trial judgment upheld by, 137
Independent Chronicle. See Boston *Independent Chronicle*
Independent Journal. See New York *Independent Journal*
Indianapolis News: Panama deal questioned by, 152; prosecuted for libel, 146; Roosevelt denounces, 153; views on *Dennis* case, 241
Indianapolis Star: view on *Dennis* case, 241
Internal Security Act, 235
Internal Security Committee (House), 236
International League of Press Clubs, 113
International Working People's Association, 127
Iredell, Thomas: denies congressional power to punish critics, 21–22; denounces critics of John Adams, 21
Ireland, 37
Industrial Workers of the World (IWW), 185, 186, 195, 281
J. Russell's Gazette: critics of government attacked by, 30; Sedition Act enforcement urged by, 34; on death of Benjamin Bache, 37
Jackson administration, 83, 84
Jackson, Andrew, 82; arrests made by, 58–59; view of martial law of, 59; in contempt of court, 59–60; martial law revoked by, 59; party of, 74; reimbursed by Congress, 61; suppresses *Louisi-*

of nation, 3–4; and struggle between Hamilton and Jefferson, 14–15; tolerance of opposing views eroded during Revolution, 5–6. *See also* Federalist newspapers, Republican (Jeffersonian) newspapers, Socialist newspapers
Press Publishing Company: indicted for libel, 164
Privacy Law: mass media and, 251
Progressive, The: enjoined from publishing article, 278
Prospect Before Us, The: and sedition prosecution, 44
Providence *Journal*: on *Marchetti* case, 268–269
Pulitzer, Joseph, 160, 161, 166; Denver *Republican* denounces, 163–164; indicted in District of Columbia, 164; indicted in New York, 165; indictment of quashed, 167; press defends, 161, 162–163; prosecution of suggested by Roosevelt, 155–156, 157; Roosevelt message on, 156–157

Quebec, 6

Railroad Strike of 1877, 116, 117
Ramsay, Charles: editor of Cincinnati *Republican*, warns abolitionist editor, 89–90
Randolph, John: attacks war hawks, 49
RCA, 286
Red Lion Broadcasting Co. v. FCC, 266
Reed, Stanley, 238; *Pennekamp* opinion of quoted, 228
Reporters and confidential sources, 271, 275–277
Reporters Committee on Freedom of the Press, 270
Republican (Jeffersonian) editors: targets of Naturalization Act, Alien Act, and Alien Enemies Act of 1798, 23
Republicans (Jeffersonians), 29, 30; views on Sedition Act, 34–35; views on freedom of speech and press, 25
Republican (Jeffersonian) newspapers, 35, 37, 280; accused of conspiracy, 28; Bache defended by, 36; Duane defended by, 43; effect on of Sedition Act prosecutions, 44; mob attacks on Federalist papers excused by, 53, 54, 55, 56; outnumbered by Federalist papers, 29; sedition bill ridiculed by, 25, 33
"Revenge Circular," 118–119; August Spies author of, 118
Revolutionary Age, 207
Rhode Island, 56
Richmond, Va., 21, 84
Richmond *Compiler*: on abolitionist mail, 87
Richmond *Enquirer*: bill to curb contempt power reported by, 77; Mexican War favored by, 102; on abolitionist press, 92
Richmond *Examiner*, 44
Richmond Whig: acquittal of Judge Peck criticized by, 75; approves ban on abolitionist tracts, 83
Right of reply, 264, 265, 266. *See Miami Herald v. Tornillo*
Rights of Man: praised by editor Philip Freneau, 15
Right to know: rejected by Supreme Court, 273
Rivington, James: press of destroyed, 5
Robbins, Asher: acquittal vote for Judge Peck noted, 75
Roberts, Owen J.: *Associated Press* dissent of quoted, 223
Robinson, Douglas, 151, 155, 156, 157, 158, 163
Robinson, John M.: excused from voting in Peck trial, 73
Rocky Mountain News. See Denver *Rocky Mountain News*
Roosevelt, Franklin D., 221, 222, 234; press freedom extolled by, xii
Roosevelt, Theodore, 145, 147, 148, 149, 152, 167, 188; congressional message of, 156–157; corruption in Panama arrangements denied by, 153, 156–157; government libel prosecution by, 146; W. R. Hearst attacked by, 171; judge at-